D1614732

CELEBRITY, PERFORMANCE, RECEPTION

By 1800 London had as many theatre seats for sale as the city's population. This was the start of the capital's rise as a centre for performing arts. Bringing to life a period of extraordinary theatrical vitality, David Worrall re-examines the beginnings of celebrity culture amidst a monopolistic commercial theatrical marketplace. The book presents an innovative transposition of social assemblage theory into performance history. It argues that the cultural meaning of drama changes with every change in the performance location. This theoretical model is applied to a wide range of archival materials including censors' manuscripts, theatre ledger books, performance schedules, unfamiliar play texts and rare printed sources. By examining prompters' records, box-office receipts and benefit-night takings, the study questions the status of David Garrick, Sarah Siddons and Edmund Kean, and recovers the neglected actress, Elizabeth Younge, and her importance to Edmund Burke.

DAVID WORRALL is Professor of English at Nottingham Trent University. He is the author of *Theatric Revolution: Drama, Censorship and Romantic Period Subcultures, 1773–1832* (2006), *The Politics of Romantic Theatricality, 1787–1832: The Road to the Stage* (2007) and *Harlequin Empire: Race, Ethnicity and the Drama of the Popular Enlightenment* (2007). He has held fellowships from the Leverhulme Trust, the Lewis Walpole Library, the Folger Shakespeare Library, the Huntington Library and the Library Company of Pennsylvania.

CELEBRITY, PERFORMANCE, RECEPTION

British Georgian Theatre as Social Assemblage

DAVID WORRALL

CAMBRIDGE
UNIVERSITY PRESS

University Printing House, Cambridge CB2 8BS, United Kingdom

Published in the United States of America by Cambridge University Press, New York

Cambridge University Press is part of the University of Cambridge.

It furthers the University's mission by disseminating knowledge in the pursuit of education, learning, and research at the highest international levels of excellence.

www.cambridge.org
Information on this title: www.cambridge.org/9781107043602

© David Worrall 2013

First published 2013

Printed in the United Kingdom by CPI Group Ltd, Croydon CR0 4YY

A catalogue record for this publication is available from the British Library

ISBN 978-1-107-04360-2 Hardback

Contents

v

Figures

Preface

This study arises from a number of research problems I encountered while writing my three earlier studies, *Theatric Revolution: Drama, Censorship and Romantic Period Subcultures, 1773–1832* (2006), *The Politics of Romantic Theatricality, 1787–1832: The Road to the Stage* (2007) and *Harlequin Empire: Race, Ethnicity and the Drama of the Popular Enlightenment* (2007). What the books did not solve was the question of how to conceptualize for analysis theatrical performance in the state of its historical activity. *Celebrity, Performance, Reception* is an attempt to evolve a working, predictive, method of theatre history which can then be further adapted by other scholars to suit a range of performance types.

I am grateful to Nottingham Trent University for its continuing support and for providing a lively research culture. My thanks also go to the Huntington Library and Art Gallery, the British Academy, the Lewis Walpole Library, the Houghton Library and the Folger Shakespeare Library, all of which awarded me the vital research grants enabling the archival visits on which this monograph is based. All of their staff are wonderful, patient and brimming with knowledge.

My greatest thanks go to Georgina Lock, who has enriched my life beyond anything I ever imagined.

Introduction: theatre, performance and social assemblage theory

The research questions analysed in this book are directly related to the size and complexity of eighteenth-century British theatre. *Celebrity, Performance, Reception*'s underlying assumption is that, at least as far as any robust empirical method of recovery is concerned when linked to figures for consumption, Georgian theatre was the nation's dominant culturally expressive form in the long eighteenth century. The book argues that social assemblage theory, a theory of social networks and social complexity principally developed by Manuel DeLanda, provides the most effective analytical and predictive bases for modelling how theatre functioned.[1] The theory of performance set out here is derived from a novel transposition of a theory of social structure into the discipline of theatre history.[2] The book is about the application of this theory to a particular set of materialized, fully historicized, empirical conditions rather than a study of its epistemological genesis or variants.[3] It should be emphasized that assemblage theory does not subsume or provide autonomous alternatives to other critical theories of inquiry. Methodologies based on gender, class, racial, political and other modalities of ideology can be – and should be – enlisted to analyse any or all of the components within the assemblage model; indeed, many of them are also employed in this book. Essentially, assemblage theory provides a predictive explanation of materialized social complexity. It does not particularly offer to explain the origins of those complexities.

Although the overall framework of assemblage theory will be outlined more extensively below, it can best be summarized by its insight that 'The identity of an assemblage is not only embodied in its materiality but also expressed by it.'[4] This enables *Celebrity, Performance, Reception*'s principal methodological proposition that all physical spaces, locations and embodiments of performance are expressive and comprise population components within a connected social network or assemblage of production and reception. DeLanda's subsidiary insight, integral with the first, is that assemblages are subject to 'defining processes in which specialized expressive media intervene, processes which consolidate and rigidify the identity of the assemblage or, on the contrary, allow the assemblage a certain latitude for more flexible operation while benefiting from genetic or linguistic resources (processes of coding and decoding)'.[5] In other words, 'specialized expressive media', such as theatrical performances, through processes of coding and decoding located at the performance and reception location, allow emergent differences to develop, permitting the overall assemblage to become more (or less) homogeneous or heterogeneous. This mechanism of difference operates throughout the assemblage's components. The overall cultural effect constitutes the assemblage's identity, where 'every social entity is shown to emerge from the interactions among entities operating at a smaller scale.'[6] The persistence of both private and public theatrical performances as a cultural practice means that this particular assemblage has always been in a state of activity in Britain since 1660.

The background to these new theoretical models derives from assemblage theories originating in the work of Gilles Deleuze and Félix Guattari, and subsequently adapted by Manuel DeLanda in *A New Philosophy of Society: Assemblage Theory and Social Complexity* (2006), the essays collected in DeLanda's *Deleuze: History and Science* (2010) and further redefined by him in *Philosophy and Simulation: The Emergence of Synthetic Reason* (2011).[7] These have then been adapted by me to apply them more coherently to theatrical performance in general and specifically to the circumstances of late Georgian London.[8] Although many other more philosophically oriented directions of performance theory are available or under inquiry, the principal benefit of applying these particular frameworks is that they help model Georgian theatre in the state of its contemporary activity; that is, as a working and materialized economy of performance.[9] *Celebrity, Performance, Reception* is particularly unusual in offering a theory of performance reception as well as performance production. Nevertheless, it is not intended that this book will particularly seek to articulate or discriminate between different epistemological incarnations of Deleuze, Guattari or DeLanda.

As an intriguing parallel strand situated in a complementary relationship to assemblage theory, Bruno Latour's actor-network-theory (ANT), as principally developed in *Reassembling the Social: An Introduction to Actor-Network-Theory* (2005), similarly proposes that social structures are always in process, determined by factors which particularly include interactions between non-human 'actors' (or agents) and the connected micro and macro movements of 'the social' (as Latour terms it) in combinations of both human and non-human agency. Latour's ANT provides an alternative, perhaps more foundational, account of assemblage theory, arguing that the social comprises networks (or assemblages) of connectivity (including non-human agents) rather than fixed or determined structures (see Appendix). What they have in common is that they describe the social as a series of interactive economies of culture which might also now be mapped as materialized networks or topographies of Georgian theatrical performance. ANT provides a minimal description of the structural pre-conditions for ways of thinking about the relationship between theatrical performance and the social, although it is not in itself, at least in its articulation by Latour, a sufficiently developed theory to be readily adapt-able to the context of Georgian playhouses, performance texts and players.[10]

Social assemblage theory provides an essentially post-structuralist empir-ical method to model an economy of theatrical culture in which meanings are continuously created, modified and displaced within complex networks comprising hundreds of thousands of individual people and even more combinations of text connected to built playhouse environments.[11] At its most reductive, the majority of the research questions raised in *Celebrity, Performance, Reception* are connected with the outcome of the two inter-secting dimensions basic to the idea of theatrical assemblage theory pre-sented here. One dimension is materially quantitative and is concerned with plays, performances and actors. The other dimension, similarly mainly quantitative, is chronological and is concerned with the material location of performance venues (the latter of which includes the dates of perform-ance). At the moment, a set of theoretical frameworks has yet to be evolved suitable for understanding what might be derived as a viable and compre-hensive cultural history extrapolated from the magnitude of contemporary theatrical performances.[12]

Since *Celebrity, Performance, Reception* is a book broadly situated within the discipline of literary studies, there is also a crucial literary theoretical problem which needs to be resolved. This principally concerns the actuality (or material status) of dramas not performed. These issues also provoke significant – even profound – implications for the status of literary texts in general where they are not materialized at locations with specifiable pop-ulation densities of reception or where they are imperfectly placed on uncertain population gradients within the assemblage.

Assemblage theory as developed in *Celebrity, Performance, Reception* proposes a relationship between 'real' texts (that is, those bordering on the virtual) and 'actual' texts (that is, those with a traceable material purchase on specific components of the assemblage population or on the gradients of difference operating within the assemblage) where relays and transpositions across both categories produce differences in exterior relations. My modelling of this relative distinction between real (or virtual) assemblages of reading and actual assemblages of performance (theatrical assemblages) develops DeLanda's adaptations of Deleuzian ontology. DeLanda indirectly initiates this major development for conceptualizing assemblages of readers of texts in contrast to theatrical assemblages where performance texts are materialized at the theatrical venue. According to DeLanda, 'the Deleuzian ontology is flat: the world of actual assemblages forming *a plane of reference*, that is, a world of individual singularities operating at different spatio-temporal scales, to which we can refer by giving them, for example, a proper name; and the world of diagrams defined by universal singularities forming *a plane of immanence*, a plane that does not exist above the other plane (like a genus that is ontologically "above" a species) but is like its reverse side. A single flat ontology with two sides, one side populated by virtual problems and the other by a divergent set of actual solutions to those problems.'[13] It is this idea of a plane of 'real' (or virtual) texts connected to an adjacent plane of actuality (the materialized exterior relations of the text) that allows us to model how play texts in performance can be linked to distinctive social assemblages actualized in density and located within knowable populations of the assemblage.[14]

When a further dimension of scale (meaning organizational complexity) is discussed later in this Introduction, the conceptual framework of Georgian theatrical assemblage will be complete. However, to return to the literary studies problem, the most readily accessible example of a late Georgian dramatic author who produced real or virtual plays is Joanna Baillie, someone whose dramatic works had a strong real or virtual presence yet whose play texts were seldom materialized at performance locations. Baillie's three-volume *Series of Plays: In Which it is Attempted to Delineate the Stronger Passions of the Mind – Each Passion Being the Subject of a Tragedy and a Comedy* (1798–1812) was widely read, but its dramas were infrequently performed. The American theatre manager William Dunlap's recollection of a rare 1801 Boston, Massachusetts, production of one of her plays referred to '"De Montfort," one of those grand and truly poetical, as well as philosophical dramas, written by Joanna Bailey [*sic*], to portray the progress of the passions, [which] was performed, but failed . . . It would not have done so in the time of Addison.'[15] While Dunlap helps us materialize an unusually elongated contemporary transatlantic reception environment for Baillie (the network he accessed had clearly stored along its links knowledge about both her plays and her reputation), this particular performed play has a very low density of population component because it had few materialized presences in theatrical assemblages. The single Boston performance 'failed' and there seem to have been no other performances thereafter, although, quite clearly, the overall Boston theatrical assemblage prospered. Of course, there would have been many contemporary readers of Baillie, but, unless some methodology can be devised to reassemble their material density, they remain highly diffused and disaggregated – that is, real but virtual. As DeLanda cautions, 'in assemblage theory expressivity cannot be reduced to language and symbols.'[16] This flat but materialized ontology is a general condition of text and not something exclusive to Baillie or to the closet drama genre in which she usually wrote.

Play texts performed at locatable venues have a higher actuality than those which remained read but unperformed unless their population densities can be precisely located – assuming date and venue records of reading exist with some degree of meaningful specificity. However, *Celebrity, Performance, Reception* often discusses plays with few performances because such plays demonstrate important aspects of the materialized nature of the theatrical assemblage. Joanna Baillie would be a good example of a playwright whose dramas, in general, have a low level of actuality and comprise a highly molecular part of the overall assemblage. When Dunlap wrote that Baillie's *De Montfort* 'failed' at Boston, it is striking that he is primarily referring to its performance existence on the plane of the actual and that the high esteem in which he otherwise held what he describes as her 'grand and truly poetical … philosophical dramas' represents his individual sense of their real or virtual existence. It is these crucial processes of materialized performance reiteration (play texts repeated at physical performance locations with defined populations) which permit the development of difference within the assemblage.

The centrality of theatre in Georgian culture is precisely a function of the scale of its materialized presence and the complexity of its organization. Theatre had a pre-eminent cultural status. Unlike the general print culture of books, journals and newspapers or the circulation of painted or printed images, not only did theatre achieve massive cultural focus on account of the concentration of large audiences within the metropolitan playhouses (along with many other smaller audiences dispersed across provincial or regional theatres), but also the scale of its presence and economic impact can be quantified with greater levels of accuracy than is the case with other contemporary cultural forms. Following the traces of materialized performances necessarily reverses some expectations of literary value. To the example of Baillie could be added the dramas of the author of *Political Justice* (1793), the philosophical anarchist and novelist, William

Godwin, whose lifelong interest in playwriting, despite his largely advantageous social connections, resulted in just two plays put into contemporary performance, *Antonio; or, The Soldier's Return* (1800) and *Faulkner* (1807), with the plays receiving, in total, four nights of performance.[17] However, as David O'Shaughnessy's monograph *William Godwin and the Theatre* (2010) notes, Godwin's extensive diary shows that he attended the theatre 'almost 2,000 times over half a century', seeing still identifiable plays, often in company with identifiable parties of friends (including the playwright Elizabeth Inchbald and the feminist, Mary Wollstonecraft).[18] As far as theatrical assemblage theory is concerned, Godwin's significance undoubtedly resides not in his standing as a playwright but in his extensive and well-documented participation in contemporary London's audience populations. In general, social assemblage theory provides a robust methodology for examining the cultural mechanisms of how theatrical texts were disseminated across a continuum of difference to audiences whose collective identities can be quantified at materialized locations, very often as recurrent multiples of theatre capacities and sometimes as absolutely quantified figures of attendance.[19]

One particular (and popular) literary methodological *cul-de-sac* needs to be discussed at this point. The seductive possibility of adapting to theatre history theories of generalized linguistic 'performativity', *pace* Judith Butler after J.L. Austin, a term understood as being adjacent to, or even subsuming, theatrical performance, has engaged much recent critical attention.[20] For example, Romantic period studies, an industrious subdiscipline within English literary scholarship, has found it particularly problematic to engage with performativity so as to be able to distinguish it from (or subsume it under) theatricality. Alexander Dick and Angela Esterhammer's judicious overview fronting their collection *Spheres of Action: Speech and Performance in Romantic Culture* (2009) remarks about this problem of conceptualizing performance with reference both to theatre and to poetics, 'that action can be defined neither in purely abstract nor in purely material terms; rather, agency always comprises a tension between material and abstract forces.'[21] By comparison, Lilla Maria Crisafulli and Keir Elam's introduction to their promising collection, *Women's Romantic Theatre and Drama: History, Agency, and Performativity* (2010), more ambivalently states that 'performativity' can sometimes be little more than Joanna Baillie developing 'a persuasive liberal rhetoric' for her plays while on other occasions it denotes 'the social habitus of the characters and the semiotics of the actors' "doing things" on stage'.[22] Dick and Esterhammer's analysis of the problem arguably helps prompt how social assemblage theory might be the critical paradigm best able to propose a robust methodology capable of harnessing such divergences while still retaining their original dynamics and permitting new spaces for interpretation.

Since just about anything can be performative (and nothing appears to be non-performative), the invocation of 'performativity' as a theoretical term to cover any kind of textual utterance, including that which takes place in theatres, has rendered it all but redundant.[23] Of course, the attractiveness of performativity to conventional literary studies is easy to see. Literary critics tend to concentrate on authors and their texts as the primary producers of meaning and have only afterwards surveyed readers (the reception environment) as the secondary agents engaging with the performativities alleged to be contained within the text's utterances. Overall, it is generally the case that in modern English literary studies focused on this period, a great deal is known about the production or supply side of literature, but considerably less quantitative information is available about literature's consumers (the demand side). With theatrical performance, however, and especially with respect to Georgian Britain, the reverse is true. The scale and complexity of Georgian theatre makes it essential to study the performance base, including the reception environment.

Although readers – as opposed to theatre-goers – are proposed as comprising the principal reception environment in William St Clair's magisterial *The Reading Nation in the Romantic Period* (2004), his analysis is relevant as a point of empirical contrast. St Clair employs high-quality quantitative information about the balance between the production and consumption of poetry, novels and literary periodicals but, perhaps unexpectedly, makes the strategic decision to ignore almost entirely the production and consumption of printed plays (with the exception of Shakespeare). Perhaps this is a reasonable assumption (since plays are intended mainly for performance), yet some knowledge of the availability of printed play texts would help balance the picture St Clair so brilliantly presents. In the case of his single significant discussion of drama, concerning stage adaptations of Mary Shelley's *Frankenstein* in the early 1820s, St Clair makes the point very forcibly that, as far as reception by the general population was concerned, theatricalized versions quickly swamped that fiction's original identity as a novel.[24] Otherwise, very little can be extrapolated from St Clair about reprintings of the standard performance repertoire in Britain or about the print fortunes of new writing for the stage. Nevertheless, the overarching conclusion of *The Reading Nation in the Romantic Period* is that much that was previously imagined as the voluminous contemporary readership for the major Romantic authors (with the notable exceptions of Byron and

Scott) has now to be scaled back. The print runs of some of the major writers, often only between 500 and 1,000 copies, were sometimes financially sponsored by the authors themselves and, on occasion, as notoriously in the case of the quarto edition of Wordsworth's *Excursion*, often sold very slowly indeed.[25] In other words, reader densities, disaggregated as they were by publishers' increasing ability to reach markets on a national scale, are difficult to actualize as far as retrievable traces are concerned. H.J. Jackson's *Romantic Readers: The Evidence of Marginalia* (2005) helps materialize and triangulate some types of knowledge about contemporary readers by tracing specific interactivity between books and readers in the same period – in this case as exemplified in the habit of annotating books with marginalia. As such, Jackson's study provides a slightly different avenue towards establishing quantitative (as well as qualitative) methods of assessing literary reception.[26]

Reception figures for drama do not combine in the same way as the reception characteristics of readers because audience numbers are the primary indicators of the scale of theatrical reception. However, plays were printed in abundance. In general, by the late eighteenth century, most plays produced by Covent Garden or Drury Lane – the principal venues for new writing for performance – found their way into print and also tended to be reprinted. For London's emergent playhouses, such as Sadler's Wells or The Royalty in Tower Hamlets, printings were more occasional but still persisted as a theatre practice. A revealing example is a single 1792 entry in a Drury Lane company ledger book which records a payment for printing '3500 Books of Cymon', David Garrick's successful farce of 1767. This made Drury Lane's 1792 printing the eighth reprint (and not a run-out of old stock). Moreover, as well as direct selling at the theatre, a single night's royal command performance of *Cymon* (billed with James Cobb's musical adaptation of Karl Ditters von Dittersdorf's, *The Doctor and the Apothecary*, 1788) brought the playhouse receipts of £552. 15s. 6d. (plus a further £1. 4s. 0d. not accounted until the next day, inexplicably handed over by a justice of the peace because of 'the Hurry last N[t.]'), implying an audience full to bursting at around 2,500 people.[27] In other words, by whichever criteria one employs, whether measuring theatre audiences by their appetite for reading or by their theatre-going (*Cymon* was a shilling a book, the same price as entry to the playhouse gallery), the raw volume of contemporary theatre audiences' appetite for drama rapidly reaches multiples of thousands. *Cymon*'s successful Drury Lane revival in 1792 meant that the playhouse could schedule it for as long as it drew audiences, the playhouse carefully pairing Garrick's farce with different mainpieces or afterpieces so as to refresh and attract multiple audience segments while, at the same time, steadily reducing its stock of 3,500 texts.

The financial incentives for authors to write convincingly workable plays for performance were also considerable, acting as autonomous catalysts impelling the growth and success of the theatrical economy and propelling its status as a sustained and distinctive social assemblage with its own populations and arrays of performance locations. George Colman the Elder's moderately successful adaptation of a Voltaire comic original, *The English Merchant* (1767), apart from a customary pirated Dublin edition, was printed twice in 1767, again in 1774, and, after the author's death, was gathered by Elizabeth Inchbald for her 1811 edition of *Modern Theatre*. Whatever sum Colman received directly for the copyright of *The English Merchant* probably pales into insignificance against his earnings from its theatre performances. Around the same time that the publishing family of Lowndes – who printed the 1792 *Cymon* – customarily paid authors of novels between £5 and £10 for copyright, Colman received £341. 18s. 0d., net of the playhouse house charges, for his three *English Merchant* author benefit nights.[28] In other words, the reception characteristics of drama in performance were entirely different from those associated with the production of books for reading. Understanding the different economic forces encountered in this theatrical reception environment helps differentiate it from the production and reception context of most of the works of literary fiction or poetry produced at this time, particularly when estimating their places as virtual or actual texts in DeLanda's sense.

Despite the availability of a great deal of quantitative archival information about theatrical consumption, and despite some excellent studies of individual performers such as Garrick, Siddons and Kean, the dominant critical methodology has tended to focus on playwrights and their texts (closely followed by celebrity performers). This is a trend not noticeably countered by the excellence of late twentieth-century research comprehensively recovering the longitudinal extent of the generality of performers within the theatrical profession, notably in the sixteen volumes of Philip H. Highfill, Kalman A. Burnim and Edward A. Langhans' *A Biographical Dictionary of Actors, Actresses, Musicians, Dancers, Managers & Other Stage Personnel in London, 1660–1800* (1973–93). Insofar as literary studies can be described as a branch of theatre studies (or vice versa), a situation of critical asymmetry has arisen, in which playwrights and play texts have provided the primary context for scholarly inquiry. The extensiveness of the theatrical personnel collated by Highfill *et al.*, and the many performances recorded as constituting their professional careers, is an absolute indicator of the complexity of the theatrical assemblage.

Having set out the production context, what happens at a performance can now be described, keeping in mind the point made earlier that the materialization of texts in performance constitutes a plane of the actual connected to a plane of the real (or virtual) and that this comprises the principal bases of the relationship between text and performance in the theatrical assemblage.

On the demand (or reception) side, performance meanings are always distributed at the location of the performance venue rather than residing principally in the fixed status of the authorial text. Within this structure, the performers are the primary producers of performance meaning although they have no connection to its reception characteristics, which, of course, are displaced towards the context of the audience. In the terminology of assemblage theory, texts are progressively decoded and deterritorialized of their authorial or original contextual meaning with each and every performance and then recoded and reterritorialized by the collectivity of the performers and the audience at every live performance. David Garrick's quelling of a near-riot at a performance of Edward Moore's *The Foundling* (1748), discussed in Chapter 3, would be one example – albeit a fairly reductive one – of the spontaneous reterritorializing of performance texts by one particular population component within a contemporary theatrical assemblage. In the Georgian period, in the overwhelming number of cases, performances can be located with great precision with respect to the identities of actors, texts performed, and the date and location of the performances. This potential for quantitative specificity is why the particular emergence in the eighteenth century of celebrity performers as a palpable cultural force, dependent upon the reception side of cultural production, has been interrogated so frequently in this book. Indeed, the role of celebrity performers provides particularly useful sets of information for understanding the social structures involved with performance reception.

As we have emphasized that performance meaning depends upon performance location, the principal structure of the theatrical assemblage can now be described. All theatrical performances take place along two axes. One axis is spatial and is defined by location; the other axis is temporal and is defined by chronological moment. These two axes are the basic components generating the meanings and values resulting from theatrical difference. They are what Latour calls '*translations between mediators that . . . generate traceable associations*' and on which ANT is built.[29] DeLanda, following Deleuze, calls them '*relations of exteriority*'.[30] In order to be evidential, the spatial and temporal locations of performance need to have been recorded, because, unlike organisms or material compounds, the unmediated trace of performance did not persist in the Georgian and now only exists in the form of their historical '*traceable associations*' known to have been materialized at their performance location.[31]

The outcome of the intersection of these two dimensions (of perform- ance production and of performance consumption) can be described in any number of ways, but perhaps their most notable feature is the non- linearity emphasized by Deleuze, Guattari, Latour and DeLanda in their descriptions of the structure of social assemblages. This engenders another principle about performance history. Two performances of the same text can never take place in the same geographical and date location; therefore, their cultural meanings cannot coincide. Cultural meaning shifts with every performance. The volume and organizational complexity of the overall assemblage of eighteenth-century playwrights, playhouse managers and performers, all incentivized to produce and perform dramas at built physical locations for playing in front of live audiences, gave rise to a critical density of audience and performer populations not normally associated with groups of readers. The co-presence of performers and audience, materialized at the performance locations, shared uniquely presented reiterations of performance texts. The audience's fleeting pres- ence as a materialized collectivity, particularly in the case of the large metropolitan playhouses, has a higher density than that which could feasibly be evidentially identified by specific dates and locations for dis- aggregated sets of readers. Again, the mechanism of performance differ- ence, perpetuated throughout the materialized Georgian theatrical assemblage, is generated by reiterated performances which produce this difference through successive routes, networks and sequences of territori- alization, deterritorialization, decoding and encoding.

An insistence on historical specificity is a major strength of DeLanda's development of assemblage theory: 'Every assemblage must be treated as a unique historical entity characterized both by a set of emergent properties (making it an individual singularity) as well as by the structure of possibility space defining tendencies and capacities (a structure defined by universal singularities).'[32] Transposed to performance theory within the Georgian, performance is uniquely an 'individual singularity' taking place within a space of emergence (which is the playhouse venue). At this point, it is probably worth extrapolating further (and perhaps reinforcing) the descrip- tion of how this theoretical model functions.

While Georgian performance did not (and does not) persist, its high degree of materialization at the performance venue increased the density of theatre's social assemblage. The audience and the performers retain their capacity to store individually the performance's narrative while decoding and re-encoding its meaning. In addition, the physical congregation of audiences into audience crowds also enabled actual co-presence, increasing the density of the episodes of decoding and providing favourable circumstances for their reiteration as new encodings along social networks. Discussion and social interaction, not merely spectating, feature noticeably in Thomas Rowlandson's etching, *Comedy Spectators: Tragedy Spectators* (1789) (Figure 0.1). This degree of density in the assemblage at the point of performance makes it rather different from the lesser levels of the intensity of, say, the ideas present in a book (including printed plays, of course), which generally lack the immediate co-presence of the other parts of the assemblage population.

From the Western early modern period onwards, it is the playbill, newspaper advertising or a combination of these two artefacts which usually provides the most comprehensive and quantifiable record of past performances and the assemblages to which they related. They are the keys to our knowledge of how past performances were materialized.[33] The double archival layer of playbill and newspaper advertising empirically demonstrates the quantitative component out of which divergences or convergences of cultural meaning arose. Of course, performance is always the outcome of an interaction between the performer and the dramatic text, with the latter being the artefact within performance most commonly recovered and accessed. However, to this combination must be added the audience who are co-present with the performers at the venue. Theatrical economies are true cultural economies because these three principal components (performance, dramatic text and audience venue) constantly move through shifting degrees of meaning or value materialized at the performance location.

Within *Celebrity, Performance, Reception*'s model of assemblage theory, the dramatic text in performance occupies what DeLanda calls the expressive role within the component of the assemblage, with the combination of performance, text and location giving the assemblage its contingent identity.[34] The performance text (which might be song, dance or pantomime as well as the spoken word) is a part of – as DeLanda puts it – the 'defining processes in which specialized expressive media intervene, processes which consolidate and rigidify the identity of the assemblage or, on the contrary, allow the assemblage a certain latitude for more flexible operation while

COMEDY SPECTATORS.

TRAGEDY SPECTATORS.

0.1 Thomas Rowlandson, *Comedy Spectators: Tragedy Spectators*, S.W. Fores, 8 October 1789, etching, hand-coloured. Visual records frequently show audience reception as reactive and socially dense.

benefiting from genetic or linguistic resources (processes of coding and decoding)'.[35] It is DeLanda's persistent return to the materiality of the assemblage, particularly its population density and ability to store and transform information along its networks (a characteristic also emphasized in Latour's ANT), which renders it so applicable to theatrical performance.

Crucial to the operation of social assemblage is that its material components (including non-human actors such as buildings, physical locations and economic forces) help comprise the assemblage's expressive identity. In the sense of the theory proposed here, the assemblage is the outcome of the interaction between the performer in the playhouse, the playhouse itself and the playhouse audience (which is why it is always, precisely, a *social* assemblage). All of these components contribute to giving the assemblage both its identity and its emergent possibilities. The accumulation of meaning via textual codings and subsequent textual decodings, through performance joined to specific performance populations, also necessarily involves a non-linear model of cultural production. Audiences are disaggregated individual 'actors', whose collective identity is present in variable densities of formation gathered at playhouses at specific date locations and also, in weaker configurations, capable of accessing social networks beyond the theatre, and of storing and modifying experiences encountered during their co-presence with other parts of the assemblage population.

In short, in the case of theatrical performance, audience decodings have density and co-presence. Secondly, their historical moments can be empirically traced. Thirdly, the materiality of their implicit cultural meanings can be analysed. DeLanda gives as his description of this process: 'The combination of recurrence of the same assembly processes at any one spatial scale, and the recurrence of the same kind of assembly processes (territorialization and coding) at successive scales, give assemblage theory a unique way of approaching the problem of linking the micro- and macro-levels of social reality.'[36] These basic processes, reiterated but not repeated, act as performance's continual economy of difference.

To put it another way, all the theatrical performances referred to in *Celebrity, Performance, Reception* are functions of these shifting (textual, chronological, geographical) social assemblages and of the material dimensions in which they were embodied. Collectively, they constitute not only the expressivity of the assemblage but also its identity.[37] In other words, particularly with respect to the issues of celebrity discussed in Chapters 3 and 4, all of the parts of the assemblage construct the assemblage's identity. No performer possesses the perquisite of conferring homogeneity of reception on large and complexly organized theatrical assemblages. On the contrary, it might be said that the physical configuration of the playhouses (which might include factors such as the scale and frequency of performance as well as less visible legal and economic determinants) conferred celebrity.

Although it is not the intention of this book to get too involved with the critical discourses inevitably attached to social assemblage's theoretical histories or contexts, DeLanda makes the helpful formulation that 'Cultural replicators may be viewed as having phenotypic effects similar to catalysis.'[38] The attraction of transposing DeLanda's (and Deleuze and Guattari's) insights, often adapted from metaphors of genetics, from social theory into theatrical history should not be too surprising since performances and performance receptions constantly mutate and evolve, progressively territorializing, deterritorializing and reterritorializing in precisely the manner attributed to changes within social assemblage. Dramas in performance, even such canonical stalwarts as Shakespeare's *King Lear*, always operate within well-known underlying fields of reception difference and mutate from their genotype, even though their textual, temporal or physical proximities might seem very confined and constricted. To take a simple example, while Covent Garden and Drury Lane in the Georgian era were unlikely to programme *King Lear* on the same night, Shakespeare's tragedy regularly appeared in both of their repertoires. However, although this may sound like a familiar process of literary canon formation, even here one swiftly enters into less well-known territory. For one thing, the version of *King Lear* playing throughout this period used Nahum Tate's 1681 happy ending, an adaptation now little known yet one resonant with reigning conservative ideologies as much as the inflections of lost Shakespearian originals.[39] Much that was commonplace about this repertoire has long been forgotten; the genetic structure of the canon has mutated even though the original genotypes were once widely distributed.

Mutations in the performance genotype caused massive changes in the repertoire including how it was programmed. Staples such as George Lillo's seasonally performed *The London Merchant, or The History of George Barnwell* (1731), as well as the similarly seasonal pantomime harlequinades exploring specifically British developments of Italian *commedia dell'arte*, are now rarely studied. However, both were almost as likely to have been performed in New Republic America as in London's patent or 'illegitimate' playhouses or in the provinces.[40] Indeed, if one had to search for readily recognizable features common to both Georgian and modern British theatre programming, it is probably only the consecutive nightly runs of the seasonal pantomimes which mirror today's scheduling practices. The distribution of this genotype has also brought about its mutation. These materialized changes in the structure of the theatrical assemblage are apparent to everyone even though, if we were to open a copy of *George Barnwell* today, there would be relatively little which would make us aware of its past place in the repertoire.

Other scholars have added important strategic insights into the social function of theatrical performance. Working apparently independently of Deleuze and Guattari's formulations, as well as Latour's, the theatre historian Joseph Roach has noted how theatrical performances mark processes of 'internal cultural self-definition ... [which] these and other performances produced by making visible the play of difference and identity within the larger ensemble of relations'.[41] Roach's insights have also recently been influentially expanded by Kathleen Wilson within a critical context cognisant of Deleuze and Guattari's work but made even more specific to eighteenth-century theatre.[42] There is much which may be added, but the underlying proposition is that social assemblages describe active and materialized economies of cultural difference, always present and actively working.

If we move from these general characteristics, some specific examples will help demonstrate the stability of social assemblage theory as a way of modelling the culturally complex topographies of Georgian performance as well as introducing a more expanded idea of what might be included under the heading of theatrical assemblage.

If this book's primary theoretical formulation is that there existed a recoverable economy of cultural difference perpetuated through theatrical performance, its second formulation is that some reckoning needs to be made of the scale of Georgian theatre. Scale in the sense of simple quantification is not particularly informative. Nevertheless, it provides a good indicator of the existence of what the theory terms population densities and population 'gradients' between the different parts of assemblages. 'Gradient' is a useful term employed by DeLanda to describe the internal 'capacity' within an assemblage and enables us to model how difference flows between the connections of an assemblage or social network. Capacity, in turn, can also indicate the propensity to mutate, activate or regenerate difference: 'The capacity of intensive difference to act as energy storage devices will play such a prominent role in the explanation of emergence ... that it will be useful to have a more compact term for them. We will refer to them as *gradients.*'[43] Within the assemblage are internal capacities for change but also different relationships between higher and lower levels of gradient as well as different levels of organization. Gradient is most easily visualized with respect to human agency as a simple thermodynamic.[44] Although a novel proposition when applied to cultural studies, this has the virtue of concentrating on the materialized properties of the assemblage.

At its most reductive, one might picture gradient as thermodynamically active differences in heat generated by large collections of audiences in the big Georgian theatres, with each section of the auditorium differentially vociferous or boisterous, broadly in accord with their class or social segment. Each area of the auditorium deployed different repertoires of participation in their overall collective co-presence, raising an absolute thermodynamic increase located at the built space of the venue. The energetic interactivity and physical proximity of Georgian audiences can easily be seen in Thomas Rowlandson's etchings, *The Boxes: O woe is me t'have seen what I have seen seeing what I see* (1809) and *Pidgeon hole: a Convent Garden contrivance to coop up the gods* (1811), which, when put together, show an entire vertical elevation of the auditorium (Figures 0.2 and 0.3). These are the raw indicators of the co-presence of populations within assemblages. This simple calorification of human bodies gives some indication of the density of their collectivity or co-presence and the mass of their organized connectivity within the assemblage. Indeed, it happens to be the case that the hot and crowded conditions of Georgian theatre audiences were a ubiquitous feature of contemporary anecdotes about theatre-going and were often represented in caricature prints.[45] The historical consequences of these material pressures are explicitly concrete and irreducible. For example, the diary of the composer John Marsh records that it was the early June 1791 heat of the old Chichester, Sussex, playhouse and its coincidence with a packed performance sponsored by 'Ld. Newark & the Officers of the [Queen's] Buffs' (including playing by the regimental band) which led to an entirely new public theatre being built in the city by tontine subscription: 'Of course, it was very hot, disagreeable wch I believe made the expediency of having a new & more comodious [*sic*] House so apparent, that a proposal, wch had been sometime before made, was almost immediately received & acceded to, so that this was the last time of using the old Theatre.'[46]

In this particular example, there is a straightforward connection between the thermodynamics of congregated human density and the building of an actual physical space for a new Georgian theatre.[47] Marsh bought several £40 tontine shares for himself and on behalf of his two young sons to construct Chichester's new theatre, although, at the time of the compilation of James Winston's notes (*c.* 1802) for his *Theatric Tourist* – which record the new playhouse – the theatre was still too hot, and Marsh reported going in 1805, keen 'to see y^e improvement in the Theatre lately made by

0.2 Thomas Rowlandson, *The Boxes: O woe is me t'have seen what I have seen seeing what I see. Shakespear* [sic] / *Opie inv.* [printed in reverse], 12 December 1809, etching, hand-coloured. Covent Garden theatre in the aftermath of the 1809 'Old Price' riots. Although three watchmen with clubs are dispersed into the auditorium, the audience engage in more predictable social interactions. Note the two black men and a turbaned man accompanied by a young white woman, bottom row, second box from left.

0.3 Thomas Rowlandson, *Pidgeon hole: a Convent Garden contrivance to coop up the gods*, Thomas Tegg, 20 February 1811, etching, hand-coloured. The picture caricatures the dense occupancy of the alcoves visible in *The Boxes* picture.

Mr. Collins, by putting a ventilator in ye ceiling'.[48] Eventually, gas lighting (introduced into London theatres around 1817, but for ambient rather than stage lighting) intensified these thermodynamics, with the popular singer Jacob Beuler even creating a comic sketch, 'A Peep at a Play', which coupled traditional theatre overcrowding – '(*Spoken*) O dear, O dear! Don't push so. – I shall be killed. – I shall be squeezed to death . . . . O gad! It's enough to make me *cross*, I've split my *inexpressibles*' – with the latest effects of gas illumination – 'Bless me! The heat is so very *opressive* [*sic*]! I can hardly *bear* it, I fancy it is the gas. – Phoo! The gas makes it *lighter*.'[49]

The innovative take-up of gas lighting so quickly by the theatres is also an important indicator not only of the economics at work within the populations of the assemblage but also of the layers of organizational complexity across its networks. Crucially, developments in theatre lighting were not restricted to the West End but were mirrored across London's theatrical assemblage. By 1817, for example, the Royalty Theatre in Tower Hamlets had 'Gas Lights . . . in the exterior and interior of the Theatre', and, remarkably, by 1820 the playhouse owned – and ran – its own gasworks (which it later sold as a job lot with the theatre).[50] As DeLanda puts it, 'At any level of scale we are always dealing with *populations* of interacting entities (populations of person, pluralities of communities, multiplicities of organizations, collectivities of urban centers) and it is from the interactions within these populations that large assemblies emerge as a *statistical result*, or as collective unintended consequences of intentional action.'[51] In other words, thermodynamics, whether in the metropolis or in the provinces, is a reasonable proxy for co-presence and population density within contemporary theatrical assemblages.

One final example in this Introduction will serve to show nearly all of these components in operation. In late August 1779, George Colman the Younger, then working at the Haymarket under his father's management, wrote the comedy, *The Separate Maintenance*, as a final production before his season ended (on account of the two winter playhouses reopening in mid September). Featuring marital estrangement, aristocratic infidelity, a female tragic playwright and a French dilettante, Colman's comedy covered a range of issues illustrative of the complexity of late eighteenth-century metropolitan culture.[52] *Separate Maintenance*'s gently satiric narrative tells us much about metropolitan manners, with Colman teasing the audience about the city's latest affectations. For example, Mrs Fustian, the playwright ('The Title of my Tragedy is Cyrus Son of Cambyses'), calls on the estranged Lady Newberry at her salon:

ENTER MRS. FUSTIAN . . . I have brought a Tragedy – Your Ladyship wished to hear it, and knowing there wouldr be a numerous and brilliant Audience I thought a fortunate opportunity – Reading plays in polite circles is all the mode at present.
LADY NEWBURY: Oh! True – your Tragedy! Do you mean to read it all thro' Mrs. Fustian
MRS. FUSTIAN: All thro'! – why yes, if your Ladyship pleases.
LADY NEWBERRY: Because a Tragedy must be rather long I suppose. . .[53]

Almost incidentally, Colman's reference to the fashion for 'Reading plays in polite circles' catches another dimension of the theatrical assemblage. The presence of informal play-reading groups as part of literate social networks was later made the subject of James Cobb's farce, *English Readings* (1787), another Colman Haymarket production but this time satirizing the percolation of the fashion into provincial England ('Captain Wilmot: But tell me, Kitty, how did this *rage* for English Readings reach a town so far from London? Kitty: Mrs Poplin, the Irish mantua-maker, who came down from London, introduced it').[54] Colman's incorporation of amateur reading groups as a minor textual subtheme present in both *The Separate Maintenance* and in Cobb's *English Readings* is a good incidental example of how fashionable knowledge was disseminated across the theatrical network, giving specific audiences an awareness of popular cultural practices, such as changes in fashions of reading.

In this case the production of these two plays shared the same playhouse space (the Haymarket) but at widely separated temporal reception locations. This simple example demonstrates the ability of the network both to store knowledge (e.g. about the popularity of reading groups) and for its links to help deterritorialize original cultural value. In this analysis, fashionable metropolitan reading groups have been deterritorialized by provincial emulation. The specificity of amateur reading groups described as 'all the mode' or '*rage*' makes it clear that the Haymarket was a part of this process of the deterritorialization of fashionable practices and habits, disseminating them across the networks of the assemblage. Or as DeLanda puts it, following Foucault, 'The birth of fashion . . . had deterritorializing effects.'[55]

This low-key example of metropolitan and provincial reading groups (some of them clearly play-reading groups), all referenced in multiple performances at the same theatres, tells us much about the complexity of the society reflected in the Haymarket's repertoire. However, to this must be added several other layers of components within the assemblage. The physical nature of the Haymarket contributed substantial parts of its expressive identity, even if it is not always easy to know what these specifics, apart from audience density, might have been. One of the few things known about *The Separate Maintenance* production is that a contemporary newspaper reported it was 'ornamented with a most elegant scene in which Lady Newbery [*sic*] gave her fête, painted by the artist Mr. Rooker'.[56] Michael Angelo Rooker (1743–1801) is one of only a few Georgian scene painters for whom some kind of connected biography can be provided. The notice of his work for this play is a reminder that this drama was a physical construction, occupying three-dimensional space and operating across several levels of symbolic imagery, implying a number of layers of social construction and economic identity.[57]

That the Haymarket was a complex physical assemblage whose theatrical performances were part of an extensive network of exterior relations within the metropolis can also be deduced from newspaper reports and advertising about *The Separate Maintenance*. Newspapers are a key aspect of the Georgian theatrical assemblage, providing the means to react to (or deterritorialize) performance meaning and to store the history of those performances across their networks. *The Public Advertiser*, using a text possibly

provided by Colman himself, gives some impression of a disrupted first
night for the play where, 'notwithstanding the intense Heat of the Weather,
a most brilliant and crouded Audience [attended], insomuch that not one
Seat in any Part of the Theatre remained unoccupied ... The Prologue
spoken by Mr. Palmer, in its Conclusion, alluded to the Author's being
deprived of the Assistance of Mrs. Abington, by the Menaces of the *Family
Compact* of the two Kings of Brentford, whose *united* Sceptres rule our
Winter Theatres. The Audience shewed their Dislike to Monopolies by
repeated Plaudits, and insisted on the Speaker's repeating the Lines ... In
the fourth Act a violent Contest arose in the Theatre. On Mr. Edwin's Song
being encored a Fray ensued, and a Person was pushed out of the Pit. The
Comedy was greatly applauded by a prodigious Plurality; but it appeared a
few single Men came determined not to like it.'[58] The density of the
population component within the theatrical assemblage, registered by *The
Public Advertiser*'s combined references to an extreme thermodynamic,
the presence of disruptive 'single Men' in 'a violent Contest' or 'Fray',
together with a straightforward headcount of the audience ('not one Seat in
any Part of the Theatre remained unoccupied'), establishes a sense of the
scale and social complexity of the event as well as an indication of the several
layers of population component present at the theatre. Newspapers acted as
supplementary technologies for the theatre's social network, deterritorializing the actual, physical, social networks co-present in the theatre and
redistributing knowledge of the Haymarket's several audience factions.

   However, *The Public Advertiser* reports also describe an additional social
level of organization within the assemblage by reporting the (now lost)
prologue and how it referred to 'the Menaces of the *Family Compact* of the
two Kings of Brentford' who 'rule our Winter Theatres'. The 'two Kings of
Brentford' is an allusion to George Villiers, Duke of Buckingham's popular
comedy, *The Rehearsal* (1672), and was Colman's satire on the two patent
theatres.[59] Part of the complexity of the theatrical assemblage as it operated
arose from the institutionalized powers wielded over the Haymarket, within
which the theatre was situated, both physically and legally. The 'two Kings of
Brentford' are reminders of the non-human actors determining how the
Haymarket functioned. The first of these actors was the Lord Chamberlain's
power of censorship (a statutory intervention which has ensured the preserva-
tion of the unique manuscript), but there were also indirect pressures applied
by the patent owners 'whose *united* Sceptres rule our Winter Theatres'. In
these examples, the assemblage model provides vivid explanations.

   Although ultimately responsible to the magical body of the King, in
Britain monarchical or noble offices were devolved or deterritorialized

towards aristocratic or commoner officials in a fundamental separation of the role from its incumbent. In this sense, censorship was not vested in the King but in the office of the Lord Chamberlain, with day-to-day scrutiny of play texts further devolved to the Examiner of Plays, at that time, John Larpent. This devolution and separation of office from incumbent is one of the most basic pieces of organization denoting a social structure's status as an assemblage: 'At the smallest scale an individual organization can be said to be deterritorialized if the resources it controls are linked to an office as opposed to the incumbent of that office.'[60] Paradoxically, the monarch's need to devolve offices was countered by the royal theatre patentees' reliance on the authority of his personal fiat since (theoretically) the patent vested in them ceased on the death of the reigning monarch. In practice, theatre audiences well understood the complexities of the magical body and its devolved attributes. During a period of largely female-led pro-Queen Caroline agitation, a performance of Robert Dodsley's *The King and the Miller of Mansfield* (1737) at Drury Lane in April 1820 was interrupted by a boy in the audience who knew what was at stake: 'At the commencement of the second [act when] the King's health [was] being drunk, a boy in the gallery added "The Queen". Not a word more was heard.'[61] The manager James Winston's diary vividly captures this moment when even children understood (and felt empowered to intervene against) apparent disconnections between the symbolic statuses of George IV and his estranged queen, and the materialization of their textual symbolic registers in performance among a co-present audience population.

To return to the 1779 performances of *The Separate Maintenance*, the Haymarket's particular ire seems to have been raised by the contractual restrictions placed by the patentees on the famous actress, Frances Abington, which prohibited her freelancing appearances during the royal theatres' closed season. Interestingly, it is again the public dissent displayed directly by the audience in the theatre that night, when 'The Audience shewed their Dislike to Monopolies by repeated Plaudits', which gives some glimpse of the audience's ability to display collective disapproval and, much like the boy's impact on the audience at *The King and the Miller of Mansfield* in 1820, to act as a fleetingly composed politicized network. A couple of the other London newspapers, although clearly fed a précis of *Separate Maintenance*'s text by Colman, also comment on how 'The Witticisms that struck us most were the Allusion to the theatrical Coalition, in the Prologue', one calling it, 'a poetical *Manifesto*'.[62] Situated as it was in the West End as an anomalous playhouse not directly competing with the patent houses (because it performed only during their closed season) but lacking the royal patent to perform the spoken word (although still remaining subject to the Lord Chamberlain's interdictions), the Haymarket stood in a complex relationship of permission and prohibition, satire and protest. Yet it was also directly networked by links related to the newspapers, the patentees, the actors' lives, and the political and social perspectives of the Haymarket audience's attitudes to topics such as marital disharmony, fashionable reading, monopoly power and the permissibility of dissent within the playhouse space. It is all of these layers which form the identity of the assemblage and comprise the exterior relations of *The Separate Maintenance*'s Haymarket performances, a play whose array of actors, as actants, is greater than the sum of its role as a real (or virtual) play text.

CHAPTER ONE

Theatrical assemblages and theatrical markets

If the Haymarket's *The Separate Maintenance* provides a good example of the social complexity of a single production, the contrasting performance spaces of country-house private theatricals and London's larger public theatres present examples of the extremity of gradients of difference across the physical components of the assemblage. These are not just limited to the performance spaces themselves but include levels of audience density and co-presence in the reception environment, as well as the existence of active economic markets across the assemblage. With its recognition of the role of audience populations across the assemblage, the theory helps connect individual private and public performance spaces as cumulative examples of materialities structuring the overall theatrical assemblage and its array of social networks.

Although a general appetite for theatre led to the building of bigger and grander private theatres, such as that at Brandenbourgh House at Hammersmith, it is generally the case that diminished scale is permanently engineered into most country-house theatricals.[1] On the other hand, of course, while the physical size of the main metropolitan theatres conferred greater capacity, the spaces were not always full. Nevertheless, over some extended periods, as in Edmund Kean's first season at Drury Lane in 1814 discussed in Chapter 3, performance populations could reach considerable percentages of the total available London population demographic. The overall volume of the performance spaces (the seats) on sale implies an audience co-presence and density enabling the capacity for considerable processes of cultural change through sequences of deterritorialization and decoding.

An underlying capacity to initiate change is inherent within all populations of assemblages and all assemblages, however small, have populations. Although population mass is not in itself an indicator of a capacity to change, differentials within that mass create the capacity to facilitate mutation.[2] Compared to the largest of London's public theatres playing their standard repertoire pieces to audiences frequently given to fractious (indeed, heated) social exchanges expressive of their heterogeneity, the smallest of Britain's venues (and the most culturally and geographically distant from the big metropolitan spaces) were rural private-house theatricals. There, intersections of venue, performance and audience created social assemblages much more homogeneous and exclusive than existed at their larger urban public counterparts.[3]

All such theatrical assemblages have a singular historical identity, knowledge about which can be derived from studying the intersection of the performance and physical venue. Assemblage theory makes the links between extremely diverse types of theatrical space more comprehensible by indicating their inherent capacity to bring about change in the larger assemblages to which they are connected (as well as vice versa). Typical mechanisms of change would include alterations in patterns of linguistic usage, different attitudes towards sexual or cultural politics, different receptions of economic influence, or varying legal and political affiliations. In these dynamic diagrams of connected networks, the largest assemblages are always connected to the smallest and the smallest to the largest.[4]

Structures expressive of identity are materialized at the performance venues as capacities stored within the theatrical assemblage and diffused along its networks. As DeLanda describes it, the assemblage itself 'is a concept that allows us to retain both irreducibility and decomposability ... [as] a concept that makes the explanation of synthesis and the possibility of analysis intelligible'.[5] With private theatricals providing some of the most attenuated population examples of theatrical assemblage, their connectedness within the theatrical system as a series of possibility spaces allows us to decompose and synthesize their place in it. Differences in scale are important because they are the best indicators of the gradient's levels of the organization, density and complexity enabling the assemblage's capacity for change even if those capacities may be dormant, deferred or only gradually emergent. In visualizing how the smallest private theatrical can be empirically linked to the largest of the metropolitan theatres, it may be useful to think of them as connected within a diagram or circuitry of assemblage, the shape and composition of which are not of any consequence as long as the circuit remains connected across the network.

One of the most extreme and homogeneous types of historical theatrical assemblage that I have been able to locate is a comedy performed at a country-house private theatrical in 1693. The play of *The Discreet Lovers or the Cully Squire*, provisionally attributed to Spencer Cowper (1669–1728),

exists uniquely in a Huntington Library manuscript of its prologue and
epilogue. The rest has been lost. It was 'writ ... at y^c request of several
Ladies and Gentlemen [and]... was afterwards represented by them'. The
remaining few hundred lines of verse tantalizingly summon up a private
performance at an obscure country house in or near 'Hartford' (or
Hertford), England. The author spoke the prologue and 'Arabella', apparently one of the 'several Ladies and Gentlemen ... [who] afterwards
represented' it, spoke the epilogue. *The Cully Squire*'s subject, content
and audience are probably irrecoverable, yet it is clear from Arabella's
final lines that this was a closed circle which encompassed the writer, the
players and the audience: 'All that we can to please you we have done: / I'm
sure at least your entertainment's now, / For it was writ only for us, and
you.' The homogeneity of meaning enclosed within this performance, 'writ
only for us, and you', is a matter of speculation because its parameters of
exterior relations are extremely bounded. The title may suggest that *The
Cully Squire* included some self-satirizing of the author's and players' own
class but the rest can only be guessed. Yet the articulation of *The Cully
Squire* in performance at Hertford also signals the gradient of a high-status
population within this assemblage by virtue of its materiality within an
exclusive private venue and equally exclusive audience ('writ only for us, and
you'). However, as an actualized text in performance, datable to 1693
and located at Hertford, England, *The Cully Squire*'s single performance
had greater density and co-presence of audience population than that found
in the private theatrical fictionalized in *Mansfield Park* or in Joanna Baillie's
unperformed plays. While one existed on an actualized plane of immanence, the others remained real but virtual.

It would be difficult to imagine codings so precise – and options for
alternative decodings so starkly limited – as those which occurred within
that almost certainly unique performance at Hertford. In this way it is starkly
different from the diffused and disaggregated sets of readers of Jane Austen's
novel. *The Cully Squire* sets a good proxy for what one might understand as a
limit on possible performance codings and decodings. Yet it was also part of a
gradient of larger and denser populations within the overall assemblage. As
DeLanda puts it, 'The more homogeneous the internal composition of an
assemblage and the better defined its outer boundaries the more territorialized
its identity may be said to be.'[6] However this assemblage stored or reiterated
its experiences, almost all memory of it has vanished, save for the solitary
Huntington manuscript, on account of its limited connectivity to other parts
of the assemblage with greater population densities and, therefore, more
capacity to store and modify knowledge.

That the Hertford theatrical remained connected to other parts of the assemblage as a meaningful social network (albeit one operating at an almost virtual level) is indicated by its gathering of co-present performers and an audience at the venue (the minimum conditions conferring its singularity as a theatrical identity). *The Cully Squire* was also linked to other recognizable symbolic social registers such as the author's willingness to adopt the contemporary conventions of including a prologue and an epilogue (including the convention of having the epilogue spoken by a woman). These are straightforward textual markers demonstrating connectedness to larger and denser populations of the assemblage beyond the house at Hertford. Of course, the presence of lower- and higher-density populations within the gradients of an assemblage does not necessarily demonstrate where its most territorialized components are located. However, the acts of social segregation at *The Cully Squire*'s performance (it was specifically a *private* theatrical 'writ only for us, and you') achieved a degree of territorialization of its immediate reception environment substantially different from the processes of deterritorialization encountered at performances available to the paying public at the big metropolitan theatres. Such cultural dominance is generally an homogenizing characteristic, derived from the absence of those heterogeneous elements within the assemblage which might threaten its stability. In the absence of viable traces of exterior social networks, these features set an absolute limit on the cultural intervention of this private performance.

The highly attenuated nature of *The Cully Squire*'s reception context at its Hertford performance demonstrates an extreme example of the population of audiences. Even for other private performances, better records exist, helping us trace more fully the materiality of the extensive social networks connected to this type of theatrical. A good example would be the range of private theatrical performances at Irish townhouses and rural estates referred to in the amateur actor Samuel Whyte's (1734–1811) *The Theatre: A Didactic Essay. Including An Idea Of The Character Of Jane Shore, As Performed By A Young Lady In A Private Play, &C. &C* (Dublin: 1790) and (essentially his expansion of it) *The Theatre, A Didactic Essay, In The Course Of Which Are Pointed Out The Rocks And Shoals To Which Deluded Adventurers Are Inevitably Exposed* (1793). As a socially well-connected schoolmaster in Dublin, Whyte both acted in and wrote prologues and epilogues for a range of private theatrical stagings including *The Beggars Opera, Henry IV*, Garrick's *Bon Ton, or, High Life Above Stairs* and Rowe's *Jane Shore*. Whyte's awareness of the colonial context in which he wrote and performed is a fascinating question, beyond the scope of this book, but the social networks surrounding all Georgian theatrical assemblages are rarely simple structures to evaluate because of the evolved complexity of the system in which they were situated.

Connections across the links of actualized networks always reveal differences within the assemblage. Little is quite what it seems. Whyte's record of an apparently genteel 1776 private staging of *Comus: A Masque* (1772) – for which he wrote a new prologue and epilogue as well as played the title role – at Marlay Hall, Dublin, the home of the banker, David La Touche, probably refers to a performance of Covent Garden's risqué version as then popularized by the ex-courtesan singer Anna Catley rather than to Milton's masque of moral rectitude.[7] In other words, the reception environments of private performances are as unpredictable as those of the public venues, and what may now appear canonical texts had already mutated. In some cases the density of the layers of performances within the Georgian theatrical assemblage means that reception difference is generated right across the networks connecting the assemblage. This can be illustrated by the example of Mary Berry's *Fashionable Friends*, which was performed at both a private and a public venue. *Fashionable Friends* was a farce written for an 1801 private theatrical performance at Horace Walpole's Strawberry Hill house (by then bequeathed to Berry) and originally supplied with an epilogue composed by Joanna Baillie and spoken by Berry's sculptor friend, Anne Seymour Damer. Although little is known about its private performance, its indelicate plot of intriguing married couples ('Marriage has cured me of nothing but respect for my own wife') did not transpose itself very well to the West End stage, possibly due to its contemporary public association with the Prince of Wales' Pic-Nic private theatricals, possibly on account of its homoerotic undertones.[8] Again, the social network afforded by increases in the variety of the newspaper and periodical press meant that the play's homogeneity of reception at its single private performance was markedly deterritorialized and recoded when it was performed for three nights at the 3,000-seat Drury Lane theatre.[9] As *The Director*, one of London's new literary weeklies later recalled, 'a dramatic performance [of], *the Fashionable Friends*, sanctioned and approved in a private theatre by individuals in the first rank and talent … [was] soon after rejected and irretrievably condemned by the *mobility* of Drury Lane theatre, as immoral and indecorous.'[10] Although it was much more common for the West End repertoire to find its way into private theatres rather than the other way round, even in this example both sets of performances remain connected, although in different positions on the population gradient.

Such connections between private and public theatres demonstrate the presence of active difference within the assemblage across sets of tangible links materialized at the performance venues. The assemblage model accounts for this diversity, with, for example, the two productions of *Fashionable Friends* demonstrating DeLanda's formulation that 'The identity of an assemblage is not only embodied in its materiality but also expressed by it.'[11] In other words, although both Strawberry Hill and Drury Lane performed the play, the identity of the parts of the population gradient they inhabit is embodied and expressed by the two playhouses' temporal locations and not exclusively contained in the symbolic register of the play's text. Whatever homogeneities of meaning and exclusivity of codings were present at Strawberry Hill were countered by the steeply deterritorializing re-encodings at Drury Lane, which had a higher population density and, therefore, a greater capacity to mutate cultural meaning. Although the Strawberry Hill audience may have been well connected to each other across the homogeneity of their own social network, their reactions counted for little among the much larger and denser audience populations co-present at the Drury Lane performances. In other words, it is not necessary to ascribe any particular sets of cultural value to the reception environments at Drury Lane or Strawberry Hill, but in the absence of evidence of extensive and dense social networks with materialized links, only the West End performances resulted in perceptible mutated or deterritorialized meanings at the reception location.

While it is easy to visualize these extremes of performance reception between an aristocratic, semirural, private house and one of the big urban public theatres, the boundaries between them were not symmetrical during the Georgian period. Some of London's private theatres (but not Strawberry Hill) charged for admission to spectate and for the opportunity to act. As early as 1802, an anonymous commentator alluded to 'several private theatres in the metropolis . . . in Berwick-street . . . Green-street . . . [and] elsewhere', with reports by the end of the 1810s referring to how apprentices or bakers' boys paid to perform in *Macbeth* in a private theatre off the Strand.[12] Some of these London private venues were more well-heeled than others. In 1799 there was a project to establish a private theatre paid for by subscription membership (a 1 guinea joining fee plus 2s. a week) in Lambs Conduit Street, Camden, which allowed for forty male and eight female performers at which 'every member shall be obliged to play some character or other . . . once in three months.'[13] By the late 1820s, William Thomas Rede (whose actor brother had written a manual for Georgian performers) listed half a dozen such venues across London including The

Minor, Catherine Street, Strand (the venue almost certainly visited by John Keats in 1818); the Theatre, Berwick Street, Soho; Pym's Theatre, Wilson Street, Gray's Inn Lane; The Shakespeare, Curtain Road; Wilmington House, Wilmington Square; and the Theatre, Rawstone Street, Islington. These were theatrical spaces 'let by the night or week, for either public or private performances, or most usually for public performances (admittance being had by *tickets* sold at places in the vicinity) by amateur actors'.[14] With most of these private playhouses open by the 1820s, judging by the frequency of their plebeian locations and the fact that by 1831 London could support at least one journal regularly encompassing private performances (*The Acting Manager; or, The Minor Spy. A Weekly Review of the Public and Private Stage*), it is likely these private theatres were fuelled not only by the gradual, *de facto*, deregulation of the patent monopolies but also by a general diffusion of interest in theatricality, perhaps most readily understandable as propelled by the popularity of Edmund Kean's status as a proletarian tearaway star of the stage. Whatever their origin, they contributed to the density of the assemblage population, particularly with regard to the complexity of its activities as a market (as defined below).

To these metropolitan private theatres must also be added a surge in London's regular and irregular public theatres as they tested the strangle-hold of the patentees. They are important to list because they provide some idea of the scale and complexity of the levels of social organization required to perpetuate all of these venues as performance spaces. Although some only opened seasonally, or only occasionally obtained licences from local magistrates, as early as 1812 the capital's total theatre capacity was estimated at 29,500 seats for sale.[15] By 1836 London's new playhouses included the Adelphi, Strand; Astley's Amphitheatre, Westminster Road; City Theatre, Milton Street, off Fore Street; The Clarence, King's Cross; Fitzroy Theatre, Tottenham Court Road; The Garrick, Leman Street, Goodman's Fields; The Haymarket; London Bridge Theatre, Tooley Street, Borough; New Queen's Theatre, Windmill Street; The Olympic Theatre, Wych Street; The Pavilion, Whitechapel Road; The Queen's, off Tottenham Court Road; Sadler's Wells; The Sans Souci, Leicester Place; The Strand, off Surrey Street; The Surrey, Blackfriars Road; The Victoria (ex-Royal Coburg), The Cut; and The Westminster Theatre, George Street.[16] In total, they not only provide compelling evidence of the massive deterritor-ializion of the Georgian repertoire but also give a rough idea of the density of the populations frequenting the theatres and the degree of their collective audience co-presence.

In their wake came new journals devoted to theatre which extended their social networks. One such publication was *The Stage* edited by T.J. Wooler from premises in Catherine Street, the same thoroughfare occupied by The Minor private theatre. Begun in December 1814, it was eventually halted on account of its copyright infringement of John Poole's farce, *Who's Who*, ultimately resulting in Wooler's moving on to begin the famous radical journal, *The Black Dwarf* in 1817. Given Wooler's radical leanings, *The Stage* characteristically championed Kean ('To sum up all in a few word. – We believe the character of *Richard* is played beyond all comparison better by Mr. Kean, than by any other actor now on the stage'), but it also ran a series of anonymous articles on theatre's democratic origins in classical times, idealistically claiming, 'nor was there a Grecian sailor who did not taste the beauties of Sophocles and Euripides'.[17] Not unexpectedly, *The Stage* also commented on the usual Georgian theatre crush ('the pressure of an immense crowd, – a crowd through which it is scarcely possible to force a passage').[18] These public and private emergent metropolitan playhouses also spawned their own disturbances, which, in turn, were reported in the new theatrical journals. A typical incident was carried in *The British Stage, and Literary Cabinet*'s report of how 'A serious riot took place at Bologna's Theatre in the Strand, called the Dominion of Fancy', another fugitive theatre, like The Minor or The Olympic, only a few hundred metres away from the two patent theatres.[19]

All of these examples give some sense of the mass heterogeneity embedded within Georgian theatrical performance even when restricted to its London manifestations. However, the density and complexity of the population gradients encompassing the exclusive private theatres, the paying private theatres and the wave of emerging public playhouses were not accompanied by much in the way of the textual standardization of the plays they performed, even though printed editions were often plentiful and compare extremely well in their print runs with novels and poetry. In other words, differences generated within the theatrical assemblage were also present at the level of the texts the players used on stage. As with Tate's *King Lear* or Milton's *Comus*, even plays now of high canonical or critical interest were not then always what they seemed. Wooler's *The Stage* was typical in commenting ruefully about Covent Garden in 1815 that 'The only novelty at this theatre for the past week, has been the revival of the *Tempest* – not the *Tempest* of Shakespeare, but as altered by Dryden.'[20] Departure from the canon and from standardized texts was widespread, indeed, almost universal. Performance difference was not just limited to incessant movement in temporal and spatial locations but was also a characteristic of the texts in the repertoire.

Any assumption that standardized texts were used in performance even in the late Georgian period needs considerable caution, despite the presence of series such as Bell's British Theatre (begun in 1777), which provided a parallel stream of texts to complement those regularly produced by the theatres themselves. Indeed, the eventual standardization of performance texts probably had more to do with the cumulative impact of substantial (and substantially later) series such as 'Duncombes' Edition' of New British Theatre (532 vols., 1825–65) or Cumberland's British Theatre (1829–75) than it did with anything available in the Georgian period. The use of manuscript transcriptions was endemic and certainly not confined to provincial or poorer playhouses. After its disastrous fire of 1809, in 1812 Drury Lane was obliged to borrow play texts for its reopening from the Lyceum Theatre at the bottom of Bow Street. In all, the playhouse borrowed about ninety mainpiece 'Printed Plays' and about sixty afterpiece 'Printed Farces' but also about forty-five 'M.S.S.', all of the latter evidently for use as performance texts because their titles do not replicate the listed Lyceum-owned printed editions obtained by Drury Lane. The existence of a considerable body of the theatre's acting repertoire in manuscript form is an extraordinary reminder of contemporary casualness towards textual fidelity and a marker of how reception difference was enabled even at the level of the performance texts.

The presence among the Lyceum 'M.S.S.' of plays such as Sheridan's *School for Scandal* and James Cobb's *Siege of Belgrade* (1791), both of them standard repertoire pieces easily available in print, argues that, quite apart from issues of cutting for purposes of shortening, textual faithfulness was often disregarded.[21] Payments made for writing out parts occur fairly regularly in contemporary theatre ledger books, although these appear only to represent special moments when playhouses resorted to outsourcing scribes rather than using their permanent staff to perform this function. One must assume that the use of manuscript actors' 'parts' was commonplace and that performers did not always have access to printed plays, particularly for their individual roles.[22] In other words, the textual codings delivered in performance, even though one might calibrate their occurrence very precisely by the title and venue set out on the playbill, cannot be reliably or consistently extrapolated from a knowledge of the printed texts available today, either in their original printings or modern editions, or through databases of print facsimiles such as Eighteenth Century Collections Online (ECCO). However, in tension with this performance heterogeneity was the persistence of a gradually increasing trend to settle on textual standardizations, although it is particularly important to remember that the national distribution of drama (which is itself a feature of the contemporary theatrical assemblage) meant that such fashions were adopted unevenly across the country. Again, social assemblage theory is helpful in providing a conceptual model for how performance difference arises as an active economy within the assemblage, not only due to the scale of the overall theatrical enterprise but also on account of its complexity and non-linearity of production.

Outside London, in the rural and provincial hinterlands, the assemblage model helps register connections across the metropolitan and regional theatres while also accommodating their actual difference. In this model, standardized texts representing the canon were likely to have had only a real (or virtual) presence inhabiting a subsidiary or deferred plane of existence relative to the actualized performance texts presented at the performance location. Actual performances on the touring circuits only slowly adopted standardization. However, any topography of the social gradients between metropolitan and rural performances also needs to take into account that the populations of performance text (the available texts as acted), even within the metropolitan centres, would inevitably have included a fairly high degree of erroneous manuscript transcription.[23] Again, the theory reminds us that the materiality of a playhouse such as Drury Lane expresses this particular limit on its identity or authority as a theatre where textual fidelity was practised or endorsed. This flattening of the possible ontological gradients concerning the texts in contemporary performance (and of topo-graphical gradients within the shape of the assemblage) is a recurrent feature of the model because the theory materializes its degrees of difference.

Indeed, some of the more regionally distant parts of the overall assem-blage were surprisingly advanced advocates of the modernizing fashion of standardization still only tardily present in London's patent theatres. In the rural hinterlands of Lincoln in 1809, for example, local playgoers set up a short-lived theatrical journal through which to calumniate the manager of the touring circuit (Thomas Robertson) for performing casually delivered dramas, with the editors carefully enumerating incorrect lines in the touring company's performances of *Richard III*.[24] In this instance, enthusiastic rural audience elites clearly demanded a literary fidelity which the players were demonstrably unable to deliver. Their advocacy, deep in the provinces, demonstrates not only the unpredictable pathways of connectivity within the network but also how the metropolitan 'centres' were not centres in the sense of literary integrity. Assemblage theory helps model this past national distribution of theatricality back to the identity of the original sites of performance while alerting us to the possibility of specific differences remaining connected across the populations of performers, audiences and playwrights.

Much of the above cautions us that our knowledge of modern theatres and their current practices cannot be easily transposed back into late Georgian Britain. This is not only on account of the modern unfamiliarity of the repertoire, the restrictive practices over genre within the Lord Chamberlain's remit, contemporary customs of doubling plays, or casual attitudes towards textual fidelity. Coupled to these practices was a lack of direct state support (apart from the crucial monopoly status conferred on Covent Garden and Drury Lane) or of indirect infrastructural subvention, creating the market-driven model of theatricality which became overwhelmingly Georgian drama's most dominant structural feature.[25] A dramatic topography of rural and metropolitan private and public theatres supplemented by fleeting companies of strolling players and touring companies, together with all their individual transactions connected with the production and staging of drama, constitutes the actualized structure of this assemblage. The role of closet or unperformed drama in the formation of this assemblage is vanishingly residual. Since issues such as celebrity or the viability of all theatrical productions are related to the workings of this theatrical economy, the issue of markets and marketplaces needs to be particularly carefully defined.

'Market' in *Celebrity, Performance, Reception* is intended to mean a complex of concrete individual singularities within a set of materialized universal singularities – in other words, the 'market' as part of an assemblage (or an assemblage of assemblages) rather than as a reified, centred object.[26] This is why this book refers so frequently to actual, irreducible, market transactions of money in the theatres; that is, to markets as sets of 'concrete organisations . . . located in a concrete physical locale'.[27] As such it differs markedly from Matthew Rowlinson's *Real Money and Romanticism* (2010), where no individual *£.s.d.* transactions are referenced.[28] Wherever possible, *Celebrity, Performance, Reception* cites real transactions because theatres, whatever their creditor obligations, operated as cash enterprises with their income deriving exclusively from box-office receipts obtained on the night of the performance. Benefit nights, for example, were elaborately constructed around this assumption. For the model of markets as assemblages, the theory suggests that all theatrical market transactions relay between the microlevels and macrolevels of the market's gradients. These transactions are extremely numerous and take place at multiple levels. These included different rates of payment at the level of the individual actors or actresses (for their benefit nights, for example), for individual playwrights (for their copyright or author benefit nights) and even individual members of the audiences (who paid a variable tariff of charges ranging from benefit-night 'Tickets' to half price for afterpieces, differentiated for different parts of the auditorium).[29] These can all be categorized as individual (or micro) singularities positioned within a universal – or macro – singularity of a marketplace of theatres constituted as the built spaces open to the paying public.

Although these striations might appear overintricate or complex, they are still insufficient to illustrate the range of physical individual singularities within the market. For example, even where no documented evidence of the financial outcomes is extant, benefit nights are usually quite well recorded right across the national spectrum of playhouses, indicating at the very least an inversion of the normal monetary arrangements for those types of performance on those nights. Many other practices can never be confidently captured because of the scale and organizational complexity of the assemblage. To take a simple example, the mid-eighteenth-century itinerant actor, George Parker, asserted that the manager of the Gosport, Hampshire, theatre where he then worked, 'In order to cheat his Company . . . kept two Stock-Books.'[30] Within this set of theatrical markets, in the case of London, additional macro-elements, such as monopoly exclusivity over the financial contracts to perform the spoken word, would also have to be included as part of our understanding of their economic status. Preserving this sense of the individual agency of actualized participants is crucial: 'The picture that emerges from this treatment of the micro-macro problem is one of fully embodied historical actors operating at many different scales while constantly having to perform maintenance operations to preserve their contingently produced identities.'[31] The constant flow of individual market transactions across many playhouses and across many seasons all confer on the assemblage this disaggregated but materialized structure, of which theatrical performance was both the aim and the outcome.

Of course, as mentioned above, London theatre was not a free market. Rather, its economics was derived from the context of the monopoly holders who operated a cartel. The notion of a cartel of patentees trading under exclusive and highly specific licences strongly suggests that, as social assemblages themselves, the study of their day-to-day practices materialize and make visible other sets of economic forces expressing their actual identity. The remark of one contemporary commentator that these were 'theatrical cartels for over-ruling merit' not only typifies how non-human actors (through the economic impact of the patents) altered the shape of the theatrical assemblage and that of their reception populations, but also demonstrates how even this cultural homogeneity could be challenged by the presence of a minority of heterogeneous actors (in the ANT sense).[32] Nevertheless, the influence the theatrical monopolies exerted over individual careers, while it is beyond quantification, would be foolish to underestimate. Applying the term to twentieth-century Italian-Americans, Charles Tilly usefully describes the resulting social and economic distortions of the labour market as 'opportunity hoarding', where 'Network, valuable resources, and sequestering combine into effective opportunity hoarding when together they yield advantages in relations with actors outside the network.'[33] The operation of economic determinants as particularly important forces shaping the assemblage, particularly at a microlevel, will be examined throughout this book.

However, given the obvious impact of the London monopolies and their overwhelming concentration in Britain's most well-populated city, the projection of drama into the provinces was also a viable route for those wishing to produce theatrical performances. Each theatre and strolling company constitutes part of this theatrical market in an assemblage of assemblages. Again, modelling Georgian theatricality from modern customs or perspectives needs to be treated with caution, even though this may seem counter-intuitive. Although the picture of Georgian London's public and private playhouses closely matches the highly distributed availability of theatre in the capital today, the analogy does not hold good for the English provinces. Put broadly, the amount of live theatre available in Georgian rural England at known physical locations was much greater than it is today and was as much a typical activity of small towns or villages as of large cities.[34]

De-centred models best reconstruct the shape and topography of the national distribution of Georgian theatricality. The scale and diversity of the national inventory of playhouse spaces provided the material sites for the theatrical disequilibrium in which emergent cultural meanings could be precipitated. Most cathedral cities – Lincoln is one example already referred to – and many of the English provincial towns with markets, particularly those which also served as centres for seasonal fairs, assizes or horse racing, were visited by at least one touring company, which would stay for between two and eight weeks per year, performing perhaps three or four nights a week.[35] Even extremely small villages sometimes supported productions brought to them by touring companies or 'strollers', as they were inevitably termed.[36] Private theatres in small towns were also just as likely to mix professional with amateur actors as the better-known metropolitan private theatres such as the royal Pic-Nic Club of 1802, based off Tottenham Court Road, or Elizabeth Craven, Margravine of Anspach's aristocratic theatricals in 1780s Hammersmith.[37]

In London, on the other hand, while the total amount of theatre was not as great as it is today, it was still impressively large. The two royal theatres, *c.* 1800, had combined annual turnovers approaching £100,000. In addition to actors, dancers and musicians, they also employed many local services and tradespeople ranging from coal merchants through to textile suppliers, 'colourmen', 'tinmen', glaziers, embroiderers and even fruit sale franchisees. In other words, amazingly cash-rich by virtue of their daily takings, the two winter season theatres were enormous capital undertakings concentrated in a tiny area of London. Taking a datum point of *c.* 1800, and including only the two winter-season patent houses of Covent Garden and Drury Lane, plus the summer season Haymarket theatre, the annualized number of theatre seats available for sale in London was well in excess of one million. This figure does not include the extra capacity brought by the emerging, if sometimes intermittently operating, playhouses in the West End such as the Adelphi, Lyceum and Olympic, as well as those only slightly further afield such as Sadler's Wells to the north, the Royal Coburg and Surrey Theatre to the south, and the Royalty in Tower Hamlets in the east, all of which held average audiences of 1,800.[38] This annual figure of around one million theatre seats on sale equates quite closely with the then population of greater London, which stood at 1,096,784 persons at the 1801 Census. By 1815 the population of London had reached a little over 1.4 million.[39] In other words, during this period, the total population of the capital city more or less mirrored the annual number of theatre seats available for sale within it.[40]

These figures are important because they demonstrate the number of theatrical performance experiences capable of being disseminated and consumed in London and are an absolute indicator of the complexity of the assemblage and its capacity for performance and reception difference, as well as its levels of micro- and macrogradients of organization and population density. Everywhere one turned, there were myriad types of theatrical performance available, occasionally glimpsed as microniches of theatricality such as the series of 'Animated Lectures on Modern Characters' delivered 'By Ladies only' at Greenwood's assembly room, Haymarket, in the early 1780s.[41] Within the framework of the theory, they quantify (because they materialize) the gradients of theatricality within the city with respect to other types of social assemblage. The number of available seats for sale, as well as being indirectly suggestive of the totality of the built environment supporting the theatrical assemblage, is also an important indicator of capacity. Again, capacity is a key descriptor because it denotes the existence of a facility for change within the assemblage (what DeLanda calls the 'mechanisms of emergence'), if we remember that each individual in every seat at every performance (and every performer) decodes, deterritorializes, and then re-encodes or reterritorializes the performance meaning.[42] To adapt DeLanda, one might express this seating capacity (which implies the levels of organizational complexity related to it) as an absolute indicator of theatrical difference.

Without the distorting effects of state subsidy, or even substantial courtly favour, market forces, over the long term, produced an audience capacity in the playhouses which closely mirrored the actual take-up of the theatrical experiences they set out to offer. In other words, one must assume a more or less efficient theatrical market. As stated before, unlike the case obtaining in many other areas of literary reception, for this historical period the survival of playbills in association with newspaper advertising has preserved the raw data, allowing specific dramatic texts in performance to be assigned precise venues by date and by location, and for some indication of the scale and complexity of the theatrical assemblage to be estimated. While the sizes of the audiences per night within the theatres might be open to dispute (although some estimation is given below), the quantity of the performances at the major playhouses in London (as well as some of the major provincial or regional centres) is hardly ever in doubt. By comparison, although a case could be made for locating some acts of reading, writing or conversing about literature with some limited degree of specificity, as far as theatre shows are concerned, only a relatively small number of performances are incapable of being located or determined.[43]

The figures for the scale of Georgian London's theatricality may be surprising. Theatre's critical mass both structured and propelled its ability to reiterate theatrical texts on a huge scale. As far as the capital's broader cultural history is concerned, particularly as it has been much revisited by modern historians, the Royal Academy exhibitions (then held at Somerset House a few hundred metres from the two patent theatres) achieved a far smaller scale of cultural impact by comparison. Its principal density as an assemblage was clustered within a fairly homogeneous population component which had the financial and other cultural resources to commission and purchase oil paintings, prints and sculptures. The expectation of royal financial assistance, as Holger Hoock notes, was at the core of the Academy's foundation.[44] When compared to the scale of the visual spectacle and capitalization presented in the nearby theatres, the influence of paintings was low (prints, circulated to disaggregated sets of consumers, function in similar ways to readers of books). However, the Academicians and theatres interacted in a manner which, in the very long term, has become culturally decisive, privileging painting as if it created, rather than mirrored, the centrality of theatre within the culture. Artists such as Sir Joshua Reynolds or Thomas Lawrence sought out the rising stars of the stage for some of their most successful portraits. Subsequently, the gradual, almost imperceptibly slow return of their paintings into modern public galleries has distorted our sense of the original balance between the artists and the theatres on which their work depended. Crucially, the pervasive modern unfamiliarity with both the repertoire and the scale of Georgian theatre has produced a cultural distortion of the past. It was the volume, frequency and reiteration of theatrical performance within Georgian society that created a cultural economy which comprehensively mediated, reflected and produced a variety of perspectives on politics, empire, sexuality and celebrity.

Given the rebalancing of cultural history needing to take place, there follows here some attempt to put a sense of the number, the dimension and the overall configuration of the personnel involved in London's theatre industry. Even to speak of the 'personnel' of theatre is to reinforce a sense of theatricality's mass, physically collective movement, an aspect of its presence as an assemblage not easily isolated or made reducible to its more accessible components of singular celebrity or canonical play texts with their virtual symbolic registers. We have given some outline indication of London's theatre capacity, and this process of recovery begins with defining some idea of the numbers of people involved in the world of Georgian theatre. Invariably, if ironically, it is easiest to start with a celebrity.

In the summer of 1814, at the end of Edmund Kean's first Drury Lane season, one of the playhouse's three accountants (or 'Assistant Treasurers'), Edward Warren, was given the job of calculating the theatre's total audience numbers in order to assess the box-office impact of the new star. According to his figures, the theatre audience that year came to 484,691 persons across 235 nights of performance, an average – according to Warren's estimate – of '2063 [people] Nightly', or about two-thirds of the theatre's capacity, a fairly low average explained by Kean's starting about halfway through the season, offsetting some pretty dire numbers in the early box-office receipts.[45] Although this number obviously includes persons who made repeat visits, it equates to 35 per cent of the capital's population. Of course, only 300 metres away, Covent Garden was running approximately the same length of season and deploying approximately the same audience capacity, although, understandably, the presence of Kean over the road would have diminished their actual audience numbers. Nevertheless, even taking just these two playhouses on their own, the total number in the audiences that season must have been around 800,000. By and large, and although successful plays were run for as long as box-office receipts stayed healthy (especially during the period up to 1794 when author payments remained largely based upon authors reaching their benefit nights), the usual Georgian practice of running two shows in tandem per night (the mainpiece and the afterpiece) also meant that the total number of different plays performed was much greater than it would be today.[46] Apart from the seasonal pantomimes or equally seasonal, morally improving stagings of *George Barnwell*, there was little concept of a single play having a 'run'. The Drury Lane prompter, William Hopkins, carefully wrote at the end of his seasonal diary for 1770–1 that the playhouse had staged '61 different Plays / 37 different Farces / 190 Nights in all', just as for the 1772–3 season he recorded '63 different Plays / 36 different Farces / 188 Nights in all'.[47] In other words, each royal playhouse's season generated the performance of around 100 different dramatic texts. While there would have been some degree of overlap, the presence of the two playhouses in competition for the same audience meant that the diversity and distinctiveness of the repertoire were prioritized.

By contrast, the annual average paying audience for Royal Academy exhibitions was only around 60,000 persons, actually peaking during Kean's years at 79,000 in 1814 and 80,000 in 1817.[48] No doubt many of these Royal Academy spectators aimed to combine their visit to the exhibition with a theatre visit to see Kean. This could be done by simply walking across the present-day Aldwych, up Bow Street and into the Drury Lane theatre entrance. The simple evidence of their two income streams corroborates much of this narrative of their relative cultural profile. The highest revenue received from Royal Academy admissions up to 1818 was £7,500 in 1817, although these figures were not net of expenses.[49] By contrast, even the middling Drury Lane season of 1795–6, before the full flight of Dorothy Jordan's career and during a period of unusual political tension, made the playhouse a surplus of £8,524 on a turnover of £52,620. 19*s*. 6*d*.[50] In any analysis of the theatrical market – or assessment of the determinable capital inherent in theatre – gross turnovers are absolute indicators of economic activity as well as, indirectly, of cultural complexity. Of course, the two sets of institutions were far from being like-for-like and, in any case, treating them as distinctive assemblages muddies the incessant trafficking between the two. The Royal Academy exhibitions were originally devised as a means of generating funds for painters living in reduced circumstances, and hence they followed a largely charitable calling, despite their increasing role in showcasing the Academy's artists and clinching convenient sales. However, even within its welfare function the Royal Academy stands slender comparison with the royal playhouse theatrical funds discussed below. Buoyed up by their exclusive monopolies, the two patent theatres were straightforwardly commercial enterprises. That the Royal Academy was unwilling, or unable, to run its site to accommodate permanent exhibitions was, in itself, a function of its culturally limited role in comparison to the patent houses' double ability to run forty-week seasons with tens of thousands of audience a few hundred metres up Bow Street.

Although these types of comparison may seem unfair, the programmes, schedules and missions of these institutions are reflections of underlying economic determinants which specified the limits of their relative cultural roles in the metropolis. They also denote the relative complexity – or simplicity – in their role as social assemblages within the capital. The Royal Academy's relationship with the royal theatres was one which allowed it to access the greater cultural mass of London's theatrical assemblage, but the absolute cultural impact of the Royal Academy was inevitably restricted by the nature of its economic profile. Even if one includes those grander Royal Academicians who could employ apprentices, the painters did not have much in the way of employees. Operating largely as a restricted access guild under direct royal patronage (the 'King's Artists' of Hoock's title), the Academicians both devised and perpetuated their own cultural constraints. A scrutiny of the playwright-manager Richard Brinsley Sheridan's first season at Drury Lane shows that the theatre that year employed forty-eight actors, thirty-six actresses, six male dancers, fourteen female dancers (including two children), thirty dressers, fourteen doorkeepers and twenty-three musicians in the band.[51] The evidence of records in the Covent Garden ledger books (which provide figures for individual salaries, week by week) suggests that all ranks of Georgian theatre employee tended to remain employed by their playhouse for at least the duration of a season and very often for much longer. What would today be described as the labour intensity of the theatrical employment market generated important social developments around actor welfare. The most important of these was the theatrical funds.

The theatrical funds are exceptionally clear indicators of the density and complexity of the theatrical assemblage and how it self-generated a system to allow it to cope with the actors and performers it employed. They have important implications for how one understands theatre as a gendered workplace in the Georgian. It was David Garrick who first proposed, as early as 1753, a 'Theatrical Fund' to which performers could contribute as well as derive benefits in times of need, although this initiative was not implemented until December 1765, when Drury Lane and Covent Garden both founded, within ten days of each other, funds intent on meeting similar objectives.[52] James Winston, in *The Theatric Tourist* (1805), records the establishment of similar theatrical funds in Norwich and Bath.[53] The eventual Royal Charter of Incorporation of the Covent Garden in 1776 and the Drury Lane Fund's promulgation as an Act of Parliament must locate both of these institutions among the beginnings of modern British workplace welfare legislation.[54]

The nature of the gender balance of professional performers meant that, from the outset, the theatrical funds were obliged to benefit women performers to the same degree as their male colleagues. The surviving 'Proceedings' of the Drury Lane Theatrical Fund for the period 1781–9 make it clear that benefits were disbursed to both sexes under roughly equal conditions. The scheme's condition that members needed to have paid subscriptions for 'Five Successive Seasons' tells us much about expectations of employment stability.[55] Scrutiny of the records of disbursement reveals that such conditions were regularly met. Indeed, the theatrical fund's support by providing annuities in cases of 'Age, Infirmity, or Accident', *de facto*, meant that it operated almost as a kind of virtual unemployment benefit. These benefits could be accessed from any theatre as long as the five-year, graduated contribution requirement had been met and subscribers had maintained payments while in their new employment (although contributions were set proportionate to 'the rate of the highest Salary, by him or her received' while at Drury Lane).[56] The Drury Lane Fund's end-of-year running balance of £344. 19s. 0d. in 1783 was only equivalent to the proceeds of about one or two nights' box-office receipts, but it was clearly sufficient to discharge their obligations, and both theatres' funds held considerable reserves in equity stocks.[57] By the standards of the era, these were excellent employment perquisites, not only permitting a considerable level of personal independence but also meeting many of the challenges typical of the Georgian world where the threat of poverty, the debtors' prison and illness stalked the lives of virtually everyone. The funds have considerable implications for what is understood about the equality of women in Georgian Britain.

The presence of the two London theatrical funds necessitates a radical rebalancing of any assessment of the theatrical profession. The recent critical tendency to picture feisty Georgian actresses precariously negotiating new sets of gendered cultural relations looks rather less challenging when one knows that their personal financial provision sometimes included the prospect of an annuity.[58] By 1813, the Drury Lane maximum annuity was £70 and the minimum £30.[59] Around that time, it is estimated that

£15–£20 per year was considered a low wage for a single artisan, and close to £40 was needed to keep a family.[60] Access to the funds as a subscriber was available to all types of performers of both sexes, including singers and prompters. Indeed, for the Drury Lane Fund, although there was an upper-earnings means test set at the extremely high bar of £300 per annum of household income if cohabiting, it was stated that, otherwise, 'married subscribers to the Fund shall be considered as separate parties, and as such allowed to claim under the foregoing Articles'.[61] Even taken on its own, this single provision marks out the distinctively new social and gender boundaries which resulted from the almost equal distribution of men and women in the performance workplace.[62] That actresses of modest means made it their business to access such benefits is very clear. When she worked as a middling-level actress during the early 1780s, Elizabeth Inchbald very carefully paid 1s. 6d. each week into the Covent Garden Fund, no doubt making a considerable sacrifice at a time when her wage (payable only during the season) fluctuated between £2 and £3 a week.[63]

The reach and flexibility of the theatrical fund welfare provisions can be illustrated by two actual case histories drawn from the Garrick Club's set of Drury Lane Fund 'Proceedings'. Around the time Elizabeth Inchbald was paying into the Covent Garden Fund, the widow of Joseph I. Gawdry (or Gaudry, d. 1782) and the actress Mrs S. Ward both made claims for – what amounted to – death-in-service and sickness benefits respectively. Following her singer and actor husband's death, Mrs Gawdry was forced to find work as a governess in Ireland 'at a Sallary of Eight Pounds per An^m'.[64] However, she also received from the fund an 'Annuity in behalf of her Children', derived from her husband's payments into the fund. A few months later she reported back to the committee saying that her circumstances had changed, and, by 1790, her daughter, Anne (c. 1780–1849), was herself dancing at Drury Lane, playing among other things the cross-dressed role of 'Blunt's Boy' in *Love in Many Masks* (1790), John Philip Kemble's adaptation of Aphra Behn's *The Rover*.[65] In other words, the theatrical fund not only rescued Mrs Gawdry from the relative poverty of teaching, but also enabled her to retain sufficient financial independence to return her family back into the profession. Appearing on the same *Rover* bill, Mrs Ward (playing Angelica) also had a history of having made an application to the fund. Around the time Mrs Gawdry's case had come before the committee, Mrs Ward made a claim on the grounds of persistent ill health. To determine Mrs Ward's claim, the committee requested further information about her circumstances, commissioning a medical report. Ward was only in her thirties and the fund was understandably cautious about committing to paying a lifetime annuity. Mr Pilliner, an apothecary, submitted a written report declaring the 'case is . . . Nervous but is chiefly that Species which are call[ed] Hysterical she has lately had an Hysteric Fit . . . [and is] now troubled with lowness of spirit Tremors and Pain in the Head.'[66] The committee rejected her claim, concluding that 'the Directors think a Nervous case in a Woman of Thirty Six scarcely Infirmity Sufficient to claim upon.' While there is much of interest here about the gendered psychopathology of contemporary medicine, after she first filed her claim and while the committee was awaiting Pilliner's report, they agreed that 'her An[nuit]^{y} be continued' – that is, the fund made payments to her on an interim basis.[67] Pilliner's designation as an apothecary also meant that his work fell under the fund's articles, which undertook to pay, in whole or in part and if approved by the committee, an apothecary's final bill.[68] Indeed, the paper trail of the Drury Lane Fund 'Proceedings' strongly suggests that interim or temporary benefits were usually paid promptly at the claim stage and modified or rescinded afterwards when the claimants' true circumstances had been ascertained. Quite clearly, by 1790 Ward had recovered sufficiently to play Angelica in Kemble's *Rover*, and although she would have been disappointed at having had her request for a permanent annuity rejected, it seems likely the fund's temporary payments gave her some relief from hardship at what was obviously a difficult stage in her career.

The importance of the theatrical funds as they evolved into these surprisingly elaborated forms – which incorporated such things as interviews in the workplace (often held in Drury Lane's green room), medical reports, interim payments, and the provision for both lifetime annuities and short-term sickness benefits – is indicative of the larger and more significant cultural economies at work in Georgian theatre and demonstrates its complexity as an assemblage and how such workplace innovations developed. Although Elizabeth Inchbald was herself a struggling subscriber to the Covent Garden Fund in the early 1780s, ironically the newly opened theatre in Philadelphia in 1794 staged her *Every One has his Fault* (1793) 'In aid of a fund about to be established for the relief and support of those who from age and infirmities may be obliged to retire from the stage'.[69] By 1811 even a speculative project to build a 1,000-seat, private-subscription theatre in Marylebone, London, aimed to include within its articles of establishment a £1,000 'Fund for the relief of Performers, who may have claims from length of Service, Merit, or Misfortune'.[70] This distribution of theatrical benevolent funds attempted to enfranchise all levels of the profession. Although they worked at Drury Lane, neither Mrs Ward nor Mrs Gawdry were particularly high-profile actresses, yet the depth and relative administrative sophistication of the theatrical benevolent organizations which arose to meet their welfare needs demonstrate the labour-intensive nature of the capital's theatrical culture. The Royal Academicians came nowhere near approaching the theatrical funds' systematized levels of provision and support. Unlike with the painters, the theatres' rolling current account balances of a few hundred pounds could easily be boosted simply by declaring a few benefit nights on behalf of the funds.[71] Indeed, the fame of theatrical celebrities furthered the cause of the funds.

Still on the upward curve of her rise to fame, on Monday, 19 May 1783, Sarah Siddons played in Rowe's tragedy of *Jane Shore* (1714), paired with John Dent's farce, *Too Civil by Half* (1778), in a benefit for the Drury Lane Theatrical Fund. The fund took from this performance £251. 19s. 10d. 'Nett' after £62. 15s. 2d. 'Expences'.[72] Siddons had been ill at the end of the previous week, causing the performance immediately preceding this one to be precipitately cancelled.[73] A letter sent from the committee to Siddons shortly afterwards, thanking her for performing on the fund's behalf, provides a fascinating perspective on the committee's attitude to her rising celebrity. At first sight the letter seems innocuous. It elaborately, even obsequiously, notes how 'your own Indisposition was forgotten while you thought on the Illness of others'.[74] However, its transmission also gave the fund an opportunity to send Siddons a reminder of her own professional fragility, even as a rising star.[75] The previous night's cancelled benefit (for which lucrative 'Tickets' had to be refunded) perhaps prompted the committee to signal subtly to her the importance of the Drury Lane Fund's role within an otherwise precarious profession where illness could so devastatingly strike.

Without at all being comprehensive, these diverse sets of information and numbers about theatres, personnel, revenues and benevolent funds help describe the underlying shape and capacities which comprise the components of the theatrical assemblage, materializing them at their performance locations and correlating them against some of the principal types of financial transactions structuring its role as a market.

CHAPTER TWO

Georgian performance and the assemblage model

We have outlined some of the structural features of the theatrical assemblage in the Introduction and Chapter 1, and the purpose of this chapter is to examine Georgian theatricality at the level of the performance and to analyse some specific plays in relationship to the overall theory and its materialization in stage performance. Such a study is essentially an examination of the intersection of three components: actors who played roles, authors who provided the texts, and, finally, venues in which performances were acted. The venue component needs to be explained further because it was the spatial and temporal point of conjunction between the performance and the audience caught in the actual moment of its production. Although the model accommodates the presence of authors, performers and performance texts, the audience component provided the assemblage with the greatest proportion of its population density together with several implicit levels of economic and social complexity. For their part, authors and performers comprise an array of individual singularities (of talent, of professional experience or of expertise, for example) enfolded within a stratum of universal singularities (of playhouses, of audiences and even of generic categories).[1] Within the framework of the theory, 'the ontological status of assemblages, large or small, is always that of unique, singular individuals', with the latter phrase meaning individual entities as well as individual persons.[2] The playhouses' built spaces, audiences and generic setups, together with their links to outlier social networks (such as newspapers), comprise the assemblage's sets of '*universal singularities* because they are singular or special topological features that are shared by many different systems'.[3] As defined above, the playhouses' materialization of author, performer and audiences as assemblages generated the cultural differences which constitute the assemblage's identity.

   Given that performances are reiterations but not repetitions, and that audiences make socially or economically active decisions to attend, Georgian theatre can precisely be described as an economy of culture configured around changing networks of economic, social and political negotiations and transactions. The numerical volume of performers (a term including dancers, singers and musicians as much as actors or actresses), together with the vast number of performances on offer, made it difficult for individual performers to stand out. Of course, their dispersal across extensive provincial circuits hindered their finding national pre-eminence except when they appeared in London. The necessarily collectiv-ized or ensemble methodology of theatres also inevitably required a broad company base of effective and attractive performers capable of providing mutually supportive roles.

When coupled to an extensive, rapidly changing repertoire, the profes-sional lives of performers presented a never-ending succession of challenges. Each performance was a new event, precisely a reiteration without being a repetition and, from a historical perspective, due to the number of tran-scription errors likely to have been in the texts (quite apart from abbreviated or augmented adaptations then in favour), the lines actually uttered may bear only a modest relationship to the texts we might study today. Indeed, for many modern scholars, Georgian theatre manifests as unfamiliar terrain, with respect to not only the contemporary national distribution of its playhouses but also the types of plays and general nature of the assemblage in which they existed.

The eighteenth-century British stage has become notorious for its lack of canonical writing, but it is not until one considers the implications of the factors outlined above that the reason why drama texts struggled for ascendancy becomes clear. With only the two London playhouses holding the licence to perform the spoken word, and with some areas of dramatic discourse prohibited through censorship interventions, the vector through which new writing in the genres of tragedy or spoken comedy could emerge remained highly restricted. Additionally, the persistent presence of mutant texts performed on stage made it much less easy to identify the type of writing capable of reaching critical acclaim and new audiences. What is also less quantifiable is the overall impact of those one hundred 'different Plays ... [and] different Farces' – doubled when one includes the other patent house – which were the regular offerings of the two principal London playhouses. The constant churning of the repertoire only gradually threw up Shakespeare as a figure around whom theatre programmers could con-solidate, and then only with the Bard's works resolutely coalescing around *Richard III, Othello, King Lear* and *The Merchant of Venice*. Less frequently commented on, although perceptively noted in Judith Milhous' important essay on Georgian theatre finances, is the fact that new plays were greeted with an audience enthusiasm immediately measurable (and therefore poten-tially lucrative) in buoyant box-office receipts for first nights.[4] These com-plexities of the marketplace make it particularly difficult to isolate star performers, much less star writers.

Paradoxically, failures could sometimes be successes if taken in raw box-office terms. Hannah Brand's *Huniades; or, The Siege of Belgrade* (1791), when it played at Drury Lane's then temporary home at the Haymarket – a much smaller venue – grossed the remarkable sum of £365. 10*s*. 6*d*., a figure which belies the evening's overall, near-theatrical disaster when the essen-tially amateur actress Brand performed in it herself although stricken with a heavy cold. Despite its single West End performance, *Huniades* actually sold respectably enough. The previous night, David Garrick's *Cymon* (1767), paired with Henry Fielding's [*An Old Man Taught Wisdom, or,*] *The Virgin Unmask'd* (1735) – part of the same revival of the Garrick play for which the theatre printed 3,000 copies – took £393. 16*s*. 0*d*., but, the day before that, at another performance of *Cymon* – this time paired with James Cobb's unprinted farce, *The Humourist; or, Who's Who* (1785) – the theatre took less money than on Brand's night (£352. 10*s*. 6*d*).[5] Across the three nights, including the misfiring London debut of *Huniades*, the theatre itself took around £1,100. These programmes are not exceptional in their configuration. Lucky quirks boosted receipts even more. The 1796 first night of George Colman the Younger's successful *The Iron Chest* (based on Godwin's novel *Caleb Williams* and paired with the pantomime, *Harlequin Captive*) took £468. 13*s*. 0*d*., but scarcely more than a fortnight later, on what proved to be the first and last night of William Henry Ireland's – by then notorious – Shakespeare forgery, *Vortigern* (paired with Prince Hoare's *My Grandmother*), the box office jumped to £557. 15*s*. 6*d*. Again, these receipts for performances of two first-night plays in the spring of 1796 at Drury Lane grossed over £1,000 at the box office.[6] Examining just these five nights of programming, one is plunged into a world filled with the inferred presence of audiences of considerable magnitude, with the playhouse receipts totalling over £2,100 in just these examples, but with very little modern critical or methodological purchase about what was being per-formed or why.

In order to explore the production of Georgian drama at the level of the performances, the rest of this chapter will examine two now forgotten – but then popular – plays about war. As Chapters 5 and 6 will demonstrate, military conflict, either as an aspect of diplomacy and imperial expansion or simply as one of the most pervasive contexts of contemporary civilian life, was frequently represented on the stage. This theatrical pervasiveness makes dramas about war particularly reliable indicators for describing some of the professional production circumstances of London theatre in the 1780s and 1790s. By following two plays, it is possible to contextualize plays in performance and to extrapolate something of their exterior relations with the assemblages and social networks surrounding them.

On 10 May 1793, a few months after the outbreak of the war with France, the low-comic actor Richard 'Dicky' Suett (c. 1755–1805) performed for the first time the character of Mr Indigo in Samuel Birch's new two-act comedy, *The Mariners*. The venue was the Haymarket theatre, at that time rented by the Drury Lane company while their own theatre was rebuilding. Birch's farce was a late-season comedy, making fun of anxieties about a French invasion and portraying trigger-happy provincials and incompetent militia-men nervously acclimatizing themselves to war. *The Mariners* is sympto-matic of the way drama functioned in late Georgian London, sustained by its strikingly memorable actors and its conscious and subliminal links with the metropolis' newspapers. *The Mariners* almost seemed to represent the present as if it were in process. Unfamiliar as it is today, even a piece as slight as *The Mariners* prompted the Drury Lane company to produce a booklet of the song texts, while Thomas Attwood, their composer, published the engraved music (at an expensive 8*s.* per copy) in an arrangement for the domestic instruments of harpsichord and bass continuo.[7] Such printed supplements to performance, ranging from full texts of plays through to scenic descriptions of pantomime, were abundant at the time, extending the reach of the performance into the general print culture and making the songs and music available for domestic performance.

As to its genre, Georgian comedy was deeply revealing of national characteristics. Jean Marsden has argued that eighteenth-century stage comedy was thought almost uniquely to reflect the irreducible elements of the British national character. Since comedy drew freely on incidents from ordinary life, the presence of a virtuous theatrical comedy reflected directly on the moral temperament of the nation.[8] The issues thought to be at stake were of considerable magnitude. Henry Home (Lord Kames) specifically connected the vitality of Athenian satiric comedy with the progress of democracy. Comedy's proximity to the authenticating language and political perspectives of ordinary people, he argued, presented useful indicators of the health of the state: 'Athens was a democracy; and a democracy, above all other governments, is rough and licentious. In the Athenian comedy neither Gods nor men are spared.' By marked contrast, and making connections with the vitiated British slaving cultures of his own times, Home considered that lack of jovial humour signalled the absence of moral sentiment: 'the rough and harsh manner of our West-Indian planters, proceed[s] from the unrestrained licence of venting ill humour upon their negro slaves.'[9] If the presence of comedy in a society could hardly be very realistically deployed as a corrective to slavery, Home's subliminal recognition that theatricality acts socially via systems of coding and decoding emphasizes the particular role of the performer and performance in the collective environment of a playhouse.

A suggestive set of descriptions for performers' roles is included in Gilles Deleuze and Félix Guattari's *A Thousand Plateaus: Capitalism and Schizophrenia* (1980/2004). Although often exasperatingly indirect, Deleuze and Guattari's identification of what they call 'the stagemaker' borrows key elements of its terminology from theatrical vocabularies.[10] The stagemaker is any animal taking to a stage or a platform (Deleuze and Guattari expound on birds singing from branches), uttering or declaring itself, adapting what it has heard and then reiterating its new invention. Their suggestive example of children's nursery rhymes, with their subtle modulation from street to street and neighbourhood to neighbourhood, stresses how performance changes with reference to spatial and temporal dimensions. However, it is Deleuze and Guattari's particular configuration of such processes as acts of territorialization and deterritorialization that holds the greatest theoretical potential on account of its implicit incorporation of the material context of such utterances.[11] While the role of materialized reiteration is only hazily conceptualized by Deleuze and Guattari, Manuel DeLanda's formulation that 'The identity of an assemblage is not only embodied in its materiality but also expressed by it' provides the conceptual breakthrough allowing the performer (the 'stagemaker' in Deleuze and Guattari's terminology) to be linked directly to the venue of performance as well as to a networked relationship with the greater performance context, including that of the assemblages of the larger contemporary culture.[12]

Without rehearsing here all the steps of their argument in the chapter, '1837: Of the Refrain', Deleuze and Guattari describe how acts of utterance delineate territory between speakers and audience ('The territory is first of all the critical distance between two beings of the same species'). This 'has two notable effects: *a reorganization of functions and a regrouping of forces*', resulting in a 'territorial assemblage [which] is inseparable from lines or coefficients of deterritorialization, passages and relays towards other assemblages'.[13] When combined with the implications of DeLanda's formulation concerning materialized networks of assemblage, the rudiments of a true Georgian (theatrical) actor-network-theory can now be put in place.

Georgian theatre materialized, in front of specific audiences, texts otherwise remaining real but virtual. Repeatedly reiterated at traceable performance locations, the symbolic registers of play texts, connected by the
performer to the reception environment, could develop highly nuanced
meanings. In turn, these were capable of being networked and stabilized
across the entirety of the assemblage populations. For example, theatre was a
major agent mediating the dissemination of examples of the national
characteristics defining and differentiating British distinctiveness. Perhaps
surprisingly, such characteristics were not exclusively vested in the repetition of high canonical tragedies but, rather, in contemporary proliferations
of preludes, interludes, farces, comedies and operas, whose representation
relied on middle-ranking actors and actresses. One could begin with just
about any 'stagemaker'. No matter how obscure, they were all integral
components within the theatrical network and its national social assemblage
reiterated through the inventory of playhouses.

To return to Birch's *Mariners*, Dicky Suett was himself a fairly ubiquitous comedian, later remembered fondly enough by Charles Lamb and
William Hazlitt and more pragmatically noted by contemporaries. In the
early 1780s he acted with Elizabeth Inchbald, knowing her sufficiently well
to borrow a guinea from the energetic but hard-pressed actress.[14] According
to one commentator, Suett was 'a pleasant entertaining comedian' but with
a strikingly ungainly physical appearance ('His figure ... too thin for its
height'). However, his actor's portfolio of predictable stage mannerisms
('His turned-in tottering knees and lathy body, when performing old men')
was probably sufficient to endear him to audiences and make him immediately recognizable. Revealingly, Suett was also said to be prone to 'saying
more than is set down for him'.[15] Again, one does not need to wander too far
from the basic principles of assemblage theory (via Deluze and Guattari, via
DeLanda) to realize that Suett was, indeed, a 'stagemaker', elaborating his
own particular utterances by 'saying more than is set down for him', as he
acted in a sequence of performances of Birch's drama, drawing steady
Haymarket crowds.

The situation of *The Mariners* as a new farce, with Suett one of its live
performers, helps materialize the setting of this long-forgotten drama.
Although then occupied by the Drury Lane company, the Haymarket
was normally London's principal summer-season playhouse with a capacity
of some 1,800 people.[16] At that moment, with only the battle of Aix-la-
Chapelle of 2 March 1793 marking any notable British success against the
French, *The Mariners* was just the latest drama on the London stage
reminding audiences of the proximity of Britain's enemies. It was part of

a recurrent group of dramas about invasion, a sequence which included, for example, R.B. Sheridan's earlier but more enduring comedy, *The Critic; or, A Tragedy Rehearsed* (1781), written for Drury Lane at a time when Britain's catastrophic engagement in the American War of Independence made the nation fearful of hostile alliances between France and Spain. The tragedy referenced in the title recollected the Spanish Armada's appearance off Tilbury fort in 1588.[17]

This issue of repetition or, rather, as far as Georgian dramatic perform-ance is concerned, *reiteration* is important because it is the principal characteristic whose territorializing effect confers stability on the assem-blage.[18] In the context of the early summer of 1793, Dicky Suett's interpre-tation of Birch's Indigo embodied and reflected sets of collective anxieties prevalent in these dramas of Georgian Britain. *The Mariners* presented an array of perspectives and challenges faced by Britain in that first full year of war. Although details of Suett's actual performance are now lost, the suggestion that he habitually said 'more than is set down for him' adds an extra dimension to the text now preserved among the Lord Chamberlain's papers. Towards the opening of the play, Indigo takes up a newspaper and reads aloud:

> let's [*sic*] me see – "Theatrical Intelligence" – New Comedy – Psha! Psha! "Hasty sketch of Friday's debate – Negativ'd without a division" – ay all of a mind, that's as we should be in times of danger for as our Poet has it – "come three quarters &c." – Oh come, come here it is, hey! Stop, stop what's all this? "Communication from our resident correspondent at Cork" – "We are credibly informed that some French Vessels have been discover'd making soundings in the Irish channel, but a thick Fog coming on, they were able to disperse unmolested, Ay, ay, they have been making their soundings too, in Old England, but damme! They found us too deep for them – "[19]

This short passage introduces much which is typical about this type of drama. Mary A. Favret's *War at a Distance: Romanticism and the Making of Modern Wartime* (2010) argues that newspapers, clocks and even post-boys helped regularize and structure the period's public and private responses to war, but theatre uniquely provided a living embodiment of texts about Britain's military conflicts through the representational capacity of actors in performance.

Newspapers, clocks and post-boys are readily recognizable subsidiary parts of the networks comprising the contemporary assemblage, but repre-sentational acting (done differently every day – particularly so in the case of Suett's interpolations perhaps) provided markedly higher degrees of actual-ized co-presence among the participant audience at the time of performance, as datable by time and locatable by place. Theatre audiences are the principal components – along with performers and authors – of historically identifiable populations known to be active within this information network. High degrees of co-presence indicate the density of the assemblage and its ability to store knowledge about itself capable of being relayed to other parts of the assemblage. Low-density technologies within the network in the shape of newspapers, clocks and post-boys increase the capacity of the assemblage to change over time and in unquantifiably disaggregated densities of population. However, the concentrated focus of theatrical performance, with its inbuilt differential for reiterating texts through new performances or interpretations, provides high degrees of population component present at recoverable moments and in recoverable places.

Dicky Suett's performance, possibly exaggerated in its topicality by his own textual interpolations, must have embodied in its very comic physicality many Londoners' reactions to the fear of imminent invasion. Performance and processes of enactment made war feel more proximate, not least by virtue of the frequency of their repetition as subjects of stage plays. The theatres, as will be shown in Chapters 5 and 6, were filled with such representations, not least because of Britain's ceaseless eighteenth-century engagement in war and military conflict.

Birch's farce illustrates the interconnection of several discourses and networks symptomatic of a sophisticated and complex metropolitan society in the immediate aftermath of a declaration of a state of war. In this example, a live actor reads from a newspaper and, from the stage, creates (or recreates) alarm and misgiving about a potential French invasion, articulating and embodying processes of fear and anxiety ('Stop, stop what's all this? ... but damme!'). Belying their fictional status, Indigo's words were grounded in vivid contemporary perceptions of the French threat. Although Mary A. Favret has written that, 'after the defeat of Stewart loyalists at Culloden in 1745 [*sic*], distance – either geophysical or temporal – was increasingly built into the British nation's understanding of war', Suett's Indigo is a reminder that the Jacobite rising still stood within living memory and that a stage character could claim, however preposterously since he never went further than Kentish Town, some experience of it, declaring, 'I never alarm myself without a Cause, why do you know I have the very musket by me, that I march'd with in the Rebellion.'[20] Far from war being unfathomably distant, Suett's facility for feigning old men (with 'tottering knees and lathy body') embodied something of a wider communal memory of 1745, here summoned up by an actor only in his forties pretending to be in his seventies. Theatre's conjuring up of this illusion of presence worked through a number of channels simultaneously.

Birch's use of a newspaper as a stage property not only provided a point of interpolation between the safety of the Haymarket and the indefinable proximity of the French enemy but also served as a reminder of how theatricality was itself consciously a subject of *The Mariners* ('– "Theatrical Intelligence" – New Comedy – Psha! Psha!'). Indeed, it is arguable that the entire farce itself was comprised precisely of 'Theatrical Intelligence', incorporating, creating, narrating and projecting different potentialities and variant outcomes. For an hour or so on the Haymarket stage, Dicky Suett embodied, as much as he caricatured, theatre's perspective on the British national character as a literate, politically savvy population, publicly capable but privately worried. While the invasion fears of the 1790s were not the sudden alarms of the 1580s or the fractures exposed in 1745, they were extensively signalled ahead in the press and on the stage through early-summer dramas like *The Mariners*.

Using a newspaper as a stage property was nothing new, but this too emphasizes the actuality of public networks of information beyond the confines of the playhouse.[21] Newspaper columns specifically headed 'Theatrical' or 'Green Room' were commonplace, and the theatres themselves were closely linked to London's daily press. By 1797, Drury Lane was spending around £750 annually to advertise its productions in no fewer than ten London newspapers, including the loyalist *True Briton & Sun* and the rapidly establishing London *Times*.[22] As well as carrying advertising of playbills, newspapers also habitually inserted snippets about theatrical comings-and-goings between news items, even where no theatrical subheading or heading was carried. Indigo's reading seems to reflect this practice with his dismissal of the 'New Comedy' reported under 'Theatrical Intelligence', ironizing his own situation of an actor acting in a new farce. Birch's use of such a template makes implicit the audience's understanding of how information appeared in newspaper format as part of a wider social network whose circulation, at least in part, would have facilitated the decision to spend evenings at the Haymarket.

In his speech, Suett moves seamlessly to the parliamentary reports, apparently commenting on how a time-wasting and frivolous debate has been obstructed now that party politics are set aside in order to prioritize the organization of the war effort. Picking up something of the urgency mirrored in the newspapers, Indigo's eye is then caught by the newspaper's Cork correspondent, who reports an incursion of enemy vessels into the Irish Sea. To Londoners, this would have triggered anxious responses about the possible complicity of Irish nationalists and fears of their alliance with France; this figured in *The Mariners* as reports of vessels 'making soundings', presaging a possible invasion. Indeed, it is the resulting confusion around scares of French landings which forms the basic comic material of the farce: 'French – they are all French in disguise, my life for it – French soldiers landing by degrees in this way round the Coast, and this storm for any thing I know, made a pretence to cover the design.'

The Mariners' importance lies in its typifying the mediation of theatre in disseminating British social and political life and presenting it to large numbers of the metropolitan population co-present with each other at its performances. It was exactly 'Theatrical Intelligence'. Kathleen Wilson has made the first important formulation that 'the English stage [w]as the leading site for the enactment of superior national virtue and character', where 'theater was able to transform historical idealizations into historical "realities" that helped structure and confirm English beliefs about their own distinctiveness and destiny.'[23] One could add much to this, including noting the subtlety of how *The Mariners* also glances at British psychological timidity before going on to assert the values Wilson correctly identifies as comprehensively present on the Georgian stage. Within assemblage theory, the relationship between the theatres and the 'Theatrical Intelligence' columns of the newspapers demonstrates the existence of a social network connecting populations across the theatrical assemblage (e.g. readers, writers, theatre audiences and playhouse personnel both in and out of the performance environment). Within this assemblage London newspapers acted as nodes within the network, storing reputations for current and future reference and providing capacities linked to the theatrical performances. Reviews, managers' puffs and advertising, as well as the specific columns entitled 'Theatrical Intelligence', all filled this role. At even lower densities of assemblage (and with less possibility of recovery), the storage of reputations was also facilitated by audience members conferring with friends during or after the plays or even discussing newspaper theatrical anecdotes. Sometimes (as with the example of Edmund Kean discussed below in Chapter 3), these information networks operating at lower densities were able to provoke the emergence of higher concentrations further up the assemblage's gradients as more links were established across the network's diagram of connectivity.

Completely integral to *The Mariners'* place in the theatrical assemblage was the physicality of the playhouse itself. This was George Colman the Younger's Haymarket theatre, variously known as The King's Theatre and The Little Theatre in the Haymarket. It was part of the national inventory of metropolitan and provincial playhouses that provided the physical spaces of possibility in which, with each performance, cultural meaning shifted. Although the circumstances were different that year on account of the Drury Lane company using its premises, the Haymarket normally had an anomalous relationship with the two monopoly theatres, tending to avoid rather than confront by legal challenge the archaic principles of their patents. Its mismatch within this very specific theatrical assemblage is a crucial indicator of the capacities for emergence stored within the assemblage and materialized in its operating status. Usually, Colman's Haymarket mopped up the capital's ever-present theatrical audience during the summer season when Drury Lane and Covent Garden were closed. As a result of the anomaly which normally restricted the Haymarket to musicalized drama or pantomime and then only for the summer, Drury Lane rented the playhouse during their rebuild, transferring their patent to perform the spoken word to new physical premises on a temporary basis during the winter.[24] DeLanda's formulation is that 'Every assemblage must be treated as a unique historical entity characterized both by a set of actual emergent properties (making it an individual singularity) as well as by the structure of the possibility spaces defining its tendencies and capacities (a structure defined by universal singularities).'[25] The Haymarket's position is clearly sufficiently complicated for it to be easily seen that it comprised an individual singularity within the universal singularity of a dominant local monopoly system of playhouse spaces.

If the Haymarket was beset by a series of material conditions affecting its day-to-day operation (and the Lord Chamberlain's censorship should be added to the list), the playhouse was itself part of a built inventory of established or temporary theatres in a national network of theatricality. Indeed, Drury Lane's rebuild and their tortuous financial circumstances are themselves indicative of a propensity for private financiers to improve the national theatrical infrastructure. Capacities for emergence were materialized at the playhouse sites themselves, these being the principal physical components expressing the identity of the assemblage. As referenced above, the inventory of theatres in Georgian Britain was undergoing a manifest physical transformation at unprecedented rates, a process which can be usefully registered by examining changes in the exteriors of theatres. The network of provincial playhouses, as well as the layers of the touring circuits mapped over them, gives some idea of the topographical extension of the assemblage, which existed not as a standardized sequence of performance spaces sited at regular intervals across the nation but rather as a complex diagram of connection encompassing the various types of private theatres (paying, subscription and domestic) as well as the regular public playhouses. To this diagram must be added the theatres' material expressivity. Georgian playhouses as built environments exhibited their identities as sets of ordinal points, rather than cardinal points, across the topographies of the assemblage. In the provincial and regional towns, as much as in London, the theatres were built around points of collective assembly, often as the outliers of other activities. The reasons for their location differed according to their material context, from the maritime activities of ports, the institutionalizing processes of assize courts, the economic determinants of food and produce markets, or even leisure activities such as horse racing or visiting medicinal spa waters. In other words, the integrity of theatres as spaces of performance acted as intensifiers of difference, their asymmetry (of design, of rationale for construction, of location) generating morphogenetic characteristics across the whole assemblage.[26]

Even a cursory glance through the engravings commissioned by James Winston for *The Theatric Tourist; Being A Genuine Collection Of Correct Views, With Brief And Authentic Historical Accounts Of All The Principal Provincial Theatres In The United Kingdom* (1805), particularly Daniell Havell's unused watercolours assembled for the project (now lodged at the Harvard Theatre Collection), reveals an expanding theatrical built environment stretching across provincial England. Many of the theatres Winston portrayed are fairly plain buildings, sometimes with blank facades, and sometimes boasting porticoes or rudimentary verandahs to protect entering or exiting audiences from the worst of the weather and allow conversational exchange. An etching of the Norwich theatre, around 1802–5, shows how external structures for informal gathering were a continuation of their internal spaces of box and box lobbies (Figure 2.1).

Fairly typical was The Theatre in Edmonton, Middlesex, which Winston described as 'a barn but recently erected' with only a lyre mounted over the main window to indicate its cultural purpose.[27] Even some of the grander resort towns had theatres with plain exteriors. Save for two doors marked 'Gally./Pit' and 'Boxes', the Theatre Royal, Bath, had a blank facade, giving 'the frontispiece a heavy appearance'.[28] In London by 1815, the newly built Olympic Theatre in Wych Street, a few hundred yards from the Theatre Royal, Drury Lane and constructed from an old man-of-war, had an open verandahed frontage (as did Drury Lane itself), while the Royal Coburg (now The Old Vic) of 1818, built directly to the south over the newly built Waterloo Bridge, featured a compressed pastiche of a classical portico. In other words, although the performance action materialized on stage through successive reiteration was expressive of the theatre's identity as an

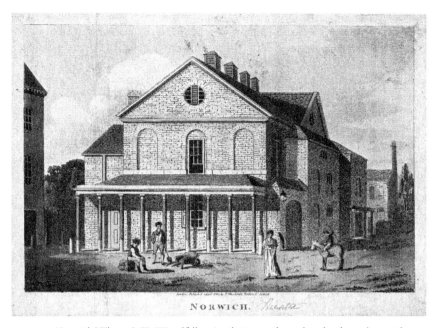

2.1 *Norwich [Theatre]*, T. Woodfall, 1 April 1805, etching, hand-coloured, pencil
inscription. This illustration, possibly by Daniel Havell, appeared in James Winston's
*Theatric Tourist; Being A Genuine Collection Of Correct Views, With Brief And Authentic
Historical Accounts Of All The Principal Provincial Theatres In The United Kingdom*
(1805). *The Theatric Tourist* doubles as an informal census of the provincial theatrical
infrastructure around 1802.

assemblage, this was also materialized as a component continuous with the
functionality of the playhouses' skeletal hardware of stone, bricks or timber.
In the Georgian period, playhouse exterior architecture was not usually
expressive of its interior function in the way we understand it today. Even in
the smarter locations, theatres could easily be mistaken for townhouses or
public buildings. James Winston noted that in the countryside theatres
were often actually barns (Penzance, Cornwall: 'being the Attached Stable
and Granary loft to the Principal Inn The Theatre is above the Stabling –
Dressing Room in [the] roof').[29]

Every performance (reiterated, not repeated) at these playhouses generated a unique performance meaning materialized at the venue, a reception
environment of intensive difference in relationship to the ordinal points of
their location or the expressive qualities of their built environment. As far as

the Georgian provincial playhouses were concerned, every individual singularity was part of a gradient of connected relationships with all the other theatres (plus their audiences, writers and performers) dispersed across the whole of provincial and regional Britain. While they clustered in a group in London (although even there they spread northwards to Islington and eastwards to Tower Hamlets) and constitute an assemblage of assemblages, each with its own expressive identity (e.g. patent and non-patent, regulated by the Lord Chamberlain, restricted to musicalizations), the overall assemblage comprises multiple sets of intensive difference mapped across the country. These continuities and discontinuities ultimately gave the assemblage its overall spatial and material identity as a series of ordinal rather than cardinal points.[30]

On the stages of all of these theatres were living players. At the Haymarket, as in the other playhouses both private and public, the performers and audiences gathered there comprised the assemblage's density and facilitated its capacity to network with other populations within the assemblage. Occasionally, these can be glimpsed in riotous proximity. The itinerant mid-eighteenth-century actor, George Parker, picking up work in Gosport, Hampshire, related how 'Our house in this place was chiefly supported by Jack-Tars – a whimsical race of mortals. These jolly Britons used to sing and drink flip during the performance of the play, and hand occasionally on the stage bowls of punch to the Actors; no unwelcome feast to the poor people, who were starved by the rapacity of the unfeeling Manager.'[31] As well as the physical components of the social networks indicated above (newspapers, advertising, theatres grouped closely within the metropolis, playhouses distributed across the provinces), both the actors and the playwright's texts (interpolated with Dicky Suett's and other performers' now irrecoverable improvisations) all collectively maintained and promoted the assemblage's continuity through nightly reiteration. Added to the production of new texts for performance, there were new interpretations of old performance texts (the eighteenth century was rife with adaptations, from Molière through to Shakespeare and the other Elizabethan writers), and to all of this must be added the practice of performing two plays per night, creating a dazzling proliferation of performance and reception difference.

The difference between the status of texts for readers and texts for performance at theatrical venues has already been alluded to in relation to William St Clair's study of Romantic period readership. *Celebrity, Performance, Reception* has argued that performance meanings are distributed at the location of the performance venue rather than residing in the symbolic registers of the authorial text. Prior to discussing the Drury Lane company's production of *The Mariners* and other plays more closely, it is appropriate to set out the ontology of this difference between texts which are read and texts which are performed in theatres.

Within the ontology of assemblage theory, tracing the exteriority of material relations has priority when analysing historical social assemblages. The density of the populations within the assemblage confers capacity and allows the assemblage to change. To rephrase and reconfigure actor-network-theory, while there have to be performers to make the network actual, non-human actors (material properties such as location) also have to be included within the categories of things playing decisive roles in providing links across the network. As we have described the conditions existing within the theatrical assemblage – for example, its populations, its points of materialization, its local customs and practices modifying the networks, and, not least, Georgian drama's textual parameters (of fidelity and infidelity) – it is now time to turn to the author's own text and the specific performers at the Haymarket.

Bearing in mind that it is only one specific component within the overall theatrical assemblage's expressivity, Birch's text provides an important marker for contextualizing and interrogating cultural attitudes. In *The Mariners* of May 1793, even beer has become ideologically enlisted, with 'The foaming juice of Britain's vine' signifying a national plenitude contrasted to the vinous French enemy.[32] In other words, *The Mariners* is quite specifically located at a point, specifically in the West End, specifically during the Drury Lane company's Haymarket season of 1793, of mediating different responses to the onset of war. Its text reverberates with that moment. Mr Indigo turns out to be not only paranoid about invasion, carrying loaded pistols around his grounds ('let's see (searching his pocket takes out Pistols) O, I have got them, I never care to walk round my Grounds without them'), but also suspicious of the shipwrecked sailors washed up on his estate, fearing 'to be tricked at last by a Seamans Jacket and Trowsers' and reluctant to offer help. *The Mariners* stages the timid uncertainties of a British civilian population incompetently fearful of the very sailors on whom their freedom depends. When first confronting the shipwrecked Mat Mizen and his mates, who exemplify allegiance to patriotic duty ('I won't quit the Service till the danger of my Country is past'), Indigo immediately draws his pistols, mistaking them for French: 'Well how many are there of your gang, What, you thought to impose upon me, now …. {shewing him a Pistol}.' Indigo is alienated and isolated in a countryside whose inhabitants' appearances cannot make them obviously

British. The local militia are even commanded by a Prussian, Fozbourg ('Old Frederick was a great friend to discipline, he us'd to say it was better than any thing for de soldiers'), an unsettling reminder that Prussian military manoeuvres were considered much more effective than those in the British army.[33] Nor were such recent developments in Prussian influenced military expertise left unmediated by theatre.[34]

Birch's *Mariners* almost casually mirrors the widespread contemporary perception that there existed an endemic problem in the volunteer militia system intended to protect the civilian population in the event of invasion. The farce's fractious and unnerved volunteers threaten to disband as soon as Fozbourg raps the ground at their feet with his cane to marshal them into line ('I'll tell you what, if you do that again, I'll quit the Corps, I won't submit to a blow'). In short, Birch's farce was a reminder not only that Britain retained Hessian and Prussian allies, not least as semi-mercenaries in the American war, but also that these were now thoroughly dispersed into the civilian population. In contrast to Prussian military rigour, British volunteer defence forces comprised local men beyond the reach of military law and randomly led by landowners such as Mr Indigo, nervously ready to shoot on sight.

As audiences watched Fozbourg drill his incompetent and truculent volunteers, they could balance the mutinous Sheers (the one who had threatened to walk off) with the more positive militiaman, Cooper ('how are we to be taught, if we don't submit to discipline – don't spare us'). For his part, Fozbourg's apparently thorough grounding in English traditions could be signalled by his reassuring use of the local tavern, 'You shall now file off to de Bear and Ragged Staff, my head Quarters.' Although couched in comedy, some of the deeper worries about the state of the nation spilled out. Indeed, the text's symbolic registers themselves display different component parts of their imaginary populations, which, as in a work of fiction, appear to mirror different gradients within the material social assemblage.

One such component lurking very visibly beneath *The Mariners* was the age's pervasive anxiety about the calibre of British manhood, here glimpsed in the vainglorious military puffery of the dangerously pistol-wielding Mr Indigo and sketched out more fully in the timorous buffoonery of the militia. Fears of male effeminacy were rife throughout the century and endemic on the stage. Sheridan's much imitated *The Camp* (1778) had recently popularized such misgivings about military men but the anxieties can be traced much further back, at least as far as Charles Shadwell's repertoire staple, *The Fair Quaker of Deal; or, The Humours of the Navy* (1710), with its description of a new type of 'Gentleman Captain . . . our

Sea-Fops, who forsooth, must wear white Linen, have Field Beds, lie in Holland Sheets, and load their Noddles with thirty Ounces of Whores Hair' (p. 22).[35] Peg Woffington's appearance as Britannia in a Drury Lane epilogue of October 1746 not only consolidated the popularity of actresses in military cross-dress but also, of course, materialized the physicality of its appearance. In her case, Woffington's ostensibly comic role voiced ideological solidity ('Unite my fav'rite Sons, inspired by me / And draw the sword for George and Liberty!'), although even she, by that time, was building on her earlier appearances as 'The Female Volunteer' with its equivocal backstory of military uncertainty.[36]

   A principal feature in examining these theatrical assemblages is their density and constant reiteration through repeated performances in new versions. The proliferation of Georgian theatricality across many playhouse programmes provided the capacity for social perspectives to mutate at the location of their specific reception environments. The mutations are often most marked or visible in the presentation of challenges to gender roles. Forty years after Woffington's appearance as 'The Female Volunteer', a comic opera by George Colman the Younger's Haymarket company, John O'Keeffe's *The Siege of Curzola* (1786), portrayed vigorous martial female valour on a much more extended scale. Similarly produced at Colman's Haymarket, like Birch's *Mariners*, O'Keeffe's play was typical of a number of dramas dealing with masculinity and a preoccupation with military conflict. In *The Siege of Curzola*, which is based on the defeat of the Ottomans in 1571, the same year as the Battle of Lepanto, the besieged Venetian Antonietta suddenly appears on stage to rouse Curzola's female inhabitants to defend the city, the menfolk having gone off to engage the Turkish galleys, leaving them behind ('your husbands and sweethearts have shear'd off like Lubbers'): '{Enter Antonietta with a Crossbelt sabre and Harquebuss} . . . I'm a petty officer – Corporal Antonietta[,] let the Turks enter our Town if they dare – we're ready for them – fire.' Such harquebus-firing women contrast sharply with stage representations of the flat-footed and effeminized militia of Birch's farce. In this case, Britain's recurrent doubts about the militias were vividly encapsulated in *The Siege of Curzola*, in a song by Cricolo, a Venetian barber turned quack doctor: 'For my country I shoulder my musket, my razor and pestle I drop, / If an enemy ever invade us, I'll bravely go hide in my shop.'[37] Again, what is noticeable is London theatre's ability to compact these important debates about the nature of military masculinity within the guise of comedy. *The Siege of Curzola* was performed seven times in its first season (with the Haymarket's programming restricted by the shortness of their summer licence) before

being revived again in a shortened version in July 1787. However, even in its
initial season it would have been performed to some 10,000 people.

Neither were these types of drama rare. Dicky Suett of *The Mariners*
played in (and wrote the song lyrics for) the Drury Lane company at the
Haymarket's same season afterpiece, *The Female Duellist* ('Tis even so – the
spirited hero, the formidable rival and dreaded duellist was but a simple
girl').[38] In these contrasting examples, all presented to Haymarket audiences
by two different companies, the characteristics of the timidly fractious
British militiamen in *The Mariners* – depicted in 1793 at the beginning of
a formidable war – can be compared with the unhesitant volunteering for
civic defence by the Venetian women in *The Siege of Curzola*. In short, these
were plays, typical as they were, providing carefully nuanced projections of
the gendered national character. In *The Siege of Curzola*, almost as if to
recognize his awareness of sensitivities to perceptions of male military
shortcoming, O'Keeffe introduced – as a revealingly illustrative sideline to
the main action – a band of British seamen who fortuitously turn up in
Curzola to assist the abandoned and beleaguered Venetian women.

Viewed in correlation to any number of other dramas from the period,
the visibility of the patriotic politics of gender is both predictable and
repetitive, the symbolic registers of the text repeating ideological messages
which were reiterated and materialized through successive performances in
London's West End and, of course, made available for new successive
audience encodings. In *The Siege of Curzola* the women receive pithily
humorous condescension ('Ah blessings on your locks and on your fire-
locks'), while the sailors reinforce the drama's primary underlying narrative
of the distinctiveness of Britain's national character and its historic destiny,
this time 'for the honour of England's sovereign the great and glorious
Queen Elizabeth who is a woman like yourselves we'll stand by you to the
last drop of our blood.'[39] If *The Mariners* projected a number of ideological
faultlines within a country newly at war, an analysis of *The Siege of Curzola*
of 1786 demonstrated the depth of drama's ability to embody uncertainties
as to appropriate gender roles during periods of conflict.

The Siege of Curzola, much like *The Mariners*, is part of a network of
dramas performed in London that reflect anxieties about British military
readiness and the fabrication of appropriate gender roles. Recourse to
assemblage theory provides the reminder that such thematically overlapping
dramas ran on a successfully commercial basis at the Haymarket, much as
they did at other theatres. It seems reasonable to conclude that specific
populations within the assemblage (identifiable by playbill and performance
text) were sufficiently worried (or simply fascinated) by such dramas that

they consistently paid to visit them in large numbers. Within the meaning of the theory, *The Siege of Curzola* and *The Mariners* present an evidentially locatable sequence of play performances the reputations of which were relayed across the networks of the assemblage. Awareness and dissemination of their topicality, relevance and popular interest were stored by each new performance and amplified through links to the network of newspapers closely mirroring and advertising the schedules of the theatres.

Newspapers are recurrent links in the network, filling a number of roles. As with the references made in Sheridan's *Camp* to the 1588 Spanish Armada, *The Siege of Curzola* stressed historical continuities helping solidify contemporary popular receptions of British destiny. In case the public did not make the play's intended historical links independently, the Haymarket's manager took great pains to puff these aspects of the production in the London newspapers. In an issue of *The Public Advertiser* published three days before the first night, Colman fed the newspaper the copy that 'all hands are at work, and busy in clearing the decks for *The Siege of Curzola*, the gallant *O'Keeffe* Commander!' More to the point, however, *The Public Advertiser* went on to make explicit during this pre-production phase the exact connections between British history, both recent and remote, which it wanted the public to appreciate: 'The siege is, we hear, to be sustained by a *posse* of Ladies, headed by two or three British tars of the true *Elizabeth* breed, in whose reign the Adriatic exhibited this gallant action of the women and sailors; an action almost as memorable as those of Eliott and his associates at the *Siege of Gibraltar*, in the reign of *George the Third*, whom God long preserve!'[40] Giving details of the 1571 incident no doubt supplied directly by Colman, the newspaper reprinted an extract from Richard Knolles' *General History of the Turks* (1638) – presumably also the source of O'Keeffe's narrative. What is most vivid here is Colman and O'Keeffe's direct connection between the besieged Venetians of the reign of Queen Elizabeth I and the much more recent Franco-Spanish siege of British-held Gibraltar, blockaded for nearly two years until the siege was lifted during the command of the governor, George Augustus Eliott (1717–1790), in February 1783. Unsurprisingly, in view of the general argument of this book, all of this information appeared under *The Public Advertiser*'s heading of 'Theatrical Intelligence'.

The Public Advertiser's 'Theatrical Intelligence' column, as Colman knew, was an intrinsic part of the theatrical assemblage connecting him with *The Siege of Curzola*'s theatre-going, newspaper-reading audience, but it is also worth pausing to notice exactly how much cultural and political depth this drama had. Despite its unpromising generic location as a comic opera (a genre which helped the Haymarket meet the Lord Chamberlain's licensing restrictions), *The Siege of Curzola*, as much as any other drama of its period, carried an array of almost subliminal, theatricalized messages about the way in which constructions of gender intersected with the ideologies of nation.

The way social assemblage theory functions with respect to observable ideologies latent within the populations present within the assemblage is to make a point of evaluating or emphasizing the degree of their materialization, isolating their individual singularity in relationship to universal singularities elsewhere across the assemblage. As far as the role of O'Keeffe's text is concerned, to use DeLanda's coinage derived from Deleuze, it operates on a plane of immanence constantly relating with a plane of reference, or, to put it another way, a plane of the virtual or 'real' intersecting with the plane of the actual or materialized.[41] This particular theatrical assemblage of the late 1780s in which the Haymarket was positioned already had present within it a fully functional and materialized network, which included newspapers, London's cluster of other theatres, and the complex sets of subsidiary networks of actors, managers and other playhouse personnel, quite apart from the continuing presence of audiences for all of these things.

Each performance, according to the theory developed in this book, marks a changed cultural meaning, and there were many performances, even of plays such as *The Mariners* or *The Siege of Curzola*, which have now been long forgotten. The density of this theatrical network and of the assemblage to which it is attached has been stressed already with its ability to connect its populations, to store reputations or narratives, and to reproject them in newly decoded and deterritorialized forms. For the female actors and for the overall place of women in late eighteenth-century British society, theatre presented a physical environment where new modes of behaviour could be reiterated night after night and, inevitably, because of the connectivity of the assemblage, also across the assemblage's populations. While the ordinariness of both *The Mariners* and *The Siege of Curzola* has been emphasized, O'Keeffe's drama provides a particularly good opportunity to see typical portrayals of gender relations. In order to particularize the singularity of the historical moment of its performances, we must also look at the work of the women who acted in it, the principal and actual agents of its changing reiteration at each performance.

In O'Keeffe's gender configuration, women defend patrimonial territory while men abdicate their normally assigned gender roles as defenders of their womenfolk. In *The Siege of Curzola* these cultural layers are mapped over the city's imagined gendered social structure. That republican

Venetian women defend themselves against despotic Turks also marks a further religious stratification superimposed on the gendered and political aspects of the drama. In short, Christian women are shown opposing Islamic incursion. The economy of the presentation and sheer compression of all of these issues in O'Keeffe's drama is remarkable. When one of the Venetian males, Pompeio, hides in the city rather than fight the Turks at Lepanto and disguises himself in Ottoman dress, he is quickly spied by the Venetian women, who are already armed and inspirited to fight: 'Antonietta: Here he is – one of the savage Infidels – Enemies to Christianity that wou'd have destroyd our Town – fall on my Amazons.' Of course, Pompeio is able to reveal himself in good time but, despite the opera's comic structure, their confrontation rehearses these several significant layers of ideological meaning.

The Siege of Curzola presents uncompromised female militancy. While Colman (or the newspaper) called them a '*posse*' of women, O'Keeffe presents them as women abandoned by men and put into an unequivocally defenceless position, requiring them to take to Curzola's fortifications armed with their sabres and harquebuses (the forerunner of the flintlock musket): 'Scene 6 On the Works . . . . {Enter Antonietta Bab Stella and the Women arm'd . . .}.' In the finale, the departing sailors remind the Curzolan women that British male valour and Venetian female militancy create a formidable combination: 'Girls whenever your runaway Lubbers attempt to take the Command shoulder your Muskets make them strike to your flags and bid 'em remember "The Siege of Curzola".' Through such dramatic sleight of hand, O'Keeffe confirms not only the age's uncertainty about male military capability but also its crucial underpinning and endorsement by women when linked to the patriotic dependability of the typical British sailor at home or overseas.

With reference to assemblage theory, perhaps *The Siege of Curzola*'s most interesting performance characteristic is the local organization of the performers themselves. *The Siege of Curzola* repeatedly expressed these new social and political roles for women as part of its textual performativity materialized at the Haymarket enactments. O'Keeffe's particular ontology of gendered behaviour was a cultural function also performed in the lives of the theatre's actresses. Again, working within the theory, the fully historicized individual singularities of the actresses (playing in the play at the Haymarket in 1786) form part of a relay of connections with the universal singularities operative within the larger population components of the assemblage. To give an example of such individual singularities and their relationship to universal singularities, the Haymarket actresses, although not at that time personally eligible to benefit from the welfare provisions offered to female employees by the Covent Garden or Drury Lane theatrical funds, would have been aware of their existence as a universal or general singularity within their profession and eligible for them if they transferred employment. Their grouping as a nightly collectivity of women on the Haymarket stage materializes their cultural position. With assemblage theory, an empirical relationship can be established connecting the mate-rialized texts enacted with the populations within the assemblage to which their performances referred. Their performances provide a rich topography of the capacities for change vested within the assemblage. The analysis of these exterior relations starts with the professional lives of the performers.

Among the five actresses cast in *The Siege of Curzola* was Elizabeth Bannister (1752–1844), whose husband, John, played Pompeio. Her career was successful by any standards. In 1778 she was rumoured to have been 'engaged by the proprietors of the Pantheon, for two years, at the salary of *One Thousand Pounds*'.[42] At the other end of the professional scale of prestige was Giovanna Sestini (active 1774–91), principally a singer. Sestini seems to have struggled to earn more than £100 to £200 per season plus benefit nights, despite her highly fashionable Italian singing style.[43] Situated somewhere uncertainly between Bannister and Sestini in *The Siege of Curzola* can be placed the actress Margaret Cuyler (1758–1814), a regular at the Haymarket, but one who, according to contemporary accounts, mixed acting with the lifestyle of a courtesan.[44] Whatever the tensions or prox-imities involved in negotiating their relative status at the Haymarket, these actresses obviously cooperated professionally both at the Haymarket and elsewhere in London's entertainment industry. In the same year as *The Siege of Curzola*, the actress playing Teresa, Georgina George (d. 1835), sang alongside her Haymarket colleague, Giovanna Sestini, in London premieres which featured new Haydn sonatas.[45] Indeed, George's career on its own illustrates much about contemporary actresses and their employment cir-cumstances. Two years before *The Siege of Curzola*, she had appeared at Drury Lane, and secured a benefit night but suffered a net loss of £34. 11s. 6d., a 'deficiency' – as it was termed – which she was forced to reimburse promptly to the theatre. The same summer as *The Siege of Curzola*, George also sang at Ranelagh Gardens, returning there again (as well as to the Haymarket) one year later before performing in seasons at Dublin, Limerick and Cork prior to departing for Philadelphia in 1793, where she joined Thomas Wignell's newly opened Chestnut Street Theatre.[46] Quite apart from eventually risking this dangerous journey to America, Georgina George also mixed in spells at the fugitive Royalty Theatre in the East

End of London, similarly marking her willingness to embrace the full spectrum of the professional opportunities open to her as actress and singer.[47] Indeed, largely impelled by the Haymarket's licensing requirements, the musical dimension of *The Siege of Curzola*, to the success of which George contributed, provided a significant augmentation of its theatrical impact. In addition to audience figures of around 10,000 for its first season, the text of one of Teresa's songs (written by O'Keeffe) was pirated as a broadside ballad complete with the printer's anachronistic Queen Anne era woodcut portrait vignette, and entitled *The Jene Scai Quoi a New Song* (c. 1786).[48] *The Siege of Curzola*'s musical composer, Samuel Arnold, also rearranged the score for voice and harpsichord, the premiere domestic keyboard instrument of the day.[49] These types of dissemination, perhaps conveyed around both the greater metropolis and the provinces by itinerant ballad-sellers or, in the case of the harpsichord score, bought by middle-class households for domestic performance, are strongly suggestive of theatre's cultural reach and the ability of the network to store and reinforce aspects of the original performances via a further medium through which the opera continued its impact beyond the theatre.

This female ensemble's cumulative musical capability helped successfully project *The Siege of Curzola* to ever-larger audience groups – conceivably its music even reached into domestic spaces – but there were also other factors at work, both physical and moral, which projected their dramatic power to London audiences. With Elizabeth Bannister apparently happily married to a Haymarket stalwart, she seems to have appeared to her public as a kind of standard of domestic virtue, attracting very little scandal or scurrilous comment. *The Green-Room Mirror* (1786) referred to her 'chaste and syrenical [*sic*] display', and even the mischievous *Secret History of the Green Room* (1790) made do with saying, 'This lady is one among the few whose moral rectitude does honour to the Stage . . . the breath of scandal has never yet touched her name.'[50] By contrast, Margaret Cuyler's occupation of the same stage would have provided a very different perspective, accentuating perceived moral differences between the two women. Audiences would have quickly perceived that Cuyler and Bannister dramatized the difference between vice and virtue and, indeed, that the Haymarket fielded them together exactly for that dramaturgical reason. As early as Elizabeth Barry and Anne Bracegirdle's pairing at the New Theatre, Lincoln's Inn Fields, in the 1690s, actresses working together in the same company successfully amplified and contrasted their on-stage personalities to assist their prestige and marketability.[51] If, as seems likely, Sestini and Georgina George were cast alongside them to provide a powerful and professional vocal singing duo, then Bannister and Cuyler were almost certainly deliberately paired to project a visually and audibly powerful ensemble of contrasting moralities. To both complement and complete the quartet, in this particular Haymarket production, the fifth actress was Mrs [Richard?] Webb (d. 1793), a middle-aged and (by then) overweight actress facetiously described in *The Secret History of the Green Room* as, 'certainly the most conspicuous woman on the Stage' (or, much less kindly, 'uncommonly lusty and grotesque').[52] By virtue of her physical stature as much as her wealth of experience, Webb almost certainly anchored the show, acting as both foil and centrepiece for the other four actresses.

Bannister, George, Cuyler, Sestini and Webb's roles in *The Siege of Curzola* illustrate a typical rationale for female dramatic casting in late eighteenth-century London. While their career paths were as varied as their individual physical appearances and professional characteristics, they had obviously been brought together by the Haymarket manager exactly to capitalize on the type of dramatic diversity their strengths as performers could collectively offer in *The Siege of Curzola*. Such was the extent of the public's interest in theatre that their lives were the subject of public scrutiny – none of them escaped publications such as *The Green-Room Mirror* or the various editions of *The Secret History of the Green Room*, not to mention the capital's almost daily newspaper columns of 'Theatrical Intelligence'. They clearly formed an ensemble of actresses selected by Colman for their contrasting reputations, abilities and talents. Moreover, it was an ensemble that worked both in contrast and in combination, virtue and vice as Bannister and Cuyler, English and Italian song with George and Sestini. Webb's role as anchoring comedienne worked to pull them together, creating a centrepiece for the double duo. No doubt, O'Keeffe, a playwright closely associated with the Haymarket since 1781, wrote *The Siege of Curzola* if not exactly with them in mind, then certainly to fit actresses very like them. It is *The Siege of Curzola*'s very ordinariness of stature within the capital's hectic theatre programming of the late 1780s which makes it so revealing.

Not least, there were important underlying structural reasons why the Haymarket actresses worked their professional lives very differently from those in patent houses. The Haymarket's actresses would have been all too aware that the restrictive monopolies on the spoken word held by the winter-season patent houses inhibited their own ability to find work in London during the long winter season – the 'opportunity hoarding' referred to by Tilly. A structural consequence of the patent-house monopolies, which in any case worked to squeeze out competition from rising performers or innovative managers at other venues, was the sharply asymmetrical sets of actors' earnings and the profiles of their fame. As the idea of public celebrity grew relentlessly, if unevenly, during the eighteenth century, in cultural spheres as divergent as literature, boxing and self-promotion, the gap between the workings of a free market in talent and the underlying economics controlling structural formation became more difficult to transcend. The Haymarket's complex and anomalous situation within this assemblage is difficult to overstate.

CHAPTER THREE

Theatrical celebrity as social assemblage: from Garrick to Kean

The presence of 'celebrated' actors and actresses was a permanent feature of metropolitan theatre by the late Georgian. It is a subject increasingly investigated by scholars.[1] Celebrity, particularly as part of the public discourse of the theatrical assemblage, gradually transformed itself into a generically Romantic ideology of individual interpreters whose expressive or interpretive abilities distinctly exceeded all others. However special or well adapted they became, celebrities are precisely what Deleuze and Guattari call 'stagemakers' – that is, persons whose reputations are linked to emergent features of the assemblage.[2] As adapted to social assemblage theory, the role of the stagemaker is entirely related to the materiality of assemblages and their properties. Information passed along material linkages across the assemblage determines the identities of celebrity categories of stagemaker. In the cases of David Garrick (1717–1779) and Edmund Kean (1789–1833), these materialities can be described with great clarity.

As far as performers are concerned, celebrity reputations were cultivated and managed, inflated or deflated, through authorized (or unauthorized) biographies, caricature and classical portraiture, discrete anecdotage, newspaper coverage, and, not least, through conversational pastime, with all of these media filtered through to the public along an array of channels or networks.[3] Although the *OED* does not show the word used until 1849 to denote a famous person in the public gaze, the usage of the participial adjective, 'celebrated', was widely adopted in public discourse, particularly with reference to theatre workers. Early Georgian accounts show that the idea of celebrity in the modern sense of persons whose private lives, from birth to death, are considered open to public scrutiny was already familiar. By 1749, someone had published an *Account of the Life of that Celebrated Tragedian Mr. Thomas Betterton. Containing A Distinct Relation of his Excellencies in his Profession, and Character in Private Life* (1749), but even this had been preceded by Edmund Curll's *Faithful Memoirs of the Life, Amours and Performances, Of That Justly Celebrated, And Most Eminent Actress Of Her Time, Mrs. Anne Oldfield* (1731).

Curll's *Faithful Memoirs* openly announces its attempt to narrate the actress' love life and stage performances, but it also probed areas normally only of interest to close friends or family. As well as eulogies and other commemorative poems, together with a precisely itemized list of her household inventory at death ('A Gold Smelling Bottle. Six Gold Stay-Buckles and Tags . . .'), the account also included information drawn from Margaret Saunders, her ex-actress friend and confidant, as to Oldfield's appearance at the point of burial: 'As the Nicety of Dress was her Delight when Living, she was as nicely dressed after her Decease; being by Mrs. Saunder's Direction thus laid in her Coffin. She had on, a very fine Brussels-Lace-Head; a Holland Shift with Tucker, and double Ruffles of the same Lace; a Pair of New Kid-Gloves, and her Body wrapped up in a Winding Sheet.'[4] It is noticeable how neatly Curll manages the transition between the 'Nicety of Dress' adopted by the actress while alive and in the public gaze and her appearance, almost as if in a final role, 'nicely dressed after her Decease'. This kind of pathological interest in the personal and private details of celebrity performers is, of course, very familiar to modern readers. Other publications similarly made it clear that, in the modern sense, Oldfield was perceived as a celebrity: 'How have I seen the crouded Audience hang with Attention upon her Tongue, and devour her with their Eyes, whenever She appeare'd! How significant was her every Motion and Gesture!'[5]

However, the primary element in the operation of all of these cultural media is that celebrity is an absolute function of the prevailing reception environment, which includes theatre as a marketplace. A further, secondary, characteristic is that, apart from possibly the specific genre of solo shows, actors and actresses (like singers and orchestral musicians) always work alongside and in consort with other practitioners of their art, sharing the stage and usually being co-present while their colleagues are themselves presenting.

This structural combination of a reception environment (the consumers) together with the co-presence of other performers is a good indicator that celebrity is an assemblage. This pattern also suggests that celebrity relations of exteriority present the most promising perspective for analysing assemblage constructions which rely entirely on the presence of clusters, densities and gradients of population within their components. Indeed, the rise of celebrity in Western cultures is an excellent illustration of how seemingly disaggregated populations in the reception environment have capacities

mutating across otherwise scarcely visible connected networks which provide the conditions in which celebrity can thrive. These relays across social
networks, even if the diagram of their connections seems not readily
comprehensible, propagate links and nodes where information can be
stored, permitting the networks to mutate because of the assemblage's
inherent capacity for difference and emergence. Relations of exteriority
across the assemblage are the chief objects of the study of celebrity, and
not celebrity itself.[6] As DeLanda puts it in a way which can be easily
transposed to the structure of celebrity, 'it is *the pattern of recurring links*,
as well as the properties of those links, which forms the subject of study, not
the attributes of the persons occupying positions in a network.'[7] By avoiding the reification of celebrities as if they were exceptionally centred essences
of individuality, assemblage theory offers to track the disaggregated social
networks conferring celebrity on the celebrated.

The principal methodological parameter is that 'the properties of the
links cannot be inferred from the properties of the persons linked.'[8] As far as
theatre is concerned, the formulation required is that celebrity itself is an
assemblage operating within an overall theatrical assemblage. To clarify the
epistemological paradox, 'All assemblages have a fully contingent historical
identity', but 'Because the ontological status of all assemblages is the same,
entities operating at different scales can directly interact with one another,
individual to individual.' The idea that celebrities (or their followers, imi-
tators or emulators) never exist as isolated categories (for example, as specimens of 'genius') is also modified by the rule, 'At any level of scale we are
always dealing with *populations* of interacting entities.'[9] Within this flattened ontology, the most promising areas for the recovery of celebrity
populations within the Georgian theatrical assemblage are those concerned
with economic relations, since these not only reflect the complexity of the
assemblage itself but also manifest the levels of its exteriority and connection
to multiple aspects of the reception environment. Economic or market
relations happen also to have often archived some of the best-documented
traces promising empirically robust sets of data to recover the contingent
historical identity of the assemblages.

The extent and complexity of the theatrical market has already been
emphasized together with a number of the financial details which ought to
help focus the theatrical assemblage as a particular marketplace with specific
customs and practices of organization. As far as the role of celebrity
performers is concerned, the same axioms about assemblage apply.
Celebrity earnings and perquisites should not be taken as representative of
celebrity but, rather, as constitutive of the operation of that particular

marketplace. With particular reference to the Georgian theatrical market-place, constituted as it was by the multiple types of individual financial transaction noted above, the ontology of celebrity arises from the interactions within the assemblage as an emergent property, 'a *statistical result*, or as a collective unintended consequence of intentional action'.[10]

Nevertheless, performers as individuals involved in these market transactions were acutely aware (of course, as a function of the reception environment) of perceived celebrity presence as well as the public's ability to make autonomous comparisons across the immediate reception environment. The decision by the Drury Lane actress Mary Stephens Wells (1762–1829) to play Isabella in Garrick's adaptation of Thomas Southerne's *Isabella; or, The Fatal Marriage* (1758) for her 1784 benefit contrasted her sharply with Siddons' decisive interpretation of that role earlier in the same season in the same company.[11] As *The Morning Chronicle and London Advertiser*'s 'Theatrical Intelligence' columnist put it, 'she is to play the character of Isabella; that character, in which Mrs. Siddons first exhibited her uncommon powers, and recommended herself to the notice of a London audience.'[12] In a bespoke opening address written for her by Captain Edward Topham, Wells delicately voiced her predicament, 'What Stronger fears my Mind Assail / When just Comparison must Sink the Scale . . . / For Siddons pictures Isabella's Woes, / In every Gesture, Movement, look Divine / Nature has stamp'd her worth in every Line / Hard then *my* Task to follow traits like these.'[13] In the event, *The Morning Chronicle and London Advertiser*, in a lengthy analysis of her performance, thought Wells 'much too precipitate and too faint throughout'.[14] However, their sharing of the same playhouse space and adoption of the same part of the repertoire illustrates how both Wells and Siddons worked within the same assemblage, although at different levels of its reception gradients.

This compaction of the repertoire is a feature of assemblages under some circumstances. As the younger actress, Wells probably chose Isabella precisely because Siddons had renewed public interest in Southerne's tragedy, and she would have been aware of the networking role of the London newspapers storing and distributing her reputation by inviting comparison with Siddons. Certainly, Topham's address makes it clear she was managing her reputation. Indeed, the overall complexity of this assemblage is further indicated by the prologue's licensing (and payment of a 2-guinea fee) by the Lord Chamberlain on account of its constituting new writing for the stage.[15] In other words, Wells can be identified as part of the exterior relations of Siddons' place as a celebrity, in this instance with Siddons acting as a top-down causality: 'Once a larger scale

assemblage is in place it immediately starts acting as a source of limitations
and resources for its components.'[16]

The benefit-night system in which Wells acted was located within an
intricate set of these social and economic forces demonstrating the day-to-
day workings of the assemblage as a market. By returning all celebrity
performers to their financial structural base, we can analyse the nature of
the theatrical assemblage. In short, with the exception of Edmund Kean,
who entered a particularly moribund Drury Lane theatre and capitalized on
a set of dysfunctional institutional circumstances, actors and actresses on the
eighteenth-century stage generally relied upon each other as a collectivity of
professionals literally acting in consort. In view of the frequently raucous
audiences, rapidly changing programmes and demanding schedules, the
notion of a single, exceptionally individualized performance career is difficult to maintain without recourse to considering the role of the larger
networks of the assemblage in which these players were situated.

As observed in Chapter 2, Bannister, George, Cuyler, Sestini and Webb
worked together, presumably amicably, as an effective professional unit,
surviving the Haymarket's relatively short summer season by cooperation,
and maximizing their individual talents by working within an ensemble of
players. Performers such as Siddons or Kean certainly built their careers
around promoting their individuality, but they also exploited London's
unique structural circumstances of an exclusive and highly restricted set of
venues showcasing talent for the spoken word. In the case of Siddons, the
economic leverage she was able to exert was a function of the centralizing
effects of a state-protected monopoly. This metropolitan success exerted its
influences far into the provinces, as demonstrated by her summer touring.

Chapter 2's detailing of the professional roles and livelihoods of the
Haymarket's quartet of actresses in *The Siege of Curzola* is a reminder not
only of the scale of the Georgian repertoire – and its relative unfamiliarity to
the modern reader – but also of the intricacy of its networks of
collaboration. In some ways Siddons and Kean may be figured as fascinating
but untypical representatives of their profession. Marriage within the thespian profession (such as Elizabeth Bannister's to John Bannister or
Alexander Pope's to the much older Elizabeth Younge) and the ability to
retain continual employment flexibility (as in the case of Sestini and
George) were important factors enabling the survival strategies of actors
and actresses alike. Operating as a loosely collectivized, professional ensemble furthered connections already rooted in kinship by marriage or family
and helped consolidate successful negotiation of the theatrical marketplace.
The other alternatives for actresses were situated along a continuum which

included finding supplementary financial provision – for example, by operating as a courtesan – or, at the other extreme of their deployment of their heterosexuality, achieving marriage within the gentry or aristocracy. If all such strategies failed (or if players were at the beginning of their career), then provincially located routes to founding a secure professional footing were available in the companies of strolling players criss-crossing the country in material networks whose nodes were the types of provincial theatre highlighted in Winston's *Theatric Tourist*.[17]

Sarah Siddons' early experience (referred to below) in her father Roger Kemble's and mother, Sarah Ward's, travelling theatre company in the Worcestershire area gives some idea of the role of these troupes within the national theatrical assemblage. Occasionally, other travelling players can be glimpsed. At some time in the early 1790s, the ex-naval officer and itinerant actor Mark Moore, operating at the theatrical margins with his wife ('she sung well and was an excellent figure') on the Welsh-English borders, invoked his friendship with Roger Kemble's family to displace a rival theatrical troupe in Tewkesbury, Gloucestershire, who were using the local magistrates to prevent others working there. Although Moore was manipulating a highly attenuated social network in his attempt to dislodge the magistrates' stabilizing territorialization of the permission to act, the components of this assemblage were actually materialized. Facing opposition from the authorities, Moore related that he 'employed a carpenter of the name of Warren, to erect a temporary theatre, but before Warren had built it two feet from the ground, the magistrates, in order to make me fly the town, sent an invitation to Thornton and Robinson, then managers of a Company in a neighbouring town, to come to Tewksbury to oppose me.'[18] This materialization of Moore's theatre, however fleeting and incomplete, is the expressive component of this assemblage, becoming as it does the point around which his social network and its friendship memories were activated.

However, the role in this national theatrical culture of such family groups as Moore and the Kembles is much more important than simply a means of providing an evidential basis for the nurseries of celebrity. The family – whether formally or informally defined as couples in partnership with their accompanying children – was the basic collective component of many of the provincial touring companies. The strolling company run by the obscure 'Mr Kent', who visited south-east English towns (probably in the outer London area in the 1790s), featured his six-year-old daughter acting in the 'celebrated Dramatic Piece, in Four Parts (taken from the French of Madame La Comtesse de Genlis) by Mrs. Inchbald … The Child of

Nature'. Kent's company demonstrates much about the familial nature of the provincial touring companies as well as, not least, the role they played in disseminating the work of writers such as Elizabeth Inchbald. Although it is interesting that Kent advertises 'Four Parts', it seems highly probable that Inchbald's 1788 translation of Stéphanié Felicité Brulart De Genlis' *The Child of Nature* would have been cut to allow his six-year-old to play Amanthis (a role first played by the adult actress, Anne Brunton, Robert Merry's future wife). Nevertheless, however it was presented, Mr Kent's billing emphasized his company's strongest commercial feature: his family's ability to function as an ensemble, 'nor does there exist an instance of such a Piece as the Child of Nature being performed in one Family, and by Children whose Talents are not surpass'd, by the most experienced Performers.'[19]

   The distribution of such itinerant groups, materialized by the trail of playbills they left behind, provides a diagram of the Georgian theatrical assemblage. To map the distribution of such groups one would need not only the records provided in the playbills, the visual images of the built theatrical structures collected in the drawings and etchings for Winston's *Theatric Tourist*, but also what DeLanda calls an *intensive* map.[20] To use a simple analogy, a Mercatorial or extensive map describes rigid boundaries (although it actually distorts some of them at its extremes), while an intensive map is something more akin to a meteorological map recording differences in air pressure or humidity. We have no cognitive problem in mapping intensive weather maps over the more familiar extensive maps, however temporally fleeting the components of the former. Social topography works in the same way, mapping the phase spaces (areas where events happen) of intensive topographies over more concrete fixtures of extensive topographies. Structured through friendship and kinship, the itinerant theatre groups distributed across England can be historically mapped and reassembled into the areas of their intensivity. These areas of intensivity are perhaps most explicitly visible in relation to the parameters of law. As with Mark Moore's little troupe, such strolling companies frequently encountered the legal authorities and their wish to impose a territorializing stability on their own locality by persecuting itinerant heterogeneous elements perceived to be disturbing their carefully homogenized societies. Such confrontations are maps of intensity localizing gradients and populations of difference within the assemblage.

   In 1766 an itinerant theatrical troupe in the Shrewsbury area who had been arrested by the local magistrate on the grounds of their vagrancy (as all non-patent theatre actors were automatically classified) remonstrated that their company included 'two women so big with child it is at the hazard of their lives to travel, and several young children'.²¹ The pamphlet, *A Letter from Richard Hill, Esq; To His Friend near Shrewsbury, containing Some Remarks on a Letter signed by A Player Which Letter is also prefixed . . . sold for the Benefit of the Prisoners in Shrewsbury Goal* (1767) is an important document mapping an assemblage of theatrical intensity deep in rural England. Not only does Hill's pamphlet provide definitive evidence that local provincial magistrates could incarcerate, by default, whole families merely on the grounds of their earning their living as strolling players but it also testifies to the penetration into England's rural areas of knowledge of the London repertoire. Hill's fears covered a range of supposed social ills and, at the same time, reveal his surprisingly wide knowledge of the contemporary repertoire. He commented on 'the pernicious consequences which too often result from permitting such gentry among them, how many diseases left uncured, how many pockets emptied, how many minds corrupted how many apprentices and servant-maids commence *Othellos, Desdemonas, Altamonts, Calistas*, Lady *Wrongheads*, Lady *Betty Modeishes*, Mr. *Fribbles, Roman Emperors, Tragedy Queens* and what not, to their high improvement in the arts of debauchery, intrigue, dissimulation and romantic love, the great loss of their time and neglect of their masters' business' (p. 14). The repertoire to which Hill refers, with *Othello* as the most recognizable play, includes Colley Cibber's *The Careless Husband* (1705) and *The Provok'd Husband* (1728), Nicholas Rowe's *The Fair Penitent* (1703) and David Garrick's *Miss in Her Teens* (1747). Of course, one of the key issues here is the difference in standards of legal administrative behaviour between the provinces and the metropolis, demonstrating very visibly asymmetric emergence within the legal system as an assemblage. This marks another feature of the complexity of the assemblage as it related to acting. Hill's parochial authority, impelled by a blinding anti-theatricality, allowed him to sweep the strolling families into prison where they lay together – evidently as a still intact company – beyond the reach of natural justice, mercy or charity (save for the sales of Hill's own pamphlet). The extremity of Hill's actions are a reminder of the dangers potentially encountered by theatrical touring companies, which, like this one, lay at the lowest end of the professional food chain. In other words, the ability to work with collective endeavour, principally through the family but secondarily through a company, was an intrinsic benefit to those engaged in pursuing the profession of acting in England. By mapping their connectivity (their shared knowledge of the repertoire, their diverse interactions through kinship or friendship, or engagement with dominant legal frameworks), they participated in sets of materialized assemblages located at physical sites (the disputed 2-foot-high theatre or the office of magistrate or the cells of Shrewsbury gaol) which reference them to points within an overall theatrical assemblage.

The above examples are important in lending a kind of structural rebalancing which repositions the national profiles of those actors and actresses who achieved a standing akin to celebrity status. Their reputations were based upon the existence of audiences reaching far into the provincial and national regions, acting as connected outliers to the metropolitan scene. The unidentified Shrewsbury troupe of the 1760s, 'Mr. Kent's' itinerant company touring London's outer environs, Mark Moore's Welsh borders outfit, and Roger and Sarah Kemble's much more well-founded touring company all testify to the existence of a nationally distributed access to theatre figured beneath even the level of the more fixed provincial theatres recorded by Winston. This idea of intensive and extensive maps of Georgian theatricality can be summarized in DeLanda's descriptions of intensive and extensive cartographies, that 'the actual world is constituted by two separate but related segmentarities: one molar or rigid defining finished products, from atoms and molecules, to institutional organizations and cities; the other molecular or supple defining flows and thresholds that enter into the production and maintenance of the molar segments.'[22] The achievement of celebrity status is explained by this movement from molecular to molar positions in the assemblage, the molar depending on its array of relations with molecular segments.

Although the flattened ontologies of assemblage theory may be disconcerting, the connectedness of the theatrical assemblages described above (which included the obscure Mark Moore and the incarcerated Shrewsbury strollers – as well as the Haymarket's 1785 quartet of actresses) to metropolitan London's apparent centrality within the assemblage can now be described through their exterior relations with other parts of the assemblage. Indeed, the seemingly molecular components within the assemblage (Mark Moore's tiny company or the Shrewsbury troupe's fleeting constitution) always interact with the larger and more stabilized parts: 'The term "molecular" . . . refers to the smaller segments that are the component parts of a molar aggregate, but always taken as a dynamic population of interacting micro-segments, a population defined by intensive differences that are maintained through the continuous injection of a flow of matter or energy (a population *far from equilibrium*).'[23] These flows of matter or energy are particularly a characteristic of the beginnings of celebrity, although, again defaulting to the description of theatrical assemblages given in this book, performers almost never work alone on stage as soloists, and it is always necessary to position them relative to other performers.

In the archival records, what shows up time after time is that celebrity existed relative to other performers and to the reception environment rather than relative to what could now be feasibly reconstructed – other than anecdotally – as a verifiable estimate of individual talent.[24] Although the example of Mary Wells' borrowing of Siddons' most famous role illustrates proximities across differently perceived levels of talent, and that they materially interacted within the same assemblage by choosing the same part of the repertoire to project their careers, the most quantifiable method of recovering celebrity status is the examination of financial payments made to performers.

While this offers the paradox of flattening (rather than flattering) the profile of the celebrity, the complexity of the Georgian theatrical assemblage yields plenty of quantitative evidence about the crucial reception environment materialized as a market. Payments made to all performers reflected not only their individual status but also the necessity of retaining their employment within the company (a coefficient matched against the overall viability of theatricality as a commodity of consumption). If one assumes a more or less economically efficient theatrical marketplace (whose parameters include the economic implications of the state-backed monopoly acting as a non-human agent influencing human agency), then the financial and other types of material reward disbursed provide significant sets of indicators for assessing celebrity performers against others.[25]

Celebrity profiles could only be maintained in the presence of an already successful company ensemble or one with the capacity to mutate successfully. When the young David Garrick defected from Drury Lane to Covent Garden for the season 1746–7, receipts before his arrival had reached a low of £10. 9s. 5d. for one night in the first week of October when the playhouse featured Thomas Otway's *Venice Preserv'd* (1682) paired with Henry Fielding's *The Mock Doctor; or, The Dumb Lad Cured* (1732). However, the theatre's takings soared to £151. 6s. 8d. when Garrick took the role of Hamlet in the third week.[26] Nevertheless, such apparently startling individual transformations of playhouse takings need also to be assessed against the almost equally transformative profile of other players within the same playhouse, within the same season. The day before Garrick's Hamlet, the veteran actor James Quin played Richard III there with box-office takings of £125. 10s. 2d.[27] In other words, the playhouse and its constituent ensemble of regular actors continued to be as much a draw as the presence of individually notable performers amidst the playhouse's normal ensemble.

Paradoxically, the flattening of celebrity into a profile much closer to that of the ensemble or the collective group of actors is a feature most readily recognizable in the sensitive area of benefit-night performances. Benefit nights were, theoretically, evenings where some (or all) of the takings became the perquisite of one (or sometimes more) named actresses or actors. However, by the late eighteenth century, the benefit-night system had become ever more elaborated, rising in tandem with the growth of theatre audiences and the complexity of the assemblage. For the performers taking a benefit night, there were considerable financial risks. In the overwhelming majority of cases, the actors or actresses taking a benefit were charged for, in effect, the hire of the playhouse for their evening's programme. If there was a shortfall, the performer made up the difference or the 'deficiency', as it was usually termed. Eighteenth-century London theatre ledger books are littered with 'deficiency' payments. For most performers, the key element affecting profitability was the value which came through to them from what were known as benefit 'Tickets'. These were individually priced, usually bought prior to the performance and appear to have had no fixed face value. Instead, although a variety of systems existed, they provided an opportunity for the public to offer a gratuity to the actor or actress, particularly since the tickets were often marketed directly by the performer (but the receipts were tallied by the venue managers). For some idea of the fluid nature of 'Ticket' value, we may note that ten days before Garrick's retirement from the stage, the prompter William Hopkins recorded that for his benefit programme of *Hamlet* and *The Deuce is in Him*, given in support of the Theatrical Fund, 'most of the Tickets were sold for a Guinea a piece very few under half a Guinea & the whole quantity Sold in about Two hours.'[28] The playhouses had no charge over the tickets so they remained a key element in performers' financial calculations of their own profitability.

Since benefits for the two London patent theatres were usually taken in April and May, and because the season ended in June, performers planning a benefit programme needed to make careful calculations as to their strategies not only for surviving the summer but also for paying back any deficit. Although the players would not be paid again by their theatres until mid-September when they reopened, payment of deficiencies usually had to be made up within a couple of weeks.[29] Running such risks, even top-rated players needed other big-name performers in their programmes to boost the takings at their benefits. In 1796, Thomas King (1730–1805) paid Dorothy Jordan 10 guineas to perform in his *Hamlet* benefit night, Sarah Siddons also requiring payment of a further £20 to appear in this show. These extra charges levied by the two actresses were in addition to the overall charge of £200 made by the playhouse against King's receipts. At the end of the evening, this left him with a sum of £156. 12s. 0d. derived from the sale of his 'Tickets' plus a further £109. 18s. 0d. from receipts taken from that night's *ad hoc* audience (who, of course, had not paid for King's special 'Tickets' but merely at the regular rate).[30] Such crude theatrical economics enabled successful actors to levy charges on their less highly regarded colleagues, who, in turn, elected to take the risk that billing a performer with a bigger name than their own might draw in enough extra spectators to maximize their benefit receipts overall. On the night of Mary Wells' 1785 benefit in *Isabella; or, The Fatal Marriage*, for example, the actress encountered the opposite problem in 'the difficulty that occurred . . . yesterday, with regard to getting any performer to undertake the part of Nell in [Sheridan's] the Camp', Wells' afterpiece. As she was of insufficient profile to make her profit certain, it seems her fellow actresses probably decided not to risk becoming one of her creditors standing in line after she first discharged the theatre's fee.[31] The risks and calculations were complex. In King's 1798–9 Drury Lane season, for example, out of twenty-four performers who took a benefit night, only six chose not to include Jordan at the 10-guinea rate she charged, although King was the only one also to have included Siddons – despite her fee – in his benefit programme.[32] At a total charge of £31. 10s. 0d., plus the theatre's £200 fee, deploying both Jordan and Siddons could be done only by an actor absolutely confident of his following. Within this intricate thespian marketplace, all of the performers must have understood what was at stake and, to some degree or other, consented to its continuation.

The study of benefit-night performances has the virtue of demonstrating the activities of a concrete (rather than reified) market as 'assemblages made out of people and the material and expressive goods people exchange'.[33] The minute articulations and sets of implicit face-to-face negotiations required, together with their irreducible moment where the transactions were completed on the benefit night at the theatre, all provide strong evidence of the existence of this concrete and determinable market. The informal financial systems (predominantly self-administered and self-initiated, rather than imposed by managements) which developed for actor benefit nights are excellent indicators of the existence of theatrical assemblages composed of individual singularities set within a context of universal singularities where 'interactions between members of a collectivity may lead to the formation of more or less permanent articulations between them yielding a macro-assemblage with properties and capacities of its own.'[34] In other words, the macroassemblages (celebrity might be one example) are the result of these connections made within the market of the collective.

Many aspects of the financial affairs of the patent theatres are rendered intelligible by figuring them as theatrical assemblages whose economic parameters were set by the parameters which defined the nature of their enterprises. As far as the playhouses' regular weekly margins were concerned, differences between the attractiveness (or perceived profitability) of individual performers were certainly noticeable enough to be worth rewarding through increased salary, but the contribution of other performers was never insignificant. The attractiveness of triple billing the veteran Thomas King together with (although she was then perceived to be declining) Siddons – plus the star-of-the moment, Jordan – was considerable. Siddons' ability to charge double Jordan's fee is testimony to the longevity and cumulative impact of her following as well as, not least, to her own perception of how her professional status could be translated into financial remuneration. Indeed, the tensions between the repertory cast and the perceived visibility (and greater reward) of some perhaps only slightly more talented individual performers were a constant feature of the metropolitan theatre. However, while certain celebrities charged extra for their services to other performers – despite being part of the same acting company and housed within the same theatre – this was not the only system the playhouses evolved to make it financially worthwhile for the bigger names to support the lesser.

Although surviving theatre account books do not capture the minutia of the rationale behind many of the playhouses' financial transactions, it appears that one of the routes players could take to achieving a less abruptly interventionist financial settlement for their benefit-night services was for some of them to take a short-term rise in pay.[35] From the Covent Garden account books, it looks likely that Elizabeth Pope (*née* Younge) – as well as other performers of her rank – negotiated with the playhouse management rather than with individual performers to agree a special remuneration settlement to cover the benefit season. This would explain why Pope's salary in June 1791 shot up to £24 for the period 4–14 June instead of her usual £10–£12 per week during the rest of the season.[36] Pope's leap in pay approximates quite closely to Jordan's nightly charge for her services, with Pope possibly settling to undertake less fraught negotiations with the management than with an array of individual players. With this degree of complexity in the charges operative during the crucial annual benefit-night section of the season, it becomes harder to designate accurately a difference between celebrities and other types of extremely successful performers.

Thomas King and Elizabeth Pope would be two examples of players whom history has largely forgotten yet who were clearly at the top of their profession, if one examines how they functioned on benefit nights. In other words, benefit nights operate exactly as components of an assemblage, successfully operating on a day-to-day basis by dealing with intricate and shifting categories of difference. They were materialized with an exact historical specificity, and comprised multiple population components connected across a variety of gradients (of ability or of precedence, for example) which strongly feature spaces of emergence.

In the midst of these multiple sites of performance, caution is also needed before attributing celebrity status on the grounds of apparently symbolic indicators of individual standing. Although materialized, the exchange of valuable objects or valued concessions of behaviour may not determine overall standing. For example, a playhouse's willingness to pay for actresses' clothes does not necessarily indicate celebrity status or even a willingness to promote their performers' fashionable public profiles. Actresses negotiated additional terms in excess of their salaries when – and if – they could obtain them. The £60 per year clothing allowance given in 1775 by Garrick at Drury Lane to the ex-milliner Frances Abington, the sitter pictured in Reynolds' memorable *Frances Abington as Miss Prue* [in Congreve's *Love for Love*] (1771; oil on canvas, Yale Center for British Art, New Haven, Paul Mellon Collection), was all but matched only a year later by the never quite-so-well fêted Ann Barry (*née* Street, *c.* 1733–1801) at Covent Garden.[37] In 1776, the playhouse ledger book records 'Paid Mrs. Barry on Acc[t.] for finding her own Dresses £50–. –'. The tendency for apparently special perquisites to percolate quickly down to requests made by other players can best be seen by the example of the, by then, Covent Garden actress Mary Stephens Wells. Roles had been written for her in the 1780s by her lover, the Prince Regent's friend, Colonel Edward Topham, but, by 1791, Wells' career was tending to spin erratically, the casualty of unsatisfactory love affairs and debt obligations incurred on behalf of others. However, despite her professionally declining circumstances, in 1791 she secured a payment of £30 for her clothes even though her weekly wage (£6. 13s. 4d.) placed her some way below Covent Garden's then top female earner, Elizabeth Pope.[38] Working in a playhouse context founded on a legally secured monopolistic system of commercial capitalism, the performers themselves operated within a financial structure whose economy was based on the rawest of capitalist ethics. Successful exploitation of the benefit-night system, together with the rather different sorts of benefit secured by an entitling record of subscription payments to the theatrical funds, meant that the monopoly London venues potentially delivered to all performers on the patent stages a collective degree of fame and focus to assist their professional careers.

However, Georgian theatre was always a place operating under conditions of raw capitalism. Such was the pace and complexity of the theatres' financial trajectories during their seasons that not all payments to performers show up in the ledgers. The non-accountability of performers' earnings within the system can be traced at least as early as the middle of the century. Back in 1746, Garrick was considered to be a sufficiently hot property that payments to him do not show up at all in Covent Garden's account book for that year. Such off-the-record contracts must have bedevilled the attempts of the playhouse box-office keepers to maintain their own sense of their theatre's financial position, and today can play havoc with attempts to estimate earnings empirically as a true signifier of celebrity. If Garrick's contractual negotiations at Drury Lane were such that he did not appear at all on the salaried staff list, the next highest-paid male actor, Lacy Ryan, was shown as receiving £8 per week, while Hannah Pritchard, Covent Garden's top-earning female performer, was paid £6. 13s. 4d. In a clear demonstration of the intricate pecking order of performers outlined above, the veteran tragedian Quinn, while clearly not commanding quite the same unofficial terms as Garrick, received from the playhouse two non-consolidated payments of £42 and £100 in his first weeks there.[39] The fact that these payments do not recur strongly suggests that Quinn similarly argued himself into a comparable, off-the-record, agreement with the theatre. These box-office receipts, and the accounting systems underpinning them, betray the real economics of celebrity. Within a state-sanctioned monopoly system, and within a public theatre in London which could perform only censored plays, the conditions were ripe for a number of non-accountable professional strategies such as off-the-record personal payments.

Celebrity performers, in celebrity's earliest days, were only the outcome of the intersection of the overall financial strength of the twin metropolitan playhouse monopolies and their ability to reward the performers most attended by audiences. However, as far as the earliest stages of this process of celebrity development are concerned, if we consider his acting skills as separate from the managerial skills he later developed at Drury Lane, box-office draws such as Garrick exerted only a marginal effect on playhouses, while the whole system depended entirely on the overall functional integrity of its salaried company and the management system which provided the framework within which the company itself could consistently prosper.

The present-day notion of the extraordinarily talented individual super-performer is a relic of a Romantic ideology based on the supposed existence of the genius practitioner. As far as performance history is concerned, the perception of extraordinarily talented individuals endowed with special powers of textual interpretation probably dates only as far back as the career of Edmund Kean. Even the most cursory survey of Richard Cross' and William Hopkins' prompters' diaries for Drury Lane demonstrates that, throughout his professional life, David Garrick was required to draw on a broad range of managerial skills including those which were precisely contemporary insofar as they included the ability to outface and subdue restive audiences as well as negotiate truculently influential gentry. His acting skills, although obviously considerable, were additional to several other types of professional value he brought to the theatres in which he worked. Principal among these, as the Cross and Hopkins diaries reveal, was the continual recourse he had to call upon his own authoritative presence in order to negotiate – upon the spot – the roughhouse audiences typical of mid-Georgian playhouses. The visual imagery of Garrick so carefully captured – and frozen – by Sir Joshua Reynolds, and so well known to us today, belies the raucous pit of the mid-century theatre and the conditions he had to deal with.

The Drury Lane prompter Richard Cross' account shows how, in February 1748, Garrick had to confront a typically restive crowd led by one Lord Hubbard at a performance of Edward Moore's new play, *The Foundling*:

> There was a report, that my Lord Hubbard had made a party this night to hiss the Foundling off the Stage, that ye Reason was it ran too long, & they wanted variety of Entertainments. Mr Garrick was sent for, he met 'em & so far prevail'd that they promis'd peace 'till after the 9th night. however [*sic*] there was an attempt made by one cat call, & an apple Thrown at Macklin & some other other [*sic*] Efforts made by a few but without effect – Greatly hiss'd w^n give out I believe the main cause of this anger, in spite of their Excuses, was their being refus'd admittance behind the scenes.[40]

The bare testimony of the micro-movements of this event recorded by the eyewitness Cross deserves further examination, not least because the prompter's reference to the 'cat call, & an apple Thrown at Macklin' suggests that this entire incident took place when the performers were already on stage.

Lord Hubbard's making up of 'a party' means that he had obviously gone to the theatre with a prior assembled mob (perhaps of fellow aristocrats, perhaps of paid troublemakers) with the specific plan of disrupting or aborting the billed performance. That Garrick 'was sent for' suggests that Drury Lane staff felt disempowered to confront an insurgent nobleman. That Cross describes how Garrick 'met 'em & so far prevail'd' corroborates that such a meeting and set of discussions took place – and that Garrick was on hand to deal with it – although whether these discussions took place simply between Garrick and Hubbard or between Garrick and the whole of Hubbard's 'party' is not clear. Garrick's primary concern was not only to allow the evening to proceed but also to safeguard Moore's need to reach the ninth performance of his play ('they promis'd peace 'till after the 9th night'), the performance which triggered another benefit for the author. In other words, the pressures on Garrick, faced as he was with an apple-throwing mob led by a nobleman on the one hand and an author's necessity to reach his pay night on the other, were considerable.

The prompter's own reading of the incident, that 'the main cause of this anger, in spite of their Excuses, was their being refus'd admittance behind the scenes', is also significant because it is a reminder that parts of the audience were still seated on stage and could access the green-room area easily. In other words, the separation of performer and audience, which is the very foundation of the notion of celebrity status as denoting a qualitative difference between celebrities and ordinary people, had yet to emerge fully. This necessary distinction between actors as special kinds of people embodying extraordinary expressive powers could hardly function in the presence of such close and easily breached proximity. Other kinds of dangerous consequence raised by such proximities are made clear elsewhere in the same prompter's notes concerning one of Peg Woffington's benefit nights a couple of months later when, during *The Intriguing Chambermaid* afterpiece, 'As ye Curtain was rising for ye farce a Gentleman's sword was taken out of ye Scabbard & carry'd up with ye Curtain & there Hung to ye terror of those under it (lest it shou'd fall) & ye Mirth of ye rest of ye Audience – a scene man fetch'd it down.'[41] In this example, it is clear that the audience member was seated on the stage, carrying his weapon on his person and that his bearing of such a weapon is indicative of the elevated status of a 'Gentleman'.

Even in the last six months of Garrick's acting career, when one would have thought that celebrity status, if it truly existed, would have resulted in deference, Garrick was forced to play a very uncomfortable role in pacifying a riotous audience on the fourth night of Henry Bate's *The Blackamoor Wash'd White* in February 1776.[42] While Bate's farce has drawn some recent critical attention on account of its racial politics, Garrick's more immediate problem, and one which has been neglected, was a near riot by the audience, which he attempted to quell. At the previous performance, *The Blackamoor*'s third night, sections of the audience, one part led by a certain Captain Roper, threatened to riot: 'the Gentleman that came with Capt. Roper Jumped out of the Stage Box upon the Stage immediately Several out of the Pit & Boxes follow'd & some blows ensued & I thought they would have pulled the House down this lasted about half an hour.'[43] Again, the proximity between stage and audience is very marked, even in this 1776 performance so close to Sarah Siddons' rise to fame at the same theatre in 1783. However, on the fourth night of *The Blackamoor*, David Garrick – who gave his retirement final performance that June – was once more called upon to go on stage and face an angry audience. It is worth following the movement of this disturbance in full, as recorded by the prompter who witnessed it:

> They Call'd for Mr. Garrick he attended – but they would not hear him for a long time tho' [he] Attempted Several times to speak – at last some body said hear him! Hear him – Mr. G. told them that he would wait their [*sic*] all Night with pleasure if they requir'd it – hear him! again was bellow'd out – he told them he waited to know their pleasure – whether they would have the Blackamoor go on or if they would have any other Farce then a great Noise ensued; as soon as they were quiet Mr. G told them that his Theatrical Life would be very Short & he sho[ld] be glad to end it in peace – A man in the Pit said [if] you have a mind to die in Peace don't let this Farce be play'd again Mr. Garrick was on & off the Stage several times nothing would content them – at Length Mr. King told them that the Author had taken the Copy from the Prompter & was gone away with it – soon after this they withdrew so Ended this troublesome Affair.[44]

Ultimately, Garrick was unable to prevail and the performance was abandoned.[45] Not only was Garrick's failure absolute but also the event would have financially impacted on Bate as author. As his piece had already reached its third night, Bate would have received some kind of benefit payment (although none is recorded in Cross' journal), but – despite Garrick's intercession, which had worked reasonably well when *The Foundling* had been disrupted – *The Blackamoor* failed to reach its sixth-night and ninth-night author benefits. What is noticeable is not only that '[he] Attempted Several times to speak' but also that Garrick made an implicit appeal to the audience's recognition of him as a celebrated figure, reminding them that 'his Theatrical Life would be very Short & he sho[ld] be glad to end it in peace', and conjuring up an awareness of his well-publicized wish to retire. Even his self-deprecating desire to 'end it in peace' was greeted from the pit by what may be interpreted as a veiled physical threat ('[if] you have a mind to die in Peace don't let this Farce be play'd again').

If Garrick's professional career repeatedly required him to outface dangerously riotous audiences – who obviously regularly brought their swords with them into the theatre – thirty years later Edmund Kean's career was positioned to take advantage not only of the quantitative rise in the income he was able to bring to Drury Lane as an individual but also of the much calmer professional conditions within the playhouse auditorium. Importantly, Kean's ability to capitalize on his Shakespearean roles was coupled with the public's renewed appetite for rediscovering Shakespeare's texts. Imperceptibly, and despite the vivid anomaly of the 1809 Old Price riots, the change in deference towards the performer had also continued apace. Overall, the propensity of London audiences to violent disturbance was much diminished. Whereas in 1749 a French company of performers at the Haymarket had been met with open hostility when 'several strove to pelt 'em off – but some Lord & officers drawing their swords in their Defence, the[y] went on & many people were wounded', by 1812 the Drury Lane prompter (Thomas John Dibdin) entered in his journal a rather more genteel 'Riot nearly rais'd by the Obstinacy of a Lady who persisted in keeping her Shawl over the front of a box in defiance of an equally foolish Audience the performance was much retarded'.[46] With such changing cultural conditions making it easier for performers of calibre to emerge and expand their professional powers, the moment was ripe for Kean.

However, Kean's extremely good fortune was to find himself in a playhouse which was particularly moribund and had all but given up performing Shakespeare with any degree of commitment. The extent to which, as a performing company sharing one of only two patent rights to produce Shakespeare within London, the institutional dereliction of responsibility towards embodying the national playwright on the stage can be precisely judged by their rehearsal records for the Bard's plays. Drury Lane had become a company providing only the slenderest of supports for Shakespeare's works.

Kean's metropolitan advent can be very precisely dated to 26 January 1814 and his first Drury Lane performance as Shylock in *The Merchant of Venice*. Kean's Shylock, by any standards, was qualitatively different, at once creating and enshrining in literary tradition the notion of the individually interpretive performer as a major constituent of the Romantic literary ideology. The clutter of contemporary and posthumous hagiography around Kean, together with the competing contestations surrounding the impact of his private life on his public roles, has made it particularly difficult to disentangle the afterlife of his reputation. It has long been recognized that Drury Lane's decision to give Kean a chance as a relatively unknown provincial performer was part of a loose strategy of hoping some freak talent or burst of attraction would dig the playhouse out of its artistic and financial mess. However, many of the resulting attempts at analysing the beginnings of his career rest upon recirculating contemporary accounts which were almost invariably – perhaps inevitably – written when Kean's extraordinary impact was already the subject of a palpable metropolitan cultural consensus. Attempts to reassess contemporary accounts has tended towards reassembling a body of essentially secondary-level evidence concerning the beginnings of Kean's Drury Lane career. Writing in 1987, Leigh Woods has usefully commented that 'Edmund Kean stands in actors' biography as a prototype, one with which we are dealing still and will be, I think, recurrently, for some time to come.'[47] Jeffrey Kahan's recent and rather plangently readable discussion of his reputation, somewhat skittishly based upon an eclectic mix of sources, has done little to stabilize or redefine the terms upon which any re-evaluation might take place.[48] By contrast, Tracy C. Davis' analysis of factors as varied as lighting, critical memory and S.T. Coleridge's influential prejudices properly points to the existence of an array of difficulties needing to be negotiated in order to differentiate Kean's reputation from his actual performance history.[49] One promising start would be to avoid the partly self-manufactured biographical obstacle which is Edmund Kean and to correlate his emergence with the empirical evidence about his first Drury Lane appearances surviving in the playhouse archives.

   The bare testimony of the prompter's book records the exact moment of Kean's metropolitan arrival with exceptional objectivity.[50] What emerges is a picture of a playhouse heavily rehearsing its pantomimes but very rarely its Shakespeare repertoire. In the previous season, the prompter Thomas John Dibdin had occupied the Drury Lane cast throughout December 1812 with rehearsals for their (highly successful) end-of-year pantomime, his own *Harlequin and Humpo; or, Columbine by Candlelight*.[51] That month Dibdin called around twenty hours of rehearsal for the pantomime, including one at midnight on 23 December prior to its first night on 26 December 1812, and he scheduled a further two hours of rehearsal on Christmas Eve when the playhouse was otherwise closed.[52] In preparation for the end-of-year pantomime of 1813, Dibdin's *Harlequin Harper; Or A Jump from Japan* (he was contracted to devise one pantomime per year), rehearsals began on 11 December and similarly clocked up around twenty hours of rehearsal time (including a 6 pm rehearsal on Christmas Eve and another on Boxing Day when the playhouse was otherwise dark).[53]

By contrast with Drury Lane's emphasis on rehearsing pantomime (with their extremely attenuated dialogue and, hence, lack of lines to learn), and even taking into account that *The Merchant of Venice* was obviously a standard repertory piece for both of the two London patent theatres as well as the provincial theatres beyond the patentees' perquisite, Dibdin seems not to have recognized that either this particular performance of *The Merchant*, or Kean's presence in it, needed any special treatment. The only general cast rehearsals for *The Merchant* at Drury Lane so far that season had been on three (normally one-hour duration) occasions; namely, at 1.30 pm, 2 October and 10 am, 4 October 1813 prior to performances on 5 and 11 October, plus one at 10 am on 29 December 1813 before a performance of the play that evening.[54] For Kean's Shylock, Dibdin called only one hour's rehearsal, and then only on the day before his first Drury Lane performance in it, and then only for the scenes in which he would actually be involved: 'Rehearsals[:] Shylock's Scenes in M.[t.] of Venice at_____11[a.m.]'. On that day no fewer than nine players were named as absent from rehearsals, including William Elliston (later manager of Drury Lane), who was noted ('Cause') as being in 'Coventry – Snow bound', and the veteran comedian William Oxberry, 'Studying [to play] Pedillo'.[55] On the night of Kean's first Shylock, Dibdin recorded that Lovegrove (due to play Launcelot Gobbo) was unable to perform due to illness and Oxberry had to stand in for him, even though Oxberry had obviously not attended the rehearsal.[56]

Historically, the net effect of Drury Lane's *de facto* policy of not rehearsing Shakespeare with any degree of thoroughness has contributed to the myth that Kean was someone who preferred solitary rehearsal.[57] To look at it another way, the slenderness of the actual day-to-day rehearsal practice of Drury Lane for its canonical plays has become the stuff of the Kean myth. In contrast to their actual policy with respect to the performance of pantomime, the playhouse had decided not to provide its players with opportunities to rehearse Shakespeare. The cumulative picture which emerges is of a company policy understandably geared towards efficiencies of staffing and with an eye towards ensuring it was capable of staging its premier seasonal pantomime productions. Although Drury Lane's lackadaisical attitude towards performing the canon of major writers was frequently – and despairingly – noted by contemporaries, the actual underlying investment of the playhouse's personal and professional capital of acting skill has not been objectively noticed before. In other words, Kean played in a production and with a company who were professionally very experienced in their craft but not otherwise especially committed to succeeding in Shakespeare. Nevertheless, the hugely high profile produced around

Kean's spectacular acting contains something of the chiaroscuro in its popular imagery of the heroic unknown actor bringing new ground-breaking interpretations to bear.

Against such a background of routine playing, Kean easily stood out, and the subsequent positioning of him within an ideology of Romantic heroic insight followed on from that. Indeed, one of the more basic things Kean probably emphasized in his portrayal of Shylock was an elongation of the time devoted to acting it. After all, while Dibdin's dedication of a short but specific time to rehearse 'Shylock's Scenes in M^{t}· of Venice' had professionally and correctly catered for Kean's status as a performer new to working with the Drury Lane company, the rehearsal day's near-catastrophic list of absentees, together with an entirely different actor playing Launcelot Gobbo on the night, would have allowed Kean enough professional independence to project the role the way he wanted to without needing to worry about whatever the rest of the cast might have been expecting (since a number of them had not been in rehearsal anyway). Dibdin's notes give the exact time when Kean's first *Merchant* ended: '[Time] Over at Night … Play at ½ p[ast] 9[p.m.]'.[58] If we assume that *The Merchant* started at 7 pm, then the playing time of two and a half hours is consistent with a twenty-minute expansion of the performance duration compared to what was typical of the late eighteenth-century London theatres performing this play. The prompter J. Brownsmith, who had worked at Drury Lane, Covent Garden and the Haymarket forty years earlier, published his extraordinary *The Dramatic Time-Piece: or Perpetual Monitor* (1768), a work principally aimed at ensuring servants arrived punctually to collect their masters and mistresses after the show without needing to loiter in the nearest tavern. The alphabetically ordered *Dramatic Time-Piece* lists the normal duration of the 'Whole Play' of *The Merchant of Venice* as two hours and ten minutes (inclusive of any music between the acts). It seems likely that, given the circumstances of the night, Kean took advantage of the situation in order to develop and project his ground-breaking portrayal of the role.

Events such as these have served to create a misleading distance or disconnection between Kean and the theatrical culture in which he worked, emphasizing Kean as a performer of solitary and exceptional interpretive power. Of course, for the right actor at the right moment, the Drury Lane methods of working were ripe for being turned around. As far as the growth of literary Romantic ideologies around Kean are concerned, it should also be remembered how intimately linked were the subsequent profiles of the second generation of Romantic writers with Kean's entrance to the London stage. Kean's arrival helped shape and generate the reputations of the later Romantic writers, just as theirs did his, closely intertwining their collective critical destinies. In these respects, Kean's first Drury Lane Shylock finds him precisely situated as one of Deleuze and Guattari's 'stagemakers', a performer distanced from the audience yet also materialized within its reception environment.[59] In the case of Kean, Drury Lane's then current situation as a cash-generative monopoly with a recent expensive rebuild behind it has enabled a fairly good picture to be recreated of the escalation of his fame. Much needed improvements in the day-to-day management of Drury Lane's record keeping (of which Dibdin's prompter's book is a prime manifestation) captured some of the detail of his rising reputation.

With the temporal moment of dramatic performance only ever fleeting, and with the Drury Lane mainpiece finishing in well under three hours in the case of Kean's first *Merchant of Venice*, memory played tricks with contemporary testimony, not least with the influential witness of William Hazlitt. As far as the posterity of Kean's reputation was concerned, Hazlitt has been recognized as one of the most influential exponents of Kean's reputation in his recollections of his Drury Lane Shylock printed in the Preface to *A View of the English Stage* written in 1818.[60] Hazlitt's account dramatizes the difference between the actor's obscure first appearance and the heady fame which ensued. Its distortions tell us much about the eulogizing of Kean as the quintessential Romantic performer:

> I went to see him the first night of his appearing in Shylock. I remember it well. The boxes were empty, and the pit not half full: some quantity of barren spectators and idle renters were thinly scattered to make up the show. The whole presented a dreary, hopeless aspect. I was in considerable apprehension for the result. From the first scene in which Mr. KEAN came on, my doubts were at an end. I had been told to give as favourable an account as I could: I gave a true one. I am not one of those who, when they see the sun breaking from behind a cloud, stop to ask others whether it is the moon.[61]

On the contrary, Hazlitt did not 'remember it well'.

At the end of the 1813–14 season, Edward Warren, one of Drury Lane's two assistant treasurers, was given the task of compiling a body of financial data about Kean's impact on the playhouse's finances. By comparison with the records for Sheridan's term as a manager, the theatre's financial records for this period are unusually robust and well maintained. Thomas J. Dibdin's careful noting of rehearsal absenteeism was itself a subsidiary feature of an apparently new management regime, but it was also during this season that the playhouse introduced a new type of bespoke, very specialist theatrical account book bought from a commercial stationer and laid out with tables printed in red ink so that box-office treasury staff could total the receipts from the different parts of theatre. They could now enter the takings not only laterally, subdividing receipts from the boxes, pit, and 2*s*. and 1*s*. galleries, but also longitudinally, further subdividing the receipt locations by denoting 'P.S.' and 'O.P.' sides (prompt side and opposite prompt). This shows that the total receipts for that night were £164. 11*s*. 6*d*., of which £64. 17*s*. 0*d* came from the 7*s*. box seats, £73. 1*s*. 6*d* from the pit, £20. 10*s*. 0*d*. from the 2*s*. gallery and £10. 8*s*. 0*d*. from the 1*s*. gallery. Contrary to the boxes being 'empty', as Hazlitt remembered it, there were nearly 200 people in that part of the theatre. As Kean looked around him to take in the audience, the auditorium elsewhere might have looked sparsely filled, but the numbers were still considerable. High above him, perhaps looming disproportionately vast in the distance, in the cheapest 1*s*. gallery, were seated around 200 people, and below them, in the 2*s*. gallery, there were just over another 200.[62]

This chapter has demonstrated how theatre functioned as a particular type of market whose transactions were distributed across the assemblage as a series of gradients within the populations of the assemblage. As materialized at the playhouse venues, theatrical celebrity was a component attached to other components within the assemblage in an array of transactions and transportations between its molecular and molar segmentarities. The stage-maker of Deleuze and Guattari, like their image of the solitary songbird, was one among many voices making up the chorus of the forest.

CHAPTER FOUR

Celebrity networks: Kean and Siddons

Whereas both Garrick and Sarah Siddons engaged with a now largely unfamiliar repertoire, Kean's advantage was to combine Drury Lane's monopoly with a virtually single-minded advocacy of Shakespeare, cherry-picking the roles of Shylock, Othello (less often, Iago), Richard III and Hamlet. Steering clear of much of the other Shakespearean repertoire – not to mention much of the established Georgian repertoire – was important in securing his personal celebrity. That is, Kean knew what he did well and kept on doing it. The emphasis on Shakespeare transformed the playhouse, but also at work was the audience's role as a remarkable social network. This can now be partially reconstructed. The survival of the Drury Lane account books, together with increases in the playhouse's attempts at employing commercial methods of analysis, provides the evidential basis for this formulation. As soon as one analyses the careers of celebrity actors by normalizing these materialist processes of inquiry, almost inevitably they are returned closer to the mean of the overall theatrical assemblage. As will be demonstrated, this process can also be applied to Sarah Siddons' celebrity.

Implicit networks of conversation were essential to the rise of Kean's reputation and will be described in this chapter. They can be captured as interpersonal dialogues moving in a plane of immanence from real (or virtual) modalities into actualities as they were disseminated across the assemblage's networks. Conversation is a basic descriptive and structural component within assemblage theory, not only because of its status as a ubiquitous human interaction but also because this ubiquity works as an interactive assemblage, creating emergent economies of cultural difference. DeLanda refers to the mechanisms and structures of conversation several times. Drawing on the work of Erving Goffman, he writes, 'As an assemblage, a conversation possesses components performing both material and expressive roles. The main material component is *co-presence*: human bodies correctly assembled in space, close enough to hear each other and physically oriented towards one another.'[1] Technologies which defer co-presence, such as the writing of letters, deterritorialize the immediate performativity of interpersonal speech. Within the specifically theatre-going, largely metropolitan, social groups described below, one can assume that co-present conversation and deterritorialized letter-writing were the two principal physical components of social exchange and were deployed electively according to immediate ease of use. Physical public spaces within Georgian playhouses promoted human co-presence not only by structuring points of congregation but also by engineering into the buildings physical orientations capable of promoting conversation.

Pictures in Winston's *Theatric Tourist* (1805) show that even very rudimentary English provincial playhouses sometimes possessed verandahs where audiences could congregate in good weather prior to entering the auditorium. In the larger metropolitan theatres, box lobbies (the circulation areas leading into the boxes) increasingly segregated different classes of audience but were specifically designed to promote close social interaction. Writing about Drury Lane in 1813, James Henry Lawrence complained that the manager 'has accommodated his friends in the lobby with sofas, at the same time that the audiences in the boxes and pit are seated like schoolboys on benches'.[2] While Lawrence's comments were mainly aimed at the immorality implicit in offering semi-horizontal seating (reinforced by the contemporary orientalist nuances of 'sofas'), the managers clearly enabled high degrees of physical proximity between members of the box-lobby audience. These features of the Georgian theatrical built environment were geographically widespread and recurrent features of theatre buildings. Boxes and conversation were even present at the outdoor hippodromes. In September 1789 the diarist John Marsh went to Astley's Amphitheatre to see 'y[e] representation of the Demolition of the Bastile &c. & happen'd to sit in the same Box with Lord & Lady [Clotworthy Skeffington, Earl of] Massarene who (as French Refugees) were of course much interested in the subject'.[3] In America, not only were the theatres newer and greeted with greater suspicion by civic authorities than in England, but also the more extreme weather of the East Coast necessitated greater levels of public consent in order for them to be allowed to promote comfortable audience interaction. In Maryland in 1812, the building of a portico for the Holliday Street theatre in Baltimore (to 'contribute to the convenience and safety of the citizens') required a whole new local statute dictating its exact position and dimensions ('on a level with the box lobby . . . as far as the curb or curb-stones . . . elevated at least ten feet above the foot pavement').[4] Considerations of audience comfort on a large scale were carefully engineered by theatre owners. In Philadelphia, the new (post-fire) rebuild of the Chesnut Street theatre in 1821 included a lobby heated by a furnace and holding over a thousand people.[5] New Republic America's comparative unfamiliarity with cultures of theatre, yet sensitivity to the promise of its egalitarian nature, also provoked interestingly robust responses to sharp financial practices aimed at segregating audiences on economic grounds. Something of the intensity of the contemporary Philadelphian theatrical assemblage is captured in *The Cynick*, the city's new periodical aimed at local theatre-goers. Referring to the 1811 season when the city's only theatre had restricted access to the boxes to those able to pay a $300 annual subscription, *The Cynick* commented: 'During the crowded houses of the last winter, several ladies, urged by the longings of curiosity, ventured into the pit, after finding it impossible to get seats in the boxes. For weeks afterwards, their indiscretion, or what was called, their boldness, was bandied about from tea-table to breakfast, and from breakfast to tea-table, till it had completely run the rounds of scandal. Their reputation was entirely lacerated.'[6] The complexity of this exchange, with the 'several ladies' presumably discussing their seating predicament and its solution prior to their going into the pit, together with the recording of commentaries by others 'bandied about from tea-table to breakfast', serves as a fully functional example of a local assemblage directly connected to theatre. In this example the social rules of gendered personal identity have been renegotiated and the parameters of recognized decorum disrupted. Table-talk precisely acted in the assemblage as its information nodes, storing 'reputation' across a network with co-present conversation its chief channel.

This example from *The Cynick* shows quite starkly how economies of difference can quickly emerge, first materialized at the playhouse but then disseminated across the locality through varying densities of co-present conversation. With reference to social practices of conversation, DeLanda has written that 'The emphasis on the external signs exchanged during social encounters makes this research ripe for a treatment in terms of emergent wholes in which components are joined by relations of exteriority.'[7] In the case of Kean's reputation, these emergent wholes within the assemblage (in the theatrical model, the audience) can be confidently traced with respect to their relations of exteriority.

The Drury Lane assistant treasurer Edward Warren estimated that while the box-office receipts that year averaged £239. 12*s*. 6*d*. per night, the 'General Average of Kean's Performances [was] £339.10.–'.[8] The difference Kean made to Drury Lane as a financial entity after his first appearance (which did not occur until about halfway through that year's specially lengthened 220 night performance season) can be judged from this about £100 'General Average' difference. Whatever one decides about Kean's celebrity, this about £100 'General Average' difference is an absolute indicator of the magnitude of his reception environment with the co-presence of performer, performance and audience, all materialized at the Drury Lane venue. In a separate document, Warren detailed that the 4 June 1814 pairing of Kean as Iago with Samuel James Arnold's 'melodramatic romance', *The Woodman's Hut* (1814), had taken receipts of £673. 18s. 6d., just one example of the surge in income his appearances generated. For comparison, in that same opening year (using Warren's data again), a similarly late season, non-Kean, performance of Thomas J. Dibdin's *The School for Prejudice* (1801), paired with John O'Keeffe's *The Farmer* (1792), took just £74. 18s. 0d. In short, the top 38 largest box-office receipts at the Drury Lane in the 1813–14 season came from scheduling programmes which included a play by Shakespeare with Kean performing in it.[9] This lurch towards Shakespeare must be attributed almost in its entirety to Kean's transformation of the playhouse repertoire and the subsequent realignment of its scheduling choices.

Even if one takes into account that the Drury Lane playhouse Kean came to was newly rebuilt when it reopened in September 1813 after its 1809 fire and with a slightly enlarged capacity compared with the building Garrick and Siddons performed in at their height, and even if one also takes into account wartime inflation, the verified amount of Kean's box-office receipts is astonishing. However, also contributing to the rise of Kean's fame was a combination of other circumstances, much of them to do with the convergence of Kean's and Shakespeare's reputations amidst an expanding metropolitan public print culture. Kean's intersection with journalist-essayists such as William Hazlitt, and the pre-existing metropolitan market for their writings, was as important to his rise as the ability of the coherently focused, nationally distributed, theatrical companies of the mid and late eighteenth century to deliver their steady schedules of the Georgian repertoire. By strategically avoiding the discredited elements of the contemporary Shakespearean repertoire, which might have compromised the sense of newness he brought to his interpretation, Kean maximized his seriousness as an actor in a way which fitted exactly with the age's willingness to rediscover Shakespeare as the quintessential Romantic genius. Deftly ignoring *King Lear*, then still played in Nahum Tate's version (although he did briefly return to the original in 1823), or the redactions of *The Winter's Tale* promoted in Garrick's programming, Kean exactly suited the age's burgeoning interest in Shakespeare. Indeed, it was almost certainly the proliferation within the theatrical circuits of the adapted Shakespeare texts which generated a popular interest in rediscovering the originals.

Within a year, the ex-Jacobin radical activist of the 1790s turned elocutionist, John Thelwall, was advertising lectures in both London and Liverpool on the subject of Shakespeare and Edmund Kean, the series coupled with the publication of his pamphlets on curing speech impediments, in which he advocated a naturalness of 'Organization' common to both verbal fluency and Kean's acting style.[10] Indeed, that Thelwall was an early adherent of Kean is shown by the Drury Lane box-office ledger, which reveals that (providing his Lincoln Inn Fields address to the box-office keeper) he took a box in the dress circle for Kean's Richard III on 21 February 1814.[11] The interest in Kean's new interpretations of Shakespeare was palpable and percolated right through metropolitan society. Even during Kean's first season, the post-retirement Sarah Siddons was attracting audiences to the Argyle Rooms to hear her readings from *Othello*, while London's newer literary journals such as *The Examiner* were also printing semi-anonymous commentaries on 'Mr. Kean's Othello'.[12] By 1819, there was an even wider distribution of cultural activity connected specifically with Shakespeare, much of it visible in a single notice in the symptomatic publication, *The Inspector, A Weekly Dramatic Paper*, one of the metropolis' hectic new theatrical journals which help capture a sense of the public audience now accelerated by Kean's reinvigorated theatrical perspectives:

> "Shakespearian Readings" Mr. Smart, a professor of Elocution, commenced a series of readings from the plays of Shakespeare on Saturday last, at Shade's Concert Room in Soho Square ... Mr. [William] Hazlitt, Mr. [Samuel Taylor] Coleridge, and Mr. [John] Thelwall are [also] giving lectures on the plays of Shakespeare – but on a very opposite system to the readings of Miss [*sic*] Smart.[13]

Not of least significance here is London's ability to support an (alas, short-lived) weekly theatrical journal as well as the exploitative entry into efforts to cater for this audience by the formidable intellectual array of Hazlitt, Coleridge and Thelwall, the last two being a reminder of the continuing metropolitan presence of senior radicals writers from an earlier generation.

This is not the place to conjecture about the rise of Shakespeare as a national cultural phenomenon, particularly as arguments about his role in canon formation were at the time politically and economically entwined with the ownership of a new conceptualization of a British 'national drama', whose medium, the spoken word, continued to be visibly entrammelled in the century-old privileges of the two royal patent playhouses as far as London audiences were concerned. Kean's success was such that – at least in the earliest months of his Drury Lane career – he was led away from much of the older repertoire, figuring himself as almost exclusively concerned with Shakespeare's most psychologically troubled individuals such as Shylock, Richard III, Othello and Hamlet. Indeed, the degree to which Kean was able to maximize what appears to have been an almost innate talent, one capable of being summoned up with the minimum of immediate prepara-tion, was as much a feature of his Hamlet as it had been of his Shylock. Entries in Dibdin's prompter's journal reveal that although he called two rehearsals (apparently full cast) for *Hamlet* a few days before his first appearance in the role on 11 March 1814, Kean was absent with 'permission' from the one called for 10 March at 11 am. This absence fits into a pattern of his increasingly erratic approach to professionalism and for which he later became notorious. He had already missed three other rehearsals for plays for various reasons (two with 'permission', one because of undefined other 'business'). However, on the day of his first Hamlet, Dibdin held another general cast rehearsal for the play at 11 am, which Kean appears to have attended. Although Drury Lane had clearly taken some steps to ensure they could benefit from Kean's new injection of canonical depth into their programming, it may also be inferred that they had yet to learn how best to exploit his talent.[14] It might be simplistic to attribute Kean's relative failure with *Hamlet* (Hazlitt famously thought Kean's Hamlet all 'sharp angles and abrupt starts ... much too splenetic and rash') to the fragmen-tary nature of rehearsal, but, as will be seen below, his success in *Richard III* may have been assisted by more thorough preparations.[15]

Kean's rise to fame was transmitted across a specific social network whose origins can be traced back to his first night as Shylock. While Hazlitt remembered it otherwise, crucial to Kean's success, and recorded in the box keeper's book, was the presence in the audience of the Hon. Douglas Kinnaird (1788–1830) on that first night. As well as being Byron's friend, unofficial literary agent and financial adviser, Kinnaird also sat on the Drury Lane management committee.[16] In other words, it was not the absence of an audience but the presence of key members within that audience which kick-started his rise to fame. Misleadingly, in modern times Lord Byron's close relationship with Drury Lane's committee of management has helped ensure that the poet's and the actor's biographies have become intertwined as examples of Romantic profiles encompassing notions of the outlandish and exotic.[17]

Possibly tipped off by his friend Kinnaird, Byron saw Kean act no later than 19 February, when he played Richard III ('Just returned from seeing Kean in Richard. By Jove, he is a soul! Life–nature–truth without exaggeration or diminution . . . Richard is a man; and Kean is Richard'). Also there at that same performance of *Richard III* was the philosophical anarchist novelist and occasional playwright, William Godwin, who went there with his second wife, Mary Jane Godwin (Clairmont, *née* de Vial), after an afternoon spent in the company of the poet Percy Bysshe Shelley, the ex-London Corresponding Society and 1809 Old Price Riots activist Francis Place, and the writer Joseph Hume.[18] Whether they all spoke to each other is not known, but, in any event, there was present at that single performance a range of co-present, well networked, identifiable individuals capable of expanding Kean's reputation. Although he did not otherwise record the event, a Drury Lane ledger shows that Byron went back again to see Kean as Shylock on Saturday, 26 February. A letter written by Byron the next day, Sunday the 27th, claims he had largely spent the last week opting for solitude ('Hobhouse says I am growing a *loup garou*, – a solitary hobgoblin. True; – "I am myself alone"'). However, although Byron wrote that 'The last week has been passed in reading – seeing plays – now and then visitors', the picture of poetic solitude he wished to inculcate is at variance with the evidence of his theatre visits. The Drury Lane box book shows conclusively that, the day before, 'Lord Byron' took a 'Proscenium Box' as the perquisite of a subscriber (marked by a long *S* against his name) and paid £2. 12s. 6d. for the rest of his party, which equates to his being accompanied by about at least seven other people, each needing to pay 7s. for a place.[19] This forms part of the slow ascendancy of the dominant valuation of Romanticism's emphasis on solitary endeavour, not least with Byron in his letter conjuring himself for posterity as the 'solitary' muse, idly 'seeing plays'.

Another projection of the Romantic ideal of the solitary genius was perpetuated by Kean's attractiveness to the poet John Keats.[20] It has long been understood that Kean's spectacular presence on the London scene helped induce Keats' ambition to write a tragic theatrical masterpiece himself (ultimately, the abortive co-authored *Otho the Great*).[21] As soon as the revolutionary impact of Kean's Shylock became known, Keats would have been all too aware that the successful Drury Lane scheduling of his friend Charles Armitage Brown's *Narensky: or, The Road to Yaroslaf* would be cut short to suit the theatre's vertiginous turnabout to play Shakespeare rather than burletta. *Narensky* had reached its tenth performance the day after Kean's first Drury Lane Shylock, and, although it was played again later in the season, there can be little doubt its immediate progress was halted by Kean's success.[22] By the time it was staged again, the revolutionary nature of Kean's performances had been realized and the theatre's performance scheduling had undergone profound rethinking, much of it the result of reconfiguring the theatre's production planning subsequent to the impact of Kean's appearances. Nevertheless, the drift towards isolating Kean as a different kind of actor began at a moment co-existent with the beginnings of the recognition of Romanticism as a novel ideology of the projected complex self.

Of course, it should be remembered that records of contemporary perceptions of Kean's success or failure in his roles are inevitably related to the numbers of people who articulated their thoughts in writing, a deterritorialized supplement to the co-presence of the audience experience. Quite clearly, on the day of Kean's first Drury Lane Shylock – although Hazlitt exaggerates it – the playhouse was far from full, but Hazlitt's recollection has become an influential judgement, authoritatively secured on the back of his reputation as a critic. Indeed, Kean's reputation has been, even more so than that of Siddons, the result of a manifold rise in the volume and cultural significance of critical commentary which emerged during the prosperity at the end of the Napoleonic Wars and the rise in the periodical print culture. In short, they are mechanisms of emergence within the assemblage, with Kean's reputation created by the volume of critical commentary and anecdotage surrounding this emergence.

For Kean's first Hamlet, as for his other roles in that first season, the acceleration of his fame was impelled by networks of sociability within the audiences attending his performances. The influential relationship between Kinnaird and Byron has already been referred to, but with receipts totalling £660. 9s. 0d. by the time of his first performance of Hamlet, Kean's audience had expanded considerably.[23] Even the most cursory glance through the Drury Lane box book reveals not only more and more of the boxes becoming occupied on Kean's nights but also a slowly increasing number of the titled aristocrats filling them. On 19 February, for example, at the performance of *Richard III* attended by the Godwins and Byron's party, the box keeper's records show that the economist David Ricardo's brother, Joseph (1770–1847), a well-to-do Cornhill hatter, also took a box there.[24] As well as these elite and increasingly influential middle-class theatre-goers familiar with metropolitan cultural circles, on 24 February Harriet Ines-Kerr, the Duchess of Roxburghe, attended *Richard III*, the Duchess then barely a year consolidated in her new title (and the Floors Castle estate) following her husband's successful contestation of counter-claimants

(*Oxford Dictionary of National Biography* [*ODNB*]).[25] Through her family's connections with the engraver and publisher Valentine Green (1739–1813), the Duchess was also acquainted with the social circle of the landscape painter and diarist Joseph Farington. Such specific networks of cultural dissemination contributed much to Kean's later celebrity, but there were also other factors at work.

The role of Richard III, particularly during that first season, was considered one of Kean's finest interpretations. Prior to his first performance in this role on 12 February 1814, the company – apparently including Kean – had been involved in collective rehearsals scheduled on 4, 5, 7, 9 and 11 February with a further one concentrating on the '5th Act of Richard at____12' called on the day of the performance, the latter presumably a rehearsal concerned mainly with going through Kean's part in particular detail.[26] In other words, as well as having had the good fortune to struggle through and make his reputation with Shylock, much against the odds, the record of the *Richard III* Drury Lane rehearsals reveals much about his ability to benefit from the collective preparations they afforded. While the myth of Kean's solitary genius continues to present him otherwise, it seems sensible to conclude that his Richard III was precisely more memorable than his Hamlet because of the larger than usual number of general cast rehearsals scheduled by Dibdin, which included that possibly decisive fifth act final run-through on the day of the first performance. This ability of the Drury Lane company to regroup and concentrate their rehearsal time in order to maximize the advantage of their good fortune in finding Kean was an important sustaining feature of his celebrity. Again, it provides a further example of the importance of the collectivity of theatrical performers rather than the special talents of individuals. With audiences which included Byron and Godwin, their sets of influential acquaintances, and the growing presence of a socially well-connected aristocracy able to become his advocates or knowledgeable commentators, Kean was well set for increasing celebrity. A conclusive piece of evidence indicating the extent to which Drury Lane was considering how best to present him as their prime asset is shown by how, at the beginning of the 1814–15 season, their thoughts had turned to the issue of how Kean looked on stage. The playhouse's delivery book for incoming purchases shows that in October and November they received '7¼ [yards] black silk Velvet / Kean / Hamlet', '7 [yards] purple silk Velvet / Kean [Macbeth]', and '8 [yards] crimson Satin / Kean / Macbeth'.[27] Decked out in black, purple and crimson velvet and satin, Kean now looked like the star everybody expected to find.

Despite the wealth of contemporary commentary swirling confusingly around the production of Kean's reputation and its modern reception, extensive empirical evidence covering not just his clothing but also much more substantial aspects of his performance history, such as rehearsal schedules, box-office takings, audience structure and the overall financial and strategic impact on Drury Lane, necessitates a sharper definition of the loose epithet of 'celebrity' clustering around Kean. Importantly, the newly rebuilt Drury Lane of 1813, despite its relative artistic failure, had evolved a more robust set of management and accountancy practices which, although perhaps contributing little to its theatrical challenges on stage, capture many layers of its workings as an organization. By comparison, the evidence with which to evaluate the singularity of Sarah Siddons in the 1780s is much less abundant, although nonetheless suggestive.

Kean's two most celebrated performer precursors were David Garrick and Sarah Siddons, neither of whom – on a day-to-day performance basis – thought it advisable to pursue Shakespearean roles to the neglect of the conventional eighteenth-century repertoire as played in the theatres of their day. Sarah Siddons' reputation, epitomized in Reynolds' full-length portrait of her in *Mrs. Siddons as the Tragic Muse* (1784; oil on canvas, Huntington Library and Art Gallery, San Marino, California), has distorted modern perceptions about the role of celebrity performers of that era. It is worth reminding ourselves that, by and large, the term 'tragic' with respect to Siddons' repertoire did not normally mean Shakespearean. To examine the list of tragic roles Siddons performed most frequently around the time Reynolds exhibited this portrait at the Royal Academy exhibition rooms in Somerset House, only a few hundred yards from Drury Lane, is to encounter a repertoire almost certainly unfamiliar to most modern readers. For example, Nicholas Rowe's *Jane Shore* (1713), Garrick's version of Thomas Southern's *Isabella; or, The Fatal Marriage* (1758), Arthur Murphy's *The Grecian Daughter* (1772), John Hoole's *Timanthes* (1770) and John Home's *Douglas* (1757) were familiar pieces within her early repertoire. The first three were performed in the first month of Siddons' 1784–5 Drury Lane season, the one immediately following the painting's exhibition (after which it was returned, unsold, to Reynolds' studio). That same season, her chosen benefit programmes were *Douglas* on 22 December 1784 and James Thomson's *Tancred and Sigismunda* (1745) for her second benefit on 24 April 1785.

Although Siddons would go on to make Lady Macbeth perhaps her strongest role, as far as the audiences of 1784–5 were concerned, they evidently backed her decision to perform largely within the non-Shakespearean repertoire, which involved her with working extensively in the standard range of dramas available to most contemporary performers.

This issue is of some importance because, not least, it connected her firmly to an existing repertoire largely familiar to other cast members and required no specialization. This is quite different from Kean's tactic of seizing upon Shakespeare, an author then languishing far down Drury Lane's list of priorities, way beneath the emphasis it then placed on getting *Harlequin and Humpo* and *Harlequin Harper* right on the night. In Siddons' day, there clearly existed a day-to-day continuum along which actresses worked together in creative ensembles organized to ensure not only their own survival but also the continuing success of the playhouses in which they performed. By contrast, Drury Lane's fielding of Kean was part of a desperate strategy of chancing their luck by highlighting new performers.

However, the differences between Siddons at Drury Lane in the mid 1780s and the Haymarket quintet of Bannister, George, Cuyler, Sestini and Webb just a few years later (as discussed in Chapter 3) was not simply the result of varied levels of artistic talent but also the outcome of underlying networks of cultural and economic relations. As with Kean, the clutter of contemporary evaluations circulating in the form of newspaper reportage, reminiscence or anecdote has tended to produce a distorted projection of Siddons' acting talent, transforming her into a simulacrum of the Romantic heroine, a solitary talent substantially ahead of her fellow performers.

Upon close examination, even Siddons' well-documented ability to make members of her audiences swoon should be culturally contextualized by acknowledging a widespread affective disposition among Georgian theatre-goers. As contemporary diaries reveal, that Siddons created hysteria is beyond dispute and goes beyond contemporary journalistic puffing. In October 1783 the sixteen-year-old future American president John Quincy Adams (1767–1848) saw Siddons at Drury Lane playing the title role in David Garrick's (adapted from Southerne) *Isabella; or, The Fatal Marriage* (1757). The fastidious Adams (who, by happenchance, may also have seen Henry Siddons playing the Child) noted in his diary, 'Mrs Siddons supposed to be the first Tragick performer in Europe play'd the part of Isabella. A young lady, in the next Box to where we were, was so much affected by it as to be near fainting and was carried out. I was told that every night Mrs Siddons performs, this happens.'[28] Adams' diary entry is no less reliable than that of John Marsh, a Sussex composer and shareholder in the Chichester theatre. In March 1785 Marsh attended a private theatrical in Dover belonging to Peter Fector, a banker. The play performed was *The Orphan of China*, Arthur Murphy's 1759 adaptation of a Voltaire play.[29] What Marsh recorded there was an incident very similar to Adams' witnessing of Siddons two years earlier. When Fector, 'as he represented in y[e] last

Act a person dying in consequence of having been tortur'd, his Sister was so affected as to go into fits, on wch the Play was suddenly stopt & he arose & leap'd from the Stage into ye Box wherein she was, & was forc'd to continue for sometime assuring her he was very well & that nothing was really the matter with him, before she c^{ld} be pacified enough to be had out [of the box].' Admittedly Fector was performing in front of his sister at his 'private Theatre', but Marsh's presence along with, presumably, other guests somewhat dilutes the filial intensity between brother and sister in what Marsh simply characterized as 'an instance of Mr Fector's good Acting'.[30]

If an amateur actor in Dover in 1785 could inspire similar responses to those experienced by sections of Sarah Siddons' audiences at Drury Lane in 1783, the affective gradient between Fector and Siddons as performers cannot have been abnormally large. Although one might position these performances into a chronological sequence, as a phenomenon they are encompassed by the notion of a nationally distributed topography of theatrical assemblages where sudden effects (such as swooning) are linked as individual singularities located amidst the universal singularities of a pattern of histrionic assemblages which includes differences between, for example, public and private theatres: 'It is clear that assemblage theory, in which assemblages can be component parts of other assemblages (leading to the internal organization behind nonlinear and catalytic causality), and in which assemblages are always the product of recurrent processes yielding populations (involving statistical causality), can accommodate these complex forms of causal productivity.'[31]

The principal difference between the amateur Fector and the professional Siddons – since both induced swooning – was Siddons' increasing status as a celebrity. One of the clearest economic indicators of Siddons' celebrity was her ability to extract from Drury Lane a 'no charge' for her *Douglas* benefit in December 1784. However, while such an early-season free benefit was unusual, it was not unprecedented. Opportunities for singers who could combine their musical talents with acting were considerable. The singer and ex-courtesan Anne Catley (1745–1789) had negotiated an early-season benefit with Covent Garden, taking advantage of the special position female singers commanded in Georgian London. Writing his manual of advice and reminiscence in 1827 after a career acting in both London and the provinces, Leman Thomas Rede commented on the numerous roles by then available for 'Singing Chambermaids' and how 'First Singing Ladies are much more numerous than male vocalists'.[32] As far as a woman making a career was concerned, Rede thought that 'Any young lady embracing this line [a 'Singing Lady'], and possessed of even a moderate share of talent, could seldom lack a provincial engagement, and would stand an excellent chance of metropolitan distinction.'[33] Some eight years before Siddons' *Douglas* benefit, on 23 October 1776, Anne Catley performed Euphrosyne in Milton's *Comus: A Masque* (1772) at Covent Garden.[34] Catley was not part of the regular Covent Garden company, and it was probably this factor which enabled her benefit to be negotiated so early in the season during an era when benefit nights were normally taken in April and May.[35] Nevertheless, if salary is a marker of celebrity, then Catley's total receipts of £297. 13s. 0d. for appearing only in Act II of *Comus* were scarcely lower than Siddons' £312. 8s. 6d. for the whole of *Douglas*.

Siddons' rise was part of an emerging public lexicon which included in it the category of the celebrity performer, but, as demonstrated above, a considerable amount of caution is required when trying to equate celebrities with extraordinary individual talent. The ability of both Catley and Siddons to command early-season benefits, as well as the similarity in their benefit earnings, is one indicator of how the celebrity of performers on the patent theatre stages encompassed wide differentials of professional calling. If these highly focused manipulations of public culture were visible among the elite in the metropolis, they were also to be found manifested elsewhere, right across the assemblage as performers moved to occupy all the interstices of the capital's theatrical industry.

Twenty years earlier, the cross-dressed female marine Hannah Snell's memoir, *The Female Soldier; or, the Surprising Life and Adventures of Hannah Snell* (1750), appears to have been proficiently marketed by her publisher, Robert Walker, so that its publication coincided almost to the day with her appearances in a solo show at the New Wells Spa theatre, Goodman's Fields. Snell's London reception was the outcome of a series of specific intersections of cultural production which promoted her celebrity, not least because the private and public aspects of her sexuality were blazoned so forcefully by her career as both soldier and actress. Although Snell's ultimate financial aim was to secure an army pension, she quickly shot to fame. Walker marketed *The Female Soldier* through notices in *The General Advertiser* beginning 29 June 1750, just two days after the same newspaper had published the bill for her first night at the New Wells Spa theatre and twelve days before the same publication announced (for 'the Curious') 'A Print of an exact Likeness of the so-much-talk'd-of British Amazon, Hannah Snell' – warning prospective purchasers against 'Imposition from several Puffing Pretenders'.[36] Thirty years later in 1779, a newspaper reported a corpse found on Moushold Heath, near Norwich, erroneously believed to be that of 'Hannah Snell, who served as a marine', specifically recollecting her exclusively as 'performing the manual exercise at Sadler's Wells' (typically mistaking the precise venue).[37] Sir Joshua Reynolds' later ability to work in consort with Garrick and Siddons in the production of high-class studio oil paintings matched to accompanying prints only mirrored earlier activities such as those of the more fugitive print-makers who produced likenesses of Snell to make their prints coincide with *The Female Soldier* and Snell's cross-dressed appearances performing her speciality, the musket act of the military 'Manual Exercise' at the New Wells Spa theatre.

In other words, in both its elite and lower-class configurations, celebrity was very much an aspect of common methods of cultural production throughout the eighteenth century. However, the mechanisms at work promoting performers as celebrities were not simply matters restricted to the acquisition of favourable publicity or professional esteem. Nor were audiences witnessing the unmediated outcome of a natural, primitive, talent. In London's monopolistic system, speaking actors or actresses denied opportunities to would-be rivals by forcing them to work within predominantly musical genres. If we study the underlying economic mechanisms at work within this specific market, some of the techniques of managing celebrity can be elaborated. The sampling of a benefit night for the actress Elizabeth Pope (*née* Younge), then Covent Garden's highest-paid actress, in 11 April 1791 reveals the levels of organization and deployment of talent that were required to turn a potentially unpredictable occasion into a success.

Contemporary theatre ledger books involve immersion in an unfamiliar set of Georgian theatrical accountancy practices which give added complexity to the variable arrangements applying to benefit nights. As her choice for a benefit mainpiece, Pope selected Henry Jones' *The Earl of Essex*, a tragedy first produced in 1753 but recently updated for Covent Garden's repertoire, with her role that of Queen Elizabeth.[38] Showcasing her versatility, Pope paired Queen Elizabeth by playing as her afterpiece the servant, Kitty, in Townley's part-blackface farce, *High Life Below Stairs* (1759). Some idea of the precarious entrepreneurialism underpinning the entire enterprise of a performer mounting a benefit night may be judged by Pope's judicious pre-emptive advertisement placed in *The Oracle and Public Advertiser* newspaper on the day of the performance (although not repeated in her advertisement inserted in *The World* the same day), warning 'No Money to be returned'.[39] By choosing to perform in both the mainpiece and the afterpiece, Pope had taken control of the evening's financial outcome by limiting the number of fees payable to other performers. Her pre-emptive denial of refunds also suggests an extremely consumer-oriented business model, with

the actress quietly stipulating her terms for the evening through the medium
of the newspapers, shrewdly only selectively advertising her restrictions and
taking this sensible precaution to protect her income source. This kind of
marketing strategy extended to other aspects of her advertising. With a
similar degree of business awareness about differentiating audience segments through attractively labelled offerings, Pope had also advertised
Jones' *Earl of Essex* tagged to the subtitle, *Or, The Unhappy Favourite*, a
phrase actually taken from John Banks' 1704 tragedy, *The Unhappy
Favourite, Or, The Earl of Essex*. Such elaborate juxtapositions were no
doubt intended to draw those parts of the audience who perhaps more
readily recognized an older repertoire version of the same story, yet these
juxtapositions allowed Pope to maximize her role in Henry Jones' more
recent *The Earl of Essex*.

In short, whatever the newspapers wrote about celebrity benefit nights,
there is nothing simple about calculating either how much performers finally
earned or the transparency with which these issues can be interpreted without
access to contemporary financial accounts. According to the playhouse's
ledger, Covent Garden's total receipts for Elizabeth Pope's *Earl of Essex* and
High Life Below Stairs 1791 benefit night came to £297. 13s. 0d. (excluding a
few more pounds from 'after money' sales – i.e. half-price at half-time
admissions – normally accounted for the next day). Mrs Pope's personal
receipts for the sale of 332 box tickets and 94 pit tickets (but no gallery tickets)
came to £105. 10s. 0d., a set of figures once again suggesting that there was not
an easily intelligible relationship between the individual value of benefit
'Tickets' and the total income received from them. However, while the
proceeds of the ticket sales were her own, the playhouse also took money
from *ad hoc* theatre-goers (e.g. passing-trade, out-of-towners), who had to be
charged normal prices because they could not have anticipated attending a
benefit night. The total taken from these receipts came to a further £190. 13s.
6d., but on 2 May 1791, Covent Garden 'Paid Mrs. Pope[her] Benefit
Ballance' of £95. 13s. 0d. This suggests that, although no explicit charge was
stated in Covent Garden's books, the benefit-night terms she had agreed with
the management allowed her to receive 100% of her own 'Ticket' sales plus
50% of the rest of the playhouse receipts. The kinds of performance and
financial choices made by Pope provide a broad empirical context within
which to judge the rise of the much more celebrated actress from approximately the same era, Sarah Siddons.

As far as the late eighteenth century is concerned, and with Edmund
Kean already marked out as posing quite different problems, all of the
complexities of the configurations of acting ability, verifiable earnings and

professional pre-eminence were at their most exaggerated in the figure of Sarah Siddons. As is well known, her professional rise was mirrored by newspaper speculation as to her financial circumstances, and early on she fell foul of negative commentary. James Gillray's print caricature of her in *Melpomene* (6 December 1784), made after her alleged refusal to appear in the benefits of her fellow actors, William Brereton and West Digges, attacked her avarice, and it was well known she made lucrative tours of the provinces during the summer seasons.[40] However, what has not been examined before is the exact scale and nature of the economic leverage her celebrity brought her and how this was deployed.

Siddons' control over her own visual imagery was an underlying aspect of her professional power. The patent theatre monopolies, coupled with the size of the audience capacities at Covent Garden and Drury Lane, not only narrowly focused on an attentive audience for the spoken word but also impelled the creation of Reynolds' triumphant Royal Academy painting, *Mrs. Siddons as the Tragic Muse*. The extensive study of Reynolds' full-length portrait by modern art historians has told us much about the degree of management and deliberation with which it was both conceived and publicly presented. As Heather McPherson, Robyn Asleson and others have argued, the cultural, artistic and economic connections between Reynolds and Siddons, both of them carefully managing their relative reputations and controlling the circumstances of the production and reception of this painting, are highly complex, having much to do with the channelling and filtering of celebrity within this highly developed metropolitan market-place.[41] If much critical effort has been concentrated on tracing the origins and dissemination of Reynolds' portrait, Siddons' own awareness of the importance of managing her visual image has been less frequently empha-sized. However, as McPherson reminds us, in 1829 Siddons objected to her niece, Fanny Kemble, receiving from Sir Thomas Lawrence an amended proof of Francis Hayward's 1787 stipple engraving of *Mrs. Siddons as the Tragic Muse* on the grounds of Lawrence's polite but respectfully worded hint that Fanny had inherited the family's acting prowess.[42] Indeed, report-age about Siddons was regularly carried in the newspapers, and she grew to be adept at handling her own public relations. Hayward's stipple, published a full three years after the Royal Academy exhibition, only came about because Siddons had herself intervened to deflect Reynolds from using his favourite mezzotint engraver, Valentine Green, to manufacture the print. Even more strikingly, as early as the 1790s, Siddons – tutored by Anne Seymour Damer – took some demonstrable measure of control of the quality of the visual reproduction of her imagery by sculpting her own self-portrait bust (plaster, *c.* 1790, Victoria and Albert Museum, London).[43] Such interventions were typical of Siddons' career.

Given this high degree of professional management over her career, it is not surprising Siddons negotiated advantageous financial terms. However, what has not previously received analysis are the levels and structural mechanisms underlying her earnings. With reference to assemblage theory, the epistemological position is that 'All assemblages have a fully contingent historical identity', but 'Because the ontological status of all assemblages is the same, entities operating at different scales can directly interact with one another, individual to individual.' Celebrities such as Siddons (or her predecessors or followers) never existed in isolation, but 'At any level of scale ... are always dealing with *populations* of interacting entities.' Since celebrity is the outcome of an interaction with the reception environment, the study of the interactions materializes the history of the assemblage and the stature of Siddons' celebrity.[44]

These interactions are traceable in the historical record as part of the celebrity's exterior relations: 'Once a large scale assemblage is in place, it immediately starts acting as a source of limitations and resources for its components ... downward causality is needed to account for the fact that most social assemblages are composed of parts that come into existence after the whole has emerged.'[45] Broadly, Siddons' income has been grossly overstated since the tendency within the theatrical assemblage was for financial rewards to approach the mean for all performers across the assemblage's populations.

For May 1785, a management account book survives, giving remittance details for Siddons' tour of the theatres at Manchester and Liverpool. It is quite clear that estimates of her earnings are largely based on guesses derived from the newspapers. As Judith Milhous has argued, there is a current under-usage of eighteenth-century theatre account books as evidence in calculating the overall economics of theatre management, actors' salaries included.[46] Siddons' second biographer Thomas Campbell, in reporting her salary for Drury Lane in the season 1784–5, provided the remarkably exact figure of 23 guineas and 7s. per week.[47] However, while one assumes that this example is derived from Siddons herself, it is clear that Campbell, despite her apparent cooperation with his biographical project, generally tended to have little access to verifiable figures for her income in the 1780s. On a later occasion, in order to gather information about her pay for the period 1803–12, Campbell simply applied to the secretary of Covent Garden theatre, hoping he would deliver to him accurate notes.[48] For information about her earnings in May 1785, Campbell appears to have copied out newspaper reports, entering them into the notebook he kept for the biography. Crucially, Campbell was smart enough not to have actually used the wildly exaggerated claims about her earnings then circulating in the London press prior to her departure for Manchester and Liverpool. According to *The Public Advertiser* report which he copied out, although the figure for her salary ('Twenty-five guineas a week') was approximately accurate and correlates with Campbell's published figure, the newspaper then speculated wildly about her receipts from benefit nights and her provincial touring that season. *The Public Advertiser* assumed (correctly) that, of her two expected 1784–5 Drury Lane benefits, one would be 'clear of the nightly charge' but imagined that this, when coupled to what the newspaper assumed would be two more benefit nights in Manchester and Liverpool (both of which it believed would also be 'clear' nights), plus an Edinburgh season, would amount to £3,200 ('exclusive of presents at her benefits!!!').[49] This was the report Campbell entered into his notebook.[50]

However, the actual receipts for the two 1784–5-season Drury Lane benefit nights tell a different story. Her December 1784 *Douglas* had, indeed, been a 'no charge' benefit, making her exactly £136 from her 'Tickets' and a further £176. 8s. 6d. from the playhouse receipts. At her April 1785 *Tancred and Sigismunda*, she made £169. 15s. 0 d. from Tickets and a further £47. 15s. 11d. from other receipts, but net of a theatre charge of £106. 10s. 1d. In some ways, these two performances represent Siddons at the very height of her career, but they demonstrate that, while she took £312. 8s. 6d. for the *Douglas* benefit, her net earnings dropped sharply to £217. 10s. 11d. for *Tancred*.[51] By comparison, although she is not normally placed in the celebrity category, six years later in 1791 Elizabeth Pope's benefit gave her £200. 3s. 0d. This steep decline in Siddons' earnings from the benefits is a perfect illustration of the real economics of celebrity in the theatrical profession. The Tickets component of her receipts for *Douglas*, a sure indicator of her personal prestige and profile, was £136, rather less than the nearly £170 she earned by the same means for *Tancred*, yet the impact of the house charge produced a nearly £100 overall diminution in her income for the second benefit. In other words, while her celebrity was rising – not least signalled by the allocation of a rare late December benefit – the documentary evidence shows that her financial earnings were, if not falling, then certainly not accelerating at the rate the newspapers imagined.

In other words, rather than Siddons being part of a reified category of celebrity within an equally reified (and unquantified) 'market' of cultural value, the materialization of her earnings in absolute relation to their existence as financial transactions returns her closer to the mean of ordinary performers working within the overall theatrical assemblage.

The Public Advertiser claims have questionable validity at best. For her three-day run at Manchester, Siddons earned in total £182. 2s. While this corresponds quite closely with some of the details found in the lengthy account of the Edinburgh theatre manager, John Jackson (written nearly ten years later), of Siddons' 1784 season in that city (also in May), it differs in some crucial areas. Jackson (whose motive seems to have been to remonstrate about losses he incurred when she appeared there) gives Siddons' income for her nine nights as £967. 7s. 7d., but with only £467. 7s. 7d. of this made up from her share of the box-office receipts, the remainder being Jackson's speculative conclusion about the role of a 'gentlemens subscription' (which he estimated at £200) got up among local '*amateurs* of the drama', and a further £300 also speculatively estimated as other types of benefit-night receipts including 'presents' of plate and 'gold tickets'.[52]

In short, contrary to the newspaper reports, she did not have a benefit night at Manchester, and although her two Drury Lane benefits (even if she had 'presents') could easily have yielded £500, it seems an exaggeration to believe that Siddons could earn over £3,000 simply from summer touring. Campbell himself clearly remained sceptical about such claims. Nevertheless, the Manchester account book reveals the financial mechanisms through which Siddons was able to capitalize on her fame, amplifying the effects of Drury Lane's monopolistic cartel over the spoken tragic roles in which she specialized. The ability of a celebrity metropolitan actress to command exacting financial terms for her provincial appearances was a leveraging of her position within a metropolitan theatre protected by a state monopoly.

What the Manchester account book may also suggest is the importance of the sheer depth of her experience as an actress, drawing on negotiating tactics no doubt dating as far back as her work in the provincial touring company of her father, Roger, where she must have learned the basic raw commercial tactics of ensuring and maximizing a paying audience. As late as 1832, a witness to the Parliamentary Select Committee on Dramatic Literature, giving testimony towards their compilation of evidence for assessing the future of the patent system, recalled that when Siddons acted in her father's company in the 1760s, when touring in Wolverhampton, that company found a way of circumventing a local licensing restriction by getting the audience to buy 'a very excellent tooth-powder at 2s.1d. a box. And that tooth-powder was purchased and considered a ticket.'[53] If local licensing requirements had worked against her father in the English Midlands in the 1760s, forcing him to find creative ways of circumvention, Siddons was now positioned to capitalize on the economic and artistic side effects of the patent system, which restricted her metropolitan competitors to those few actresses able to find speaking roles. Armed with these advantages, no doubt it was comparatively easy to negotiate favourable terms with the Manchester company in 1785.[54]

One of the primary indicators of Siddons' ability to capitalize on her position as an actress – no doubt in agreement with the managers – was the ability to force up prices. Before her arrival for a three-day engagement at the Theatre Royal, Manchester, typical cash receipts were averaging around £30 per night, on prices of 3s. in the boxes, 2s. in the pit and 1s. in the gallery.[55] For Siddons' season, however, prices went up to, respectively, 5s., 3s. and 2s.[56] By comparison, thirty-five years later and after an inflationary war, the highest box prices the theatre in Liverpool could charge for Edmund Kean's last performances prior to his departing for his American tour – and with Kean in the role of Hamlet – was 4s. 6d.[57] On Siddons' first night, the theatre's total takings shot up to £148. 14s. Of this sum, Siddons took £66. 17s. in pay, the managers keeping the balance, inclusive of a £15 sum, which may have been set aside to pay the theatre owners. In other words, Siddons' share was 45 per cent of the total receipts. The second night witnessed a similar percentage split, with the house takings being somewhat higher at £171. 17s., again with £15 going to the theatre, and, of the remainder, half went to the management and 'half to Mrs Siddons [£]78.8.6'. For Siddons' third night, her payment ratio increased, although the sum she received went down, the account book noting 'Mrs Siddons half by Agreement', and the actress receiving £36. 16s. 6d., or 50 per cent of the theatre's total takings.

In other words, Siddons' earnings (according to Jackson's figures) – averaged around £52 per day at Edinburgh in 1784 and around £61 per day at Manchester a year later, but with the difference that, in Manchester, she had no benefit night and no special subscription organized by local enthusiasts. Understandably, without evidence of the quality of the Manchester ledgers for comparative purposes, and reliance only on newspaper reports, Siddons' income (and, therefore, her celebrity) has tended to become ever more exaggerated, and this has gone unchallenged in modern times.[58]

Siddons' short season was not particularly demanding in requiring her to perform new roles. Siddons (or the managers) appears to have attempted to balance the extent of her professional exertions against the possibilities of sustaining the theatre's income. Perhaps electing to maintain her stamina,

Siddons played in Nicholas Rowe's *The Tragedy of Jane Shore* (1714) twice, performing it on the first and on the third nights, with Garrick's adaptation of Southerne, *Isabella; or, The Fatal Marriage* (1757) staged on the second evening. She is unlikely to have been required to perform at all in Manchester's afterpieces, Charles Dibdin's ballad opera, *The Waterman: or, The First of August* (1774), Isaac Bickerstaffe's *The Padlock* (1768) and Samuel Foote's *The Mayor of Garratt* (1763). The dip in the third-night receipts also seems to make less likely the rumours that she was earning £1,000 for a tour. With her earnings, as indicated by her two benefits in the 1784–5 Drury Lane season, having declined, the picture of an unstoppable rise to celebrity looks questionable. Devastatingly, prior to leaving London for Manchester, Siddons had performed Rosalind in *As You Like It*, a breeches comedy role for which she was not deemed particularly suited, even at the height of her fame. Or, as the *Morning Chronicle and London Advertiser* put it, 'Did any body go more than once?'[59]

However, the principal issue at stake about Siddons' Manchester and Liverpool appearances is not the amount of money she earned but, rather, the kinds of leverage her status afforded her and, additionally, to what extent this was derived from the London patent theatres' monopoly over the kind of speaking acting roles at which she excelled. Some of the perquisites she obtained ranged from a type of reasonable nepotism – the role of Isabella's infant son in *Isabella; or, The Fatal Marriage* was almost certainly taken up by her daughter, the ten-year-old Sarah Martha Siddons (1775–1803), for which she was paid £5 – to much more profound implications for how the earnings of the Manchester company were divided up among its employees.

The percentages Siddons commanded had a number of economic consequences for the rest of the company, irrespective of the status of her separate arrangement with the management. At the front of the account book there are listed forty-two members of the company, inclusive of 'Franks [the] Hair Dresser' and ten others in the 'Band'. On at least one of the Liverpool nights the account book recorded (because it altered the playhouse's salary liability), 'Six Performers not being Wanted in the play with Mrs Siddons'. Although it is not clear which performance this information relates to, it was one of a number of impacts brought about by the terms negotiated for Siddons' visit, in this instance perhaps favouring the management through a lower pay bill but leaving company actors temporarily out of work. Quite clearly, at least some of the forty-two persons employed (perhaps not all full-time) by the Manchester company were disadvantaged by the management's decision to hold a Siddons season where she was contracted to receive around 50 per cent of the box-office takings.

At the end of Siddons' tour, the Manchester season returned to normality. Receipts slumped to their regular levels, on 29 June totalling only £24. 3s. 6d., even for Hannah Cowley's recent Covent Garden comedy, *More Ways Than One* (1784), paired with David Garrick's pantomime, *Harlequin's Invasion* (1759). A post-Siddons dip in the box office was not uncommon. Compiling his notes for *The Theatric Tourist*, around 1802, James Winston noted of Wakefield theatre's past: '1786 Bad Season after Mrs Siddons had playd one night'.[60] However, what the rest of this account book rather unexpectedly shows is that, given the right conditions, receipts could sometimes approximate to Siddons' levels even when the playhouse fielded performers of some obscurity.

Barely a month later, on 1 July 1785, *Othello* drew a box office of £57. 12s. 6d., a figure not too distant from Siddons' third-night receipts of £73. 13s. 0d. for *Jane Shore*. The clue to that night's success was that 'Major Halliday play'd Iago'.[61] This is a reference to an army officer who, in the mid 1780s, ran an amateur theatrical troupe in the Bath and Bristol area, appearing to specialize in productions of *Othello*. The actor John Bernard, who later joined Halliday's company and witnessed him playing Othello at Bath in 1786 (when Bernard acted as prompter), thought Halliday's performance 'the best piece of amateur acting I ever saw'. On that occasion, Halliday had hired Bath Theatre Royal in its entirety during what Bernard called 'an "off-night"', when the playhouse would otherwise have been closed.[62] As Halliday's Manchester *Othello* was paired with *Harlequin's Invasion* – a pantomime which was clearly a local repertoire staple – it is unclear as to whether he had brought a whole troupe or was acting in an individual capacity. Judging by Bernard's account, Halliday was already well known by 1785 in the Bristol and Bath area. His case provides a further perspective on Siddons' career, which had also recently developed professional accomplishment at Bath between 1778 and 1782.

What the Manchester comparison of Siddons and Halliday reveals is that, despite widespread commentaries in the newspapers, in mid 1785, at a time when Siddons' career afforded her celebrity status, her capacity to draw large audiences was not always unchallenged, even by comparison with an amateur actor. However, what was by then completely different was Siddons' ability to negotiate 50 per cent of the takings. Both Halliday and Siddons had experience of the provincial theatres of south-west England at around the same time, but only Siddons had been able to benefit from London's monopolistic patent theatres, which excluded many other performers.

The economic history of Georgian performance within its contemporary assemblage presents, at best, a mixed picture of celebrity distinctiveness. Whether considered from perspectives inside or outside the metropolitan acting spaces, the traceable economic associations of performers suggests a flattening of their individual profiles of talent and celebrity. Within a context where the Dover banker, Peter Fector, or the Manchester Othello, Major Halliday, could engage with audiences to similar palpable effects materialized at the performance venues, inducing swooning or capturing similar levels of box-office takings, the difference between Siddons, for example, and the rest of the profession situates her much nearer other populations in the assemblage. Indeed, given the extent of the organizational scale of contemporary theatricality in Britain, with its plethora of built performance spaces and intricate networks of companies, this flattening towards the mean of the assemblage's overall shape is perfectly predictable.

CHAPTER FIVE

A working theatrical assemblage: 1790s representations of naval conflict

'The main territorializing process providing the assemblage with a stable identity is *habitual repetition*.'[1] DeLanda's formulation helps theorize and structure the insights of Joseph Roach and Kathleen Wilson that theatre, through the repetition of performance texts at public locations, provokes the communal differentiation of public and national identity.[2] As the parameters of the theatrical assemblage have been carefully outlined in previous sections of the book, this chapter is the first one to set out the assemblage in its full working order. Of course, to '*habitual repetition*' must be added '*density*, a measure of the intensity of connectivity between indirect links', a term which, in turn, can usually be equated with the populations of the assemblage.[3] Density in the assemblage model is the coefficient of several functions, each of which is capable of being isolated for analysis and should have the property of being irreducible. At its simplest (although at a practical level it would be difficult to calculate due to the absence of a national inventory of Georgian theatrical spaces), an approximation of eighteenth-century British theatrical density can be obtained by taking any span of years and dividing the total number of theatrical performances (by date and by text) during that period into the total number of theatres in the national inventory, with the final figure adjusted for audience capacity (the assemblage's populations). Within this particularized assemblage, there are also other arrays of networks continually modifying and reconfiguring its shape and dimensions. Earlier chapters have stressed interconnectedness in the theatrical model, working with collectivities of performers (rather than single celebrities) through to the inclusion of both rural and urban private theatricals, all taken together as signifying a specific type of market. While the uniqueness of each individual performance has been emphasized, the persistence of a recognizable contemporary repertoire is also an unmistakable feature of the assemblage.

To provide a preliminary example of the repetition of performance texts centred on distinctive themes, in this case relevant to contemporary attitudes to monarchy, there were clusters of plays such as the Royal Circus' *St. George's Day; or, Britannia's Joy*; Covent Garden's *St. George's Day; or, Britons Rejoice!*; and Drury Lane's *Laoeudaimonos; or, A People Made Happy*; and *British Loyalty; or, A Squeeze for St. Paul's* (discussed in Chapter 8), all performed in the spring of 1789 and all commenting on George III's recovery from apparent mental ill health. These dramas demonstrate the assemblage's synchronicity in its ability to reflect public uncertainty about the constitutional health of the nation and present these concerns in staged representation. While some plays had only a single performance and alluded to passing news phenomena, the seating capacity of the playhouses means that their combined audience figures rapidly escalated into five-figure totals.

As demonstrated in the previous chapter, co-present audience conversation networks possessed the capacity rapidly to accelerate different perceptions of cultural value. Since cultural meaning changes with every change in the performance location (spatially or temporally), and since Georgian performances were reiterated but not repeated, each night's audience provided a unique reception environment and capacity for emergence. For example, as will be discussed below, the audience, numbering over 40,000, who went to *Nootka Sound* or its derivative, *The Provocation!*, in the spring and autumn of 1790 should be broken down into multiple reception segments of around 2,000 people (the two-thirds-full approximation of the audience capacity). Each individual audience component of 2,000 persons comprises a daily density of population within the overall theatrical assemblage carrying a capacity for new cultural meaning unique to each audience.[4]

An array of dramas about naval conflict produced in the 1780s and 1790s offers a wide range of insights as to how competing notions of nationhood and empire were theatricalized on stage in the large public spaces of the patent playhouses. The Royal Navy was the absolute basis of Britain's increasingly globalized network of national influence, and it was natural that its role in the continuing creation of empire was repeatedly presented on stage. Despite the ostensibly loyalist titles appearing on the playbills, many of the preludes, pantomimes, interludes and other types of entertainment ancillary to the mainpieces and afterpieces of the Georgian programmers managed to promote patriotism within a context which usually included some nuanced degree of dissent. In other words, they were not simple excursions into patriotism but were often surprisingly critical (or sometimes blissfully ignorant) of the forces shaping empire.

In this respect, the implications of the dramas discussed here present slightly different sets of answers to those suggested by Kathleen Wilson, who refers to 'the English stage as the leading site for the enactment of superior national virtue and character' where 'theater was able to transform historical idealizations into historical "realities" that helped structure and confirm English beliefs about their own distinctiveness and destiny'.[5] Instead of loyalist conformities, the entertainments based on Britain's never-ending series of naval conflicts offered a range of social perspectives. Not least, although full-scale partial reconstructions were sometimes used (as in the example of *The Glorious First of June* below), the theatres' use of 6-inch-high, miniaturized, painted wooden armies and navies modelling manoeuvrings of the nations at war was hardly in itself conducive to developing a credible ideology of empire building.[6]

Their topicality has meant that few of these dramas were printed, and some are now only available through the Lord Chamberlain's licensing copies (which need to be used in conjunction with playbills and newspaper comment). Although it could take weeks or months for news from Britain's furthest imperial outposts to reach the homeland, the unpredictable rapidity of the outcomes of strategic and tactical naval conflicts far out at sea ensured that the inception, production and scheduling of those theatrical performances aimed at marking or celebrating these crucial engagements proceeded at a dizzying speed. Indeed, the responsiveness of the assemblage to immediate changes in national fortune is itself a signifier of the underlying material capacities within the theatres enabling military campaigns to be represented, fully cast, costumed and musicalized, directly onto the London stages.

The origins and dissemination of maritime news was a discrete discursive process itself, often functioning in close proximity to the 'Theatrical Intelligence' columns of the newspapers. London newspapers not only provided raw factual information about the Royal Navy's movements and engagements but also, on occasion, criticized military progress (for example, deriding the inability of Lord Howe's Grand Fleet to locate the French fleet in the Atlantic in 1794). Newspapers such as *The Times* also carried regular features, often headed 'Shipping News', printing Admiralty dispatches, apparently verbatim.[7] Of course, it must be assumed that the Admiralty filtered and censored reports before they reached the press, but some of these official communiqués were also separately printed and distributed in the English provinces.[8] Occasionally, newspaper correspondents contributed further information or added eyewitness reports. What is striking is that the rationale for the critiques expressed in the theatrical texts was often far from evident in the originating Admiralty news dispatches. In other words, it seems probable that these dramas were manifestations of a more general set of civilian perspectives about the progress of Britain's military conflicts and not simply ideological by-products of newspaper reporting, as has been claimed.[9] Paradoxically, despite the state's haphazardly effective apparatus for theatre censorship, these (apparently) exclusively loyalist effusions remained surprisingly nuanced. In any event, the Examiner of Plays made few excisions to them, perhaps automatically greeting their production as straightforwardly positive expressions of maritime pride.

Their divergence from the newspaper stories or Admiralty dispatches which originally released the news, together with the materialization of divergent narratives (of patriotism or of dissent, for example) in performance, signifies theatre as a mutating assemblage. In this theatrical subset of naval dramas, whose principal components can be fully synthesized for analysis during the prolific clustering of their production in 1790s London, there was created an actualized metalevel of operations on the data reaching the playhouses' managers, ballet and scenic devisers, and script authors via the newspapers and Admiralty dispatches.

The vast geopolitical and military implications of the events portrayed in the various musicalized entertainments, preludes and interludes produced for the London stage exposes the scale of the increasingly global basis of Britain's empire. Covent Garden's 'Pantomimic, Operatic Farce', *Nootka Sound; Or, Britain Prepar'd* (1790), probably devised by their principal ballet master, James Byrne (1756–1844), is particularly interesting. It was based on an incident when two British merchant ships, the *North West America* and the *Iphigenia*, were captured off Nootka Sound, north-west Canada, by Spanish vessels headed by Captain Esteban José Martinez in 1790.[10] *Nootka Sound* not only demonstrates, at a crucial pre-war moment, the extremely extended reach of British economic and military power far from home waters, but also presents a complex example of how the country's engagement with global geopolitics was represented on the London stage.

The *North West America* and the *Iphigenia* had been contracted by the East India Company in cooperation with the – by then residual – South Sea Company 'for the purpose of supplying the Chinese market with [otter] furs and ginseng' from north-west America.[11] These elaborate networks of trade, in which Britain acted as a minor supplier to a Chinese-dominated world economy, indicate the rationale for the Nootka trading expedition, an enterprise conceived and mounted from India, reaching right across the Pacific Ocean yet actually intent on securing British access to Chinese ports at a time when these harbours were dominated by the Portuguese.[12] *Nootka Sound; Or, Britain Prepar'd* (1790) – and, of course, the incident which inspired it – demonstrated not only British imperial reach but also its brittle strength. It is probably also the case that the magnitude of the global networks of trade figured into the original rationale for a British presence on the north-west American continent must have been difficult for most of the audience or performers to comprehend. Although *Nootka Sound* was a new work commissioned for the very end of the 1789–90 season, it was performed for six nights, closing Covent Garden's year on 14 June. A benefit performance on 10 June took £250. 2*s*. 6*d*. (by comparison their *Othello* on 15 May 1790 took £203. 17*s*. 6*d*.), so that, assuming two-thirds-full houses (possibly larger on the 10th), *Nooka Sound*'s first-season audience probably exceeded 12,000 people.[13]

In the late 1780s, the best chance of Britain making an extensive commercial inroad into the Chinese market was based not on exporting domestically manufactured goods but, rather, on selling otter skins traded from local Native-American hunters. After the seizure of the ships, the subsequent claim made against the Spanish authorities for a conjectural loss of 1,000 otter pelts represented an economically strategic loss in the East India Company's abortive attempt at finding a new opening in the difficult Chinese market, whose regional hegemony was absolute and facilitated by long-established networks of Chinese imperial influence. It may be that the company saw themselves as potential colonizers, but it is also quite typical of the alternative methods favoured by Chinese economic imperialism that two precursor vessels arriving at Nootka in 1788, the *Argonaut* and the *Princess Royal*, carried with them 'near 70 Chinese, who intended to become settlers on the American cost [*sic*], in the service, and under the protection of the associated Company'.[14] The Chinese version of imperialism promoted diasporic practices which facilitated their economic hegemony by encouraging citizens to form enclaves overseas without military or political support (with the result that the Spanish quickly put them to coerced labour). This transportation of Chinese workers was perfectly suited to this kind of outward economic expansion promoted by Beijing and which the East India Company naively facilitated, in this instance deftly employing the Calcutta-built *Argonaut* to further China's economic reach across the Indian and Pacific oceans.

The seizure by Captain Martinez of the *North West America* and the *Iphigenia* at far-flung Nootka in May 1789 meant that the first contradictory and sketchy news of the incident did not reach the British government until six months later on 21 January 1790, and the details were not published in the London newspapers until *The Times* of 4 May 1790, almost four months after that.[15] However, a month to the day after the first newspaper reports, on 4 June 1790, Covent Garden staged *Nootka Sound; Or, Britain Prepar'd.*

Their 'New Pantomimic, Operatic Farce' was set in Portsmouth amidst the preparations for a naval response. Not only was *Nootka Sound* devoid of allusion to the intricate economic determinants which had carried the *Iphigenia* and the Calcutta-built *Argonaut* to icy Nootka in search of otter skins to trade to China, but its single reference to Captain Martinez came during the farce's narrative of a rehearsal for a shipboard amateur theatrical staged by sailors in which one of them (Foremast) was costumed as the Don ('You represent a more sad dog, Foremast, alias Don Martinez Ay, you blood thirsty Lubber!').[16] Of course, the readiness with which *Nootka Sound* portrayed military amateur dramatics is itself indicative of a culturally normative contemporary relationship between the military and the theatre, as extensively discussed by Gillian Russell.[17] If *Nootka Sound's* patriotism was pretty disconnected from the possibility of understanding the Nootka crisis' underlying imperial or economic imperatives, it still perpetuated a breezy version of British power and influence. The importance of its sentiments lies in their repetition to large numbers of people. In the theatres, national ideological aims were habitually reiterated in song and chorus: 'Captn Briton &c &c. Chorus / The Throne of Britannia's the Ocean / She sits there serene and majestic / Her huge floating Castles in motion / Secure her each comfort domestic. / Her Bulwark's a stout Man of War / Her Guard is a bold british Tar.' However, some of its more overbearing expressions of bellicosity were pre-emptively tempered by the Lord Chamberlain's judicious censoring (shown here with the excision struck through) because of fear of upsetting future alliances with Spain:

SEAMAN: Now, Jack Marlingspike, have at the Dons, ~~we will so manage the Guns of Brittania, my boy, that they shall strike their national honor between wind~~ & water and if ever they recover the blow sufficiently to bear down upon us again in Nootka Sound, or any place within the Sound of the British Fleet, why, I am no prophet, and Jack Marlingspike no Seaman.

However, perhaps unexpectedly, what follows in *Nootka Sound* is a succession of tropes about effeminacy. These sentiments markedly contrast with claims about the British national destiny which also repeatedly surface in the play.

On arrival at the Rodney's Head tavern, Portsmouth, the Marines officer, Cartouch, immediately deploys 'a Decoy Recruit [with] Drums beating, Fife &c. &c.' (another detailing of contemporary para-theatricality) but to little avail. Their first potential recruit, the eponymous Taylor, a reluctant and drunken local tailor, eloquently spurns enlistment:

SERJEANT: I am a Serjeant of marines who serves his Majesty (God bless him) on board the Royal Fleet now at Spithead, and you shall serve him too.
TAYLOR: Shall I? No, but I won't tho'
CARTOUCH: Why?
TAYLOR: Because I know the salt water don't agree with me – You see I'm as sick as a dog, and but half Seas over already, and, help you, Master Serjeant, I am not tall enough for a Soldier – I know I ain't – I was turn'd out of the Sussex Militia at Colchester three years ago.

In other words, structured within Covent Garden's *Nootka Sound* are all the fears of failing male valour already prefigured in O'Keeffe's *The Siege of Curzola* at the Haymarket in 1786.

Tailors were stage stereotypes for lack of masculine valour, and *Nootka Sound*'s Taylor is no exception. Eventually gulled into recruitment ('Here's a pretty rascal! Wants to mutiny already – Get along, you ninth part of humanity, or I'll run my sword in your Guts'), Taylor is immediately contrasted with Elizabeth, a sailor's sweetheart, who unhesitatingly cross-dresses to enter the navy to join her lover: 'Enter Eliza habited as a man . . . Elizabeth: . . . I have formed my resolution, and I am determined to fulfil it – I will go to the Rendezvous, enter as a Volunteer on board the Thunderbolt and then I shall have an opportunity of viewing and serving my Henry at the same time.' The staged representations of male effeminacy and female valour, repeatedly reiterated at the performance locations, provided a recurrent and familiar trope for contemporary gender roles.

Nootka Sound's ability to nuance the public's response is dramatized by the intervention of the press gang, which turn up after the departure of Cartouch's recruiting party, its colonial fractures immediately apparent in the impressing of the Irish sailor, O'Shaughnessy:

> Enter part of a Press Gang – dragging in O'Shaughnessy out of the Barber's Shop half shav'd with a Cloth about his ~~Chin~~ neck.

O'SH: Tut, man, boderation! I tell you, you don't know me atall, atall.
PIPER: Ah, what, my little O'Shaughnessy! Yes, yes, I know you well enough, my tight fellow – perhaps you forget the time you were put in Irons on board the Grampus for stealing a bag of Hollands from old Peter the Purser . . . (to Marlingspike) Now I look at him again, I do remember him on board the Warspite – He receiv'd a dozen at the Gangway for refusing to stand to his Guns of the Chesapeak [*sic*], and gave his Commander some damn'd bad language because he order'd him to reef the Topsail in a Gale of wind in the Atlantic.

O'Shaughnessy's status is as a blackfaced ('boderation! . . . you don't know me atall, atall'), double-colonized subject, literally a colonial Irish sailor but now newly press-ganged despite being the veteran of two identifiable Royal Navy warships, the *Grampus* (a 50-gun fourth-rater) and the *Warspite* (74-gun third-rater). It also seems he is a veteran of the Battle of the Chesapeake, 5 September 1781, a significant naval engagement against the French fleet, the inconclusive outcome of which and heavy British casualties resulted in bottling up Lord Cornwallis' forces at Yorktown, Virginia, during the American campaign.

Amidst these uneasy displays of effeminacy, female valour, press-ganged Irishmen and inconclusive Royal Navy engagements, *Nootka Sound* ended with patriotic songs but little further dialogue, choosing instead to have its cultural faultlines harmonized by a strongly visual ending of 'Scene the last – An Allegorical Frontispiece, thro' which is seen the British Navy lying at Spithead Enter in procession with marines, Sailors, Marine Society boys &c &c.' As referred to above, the Marine Society charity boys would have been the real thing, perhaps with all of them joining in with the 'Finale' song, 'Let's avenge the wrongs of Britain / And support her injur'd Trade', sung with 'Guns . . . suppos'd to be heard firing a Salute at Spithead', and providing containment but hardly any resolution of the problems glimpsed among the Portsmouth military and civilian populations.

Nootka Sound caught a significant pre-war mood of belligerence, a political atmosphere antagonistic towards Spanish opportunism in the North American Pacific and a national military optimism buoyed up by the strategic implications of France's increasingly chaotic revolution. Independent commentators capture the mood of the moment. In Chichester, Sussex, the musician and composer, John Marsh, noted in his diary entry for May 1790: 'About this time began the Rupture with Spain about Nootka Sound, which occasion'd a long Negotiation & great hostile preparation wh^c however at length ended pacifically, to the great disapointment [*sic*] of many Naval Officers who had been at some expence in fitting themselves out for an Expedition against the Spaniards, amongst whom was my Brother Henry, who was appointed 1st Lieutt of ye Arrogant (7th Gun Ship) commanded by his Friend Capt. Harvey of Sandwich, in which he was station'd about 3 Months at Spithead, Torbay & in ye Grand Fleet.'[18] Marsh's testimony is remarkable in accounting the implications of the Nootka Sound incident for his own family and their friends, capturing 'the great disapointment of many Naval Officers' at the peaceable negotiated settlement with Spain that October. Crucially, Marsh's anecdote corroborates the ideological sentiments of the *Nootka Sound* chorus.

Indeed, demonstrating the proximity between these sentiments and their availability in the theatre, Marsh's diary also records his going to see *Nootka Sound* at Covent Garden, watching it with Frederick Reynolds' *The Crusade* (1790), itself a hastily disguised development of an abortive Bastille entertainment abandoned because of London's glut of such shows.[19] Marsh's recollection of the unusually bellicose atmosphere was evidently also explicit in its staging. *Nootka Sound*'s political moment was immediately recognized. The newspaper *Woodfall's Register* wrote that *Nootka Sound* 'is a sacrifice to the popular passion of the times . . . The Dialogue abounds with those national Egoisms which John Bull listens to with rapture on the eve of a war, but which cannot but disgust men of liberality, who have sense enough to know that it would be no ground of national pride, much less of glory to beat an enemy professedly held in previous contempt.'[20] In the event, the dispute was settled by the Anglo-Spanish Convention of 28 October 1790, but not before Covent Garden had fielded a ballet pantomime afterpiece unambiguously titled *The Provocation!*, complete with 'Scenes &c. from the Entertainment of Nootka Sound'. Again, the complexities of the market required that any adaptation or prolongation of its run into the 1790–1 season meant that the *Provocation!* advertising had to declare its borrowings from the earlier work, causing the playhouse to state pre-emptively, 'No Money to Be returned', just in case anyone protested that they had seen some of it before.[21] As the Anglo-Spanish negotiations got under way, the political ramifications of this new drama on the Covent Garden stage came to be recontextualized into a political rather than a military sphere. One correspondent to *The Gazetteer and New Daily Advertiser* wrote, 'I saw a new entertainment called the Provocation, which I shrewdly suspect *to be got up* by the Ministry themselves.'[22] With fourteen performances before 3 November, to the 12,000 people who saw *Nootka Sound* must be added (assuming two-thirds-full houses) a further 28,000 people watching *The Provocation!* Indeed, it was revised and revived several times again as *The Shipwreck; or, French Ingratitude*, and was one of the performances seen by the Turkish ambassador in 1794 (see Chapter 6).

Nootka Sound and *The Provocation!* present fascinating examples of a mutating theatrical genotype emerging from an individual singularity (*Nootka Sound*), positioned within the universal singularity of Covent Garden's place within London's built theatrical system. They are capable of being fully isolated and synthesized. Though different, both plays were perceived along their social networks as relating directly notions of Britain's expanding empire with its global reach and military effectiveness, and how this had been coded as armed trade (literally, the *Britain Prepar'd* of *Nootka*

Sound's subtitle). The populations of the assemblage and their precise date and venue locations can be approximated as the over 40,000 people who saw *Nootka Sound* or *The Provocation!* in London over the spring and autumn of 1790. The *Nootka Sound* audience would have heard how 'The Throne of Britannia's the Ocean . . . / Her huge floating Castles in motion', and it is quite likely *The Provocation!* recycled *Nootka Sound*'s finale 'Allegorical Frontispiece, thro' which is seen the British Navy lying at Spithead'. Although these pieces were performed before the war with France, these sentiments are typical expressions of their time. Examples are plentiful. *The Siege of Curzola* had tapped into a ubiquitous cultural memory of British valour, progressively gendered ('for the honour of England's sovereign the great and glorious Queen Elizabeth who is a woman like yourselves we'll stand by you to the last drop of our blood'), while the finale of Birch's *Mariners* had proclaimed, 'The village steeple tells / Each deed of England's fame & / The golden days of old / Their frequent triumph knew.'[23] Through these reiterations and repetitions, stored at the nodes of the playhouse, ideological messages were stabilized and distributed across the networks of the assemblage through their audience populations.

Nor did *Nootka Sound*'s mutations end there. A significant feature of the eighteenth-century British theatrical assemblage was its geographical extension and ability to encompass multiple population gradients. As well as the national and regional circuits of British playhouses, *Nootka Sound* was also adapted by New Republic Americans. The John Street Theatre, New York, performed *Nootka Sound, or, The Adventures of Captain Douglas* as an afterpiece on 3 June 1794.[24] Of course, in the 1790s New York, ballet pantomimes with their emphasis on musicalized action valuably bridged a gap for the republic's non-English speakers. In this mutation, the focus seems to have been on William Douglas, captain of the *Iphigenia*, with Covent Garden's emphasis on British military preparedness no doubt discarded, particularly as the New York *Nootka Sound* was accompanied by a (presumably pro-republican) version of the William Tell story, *The Patriot: or, Liberty Asserted* ('Act Ist, the Hall and Statue of Liberty'). Although little is known about this version, from a New York perspective *Nootka Sound, or, The Adventures of Captain Douglas* would probably have warned Americans about recent British ambitions in the unclaimed Pacific North-Western territories.[25] Again, *Nootka Sound*'s deterritorialization of meaning and recoding in New Republic America demonstrates not only the connectivity of the links across the network but also the gradients of its populations, with the New York *Nootka Sound* perhaps reaching between 500 and 1,000 people at its single performance.

Nootka Sound demonstrates Covent Garden's ability to represent martial aspects of Britain's global empire, and *The Provocation!* seems to have tracked its high diplomacy. Indeed, connections between the aims of government and the practices of the theatre were already a structural precondition for most contemporary dramas because of the role of the Lord Chamberlain. However, while the interventions of senior politicians directly into theatre writing are evidentially difficult to recover, they may have occurred quite regularly, creating specific ideological inscriptions reinforcing powerful messages delivered through the reiterative capabilities of the assemblage.

One of the first people to receive reports of the Nootka naval seizure was the then British Foreign Minister, Francis Osborne, Duke of Leeds (1751–1799). Four years later, another theatre piece (described as '*a new and appoiate* [*sic*] *entertainment*'), Drury Lane's *The Glorious First of June* (1794), commemorated the victorious mid-Atlantic battle of that date and name (also known as the Third Battle of Ushant). The Duke of Leeds himself penned words for a song comprehensively encapsulating contemporary theatre's ability to reach massive and influential audiences through the performance of concise ideological mantras.[26] From the Drury Lane stage, Stephen Storace's setting of the Duke's words described how:

> O'er the vast surface of the deep
> Britain shall still her Empire keep
> Her heav'n descended Charter long
> The fav'rite theme of Glory's Song
> Shall still proclaim the blest decree,
> That Britons ever shall be free.
> . . . . .
> Hail happy Britain favour'd Isle
> Where Freedom, Arts, and Commerce smile

Although the full text of *The Glorious First of June* in which this song was performed was not printed until modern times, as usual, the theatre published a complete set of the song texts, and Storace also published an engraved musical score for domestic performance, considerably magnifying the piece's circulation beyond Drury Lane.[27] Of course, as with *The Siege of Curzola*, *Nootka Sound* and *The Mariners*, 'The main territorializing process providing the assemblage with a stable identity is *habitual repetition*.'[28]

Leeds' words succinctly encompass 'Empire', Magna Carta, the specifically British nativity of natural rights, and the country's politically and climatically 'favour'd' status, benevolence towards science (in the eighteenth-century mode inclusive of 'the Arts'), and prowess at trade. With the first charity benefit-night performance (in aid of the widows and orphans of the battle's sailors) giving Drury Lane its largest single night's takings during the eighteenth century (£1,526. 11s.), and with six more revivals in 1794 (taking more modest sums of £220–£320 per night), and assuming a full, 3,000-person capacity at the benefit and 2,000 for each revival, the total theatre audience for Leeds' song would have been around 15,000 people.[29]

Leeds and Storace's song achieved a remarkable degree of ideological compression (Magna Carta, natural rights, empire, trade, Britain's multiply 'favour'd' status etc.) of the dominant nationalism and strategic aims of a proto-imperialist government deeply engaged with managing an increasingly tough war against France. By comparison, the ability of other popular art forms to parallel the ideological work of *The Glorious First of June* was much less impressive. With news of the battle not reaching *The Times* until 11 June 1794, Drury Lane needed only three weeks to mount their production, opening on 2 July, but as early as 25 June Astley's Amphitheatre was performing a 'Naval Spectacle' based on the conflict and advertised under a 'Victory! Victory!' banner.[30] Payments entered into the Drury Lane ledger book suggest the representation of the battle was on a grand and almost realistic scale, including the deployment of four ex-sailors or other specialists 'Man^g the Yards', although the licensing copy (which did not require sight of non-textual stage business) simply indicates that the scene aimed to represent a 'Sea Fight'.[31] Pieter Van der Merwe notes that this naval engagement produced an unprecedented number of etched or engraved prints, but the delay in their production and dissemination was significant.[32]

Philippe-Jacques de Loutherbourg's dramatic oil painting, *Lord Howe's Action, or the Glorious First of June* was not exhibited (at 1s. entrance) at Robert Bowyer's Historic Gallery on Pall Mall until 2 March 1795, and its print version not published until January 1799 (NMM Greenwich Hospital Collection). Emulating the cachet of de Loutherbourg's painting but aiming for a wider audience, Robert Barker's panorama of the battle at Cranbourne Street, Leicester Square, did not open until 2 June 1795. Yet Drury Lane's *The Glorious First of June* was staged thirty-one days after the event. Nor did the drama's identifiable relationship with networks of contemporary political influence stop with the contribution made by the Duke of Leeds. Sheridan's principal collaborator on the piece was the playwright James Cobb, author of the same house's *Love in the East* (1788) and already a rising executive employed in the headquarters of the East India Company.[33] Cobb would certainly have been aware that Admiralty orders for Lord Howe's battle fleet in April 1794 specified that his ships were first to escort an East India Company convoy through the Channel while also searching for the French Admiral Vanstabel's strategically important incoming grain convoy heading from Chesapeake Bay and destined to replenish dangerously depleted Parisian food stocks. As it happened, Howe did not engage the French anywhere near the East India Company convoy, but Cobb would have appreciated the potential danger for the company's ships had the two sides fought nearer the French coast.[34]

Given the overwhelming evidence of the immediate political and ideological investment made in *The Glorious First of June* and its foremost place within the array of cultural representations accompanying the battle, it is perhaps surprising that the manuscript licensing copy sent to the Lord Chamberlain's Examiner of Plays presents a view of the British populace as markedly fractured and at enmity with itself.[35] Timothy Jenks has recently alluded to this play's portrayal of the Whig Opposition and its 'unique' role in portraying domestic civilian hardship, but it also forms part of a contrarian canon of dramas about the war.[36] With only one scene located at sea, the main plot of *The Glorious First of June* is set on land and concerns the exploitation of a sailor's family by Lawyer Endless. The village's senior authority figure is a retired and invalided naval officer, Commodore Chace ('is it not twenty years ago since that damn'd Splinter knockt me down when I was in the Dreadnought?'), who has put his lands under Endless' direction.[37] When Chace's tenant, Farmer Russett, falls into arrears because his sailor son has been killed at sea ('the old man [Russett] lost his sheet Anchor in his Son Henry – poor fellow he is gone to the bottom – and the family have ever since had wind and tide against them'), Endless threatens to 'distrain for farmer Russett's rent' while at the same time coveting Russett's daughter. Later, Endless accuses Russett's remaining son, William, of being a naval deserter, forcing Russett's daughter and widowed daughter-in-law to rush to Chace and tell him that William has actually 'gone a Volunteer to serve under a brave Captain, who honours him by his friendship'. Commodore Chace immediately exonerates William, and Endless' scheming is revealed.

What is remarkable about *The Glorious First of June* text is that, hardly a month after an episode of national martial glory, the drama portrays such inherently fractious elements of the British populace. Right at the start of the piece, Russett's wife precisely articulates the contradictory nature of domestic and national needs by wishing the family's remaining son, William, would stay at home: 'Cottager's [Russett's] Wife: Aye and I hope he'll [William] shew his love by staying at home to take care of us all instead of going to Sea again after Glory.' Lawyer Endless, like the 'curs'd land Shark' Chace later accuses him of being, is pictured as a mercantilist

systematically dismantling the social cohesion of this remote Devonshire
village, not least by attributing some of his actions to his pursuit of
Commodore Chace's interests: 'The family is viley managed – I had some
thought marrying the eldest daughter Susan and taking the farm into my
own hands – merely to manage it for your honour.' Chace's role within this
rural community is pivotal. He is not only a sympathetic landlord to
Russett, whose loss of a sailor son was a reminder to the *Glorious First of
June* audiences of the projected recipients of benefit nights, but he also
represents local justice and authority and is acknowledged in these roles by
Russett's daughter and daughter-in-law.

Given the rising tensions within British civil society in 1794, which was
connected with Pitt's campaign against seditious practices, the visibility of
the London Corresponding Society, and its alleged link to violent radicalism, what makes *The Glorious First of June* remarkable is that the play's
denouement is based on this exposure and condemnation of Lawyer
Endless. Indeed, the piece ended with a remarkable representation of the
moral economy of the mob which is worth following in full:

CHACE: Here lads lay hold of this miscreant – I have detected him [in] the worst
        Act of Oppression – in grinding a poor Sailor's family – seize him, and give
        him a good wholesome Ducking.
ENDLESS: Take care Commodore what you do – you are a Justice and must know
        this is against law.
CHACE: I'll not wait to consider whether it is Law or not – I'm sure it is Justice[,]
        Tom [Tom Oakum]. – and you shall see the Sentence carried into execution
TOM: Bless your honour once more for that I say.
ENDLESS: My Sentence! I have had no Trial – I claim a trial of my Peers.
CHACE: They are not to be found – at least I hope so.
ENDLESS: I demand a Copy of my Indictment.
TOM: He shall be ducked your honour.
ENDLESS: I move in arrest of Judgment.
SAILOR: Duck him – Duck him –
ENDLESS: I move for a new Trial.
CHACE: Execute the Sentence.
SAILORS: Huzza! & c.

With the suspension of habeas corpus on 23 May 1794, preceding Howe's
naval victory by only a few weeks, the play's fictional Devonshire dissent is
focused on Lawyer Endless' scheming to accuse William Russett of deser-
tion, a plot which would have stopped him from becoming a naval
'Volunteer'.[38] Strikingly, Endless lists through the principal civil and legal
safeguards that had just been abandoned by the government ('I have had no

Trial – I claim a trial of my Peers . . . I demand a Copy of my Indictment'). Of course, for Sheridan and Cobb, perhaps the 'worst Act of Oppression' that spring of 1794 was not the suspension bill but Endless' lack of patriotism in 'grinding a poor Sailor's family'. It is also possible to read the summary justice meted out by Chace as a condemnation of lawlessness and that the figure of Lawyer Endless obliquely refers to the lawyer Thomas Erskine's involvement with the defence of the London Corresponding Society treason defendant, Thomas Hardy. Hardy had been arrested on 12 May and his wife had died in childbirth that August, allegedly as a result of a mob attacking their home amidst the initial 'Glorious First of June' celebrations, even though their house was properly illuminated to demonstrate their patriotic support.[39]

Theatrical representations of provincial dissent were not uniquely located in the turbulent 1790s. Ten years later, one year before the Battle of Trafalgar, Covent Garden produced *The Ship and the Plough* (1804), a farce technically licensed as *The Mast and the Ploughshare; or, Britain's Best Bulwarks*, explicitly ideologically aimed at promoting understanding between farmers and the military.[40] By this stage of the war, not only had tensions between the military and farmers already been effectively censored from the Covent Garden stage during the 1801 scarcity of foodstuffs crisis, but also the longer-term impact of the war was made visible when another type of *The Glorious First of June*'s Commodore Chace figure appears on stage in the form of an 'Admiral a wounded old Tar, preceded by Servants all dressed like Sailors – Wooden legs – arms hurt &c'. In the farce, the unity of the nation is eventually symbolized by the marriage of the farmer and the admiral's offspring, whereby implicit mutual commitment to the national cause can be renewed: 'let us keep all our Quarrels for our Enemies abroad – and while we are waited at Home We may laugh at those who do threaten – now give me your Hand – here we Stand – the Mast and the Plough joined together and here no one will disapprove the representative[s] of the Bulwarks of Great Britain.' Although a restive rural population were shown contained by *The Ship and the Plough*, the extent to which disloyalty could be represented in the theatre can also be judged by correlating *The Glorious First of June* with another apparently patriotic piece, Covent Garden's *Love and Honor; or, Britannia in Full Glory at Spithead* (1794). Significantly, this 'Musical Interlude', was performed on 3 May 1794, as a celebration of the Admirals Howe and Hood's assembling of the fleet at Spithead prior to their departure down the Channel, escorting the East India Company ships, and thence to engage with the crucial incoming French grain convoy.

In other words, *Love and Honor* presented the fleet precisely before its engagement on 1 June. Again, the complexity of the theatrical assemblage in mounting these multiple representations of Royal Navy actions demonstrates different sequences and parameters within the overall assemblage, a distinctive set of spaces for emergence populated by different components of population, yet still conforming to the description that 'Every assemblage must be treated as a unique historical entity characterized both by a set of emergent properties (making it an individual singularity) as well as by the structure of possibility space defining tendencies and capacities (a structure defined by universal singularities).'[41] The sequence and distinctiveness of the dramas performed, simply around this one incident, are good indicators of the organizational complexity of the assemblage, not least because *Love and Honor* itself was almost certainly a reworking of scenery previously deployed for the Covent Garden 'Interlude', *The Sailor's Festival; or, All Alive at Portsmouth*, featuring 'The Deck of a Man of War', 'The Good Subjects of England', and an 'Irish Song', all apparently seamlessly co-opted into the piece's concluding 'Representation of The Grand Fleet at Anchor in Portsmouth Harbour'.[42] In other words, *The Sailor's Festival* was probably itself an initial theatrical response to newspaper reports in April of the assembly at Spithead of over sixty British men-of-war.[43] From a production perspective, *Love and Honor; or, Britannia in Full Glory at Spithead* would doubtless have incorporated much of the miniaturized naval scenery used earlier in *The Sailor's Festival*, and this would have been again redeployed in *The Glorious First of June* alongside the full-sized, specially constructed, rigging 'Yards' referred to below.[44]

The opening of *Love and Honor*, set in 'A Farm Yard & House with a view of the Sea Men & Women dancing', presented to the Covent Garden audience a truculent and unpatriotic rural populace unwilling to rescue shipwrecked sailors.[45] London newspapers had already reported the difficulties of assembling the fleet at Spithead during a series of storms on the approaches.[46] In *Love and Honor*, Farmer Ploughfield played an authoritarian role but was shown unable to rouse his festive farm labourers into patriotic or even humanitarian effort to assist shipwrecked sailors:

PLOUGHFIELD: For shame! After so dreadful a Storm as we have had this morning how can you think of dancing when numbers, perhaps, of poor shipwreckt sailors stand in need at this very moment of our efforts to save them and their property.

1ST RUSTIC: Why, Master, it is holiday time, you know, when we have right to sing, dance and be merry . . . .

PLOUGHFIELD: ... follow me down to the beach, as I think I spied from our Hill just now, a Ship dashing on the Rocks.

1ST RUSTIC: Now [*sic*; i.e. 'Not'] I, by Jingo, till we have another dance, so play up again, Piper.

PLOUGHFIELD: And I'll strike his pipe into shivers if he attempt to play another at present – so, follow me, I say...

As well as the vehemence of the Rustic's refusal, and a notable surfacing of the discourse of natural rights ('we have right to sing, dance and be merry'), a number of other motifs of popular dissent are present. Later, 'Lieutenant Capstone, Grapple & Press Gang' discuss the etiquette of naval impressment, rejecting runaway apprentices (for fear 'he might disgrace us in a time of action'), yet seizing a 'Pettifogging Attorney', the ubiquitous hate figure of theatre audiences ('I shou'd ... consent for keel-hauling him, in hopes ... a Sea Shark may chance to swim by and devour the Land Shark'). Amidst this incongruent display of cultural tensions, displayed yet contained, the concluding pageant of *Love and Honor; or, Britannia in Full Glory at Spithead* showed 'a beautiful representation of A Grand Naval Review, With a display of the Firing and Manoeuvring of the Spanish and English Fleets at Spithead'.[47] The old Spanish enemy shown in *Nootka Sound; Or, Britain Prepar'd* in 1790 were now the new friends floating off Portsmouth.

The rapidity and specificity with which theatres could respond to changing wartime events is also evidenced three years later by the prologue specially written by one Captain Morris for insertion into Charles Dibdin's Drury Lane musical drama, *Hannah Hewit; or, The Female Crusoe* (1797):[48]

> All their Rafts and their Floats
> And their flat bottom'd boats
> Shall not cram their French Poison down Englishmen's throats[49]

From 1797 there were increasing alarms about a prospective French invasion.[50] Pamphlets such as Commissary General Havilland Le Mesurier's *Thoughts on a French Invasion, with Reference to the Probability of its Success, and the Proper Means of Resisting It* (1798) advocated such strategies as clearing roads to assist the movement of defending soldiers, removing valuable livestock from the path of an invading army, and operating a policy of civilian non-cooperation. As early as February, the Lyceum exhibition hall displayed French drawings of the 'Bomb-Proof Rafts' said to be floating off Brest, while one week before *Hannah Hewit*, Astley's Amphitheatre featured a pantomime, *The Contrast; or, the French*

Rafts and England's Navy.[51] In late March 1798 Covent Garden staged James C. Cross' *The Raft; or, Both Sides of the Water*. A month later *The Times* reported that canals near Brussels contained invasion rafts capable of carrying 1,000 men.[52]

Covent Garden's *The Raft* celebrated the fraternization of the military and civilian populations, but with rather more insight into their uneasy tensions and excesses. Fanny's father sleeps off his drunken loyalist Sunday 'Club' nights by absconding from work the next day in the preindustrial ritual of 'Ah Saint Monday! Saint Monday! It's always the case with him after Club-night.'[53] But as with *The Glorious First of June*'s Lawyer Endless, in *The Raft* the false patriot, Busy, is zealous only in forwarding his own interests: 'Scarce time to attend to courtship now – All in a bustle – Mind employ'd a thousand ways – have fifty scheme[s] to save my Country (*aside*) and twice as many to serve myself.' Endless and Busy's anti-romantic shelving of courtship in pursuit of financial gain is a useful point of correlation with the gendered roles of the women in many of these dramas, who remain largely portrayed as willingly co-opted supporters of the national cause.

In *The Raft*, Fanny's lover is the Irishman, O'Bowling, a familiar if by then far from subtle incorporation of colonial Ireland into the war effort and a reminder of how both gender and nationality were seamlessly co-opted. Given O'Bowling's drafting into British service and the visible complicity of most female characters in these dramas, *The Raft* provides a useful example of how such fugitive pieces functioned when set to their optimum level of fictional gratification. With the London newspapers and theatres replete with invasion scare material, Covent Garden's *The Raft* concluded with a psychologically revealing theatrical set piece of French debacle. During scene 2, set on 'The French Coast – Outside of a Fort or Prison' (from which O'Bowling is freed), 'French Peasants & Artizans are seen coming down the Hills . . . bearing a Model of their Raft design'd for the Invasion of England'. In a quasi-dreamscape, *The Raft* went on to offer a denouement of victory, in which appeared 'A View of the Sea[;] Representation of the Raft, Figures seen in it, very busily employed – Fortifications on One side of the Stage, & Gunboats on the other – Cannon firing – Drums beating, &c.&c. Small English Figures Arm'd seen issuing from the other [side] Cannon fired from the Raft & return'd from the Batteries & Gunboats – at length the Raft takes Fire – Characters enter huzzaing'. Of course, the 'Small English Figures' would have literally been a miniaturized wooden army about 6 inches in height, but the intention of portraying the decisive defeat of the French invasion is clear enough. *The Raft*'s double presentation of a blatantly miniaturized wooden British army (presumably with similarly tiny 'French Peasants & Artizans'), together with the life-size reality of the human actor playing the self-seeking Busy, is a reminder of the audience's requirement both to suspend disbelief and yet recognize the theatrical representation of their current political circumstances. They could ponder Commissary General Le Mesurier's bluntly pragmatic *Thoughts on a French Invasion* (1798) while balancing it by witnessing Endless or Busy's disaffection from the public good.

In such a context of ideological commentary coupled to the organizational complexity of the overall assemblage with its ability rapidly to mutate new productions, it is illuminating to compare the differences between texts as licensed by the Lord Chamberlain and texts as performed. Caught between the licensing text and the production text, the ability of theatrical genotypes to mutate creates a clear distinction between real (or virtual) texts and texts as actualized in performance and their relative positions in the plane of immanence. G.N. Reynolds' Covent Garden *Bantry Bay, or the Loyal Peasants* (1797), about the abortive Wolfe Tone-led French landings in Ireland in late December 1796, provides an example of how a licensing text simultaneously showing the Irish not only safely co-opted but also, more alarmingly, fraternizing with French prisoners, was abandoned in favour of a sharper, more loyalist, production version.[54] With the French fleet reaching the Irish harbour on 26 December 1796, the Bantry Bay landings were rapidly theatricalized. Although Covent Garden's *Bantry Bay* was staged on 18 February 1797, by then the Royalty Theatre, Tower Hamlets, had already produced 'a new Spectacle', *Bantry Bay, or, Irish Loyalty* (later changed to *Irish Loyalty, or, The French Routed*) by early January.[55] If we assume two-thirds-full houses for its twelve performances, Reynolds' *Bantry Bay* accumulated an audience total of 24,000, while the Royalty's Bantry Bay spectacles would also have reached at least a further 4,300 people.[56]

The differences between the licensing manuscript of *Bantry Bay* (as it was then titled) and the performance version as eventually printed (subtitled 'or, the Loyal Peasants') are so numerous as to make it difficult to spot the textual similarities confirming their common origin, despite the licensing copy having been submitted only eight days before its first performance. A possible reason for the change was that, on 20 February 1797, *Bantry Bay* was visited by the King, Queen and five of the six princesses.[57] Indeed, the 'Loyal Peasants' subtitle is unique to the printed edition, with the choice of words appearing purposefully to set parameters on the relationship between the Irish and colonial power as represented on the Covent Garden stage.

Perhaps visibly outmanoeuvred by the apparently straightforwardly loyalist Royalty's versions, it looks as if Covent Garden was unprepared for the drama Reynolds had delivered to them.

Certainly, there are two principal differences which make the performance version far more ideologically loyalist. First, the licensed text attributes the defeat of the invasion to the storms which wrecked the French fleet and, secondly, this version aimed to conclude with an extraordinary festive finale depicting fraternization between Irish peasants and French prisoners. By contrast, the *Bantry Bay, or the Loyal Peasants* performance version noticeably stresses anti-French sentiment, including a reference to the closure or confiscation of the Catholic Irish Colleges in France during 1793 ('Since ever I heard they pulled down the Irish colleges, and murdered the priests, its by much ado I cou'd keep my hand from them'), in itself an extraordinary piece of defensive equivocation about Catholicism within Covent Garden's Protestant orthodoxy. Such qualifications abound in *Bantry Bay, or the Loyal Peasants*. Also seemingly dropped into the text to signal artless ideological purity is M'Huckaback, a vagabond 'north country pedlar', who calls out 'Liberty and Equality! Liberty and Equality!' as his wares, and Louisa, an Irishwoman whose 'father's religious and political prejudices ... would have sent me to America, consigned to a traitor who fled from England for sedition'. In other words, Louisa's implicitly Irish Catholic republican father has arranged his daughter's marriage to an English radical except that her 'English ship ... became the captive of a French man of war, from whom I was retaken by Captain Broadside's frigate', allowing her to be returned to Ireland as a willingly passive colonial subject. But perhaps the most overt example of loyalist placement is O'Laughlin's protest that the French 'mistook the White-boys for Jacobins; and because we sometimes play the fool, they thought we'd play the rogue'.[58] Throughout both versions runs the kind of Irish blackfacing described by Susan B. Egenolf as also pervasive in Maria Edgeworth's contemporary *Castle Rackrent* (1800).[59] In *Bantry Bay, or the Loyal Peasants*, this is typified by how the invasion news spreads among the Irish peasantry in stereotyped dialogue, 'I'll take my Oath of it; for I had it by hearsay from Darby Mulroney's own word of mouth, who had it from Jerry OBrien, and he had it from one of the Crew.' Significantly, despite the extensive textual revision between the licensing manuscript and the printed copies, this piece of banter survived.[60]

Perhaps the most significant revision, however, was the licensing copy's emphasis on the role of the weather in disabling the French invasion.[61] In the printed version the role of the weather is minimized. Scene 2 opens with a 'View of Bantry Bay – the French Fleet endeavouring to work out – a boat's crew driven in, in distress – peasants seize them'. There then occurs a comic encounter of misunderstanding between French and Irish, a mode already preceded by the drama's opening scene which predictably emphasizes colonial rustic idleness, 'Sea coast – An Irish Fair, – a Pig in a string, – a Kerry cow – several tents with Whiskey, &c. – every body idling, and nobody minding any business'. By contrast, the licensing copy emphasized the Irish readiness to fight. Its text is worth following, not only to appreciate the vehemence of their resistance to invasion but also to follow its displaced notions of Irish nationality:

> Donnel (impatient & interrupting . . .): Hold! How say you, boy? The enemy landed! (agitated) a French Fleet invade old Ireland (panting) Tell me, how far is it off? . . . Bring me my Sword! Get me my pistols – Saddle my old Team-horse – Invade my native Land! Where are my boots? My staff? My Musket? The French landed! If I had no other Arms to oppose to them, I would meet them with this Spade. . . Why, boys, wou'd you have me stand by, & see the foe carry death & revenge into the heart of Ireland? No, if they will pass, it shall be over my old body – If I cannot fight for my Country, I can die for it.

All this text disappeared in the printed copy but, in particular, what also vanished in the performance version was the role of an explicitly providential storm:

PATRICK: Hold a moment . . . till I relate to you the real situation of these Prisoners. They are not the Captives of war, but of misfortune. The Storm of last night, like that which protected England from a Spanish Armada, has totally dispersed their fleet, and we found these few defenceless men, this morning, wreck'd on our Coast.

PHELIM: Aye, aye, the Gentlemen are driven on shore by stress of weather, & as they are fallen into our hands, let no man lay this finger upon them.

DONNEL: Wreck'd! wreck'd! Their fleet dispersd! What! Have the Elements fought for us! (looks at the prisoners with compassion, approaches & shakes one of them by the hand) Gracious Providence! – Poor fellows – wreck'd! We pity distress, even in an Enemy.

While much of this falls into a familiar set of contemporary tropes about British providentiality and innate magnanimity in victory – heroic qualities here noticeably stretched to include its colony – nevertheless, *Bantry Bay*'s emphasis on the totality of the devastating shipwrecks is striking, 'The whole French Fleet. The Top sail of all of them went to the bottom – she had 100000 men onboard, & every mother's soul of them perish'd.' When put together with an efficient Irish defence organization ('Their Ships lie off the Bay, & our brave fellow Countrymen who undertake to oppose their landing, are now forming about half a mile hence'), the licensed version of *Bantry Bay* presents colonial Irish autonomy as both self-reliant and organizationally capable, although, crucially, the presence in the text of indelible ridicule simultaneously marks Ireland as a subjugated nation.

If the strains inherent in posing Ireland as both ruggedly independent and yet seamlessly co-opted into Britain's imperial aims are evident in these earlier parts of the play, the licensing text's festival of fraternization between Irish peasantry and French prisoners is even more remarkable. Whereas the printed *Bantry Bay, or the Loyal Peasants* ended with a demonstration of Irish Volunteers drilling on the lawns of the local magistrate (satirized as hopelessly late to repel the invasion: 'The Yeoman Cavalry walking down the hill – Aye, they're come a day after the fair –'), the manuscript version concluded with a dumbshow collaboration: 'Volunteers ranged round the Hall, wine offer'd to the Prisoners, who refuse it – A Harp or Violin offer'd to one of them, who takes it, begins to play, and Girls advancing, offer to dance with them, they accept the invitation & all dance a grand Ballet composed of national & characteristick dances'. This fraternization of Irishwomen with French sailors makes visually explicit the Franco-Irish social bonds actually articulated in Wolf Tone's invasion attempt. Equally striking is that, although this fraternizing festival was described in the licensing text, their intended performance in music and dance, without linguistic texts, meant that its censoring was beyond the scope of the Lord Chamberlain's powers.

The Covent Garden production clearly skirted illegality on account of its deviation from the licensed copy, although the text performed in the theatre appears in most cases to have been a reduction and restructuring of the texts as licensed rather than an expansion of them (that is, most of the text had been licensed but not in that specific order). It would have required a more forensic textual investigation than John Larpent, as Examiner, could feasibly have mounted; in any case, he could have done nothing to interdict the finale because its dumbshow status (devoid of text) was beyond his control. One may speculate that the Covent Garden management themselves thought the licensed version too disloyal for representation and self-censored it, even if the finale's song, 'And the Flag of old England shall ever prevail', was itself perhaps unintentionally grotesque given the Irish context of the drama. For whatever reasons, *Bantry Bay*'s transformation into *Bantry Bay, or the Loyal Peasants* included a major theatrical structural reversal of its dramatic form, quite apart from the many amendments made to its text. Whereas *Bantry Bay* had concluded with a scene of Irish conviviality and fraternization with the French enemy, *Bantry Bay, or the Loyal Peasants* had been rewritten to begin with its carnivalesque scene of 'An Irish Fair & every body idling, and nobody minding any business'. In other words, the Irish were rendered metaphorically blackface and the possibility of alliance with the French downgraded.

London's two Bantry Bay spectacles of 1797, and the nearly 30,000 people who saw them, demonstrate the materiality of the theatrical assemblage, the physicality of networks crossing between Covent Garden and Tower Hamlets, and the probable contingent factors of a Royal Command performance which precipitately, in less than eight days, mutated *Bantry Bay* into *Bantry Bay, or the Loyal Peasants*. The theoretical description modelling this contingency is that 'Once a larger scale assemblage is in place it immediately starts acting as a source of limitations and resources for its components.'[62] In a further demonstration of the deterritorialization of these sources of limitations, because the office of the Lord Chamberlain was displaced from the person of the incumbent, it was perfectly permissible to rewrite *Bantry Bay* as *Bantry Bay, or the Loyal Peasants* because it principally involved the rearrangement, rather than the reinvention, of its licensed texts. Of course, the real materiality of the assemblage is expressed by its physical extension. In the case of the blackfacing of colonial Irish 'Loyal Peasants', the play texts and performances in which they occurred were historically continuous with other plays performed in the British theatrical assemblage, with the theatres acting as recurrent and persistent nodes of storage for such cultural practices, materializing their visibility, and distributing and redistributing racialized and other messages to audiences.

While the principal density of the populations within the theatrical assemblage can be specified by analysing the conjunction of performers and audience at the performance locations, this can be broken down further by examining the frequency and diversity of the performance texts on offer. Examining early 1797, not even a pivotal year in Britain's war effort, provides many more examples of how the playhouses provided stable environments for the repetition and reiteration of national messages. Real blackface performance, together with another cohort of co-opted Irish characters, was present in *The Surrender of Trinidad; or, Safe Moor'd at Last* (1797), a 'new musical dramatic spectacle', celebrating the capture of Trinidad in late February 1797 and showing 'the Conflagration of the Spanish Fleet in the Gulf of Pavia, the Island's Capitulation, and the Departure of its Garrison, Prisoners of War'.[63] By contrast with *Bantry Bay*, *The Surrender of Trinidad* ran for only one night for the benefit of Margaret Martyr (1761/2–1807), who played Susan and sang a new 'Negro

Boy's Song'. By the time news of Trinidad's fall reached London at the end
of March, and Covent Garden began to devise their play for production for
the end of their winter season in early May, the country's domestic military
and political situation had radically changed because of the Nore and
Spithead mutinies on board the ships of the Grand Fleet in mid April.[64]
The principal strategic reason for British naval action in the Caribbean
throughout the late eighteenth century was to reduce French or, on occasion, Spanish, military power in the region. Trinidad, then under Spanish
control, had attracted French republican sympathizers and become a base
for marauding French privateers. Its proximity to the South American
mainland meant it could operate as a base controlling coastal waters and
strangling Spanish trade.[65] From the point of view of the British military
authorities, the Grand Fleet mutinies in home waters and the Bantry Bay
landings on the uncertain Irish colony potentially weakened the Royal
Navy's ability to confront the threat from France. Not surprisingly given
these contexts of spring 1797, *The Surrender of Trinidad* strove to indicate
the presence of Irish loyalty to the British cause (a newly arrived Irish
regiment was actually present on Trinidad but was considered too ill-
trained to serve in combat and limited to garrison duties).[66]

Mark Lonsdale's Sadler's Wells 'entertainment', *Naval Triumph; or the
Wars of Old England . . . founded on the late victory obtained by Earl Howe
over the French fleet on the Glorious First of June* (1794), had presented a kind
of double-blackfacing. In *Naval Triumph*, pro-British Irish patriots recently
returned 'From leathering and beating the Negers, an please ye, / Hurroo!
here's myself little Paddy come back –' at the surrender of Port Au Prince in
June 1794, were lubricated by 'West India Whisky'.[67] Three years later, *The
Surrender of Trinidad*'s opening eschewed racial antagonisms, where Irish
oppress other 'Negers', by creating a theatrical idyll where both types of
colonized subjects align with the British cause. The piece's opening is
located on a British naval vessel, on which takes place the following
exchange:

> Scene. The Forecastle of a Man of War. . .

> CAPTAIN CLEWLINE: Come, Lads, success to our expedition.
> JACK RATTLING: And to every expedition Old England's honour is concern'd in.
> LIEUTENANT O'LIFFEY: And little Ireland's into the bargain; by my soul but let
>   them both pull handsomely together, and the world combin'd won't over-
>   match them – But come I will take t'other tug at the Whisky Bottle.[68]

Indeed, the metaphorical Irish blackfacing of O'Liffey's 'tug at the
Whisky Bottle' was succeeded by the actual blackface role of Cymbal, a

Trinidadian black man who dedicates himself to helping the British heroine, Susan (played by Margaret Martyr), who has been captured and incarcerated by the Spanish:

CYMBAL: Stay here Missee – I shall do something to please – don't be sad – poor Black Boy bring comfort bye and bye – me love you – me love your Countree. Exit.
SUSAN: Love my Country! Then your Heart beats in unison with mine, that my dear William alone share my affections – I'd fight for one, and die for t'other.

Imprisonment not only brings about this fantasy of black patriotism ('me love your Countree') but unites it with female co-option in a role memorably figured as an interracial union of quasi-sexual and imperial solidarity ('your Heart beats in unison with mine').[69]

It would not be difficult to chart any number of fantasies about race, gender and empire figured into *The Surrender of Trinidad*'s production for Margaret Martyr at Covent Garden in the mutinous and invasion-tormented year of 1797 (for example, 'Conflagration takes place on Board the Spanish Fleet – Negro Soldiers are lead [*sic*] on who throw down their arms when Order'd to attack the English'). What is striking is the relatively naive and almost unmediated way in which such fantasies were represented, although, of course, the rigour of the Lord Chamberlain's power of censorship did much to ensure that London theatre was never completely free to initiate or promote vigorous or challenging political perspectives. But if *The Surrender of Trinidad* performed the public anxieties of a beleaguered nation beset by a long war, a fractious colony and the imminent threat of invasion, the harder rationality of the British imperial destiny could be much more explicitly stated in other plays. The Drury Lane 'interlude', *The Conquest of St. Eustacia* (1781), recalls a now fairly obscure moment when a British naval squadron under Admiral Rodney captured the Dutch West Indies island of St Eustatius in February 1781 following the severing of relations between Britain and the Netherlands. With British, Dutch, American and Jewish merchants using the island as an entrepôt to trade food and arms to the American rebels, St Eustatius was an important island, by then indulging in a well-established clandestine pattern of commerce dating back to the 1670s.[70] In the event, the capture proved to be of even greater strategic significance in a negative sense, because Rodney's preoccupation with plundering the island's assets, regardless of the nationality of their owners, made him fail to engage with the fleet of the French vice-admiral, Comte de Grasse – who subsequently recaptured St Eustatius in November 1782.

Not least, underlying all of these immediate political conditions govern-
ing the seizure of St Eustatius lay its role as a strategic island enabling the
traffic of the Atlantic slave trade. Although it was one of the lesser Caribbean
islands in terms of slave plantations, by the end of the seventeenth century
St Eustatius had become an important centre for the transit of slaves
destined for South America and, by the American War of Independence,
also an important point of transit for goods and general produce destined
for the southern British colonies of North America (so much so that it was
known as the 'golden rock').[71] Rodney's seizure in 1781 of what he deemed
'prizes' won from the enemy became a lasting source of litigation for
compensation pursued by the original owners, a situation made more
complicated by the embarrassing recapture of the island a year later.[72]
That Drury Lane's *Conquest of St. Eustacia* 'interlude', attributed to
Sheridan, would represent very few of these issues is not surprising, and it
was only performed for one evening for the actor 'Mr. Vernon's' benefit
night.[73] Indeed, the interlude existed at a delicate moment of British
imperial fortune situated between success in capturing St Eustatius – and
the possibility of Rodney going on to deliver a decisive blow to the French
West Indies fleet – and the then apparently successful resilience of Lord
Cornwallis' troops in defeating the American rebels on the mainland,
headed by General Gates, at Camden, South Carolina, in August 1780.
Even with St Eustatius captured in February 1781, however, events in
America moved rapidly, and Cornwallis' defeat at Yorktown in October
1781 signalled the end of British hopes, and, of course, the island itself was
soon captured by France.

Startlingly absent from *The Conquest of St. Eustacia* was the entire
context of the West Indian slave trade. Instead, the aspect of the incident
repeatedly emphasized was Dutch mercantilism, as emphasized by the
colony's attempts to 'shupply [*sic*] all parties at present' with the goods
and provisions which eventually provoked Rodney's invasion. The stage
'Dutch' accents of the protagonists served to emphasize their difference
from British West Indian colonists. However, the drama began with
an extraordinary caricature of national stereotypes, opening onto 'A
Rural View in the Island of St. Eustacia – skirt[?] of the Sea at a
Distance. Two Dutch Merchants sitting at a Table, smoking and two
or three Children sitting on the Ground with Pipes'. Later, 'The Children
rise & walk off very slowly smoking'.[74] The purpose of *The Conquest of
St. Eustacia* was to make clear both the Dutch lack of scruple about
choosing their trading partners and their heavy involvement with Britain's
American enemies:

VAN BRUGEN: I tell you Neighbour Spragen I'll send no more of my Goods to Jamaica – my beefs shall all to go America – the last Cargo of Tobacco from Virginia paid well.

VAN SPRAGEN: The people in America since the great vind [*sic*] Mynheer, Van Brugen are all in a great distress – it would be Charity to trade with them.

VB: Charity! Why the Man's Mad, vat has Charity to do with trade? Get Money neighbour Spragen. If the people of Jamaica were able to pay for my Goods they should have them – or Mynheer Devil if he would pay a better price than another – that's the Maxshim of Amsterdam.

Although *The Conquest of St. Eustacia* had only a single performance as a benefit late in the season, the interlude's topical location is quite specific. The 'great vind' referred to by Van Spragen marked the beginning of a notable decade of severe hurricanes hitting the Caribbean and south-east American states from 1780 onwards.[75] The 'Great Hurricane of 1780' (really a series of hurricanes) was of legendary ferocity, directly impacting on the American War of Independence by sinking an important, gunpowder-laden American cargo vessel in the Mississippi delta and foundering fifteen British warships from Rhode Island down to Daytona Beach, including the 74-gun *Thunder*.[76] *The Conquest of St. Eustacia*'s emphasis on Dutch opportunism ('Isn't it damn'd lucky we have no War with those English dogs') empha-sized the island's economic and strategic role for the retention of Britain's American colonies. Van Brugen's rejection of trade with British-held Jamaica is revealed to be a move specifically aimed at 'sending some of my pork to Myner Vashington It would be acceptable, I am told at this time'. If Van Brugen shows no scruples in supplying General Washington, he was much more cautious about accepting American credit: 'Van Brugen: ... Neighbour Spragen take care not to take any of their paper for your pork – Van Sprugen: I'll see them damn'd first Neighbour Brugen – no, no, I see how things are going with them – its very possible if I were to take their Notes I might hear of all my Shecurities being hanged before the day of payment.'

This extensive detailing of the economic and strategic background of the St Eustatius invasion – although devoid of any reference to the region's absolute dependence on slaving – is perhaps surprising in an interlude performed for only one night and which was based on events quickly overtaken by subsequent military developments. However, *The Conquest of St. Eustacia* has an important literary legacy because it is exactly these kinds of mercantilist and morally pragmatic ideologies which were more memorably criticized six years later in George Colman the Younger's enduring Haymarket indictment of the slave trade, *Inkle and Yarico*

(1787): 'I was thinking too, if so many natives cou'd be caught, how much they might fetch at the West India markets.'[77] *The Conquest of St. Eustacia* also performed another ideological work in that its island setting served to define the extent and nature of Britain's enemies and the status of its wavering allies. Upon first sighting the invasion fleet ('damn'd Rodney with an hundred thousands [*sic*] Ships'), there enters 'in a violent hurry a great many of the Inhabitants' including 'Don Varo a Spaniard – Mons Que, a French Merchant dress'd in the extreme of Parisian taste – and Oliver Cant a Bostonian Merchant station'd at St. Eustacia in the service of Congress'. One of the functions of such theatricals was swiftly to dramatize, perhaps using stereotypical conventions of costuming, the nationality of these characters and the array of political or patriotic attitudes considered appropriate for dealing with them.[78] As Van Spragen grimly put it about the fate of St Eustatius' inhabitants, 'de English only vant the French mans property Mynheer Varo's goods, and to hang Mynheer Cant – that's all.' This type of differentiation between occasional allies and sworn enemies can be taken as highly indicative of popular attitudes in early 1780s Britain.

The figure of Cant, the Bostonian merchant based in St Eustatius and apparently negotiating the importation of Caribbean commodities into America on behalf of Congress, is particularly interesting since his appearance is transfixed by that precise historical moment immediately preceding Cornwallis' defeat at Yorktown. With extraordinary clarity, and in carefully elaborated sets of dialogue, Cant illustrates the contemporary presence of a pervasive, naive British optimism about the possibility of finding lasting reconciliation with the breakaway American colonies. When the island is captured by marines (triumphantly announced by the pit band playing George Frideric Handel's 'See the Conquering Hero comes' from his 1747 oratorio, *Judas Maccabaeus*), there is a predictable display of British magnanimity, 'Marine Officer: Let us summon the Governor to surrender – take care my brave Fellows if sad necessity obliges us to storm, not to shed the blood of innocence – Strike home & do your Country honor, but spare the Aged, the Women, and the Infant – Through me you hear the Gallant Rodney speak (They all Huzza)'. This combination of a critique of Dutch mercantilism and the rendering of St Eustatius as an island overwhelmingly complicit with the enemies of Britain is accompanied by important projections of Cant as a penitent American rebel abandoned by the island's governor.

The drama mounts an extraordinary display of Cant's return to filial patriotic loyalty:

SECOND [BRITISH] OFFICER: ... What art thou?

CANT: A Villain! – one who has betrayed the best of Masters, and leagued with Wretches in accursed Rebellion – Oh Sir, I was once a Briton! Happy to call that glorious spot my home – but now the Traitor brands my name for ever, and blasts the hope of Mercy & forgiveness.

A histrionic refusal of the sympathy shown by the foppish Frenchman, Monsieur Que, accompanies this belated recognition of Cant's nativity and the 'perfidy' of Britain's eternal enemy:

CANT: Oh! thou base ungrateful Man – you who promis'd me protection, to give me up at such a Moment to the vengeance of an enrag'd Master. By Heavens I'll throw myself at the feet of my brave Countrymen – implore forgiveness, and be again restored to liberty and peace. Oh England – England! (The Frenchman offers to console him) begone thou son of perfidy & Fraud 'tis you that have undone us –

As well as being an extraordinary theatricalized projection enacting and embodying what one assumes to be Britain's desire for correction and reconciliation, the American rebel's penitence dramatizes the benefits of fidelity to the mother country and the promise of a profound and emotional reunion:

SECOND OFFICER: By Heaven my panting bosom labours to embrace him (Embraces) Thy Errors thus renounced this moment are forgiven – Oh my fancy paints the glorious day when Britain shall revive the duty of her Sons, and foul Rebellion sink to rise no more – United then we'll brave the World in Arms, and rule Britannia be echoed to the Pole – Give me thy hand – be Loyal and be happy.

If *The Conquest of St. Eustacia, The Surrender of Trinidad* and *The Glorious First of June* were productions reflecting the accomplishment of important tactical or strategic objectives, dramas such as *Bantry Bay, or the Loyal Peasants* and *Nootka Sound; Or, Britain Prepar'd* were much more concerned with the contingent outcomes of conflict. Although obscure and forgotten now, they all characterize the intricacies of the ideological workings of the assemblage. Even as single-night benefits, assuming three-quarters-full houses on these special occasions, *The Conquest of St. Eustacia* and *The Surrender of Trinidad* on their own would have reached around 4,500 people. There is something remorseless about the size and scale of the assemblage, with individual dramas readily covering wartime events now considered exceedingly obscure. Indeed, the complexity of the assemblage is expressed by the diversity of the dramas that were performed, indicating multiple organizational structures and reliable audience populations.

One such incident concerned the naval officer, Sir William Sidney Smith (1764–1840), whose maverick career included elopement, imprisonment in France on suspicion of espionage, and a spell in King's Bench prison for debt – quickly followed by promotion to Vice-Admiral (*ODNB*). In 1796 Smith commanded the 38-gun frigate *Diamond*, with orders to patrol aggressively the river estuaries of northern France as one of a pair of Falmouth-based naval squadrons operating independently from the Channel Fleet in a campaign of attrition against French coastal shipping, while protecting – and even recapturing – English vessels. In April 1796 Smith was captured while boarding a French lugger in the mouth of the River Seine, but not before his involvement in a series of spectacular actions, including a successful attack on the fortress at Erquy, Britanny, on 17 March while pursuing a French corvette.[79] The incident at Erquy, by 15 April, had been swiftly commemorated in a Covent Garden 'Prelude' or 'Operatic Interlude', *Point at Herqui; or, British Bravery Triumphant* (1796), 'Founded on the Recent and Glorious Atchievement [*sic*], at the above French Fort, of Sir Sydney Smith . . . Captain of the Diamond'.[80] With three performances, and assuming two-thirds-full houses, *Point at Herqui* was probably seen by around 6,000 people.[81]

The entire episode was little more than a skirmish with no strategic or long-term implications, but, at the very least, it showed to London audiences that British civilian shipping – as well as the Royal Navy – were at risk if straying too close to France. In *Point at Herqui*, much was made of French attacks on unarmed British vessels ('French Commandant: Ah. Ha! Bon fortune ce tems ci! Grand luck dis Time! We have take de Merchant de Angloise make de Prisonier dey have no Gun, no Ammunition, so ve conquer ma foi!') with a captured British fisherman, Napkin, retorting, 'Yes, you nabb'd me sure enough – an Armed Brig 'gainst a Fishing smack. – Damme! A Scotch Quart to a Cruet.'[82] *Point at Herqui* was also extremely specific as to its shipboard 'Scene suppos'd to be in the Cabin of the Diamond Captain. Lieutenant O'Liffey. Mat Midships &c Discover'd', with the customary inclusion of a prominent Irish officer. The drama also made much of the Royal Navy's tactical opportunism, Smith's decisiveness as a leader and the speedy surrender of the French:

SAILOR: Your Honour we larn [*sic*] some Corvettes, Briggs, Luggers and Sloops
    have been chased into Herqui & –
CAPTAIN SMITH: Bravo! Sound the Channel, and we'll attack them instantly. . .
    Skirmishes with French & English &c. . . . .Drums Beating. Fifes Playing. Guns
    firing &c. &c. A View of the Burning [of] the Corvettes, & Striking the
    French Flag on the Fort after which Enter All the Characters – Frenchmen
    Pris'ners. &c. &c.

Smith's order to 'Sound the Channel' gave some impression of the Royal Navy's determined harassment of French shipping that day, operating in the intricate and shallow inshore waters around Erquy. Not least, pre-Nelson, it provided a signal opportunity to manufacture a British naval hero.

Point at Herqui fulfilled the requirement of providing exhilarating coverage of Smith's undoubted heroism, he having, the previous year, slipped into Brest harbour in the *Diamond* before hailing an enemy vessel in impeccable French and asking for news of inbound grain ships.[83] If such naval engagements provided obvious propaganda potential, it is also beyond doubt that the Anglo-French war pitted two more or less equal imperial forces against each other over a long period of time with unpredictable outcomes. Promoting a visible set of naval heroes brought together both the visual and dramatic arts, as best exemplified by the suggestion of Nelson's prize agent, Alexander Davison, of a commemorative national naval pillar to stand on Greenwich Hill. The sculptor John Flaxman's influential counter-proposal of a monumental obelisk of Britannia illustrates the diversity of prevailing doubts and opinions about cults of national heroes, but, once again, the issue was rapidly represented on stage in Thomas John Dibdin's Covent Garden production *The Naval Pillar: A Musical Entertainment* (1799).[84] Not only did *The Naval Pillar* include a song about Sir Sidney Smith ('You all know, Sir Sydney, a man of such kidney'), but also Dibdin very carefully navigated the contemporary politics surrounding the monument project by emphasizing that it also included some measure of participation by sailors: '[T]here's a sort of court martial club, or committee, I think they call it, at the Rodney's Head, sitting in judgment upon the tars. They talk of putting up some monument in our praise – and I think it but right that we should go and see all fair and above board.'[85] In the event, Dibdin fudged the issue of what shape the monument should take by including both options: '[A] Pillar is discovered, inscribed to the memory of our naval Heroes ... At the conclusion of the Ballet, the Pillar changes to BRITANNIA on a superb throne, &c. the Apotheosis of Lord Howe appears above ... with medallions of other Admirals at the sides.'[86]

However, as well as the military successes (lesser and greater) of figures such as Howe, Smith and Nelson, the theatres also took care to illustrate glorious failures. This ability, in a time of war, to illustrate failure is yet another indicator of the organizational complexity and density of the theatrical assemblage, illustrating heterogeneity within the populations of the assemblage. Covent Garden's 'Musical Interlude', *The Death of Captain Faulkner* [sic]; *or, British Heroism* (1795), was concerned with Captain

Robert Faulknor's (1763–1795) death in an engagement off Guadeloupe, a principal military objective for British forces, as it was an island taken by the French and subsequently the subject of an arduous series of campaigns to recapture it. Timothy Jenks has recently argued that Faulknor's death established a naval counter-elite heroic, with the valiant death of an officer from the lower ranks standing in contrast to the court-martial conviction of Captain Molloy, a member of Lord Howe's fleet who had failed to engage the enemy in some of the outlier manoeuvres of the battle of The Glorious First of June.[87] Faulknor's ship was part of a West Indies-stationed expeditionary squadron under Lieutenant-General Sir Charles Grey and Vice-Admiral Sir John Jervis. Remarkably, Faulknor had recently been court-martialled (and acquitted) for killing a British quartermaster by running him through with a sword during a fit of temper during the attack on Guadeloupe in April 1794.[88] After his acquittal, in January 1795 Faulknor's frigate the *Blanche*, stationed off Pointe à Pitre, Guadeloupe, engaged with a French frigate, the *Pique*. During heavy fighting at close quarters the *Pique* eventually rammed or collided its bows across the middle of the *Blanche* with the result that its guns were unable to bear on the British ship. Captain Faulknor and other members of the crew contrived to lash the French ship's bowsprit to the remains of the *Blanche*'s toppled main mast, thereby preventing the *Pique* from manoeuvring. It was a daring and decisive action (carried out at 1 am), during which Faulknor was wounded but continued fighting before being killed an hour later. With both ships still locked together, the *Blanche* resorted to blowing out part of its own sides so as to bring two of its heaviest guns to bear on the French vessel, forcing its eventual surrender.[89]

On its first night in May 1795, *The Death of Captain Faulkner; or, British Heroism* was performed as part of a benefit night for Margaret Martyr, 'By Special Desire of His Excellency the Turkish Ambassador'.[90] Although the London theatre visits of the Ottoman ambassador will be discussed more extensively in Chapter 6, his presence is a reminder of the immediate political resonances implied by one powerful imperial nation witnessing a theatrical representation of recent martial valour by another. Although no indication of the house charge is given, Margaret Martyr's total box-office receipts of £396. 11s. 0d. suggest a full house of nearly 3,000 people.[91] *The Death of Captain Faulkner* assembled a shipful of stereotypes: the Englishman, Lieutenant Oakley; the ordinary seaman, Dicky Pounce; and the Irishman, Lieutenant O'Connor, the last familiarly signified by his propensity for alcohol and a noticeable willingness to fight:

OAKLEY: Come, O'Connor, the God of War never yet knew thee a Flincher – and why should Bacchus.
O'CONNOR: By my faith, Brother Lieutenant, Felix O'Connor will never flinch his Bottle unless 'tis empty (filling his Glass) – and as for fighting –
FAULKNOR: The less said the better! . . .

Faulknor's abrupt speech patterns, disregard for verbosity and sudden physical movements were theatrical performatives indicating the subject's heroic, impulsive temperament:

OAKLY [*sic*]: Damn speechifying! Our brave Captain. You know detests it as much as engaging at a Distance. . .
FAULKNOR: (Rising) No – (with Energy) In the Cause of our King and Country, no foe can intimidate no Danger dismay us . . .

It was by such means, and in the unlikely generic context of a 'Musical Interlude', that *The Death of Captain Faulkner* efficiently sketched out the principal personal, national and class characteristics of the British frigate's crew members.

Despite its generic limitations, *The Death of Captain Faulkner* was able to establish the role of Pounce as an interracial settler, complete with a subjugated black female (played blackface, of course):

POUNCE: Dicky Pounce, a Gentleman of the Counting House just out of my apprenticeship – A Cockney born – within the sound of Bow-Bell – and come to the vest [*sic*] Indies to pay my uncle Sugar cane a wisit [*sic*] – and now, my little black Peppercorn, I'll make thee a present (takes out a Necklace of Beads and ties it about her neck) – there now you shall be Queen of Morocco.
MORA: Ah, Massa – if ou make me Queen – vil ou be my Slave?

Pounce's Cockney transposed consonants, materialist references, plantationing uncle and unconstrained sexual desire quickly establish his mercantile social status ('Just landed from London, my pretty bit of Ebony – after a long Voyage (clasping her) will you have me for a Lover'), but this entire scene is also quite complexly dramatically established. It takes place on 'Another part of the Island' where there are 'Negroes – Men and women – discovered dancing . . . Pounce: Hah – my Merry set of Lamblacks [*sic*] – we'll shake a Leg among you. – (Pounce and Sailors run & join the Groupe [*sic*] of Negroes – dance a [*sic*] little Negro Girls and then lead them forward)'. Its ostensible purpose is not only to legitimize interracial partnerships between white men and black women but also, by localizing London's centrality, to establish Britain as the premier seat of natural rights:

POUNCE: Eh! – (aside) By the Monument this small wench is worth falling in
    Love with I must let her know something of my qualifications – ... ven I
    return to London, I'll carry thee there –
MORA: But Massa, where is London, shall I have my liberty in London.
POUNCE: My Girl, London is in England, and England is the Country where true
    liberty flourishes what sort of liberty woulds't then like Mora?
MORA: Liberty to dance ven [sic] I pleace – sing ven I please – eat ven [sic] I please –
    and go to nappy ven I please
POUNCE: Dance – Sing eat and sleep by St. Pauls the Girls Catalogue is a very
    excellent one – ....
MORA: But Massa, vite Man some times have black heart
POUNCE: Why dost think so
MORA: Because vite Man, took me from my own Country.

Additionally, this scene also performs the function of establishing a peace-
ful, convivial and interracial haven on the island of Guadeloupe entirely
separate from the ensuing naval conflict in which Faulknor dies.

Faulknor's last battle was represented on stage by 'The firing of Guns
heard – English and French Frigates come in view in the Act of Engaging –
Engagement continues 'till the French Flag is seen to strike'. Eschewing total
reliance on spectacle (of course, the 'English and French Frigates' would have
been represented by miniaturized wooden models), the Planter relates how:

> The Engagement now became furious on both sides – our main and Misen
> [sic] masts soon went over board – She attempted to board us – we repulsed
> her – She then droped [sic] a Stern – but we instantly got out a hawser, and
> again made her fast to our Capstern – it was at this critical moment when our
> brave Captain, in the very act of strenuously assisting with his own hands to
> lash firmly her Bowsprit to us, that the Glorious hero fell! – permit me, Sir, to
> pause a moment, – (wipes his eyes the other Lieutenants & Sailors looking
> downcast) –

The reportage is certainly faithful to the events, even including the detail of
how 'we blew off part of our transom Beam to get larger Guns out astern',
and crucially includes a moment of British martial sensibility ('wipes his
eyes ... other ... Sailors looking downcast'). Faulknor's death is ritualized
by the funeral and then transformed into an emblem of national mourning
validated by equal measures of valour and sensibility: 'Oakly: The Minutes
Guns are firing for the Interrment [sic] of our ever to be deplored [sic]
Commander – let us join procession to pay him the last honors &
Procession of Interment with suitable Dirge.'

It is quite likely that *The Death of Captain Faulkner*, with its exotic West
Indian setting and dancing, blackface negroes, redeployed scenery from

Covent Garden's Parisian-derived serious pantomime, *The Death Of Captain Cook; A Grand Serious-Pantomimic-Ballet* (1789), whose stage business also included an elaborate funeral ('Funeral march heard – The marines enter with arms reversed, preceded by two drums, covered with black crape').[92]

This chapter has shown the workings of the theatrical assemblage when themed around the issues of the wars and conflicts which shaped the lives of so many in the audience. The density of the assemblage, its population components and their distribution across various materialized networks in 1780s and 1790s London should not be in dispute. What is noticeable about *The Death of Captain Faulkner, The Point at Herqui, Nootka Sound* and *The Conquest of St. Eustacia* is that they were portrayals of military events whose patriotic significance was partially negated by some degree of imperial failure (the seizure of British-owned ships at Nootka, the personal death of Robert Faulknor, the recapture of St Eustatius) or negated by virtue of their being little more than heroic skirmishes (*The Point at Herqui, The Death of Captain Faulkner*). Only the event commemorated by *The Glorious First of June* could be considered a strategic victory. Nearly all of these pieces, including *Love and Honor; or, Britannia in Full Glory at Spithead* and the licensing version of *Bantry Bay*, portray specific diminutions of overt nationalist or imperialist ideologies (the truculent rustics of *Love and Honor*, the fraternizing civilians in *Bantry Bay*). Throughout them all, even in *The Glorious First of June*, the presence of social dissent and domestic fracture quickly arises within the dramas as a normal aspect of public life ready to be seamlessly included into theatrical commentary on Britain's imperial conflicts and the progress of war with France. Whatever their titles may appear to have promised, the supposedly patriotic interludes and preludes devised for the London stage in the last quarter of the eighteenth century clearly fell short of wholehearted complicity with Britain's imperial objectives. After all, in the theatres, while their soldier and sailor armies and navies were made of wood and were only 6 inches tall, they testify to the organizational complexity of theatrical assemblage capable of working within such severe limitations and with such rapidity of purpose.

There is a final comment to be made about the plays as they functioned within this particular theatrical assemblage whose parameters may be loosely defined as located in London and addressing subjects of military (mainly naval) conflict in the 1790s. The total audiences for *The Conquest of St. Eustacia, The Surrender of Trinidad, The Glorious First of June, Bantry Bay, or the Loyal Peasants, Nootka Sound; Or, Britain Prepar'd, The Provocation!, The Point at Herqui* and *The Death of Captain Faulkner* easily

exceeded 100,000 people (assuming two-thirds-full houses) and comprise
the populations within the assemblage. The degree of co-presence and
density can easily be reassembled with respect to the performance locations.
These are the decomposable and irreducible parameters of the assemblage.
The primary sources of news information on which these dramas were based
were mainly derived from the newspapers, whose 'Shipping' and formal or
informal naval dispatch columns mixed freely with 'Theatrical Intelligence'.
From these circumstances arise two principal considerations, the first of
which is the detailing of this assemblage as a concrete market which merged
patriotic ideals with economics; the second is the presence of mechanisms
demonstrating that assemblage theory models the dynamics of emergent
social ideas.

The operation of the theatrical assemblage as a concrete market with
definable populations is stressed throughout this book. These populations
comprise the identity of the assemblage and contain fully articulated sets of
ideological expressions framed within the economic spaces of the assemblage. The 2 July 1794 first night of *The Glorious First of June* was staged as a
benefit for the 'Widows & Orphans of the Brave Sailors who Fell in the
glorious Actions', and took £841. 19s. 0d. at the box office. That it was an
elaborate staging is indicated by the payment a few days later of £3. 19s. 0d.
to '4 Men for Man^g the Yards in first of June', presumably sailors or ex-
sailors hired to authenticate the show's apparently realistic warship scenes.
However, on the same day, the receipts side of the ledger shows an entry,
'Return'd by Thompson for Men that Man'd the Yards & [£]2.14.0.', an
apparent donation of much of the specialist scene-men's earnings towards
supporting the evening's charitable cause. A similar repayment was repeated
ten days later when the 'Music Band &c'. returned salaries to the amount of
£6. 12s. 0d. Indeed, the ledger shows that the total of 'Salaries taken by
Performers &c on the Fund Night [2 July] for Widows & Orphans of
Sailors on the first of June [was £]6.6.10'.[93] In other words, in a practice not
followed for regular benefits (including those for its own Theatrical Fund),
Drury Lane performers, both permanent and casual, donated substantial
parts of their night's earnings to support naval widows and orphans.

On 9 July, however, the expenditure side reveals that two dancers from a
family named 'Degville' received money for 'One night Paid for the Fund
for Relief of Widow & Orphans 2nd July to Sundry Persons Degville Senr.
6/8 D°. Junr· 6/8 ____ 13[s].4.[d]'. These were the D'Egvilles (also known as
Daigueville, Dageville or Dagueville), a family of dancers, dancing teachers
and choreographers regularly employed in the London theatres. The payments were to their founding patriarch, Peter D'Egville (*fl.* 1768–94) and his

son, James Hervey D'Egville (*fl.* 1782–1827?).[94] Although the father had first
worked for Drury Lane in 1768, an Old Bailey transcript of 1800 when the
son appeared as a witness in a trial for the murder of a fellow dancer, Louis
Barthelmichi, describes him as 'a foreigner'.[95] It seems highly likely that
'Degville Sen[r.] [and] Jun[r.]' were French and that, unlike the majority of the
rest of the Drury Lane company that night, they elected not to donate to the
charitable cause in which the British Navy had been successful in an
important strategic battle against the French Navy.

The importance of this incident is that, in addition to London's repertoire of dramas about naval conflict, all of which constitute specific components (materialized by place, date and performance) within the
contemporary theatrical assemblage, there also existed a further array of
individual singularities within the populations of the assemblage materializing otherwise hidden ideological components apparently at variance with
the real or virtual symbolic registers of the performances' patriotic texts and
their actualization in the playhouse.

To come to the second proposition, the reception characteristics here
presented in the rawest of forms by two generations of the D'Egville family,
point to a stratum of emergent possibility spaces materialized at the playhouse's marketplace, which present dissonant (financially and ideologically)
components within the assemblage's populations and run contrary to the
symbolic registers of the performance text. Indeed, they appear to be
reactive to the flow of the information originally derived from the newspapers disseminating news of the British naval victory across its networks,
and reactive to both the naval drama and its charitable cause. What this
amounts to is an important phenomenon, the creation of a type of
'Theatrical Intelligence' that is an artificial intelligence, a reprogramming
of data (the newspaper reports, the performance texts) which converts the
hardware of the performances (all of which are materialized, even down to
realistic rigging 'Yards') into new sets of perspectives, new spaces of possibility within the overall assemblage. This can be called deterritorialization,
but it also amounts to a transformation within the theatrical assemblage,
creating out of its own ideological components something which was not
there before yet whose presence is verified both by Peter and James Hervey
D'Egville's material participation in the 2 July Drury Lane performance of
The Glorious First of June and by their immediate economic transactions in
its marketplace. The theoretical background is set out at the end of
DeLanda's *Philosophy and Simulation: The Emergence of Synthetic Reason*:
'In . . . programming languages, referred to as *object-oriented*, there are no
master programs or subroutines. Control is always decentralized as software

objects encapsulating a set of operators are called into action by patterns in the very data they operate on. This implies that the identity of an application is defined dynamically in interaction with the data: if the latter changes so will within limits the application's own identity. If deterritorialization transforms a piece of hardware into software, decoding eliminates a rigid master program in favor of autonomous and flexible software objects.'[96]

CHAPTER SIX

Theatrical assemblage populations: the Turkish ambassador's visits to London playhouses, 1794

The previous chapter demonstrated that the sheer size and profile of Britain's navy, its role in the expansion of armed trade, the gradually globalizing reach of empire and the increasing engagement in military conflict all meant that these activities were inevitably represented on the London stage. As with John Marsh in Chichester worrying about his brother's naval career and the Nootka Sound crisis, perceptions of national strategic considerations – even relative to events on the other side of the planet – could reach deep into the heart of provincial England with representations of Nootka mutating across scores of reiterated theatrical performances on the London stage for many months. In other words, the individual singularity of *Nootka Sound; Or, Britain Prepar'd* and of the other plays discussed in Chapter 5, because audience populations can be quantified at precise performance locations (ordered by date and by venue), can be contemplated as specific population component subsets. These subsets represent a series of individual singularities distributed across the universal singularities of the built spaces of the theatres. The New York production of *Nootka Sound, or, The Adventures of Captain Douglas*, for example, would be a connected, networked, outlier of the London version, but there would also be other plays thematically related to this particular theatrical subset, all positioned as individual singularities, all existing with their cumulative populations distributed across the array of universal singularities The plays examined in Chapter 5, precisely because they represented a thematic corpus, all contributed to this very specific theatrical assemblage operative throughout most of the 1790s.

This chapter will add an extra layer of dramas superimposed on the previous sets discussed in Chapter 5. They constitute another, isomorphic, diagram of this particular mid-1790s theatrical assemblage. Most parts of the diagram (as befits the historical moment) overlap with the first, although, of course, not as repetitions but as new sets of emergent possibility space co-actualized in a series of unique performances (as outlined in the Introduction, the non-persistence of Georgian performance is a basic component of the assemblage), each with its own populations. The provisions of the theory allow for these new spaces of possibility to emerge from overlapping diagrams of connectivity: 'The universality of the structure of possibility spaces means that two entirely different processes can share the same diagram, or that their diagrams can overlap, so the processes share some of the same singularities. In these terms, the isomorphism between models and what they model can be explained as a *co-actualization* of the same diagram, or of different but overlapping diagrams.'[1]

In the same way that the D'Egville family were, perhaps unexpectedly, figured as distinctive ideologically dissonant population components situated amidst an array of precise theatrical markets and performances, Chapter 6 will follow the London theatre visits from mid 1794 of Yusuf Agha Effendi, the ambassador from the Ottoman Empire, demonstrating not only his personal context within Turkey's mission to Britain but also the topical and ideological formations of the plays he witnessed.

Within the theoretical model, the Ottoman ambassador is unusual in that as a diplomat he was directly linked to Sultan Selim III as part of a major conduit of strategic wartime political and military relations whose geopolitics encompassed a Western Christian imperial power and an Eastern Islamic empire. However, just as the flat ontologies typical of assemblage theory have a tendency to return celebrities to the mean of their peer group, in the same way Yusuf Agha Effendi becomes (to use the terminology of the theory) a molecular component within the populations of the theatrical assemblage in which his movements show him to be located. Nevertheless, as diplomacy between two imperial states was specifically his mission in London, his situation as a molecular component within this assemblage does not mean his theatre visits can be discounted: 'Given a population of assemblages at any one scale, other processes can then generate larger-scale assemblages using members of this population as components. This statement is correct, but only if not taken to imply an actual historical sequence.'[2] Trying to follow up or analyse an historical sequence of political or military gains or losses, for either country, resulting subsequent to his visit would be contrary to the non-linear narrative of active assemblages but, as will be shown, the Ottoman embassy was actually very carefully received by officials in London, and although it may have achieved disappointing military outcomes, the embassy's longer-term significance rests in the loose alliances and tacit understandings which ensured Turkey's effective wartime neutrality. Not least, the embassy also resituates a long neglected aspect of Anglo-Ottoman relations.

From the government's point of view, and with respect to all foreign visitors, as far as London's principal theatres were concerned, the homogeneity of the stage's ideological discourses was secured by the presence of state censorship and the granting of the patentee privileges. The massive effects of nightly reiteration, together with the flexibility and responsiveness of the theatres to military events, ensured that these apparently deterritorialized spaces of entertainment could become officially encoded, even to the extent, as with *The Glorious First of June*, of ministers writing songs for theatrical consumption. For influential foreigners, the homogeneity of message and heterogeneity of genre meant that London's theatres maximized their usefulness as extensions of diplomacy. Since it is the materiality of the playhouses in combination with their performances and audiences which constitute the expressive component of these events as well as its identity, the Turkish ambassador's visits comprise an aspect of diplomatic continuance both irreducible and decomposable. By tracking the theatre visits of the ambassador 'from the Sublime Porte' (as the newspapers usually styled him) as a fully identifiable and irreducible singularity within the components of the audience population, it is possible to examine a cross-section of the repertoire at that historical moment and to analyse its likely reception characteristics.

Not least, Yusuf Agha Effendi's theatre-going provides evidence of the scale of Britain's political, diplomatic and cultural engagement with a major Muslim empire in the 1790s. The attraction of London theatre to foreign officials on diplomatic duties was precisely that the playhouse performances were distinct assemblages within the metropolis, providing a space where deterritorialized government policy and cultural nuances could be encountered. Theatre remained constantly attractive to foreign ambassadors. In the previous chapter, it was noted that a full year later, in 1795, *The Death of Captain Faulkner; or, British Heroism* was performed as part of a benefit night for Margaret Martyr, 'By Special Desire of His Excellency the Turkish Ambassador', who was the same diplomat, Yusuf Agha Effendi, then still in post although apparently under circumstances of reduced funding. The availability of a national inventory of playhouses has also shown that ambassadorial theatre-going has not always been confined to London and constitutes a largely unknown aspect of a large set of theatrical assemblages reaching out into the provinces. As early as 1750, *Henry IV, Pt I* and Henry Fielding's *Tom Thumb* (1731) were performed at the High Street Theatre, Portsmouth, 'for the entertainment of His Excellency Hadge Mahamed

Hajee, the Algerine Ambassador'.[3] In 1761, it was probably the servants of the 'Algerine Ambassador' who triggered a payment of 3s. 6d. from Covent Garden following their master's sponsoring of a performance – discreetly and anonymously 'By Desire' – of *Henry V*.[4] The frequency of non-European diplomatic London theatre visits is difficult to estimate, but, as early as 1721, for example, 'the King of Delago in Africa' and his 'Two Princess [*sic*] Bro[rs]'. made several visits to Drury Lane. This was the year the Dutch East India Company had founded a factory in Delagoa (present-day Maputo, Mozambique). Its destruction by English pirates a year later gives some idea of the volatility of the diplomatic relations needing to be assuaged by the King and his brothers' trips to see benefit performances of Congreve's *Love for Love* (1695), Dryden's *The Spanish Fryar* (1681) and *The Merry Wives of Windsor*.[5]

The use of theatre-going as an extension of diplomacy is even more evident when Britain needed radically to reposition itself with reference to European geopolitics after the beginning of the war with France in 1793. The French war precipitated an urgent reassessment of Britain's strategic and ideological relationships not only with its friends but also with the enemies of its enemies. Notwithstanding the incipient orientalism which percolated through some sections of the arts or literature, the simple geo-political reality remained that eastward of France, at the eastern end of the Mediterranean, stood the Ottoman Empire, an unwieldy but otherwise mighty military presence that needed to be persuaded of British affection and French untrustworthiness. Not least, the strategically crucial Ottoman Empire dominated the overland routes between Europe and India. The Ottomans may not have been politically or militarily either modernized or unified, but they had the attraction of outflanking France by the simple virtue of being strategically placed between France and the growing British interests in India. This was geopolitics, eighteenth-century style. As the Levant Company had been involved in regional trade since Elizabeth I, the new war against France necessitated that any lingering doubts about Turkey's future alliances needed to be resolved in favour of Britain's strategic interests. From 1792 onwards – actually before the outbreak of war – Britain put into place the necessary, rudimentary diplomatic and military processes intended to ensure a successful and effective strategic alliance with the Ottomans. Since the state exerted such a precise level of control over the London theatres, and the state censorship system could (and did) rid the London stage of subversive or disloyal utterances, it was not unexpected that playhouses could be indirectly deployed to disseminate broad messages of British integrity, resilience and military success. Indeed, the functioning of theatres precisely as sites of social assemblage was structured into the way in which they operated by engaging live audiences with text and spectacle in real time, and, as the previous chapter has shown, many of their contemporary messages served an overtly ideological purpose. The unprecedented opening of a permanent Ottoman embassy in London in the first half of 1794 meant that cultural structures were already in place (and had been accessed before) for influencing the Ottoman reception of the British national character as represented on stage.

The presence in London in the mid 1790s of a Turkish embassy, not least as an illustration of Western and Eastern cooperation, has virtually fallen out of the historical record despite the strategic and military potential of closer links increasingly being produced between two empires of formidable size and significance.[6] As it happened, the new Turkish ambassador proved to be extremely fond of the theatre. Beginning with Thomas Holcroft's *The Road to Ruin* (1792), paired with the 'Grand New Historical Spectacle', *The Soldier's Festival; or, The Night Before the Battle*, starting on 7 May 1794, the ambassador, Yusuf Agha Effendi, attended an array of dramas coinciding with a particular upturn in Britain's military fortunes. Even taken on their own and in isolation, the range of plays the Turkish ambassador witnessed inevitably presented rapidly changing sets of military theatrical spectacles commemorating British victories. In other words, the record of the Turkish ambassador's play-going in the spring and summer of 1794 and into 1795 is an extremely good indicator of the enormous resourcefulness of the capital's theatres in projecting a coherent image of a politically stable and militarily successful nation.

The ambassador's propensity to attend, and even sponsor or endorse, London theatre was also a facet of the Ottoman Empire's ability to project its European aspirations into the day-to-day life of the British metropolis. The Ottoman embassy to London was, by some margin, better supported from Constantinople than the missions sent to the other major European capitals. Indeed, it proved to be the case that this first three-year ambassadorial cycle was the high point of Sultan Selim III's attempts both to reform his diplomatic corps and reassess Ottoman influence in Europe.[7] Ultimately, the embassy's generously funded establishment – which no doubt facilitated the ambassador's play-going – proved to be short-lived. Realizing around the middle of 1795 that the Ottoman tradition of giving foreign embassies financial assistance (something the Ottomans had always done for foreign embassies in Constantinople) was not reciprocated in European courts, Selim reduced his financial support for the London embassy.[8] However, on the embassy's first arrival in Britain, the potential for both Ottoman political reform and Anglo-Turkish military and commercial alliance seemed extremely promising to both parties, particularly in the context of an intensifying war between Britain and France.

The war with France had already initiated a series of changes in Britain's diplomatic mission in Constantinople as its effects precipitated swift revisions of Britain's strategic disposition towards potential allies and potential enemies within the context of the changing international climate. By the middle of 1794, representations of a rapid succession of battles, sieges and skirmishes had become incorporated into London's theatres in a number of variant forms. The most notable military events at that time included those which had occurred in the first full year of the war and were concerned with the aftermath of the Siege of Valenciennes. Although combat had ended in late summer of 1793, the siege continued to be the subject of several theatrical representations as the meaning of this victory embedded itself in the national consciousness. By the late spring of 1794, the British fleet (together with the Spanish) had assembled at Spithead in order to provoke a deliberate engagement with the French Grand Fleet. The most significant event of this naval conflict was the 'Glorious First of June' battle in the mid Atlantic.

Even traversing relatively narrow time bands, it can be demonstrated that London theatre had become not merely self-referentially concerned with summarizing the national mood, but also capable of deployment to shape national diplomatic ends. Yusuf Agha Effendi and his mission reached London no later than December 1793 and were (eventually) granted an audience with King George III as part of the beginning of the first permanent Ottoman embassy in Britain.[9] In the spring and summer of that year the ambassador began an extraordinary series of visits to London's places of public and private entertainment, not least visiting a number of its theatres.[10] He was a visible presence glimpsed by many Londoners, not only the tens of thousands who would have seen him in the theatre. The Sussex diarist, John Marsh, in one of his regular trips to London, records seeing him in July 1794, noting that he 'walked on the Terrace at the Adelphi . . . [and] saw the Turkish Embassador [sic] &c who lodged there'.[11]

There was much at stake in engaging the attention of the Turkish ambassador through the indirect means of drama, especially in a theatrical environment where visual spectacle – as much as speech –tended to dominate the repertoire. Successful strategic diplomatic connections with an Ottoman Empire led by a notably Western-looking sultan could fulfil many objectives, including ameliorating North African piracy through the better understanding of their Ottoman imperial centre; facilitating potential alliances or positions of neutrality with Ottoman client states, particularly with respect to Egypt; and generally offsetting French regional influence. At the end of the eighteenth century, the complex array of entrenched commercial monopolies, occasionally mismatched personalities and a fluidly developing set of political and military conditions meant that Britain's trading and strategic interests in the Middle East were particularly unsettled.[12] What Britain feared above all else was the fall of the Ottoman Empire to the Russians and the subsequent destabilization of the region, bringing with it the potential for France to take advantage of the resulting melee.[13] For the British authorities, the potentialities of such changes were magnified not only by understandable concern about the general conduct of the war with France but also by the rise in domestic political radicalism. These twin anxieties appear at their most explicit in the works of the French deist, Constantin-François Chassebœuf, comte de Volney. His *The Ruins; or, A Survey of the Revolutions of Empires* (1792) became almost an ideological handbook for anti-clerical British republicans, who widely excerpted it in their radical journals. However, one of his earlier works, *Considerations on the War with the Turks* (1788), provides an exceptionally clear French perspective on the simultaneous Ottoman conflicts of the Russo-Turkish War (1787–92) and Austro-Turkish War (1787–91). In the crisp prose style which made his writings, even in translation, comparable to Tom Paine's *Rights of Man* (1791) or *The Age of Reason* (1794), Volney predicted that 'Through Egypt we would get to India', reinstating a Suez overland route and thereby rendering commercially and strategically unviable the much longer shipping passages round the Cape of Good Hope used by Britain because of its lack of Mediterranean bases east of Gibraltar after the fall of Minorca in 1782.[14]

As early as April 1791, the appearance of a caricature print entitled *A Representation of the Turks, threatened with War, learning in a hurry the French Manual Exercise* had provided a nervously comic allusion to amateurish Turkish troops drilled, abused and ridiculed by smartly uniformed French soldiers, all observed by Sultan Selim III.[15] Until the capture of Malta in 1800 after a two-year siege, Britain was in a precarious position as far as its regional strategic interests were concerned. Indeed, the French invasion of Egypt in 1798 went on to reverse centuries of Ottoman diplomacy by obliging the Porte to seek a treaty with Russia. By the early 1790s, after Selim's accession to the throne in April 1789, when Turkey was fighting two disastrous wars against Russia and Austria over the consolidation of Ottoman territorial limits, the situation had become ripe for the Sultan to reconsider his strategic alliances. Of course, Britain was well aware of what was at stake for all parties.

As one commentator put it in 1791, well before the beginning of the war with France, 'Now seems the critical moment, to form a commercial union with the head of the Mahomedans, the Turks, and thereby to secure the interest of all the tributary nations.'[16] The instability of the Ottoman Empire – as well as the potential for exploitation of their weakness by Russia – was of continuing concern and was echoed by British commentators. One writer, who urged economic support for Turkey through increased trade, sought 'To rescue the Ottoman empire from impending ruin', fearing that its collapse would pave the way for wholesale Russian expansion and invasion ('Let us ... suppose ... that the Russian army has reached the Indus').[17] Although this commentator was clearly exploiting the divide between the increasingly rich East India Company and the much less successful (but equally monopolistic) Levant (or Turkey) Company, his careful calculations as to the potential quantities of export items (ranging from guns and clocks through to Staffordshire earthenware) reveals something of British contemporary attitudes to the East. Far from being driven by specifically ideological forms of 'orientalism', there were persuasive reasons to view the Ottomans as setting a particular range of military, strategic and economic challenges.

With Britain still fully engaged through its East India Company proxy in a long conflict with Tippoo Saib, there is no reason to imagine that it treated the political implications of the Turkish ambassador's residence in Britain with anything other than the utmost care and delicacy. As Rajani Sudani has argued, economically, industrially and scientifically, as well as by virtue of their varying spheres of political and military influence, there was too much at stake for either power to be relaxed about its regional situation and neither of them could be sure about the security of its long-term future.[18]

The strategic importance of the Ottoman Empire, together with a whole range of military, commercial and strategic issues of concern to wartime Britain, makes it difficult to overstate the significance of the first permanent Turkish embassy to London. Yusuf Agha Effendi's theatre visits, recorded in the newspaper advertising, provide a fascinating insight into his exposure to the ideological and military messages embedded in contemporary London's theatrical productions on an almost regular daily basis. Not least, his theatre-going has also to supply an absence of other types of information about his visit. The ambassador's residence was accompanied by a notable lack of presence within the formal visual record, for example. As observant Muslims, the embassy avoided visual representation. A stipple print of the ambassador's audience with George III was eventually published three years later, but a much more contemporary image was furtively produced by *The Pocket Magazine*.[19] Although aware that Yusuf had insuperable reservations about sitting for a portrait, *The Pocket Magazine* took a surreptitious sketch of him and, by the end of 1794, had provided its readers with a print.[20] With overtly satirical (rather than mimetic) intentions, as early as December 1793 James Gillray had produced an explicitly orientalist lampoon of the ambassador (Yusuf Agha wielding an enormously phallic set of credentials accompanied by French *sans-culottes* bearing his train), and a further caricature was published by Isaac Cruikshank in January 1794, both prints usefully reflecting the degree of topical interest in the Ottoman ambassador.[21] If visual representations of the Turkish embassy are scant, there is every other reason to think that Yusuf Agha impacted considerably on the middling and elite classes of the metropolitan social scene. Two musical compositions for the harpsichord or the (newly emerging) pianoforte, *The Turkish Ambassador's March* (c. 1794) by Karl Kambra and W.P.R. Cope's *The Turkish Ambassador's Grand March* (1794), were intended to mark his arrival, their scoring for domestic instruments indicating how they sought to exploit family music makers.[22]

Amidst this context of British commercial objectives vested in the Levant and East India companies, and the fears of the regional aims articulated by Volney, the onset of the war with France necessitated a rapid realignment of British diplomacy. Inevitably, pre-war theatre reflected a pre-war view of the Ottomans. Since Yusuf Agha Effendi visited London theatres so often in 1794–5, it is important to contrast the plays he saw with pre-war attitudes being represented on stage. The striking intersection of British strategic aims and London theatricality can best be examined by a play by James Cobb, a prolific playwright who also happened to work as a senior administrator in the East India Company.

The Austrian army's recapture of Belgrade from the Turks in 1789 (a city almost constantly in Ottoman hands since 1456) had been marked at Drury Lane by Cobb's comic opera, *The Siege of Belgrade* (1791). Cobb's drama, interspersed with highly successful songs by Stephen Storace, pictured the rough treatment of Austrian men and women at Turkish hands and their eventual relief by magnanimous Austrian soldiers happy to forgive their foes ('Rise, and learn, Christian revenge').[23] Benefiting considerably from Storace's music, *The Siege of Belgrade* was an immediate success.[24] Again, the scale of the theatrical assemblage and the national inventory of playhouses is important in appreciating its dissemination. In May 1792, the theatrical tontine subscriber and diarist John Marsh 'went for the 1ˢᵗ time to the Siege of Belgrade at yᵉ new Theatre whᶜ was much larger & more convenient than the old one' in Chichester, Sussex. As well as performances

in England, in 1802 it had three performances in Charleston, South
Carolina.[25]

With its seraglio, black slaves, the threatened garrotting of an Austrian
officer and, for the period, an unusually detailed set of stage directions
requiring such things as elegant Turkish costumes and tents, Cobb's *The
Siege of Belgrade* reproduced many orientalist fears and fantasies, but, in the
case of this drama about the historically liminal European position of
Belgrade, defined as being on the frontier of the Christian and Islamic
worlds, Cobb's views were not necessarily synonymous with those of his
contemporaries. The scale and position of the Ottoman Empire was simply
too vast, too important, to be reduced to a simple set of orientalist prejudices, particularly as Britain became engaged in a war with France which
necessitated securing alliances across its European strategic flanks while
providing both access to, and security for, overland routes to India. Russia
and Austria, as Turkey's habitual enemies, needed to be closely considered.
Not all European perspectives were persuaded that the decline of Turkey
implied its replacement by benign regimes. In prose fiction, the anonymous
*The Siege of Belgrade: an Historical Novel. Translated from a German manu-
script* (c. 1791) straightforwardly condemned 'the ambition of a female tyrant
[Empress Catherine of Russia], and the vanity of a capricious despot [the
Holy Roman Emperor Joseph II of Austria]' who had 'united ... to
exterminate the unoffending descendants of Mahomet ... [and] disturb
the peace of Europe'.[26] Hannah Brand's five-act tragedy based on the 1456
siege, *Huniades; or, The Siege of Belgrade* (1791), which was acted at Norwich
in June 1791 and then again in January 1792 by the Drury Lane company at
Colman's Haymarket playhouse, had made its heroine, Agmunda (played
by Brand herself), equally the victim of her fellow Hungarians and the
Turks. On the one hand, her own countrymen wished to hand her over to
the Sultan in return for lifting the siege, while, on the other hand, Mahomet
II's desire to marry her stood in defiance of her love for the Hungarian hero,
Huniades.[27]

Stephen Storace's songs for Cobb's *The Siege of Belgrade* were astonishingly successful, particularly on account of their dissemination scored for
harpsichord and pianoforte with violin accompaniment, suitably arranged
for middle-class drawing rooms and a further reminder of the centrality of
both theatre and its spin-off music-making in Georgian cultural life. Cobb's
songs from *The Siege of Belgrade* were reprinted well into the Victorian
period, and the most recent new setting of one of them appeared as late as
1950.[28] However, Cobb's portrayal of Ottoman rule ('We have groan'd
under Turkish oppression too long'), which included the conversion of a

battle-ruined convent into a seraglio in which the heroine is incarcerated, was the product of his own singular perspective on the Turks.[29] Cobb was highly placed in the management of the East India Company, entering its administrative office in 1771 and becoming company secretary in 1814.[30] For Cobb, Turkey represented territory covered by a rival British monopoly, the Levant (or Turkey) Company, founded in 1581. Much less successful than the East India Company, its profile among the diplomatic elite stood high on account of the double funding available to the ambassador to Constantinople. As they were both endangered monopolies, there was much to be gained by the East India Company's pointing out the Levant Company's relative inefficiency and linking its future to the demise and destruction of the Ottoman Empire. In the third edition of *The Wealth of Nations*, Adam Smith had drawn particular attention to the contradictions, absurdities and discouragements to free markets exemplified by the 'Turky [*sic*] trade' monopoly of the Levant Company.[31] By the late 1790s, no doubt hastened by Napoleon's invasion of Egypt, the Levant Company came under renewed attack in William Eton's *A Survey of the Turkish Empire* (1798), to which at least two members of the company were forced to make substantial replies.[32] In particular, in addition to all this pamphleteering and lobbying, the publication of G.R. Berridge's recent history of the British embassy in Turkey reveals that the East India Company opportunistically increased the reach of its influence by making unofficial, occasional payments to Sir Robert Sharpe Ainslie, the ambassador to Turkey in the years 1776–93.[33]

Central to the argument of this book is the pervasive presence of a materialized theatrical assemblage particularly visible in London and linked to networks of markets, other playhouses and media. James Cobb, the playwright and senior East India Company executive, must have known of (and perhaps even personally authorized) payments from the company to Sir Robert Ainslie as ambassador in Constantinople. This places Cobb in a key position. Not only was he directly involved at an increasingly high level in running the East India Company –which can now be clearly seen to have exerted financial leverage on the Levant Company –but also he had placed himself in a powerful position to influence the popular reception of the Ottoman Empire in Britain through his drama.[34] With the Levant Company growing weaker (especially in comparison to the East India Company), and with a number of commentators calling for an increasing volume of exports to Turkey, Cobb's depiction of an unusually dysfunctional Turkish Empire in *The Siege of Belgrade* was influential but quite at variance with other theatrical and fictional writers of the time. With his own career heavily invested in the success of the East India Company and the growing strength and durability of the British role in India, Cobb's *Siege of Belgrade* stands in a position of pivotal influence.

Despite the Turkish tents, seraglios, black slaves and elaborate eastern costumes populating Cobb's *Siege of Belgrade*, the actualities of encounters between East and West were much more complex. Orientalism, even when it was present, was accompanied by various types of projection, both psychological and imperial. When Agmunda, the heroine of Hannah Brand's *Huniades; or, The Siege of Belgrade* (played by herself), is proclaimed by her Hungarian compatriots as a potential 'Empress of the East', the Western imperial fantasy of Oriental dominion is one Brand herself invalidates by making her character's role that of a traded commodity, literally a woman about to be gifted to Sultan Mehemed II in exchange for ending the siege.[35] Brand's play ends with the siege being lifted, but, historically, Belgrade was retaken by the Ottomans only seventy years later in 1521, and the city successively changed hands over many years. To these fantasies of dominating a decaying but elusively resilient empire should be added the movements of real individuals whose lives were involved in these complex layerings of Georgian theatricality and the concerns of empire. At times, playhouse and empire intersect quite starkly as colourful figures engaged in imperial enlargement found themselves represented on the stage.

One such person was William Sydney Smith (1764–1840), a larger-than-life, swashbuckling, Royal Navy officer who eventually rose to the rank of vice-admiral.[36] In 1792, a decade after a successful American naval campaign during which he helped capture a rebel frigate, in addition to time in the late 1780s spent volunteering in King Gustavus III of Sweden's navy (incidentally picking up experience in fighting Russians), Smith had been sent to Constantinople to observe the naval defences of the Ottoman Mediterranean vassals.[37] Not least, Smith's Constantinople mission was itself a unique diplomatic occurrence. Smith's brother, John Spencer, was about to take over the role of official British ambassador to Turkey, meaning that Sydney's appointment – sanctioned by London – doubled the ambassadorial presence. Smith's duties undoubtedly included making an assessment of Selim III's new programme of warship building (using European shipbuilders), which delivered forty-six new vessels between 1791 and 1799.[38] Making his way back to Britain after hearing of the outbreak of war with France, Smith in typical maverick style bought himself a small warship in Smyrna, manned it with disparate British sailors garnered from the region, and sailed the ship homeward, destroying a number of French warships at Toulon en route. Four years later, some of Smith's naval exploits became the subject of Covent Garden's Prelude, *Point at Herqui; or, British Bravery Triumphant* (1796), as discussed in Chapter 5. Meanwhile, in London in June 1794 – no doubt invited to assist on account of his recent Ottoman experience – Smith entertained the Turkish ambassador to a lavish 'breakfast' (followed by dancing at 2 pm) on board his new command, the frigate *Diamond*, the vessel later used for the incidents highlighted in *Point at Herqui*. As well as demonstrating the extent to which diplomacy, military seamanship and theatricality could all become intricately inter-woven, Smith's movements in Turkey tell us much about the extent to which Britain was gathering the military intelligence on which to base future Anglo-Turkish diplomacy. If the Ottomans were re-equipping their navy, using European skills where required, it was important that they did not fall too far under French influence.

Smith's mission in 1792 to observe the Ottoman fleet signifies the trans-formation of Britain's relations with Turkey. Due to his naval experience, Smith combined his role as joint-ambassador with that of British military attaché, a job which, as recently as 1791–2, had actually been assigned to a German.[39] While this gradual change in diplomatic relations was develop-ing, the incumbent ambassador, Ainslie, had over many years – like other Britons posted overseas – 'assumed the style and fashion of a Musselman of rank; in fine, he lived *en Turk*.'[40] Consistent with this adoption of Ottoman habits, Ainslie's own political style was far from belligerent or confronta-tional with the Turks; indeed, he had advised his superiors in London that "[M]uch more may be operated here by civility and management than by Bearishness and Blustering.'[41] Of course, Ainslie's pursuit of his own financial interests, which clearly included payments from the Levant Company, triggered by the funds from the East India Company, may have promoted this *laissez-faire* attitude. Given changing circumstances in France after 1789, together with the kinds of French strategic thinking revealed by figures influential in the revolutionary republic such as Volney, it is not surprising Ainslie ensured that the Sultan was carefully briefed and prepared for establishing European-style embassies. For exam-ple, Ainslie persuaded the Sultan to upgrade the mission from that of envoy to full ambassadorial status, particularly ensuring that sufficient funding was provided from Constantinople to support this level of diplomacy.[42] The conjunction of issues such as Smith's naval experience and Ottoman determination to increase the status of the embassy helped ensure that Yusuf Agha Effendi, as the person appointed ambassador to Britain, was also a person with a broadly similar background to Smith's, having lately been secretary to the Ottoman admiralty.[43]

It is not difficult to see that, by virtue of their common strategic needs together with the careful preparations made in Constantinople for their mission, the Ottoman delegation to London had been very carefully established to work smoothly and effectively at both military and personal levels. Although Selim III eventually cut financial support for the European embassies, Yusuf Agha Effendi's mission had initially been provided with lavish funding, especially in comparison to the others. Since the entire delegation consisted of just three officials and two interpreters (in addition to a Christian Ottoman whose role was probably mainly commercial), it is easy to understand why it came to be so fully embedded into the cultural life of the capital.[44] As soon as the official presentation at St James' was over, the embassy began a wide range of courtesy visits of a cultural and social nature, which continued well into 1796 when the Sultan's financial cutbacks began to impact.

Perhaps one of the most revealing of these visits was when Mahmud Raif Effendi, secretary to the ambassador, gave an archery display as guest of the Toxophilite Society (then known as the Royal Company of Archers). Shot from a traditional Turkish composite bow, Mahmud Raif's arrow, 'to our utter astonishment', travelled 440 yards at a time when the best English longbow shot carried only to some 350 yards.[45] The demonstration was far from being a redundant piece of medievalism. Within the carefully modulated nuances of decorum signifying Britain's elite at play, Mahmud's prowess at archery placed him within an acceptable configuration of the fashionable gentleman of indisputably ancient and aristocratic lineage. Archery clubs, with conspicuously loyalist names such as the Royal Company of Archers, the Royal Kentish Bowmen and the Royal British Bowmen, became increasing popular among the upper classes. Feasting, conviviality and, not least, stringent property freehold qualifications for membership ensured that archery remained an elite sport. Although the demands of war meant that many clubs folded after 1794, they revived strongly after the Peace of Amiens and Waterloo.[46] Archery's association with elite young men was demonstrated to contemporaries in paintings such as Sir Joshua Reynolds' *Colonel Acland and Lord Sydney: The Archers* (1769; oil on canvas, Tate Britain) or Sir Henry Raeburn's *The Archers* (1789–90; oil on canvas, National Gallery, London).[47] Not least, archery's increasing take-up by elite women meant that it acquired a following as a healthy, outdoor pastime 'studied most by that sex for which it was least intended', with archery's close-fitting costume and upright, athletic, pose promoting voyeuristic attention. As the editor of a new edition of *Toxophilus, the Schole, or Partitions, of Shooting* (1788), Roger Ascham's

1544 seminal archery text, put it, 'The bow, in the hands of the British fair, presents a new era in archery . . . it has struck out the unknown pleasure which the king of Persia sought in vain . . . and forms a new link in the chain of society.'[48] As ever, the diarist John Marsh's record of visiting, in September 1791, 'a Toxopholite [*sic*] Society at Sarum [Wiltshire] (wch was there quite the rage)' – which included 'a Tent . . . pitch'd, with refreshments for the Ladies &c' – corroborates archery's provincial take-up.[49] In other words, with its long and prestigious Middle Eastern heritage and acceptability among sexually mixed British elites, there is every reason to think archery became an informal channel for Anglo-Turkish diplomacy in the early 1790s. The Ottoman embassy's theatre-going activities should be viewed as consonant with these other social practices. The embassy became thoroughly assimilated into the capital's cultural life. Under one of the more regular types of hospitality afforded to visiting dignitaries, in April 1794 the ambassador was guest of honour at a Mansion House dinner and ball, and in early May Edmund Burke showed elaborate deference to him when he visited Parliament to listen to one of Burke's speeches.[50] Learning that he was about to make a return visit to the Chinese Pantheon, Rathbone Place, *The True Briton* commented, 'The Turkish Ambassador continues indefatigable in the pursuit of information.'[51]

Given this degree of incorporation into the metropolitan social scene, it is not difficult to imagine the alarm when Yusuf Agha Effendi's theatre visits looked ready to backfire because of embarrassing new writing for London's prolific stage, particularly at a venue he had not yet visited. The specific form this took came in the Lord Chamberlain's interdiction of John O'Keeffe's *Jenny's Whim Or The Roasted Emperor*, a two-act farce intended for performance towards the end of August 1794, at the end of the Haymarket's summer-season licence. Although it referred to the 'Emperor of Morocco', there was no doubt that the piece was intended to take advantage of how the Turkish ambassador had gained a high public profile on account of his attendance at London entertainments. That December, *The Pocket Magazine* noted his house in the exclusive Adelphi district (where John Marsh had seen him), and how he and his entourage 'have visited many places of publick entertainment, and appear highly to enjoy our various amusements'.[52] As far as *Jenny's Whim Or The Roasted Emperor* was concerned, although Larpent certainly had the power as Examiner to interdict plays, in this instance he referred it to the Lord Chamberlain himself, James Cecil, Marquess of Salisbury, because 'The general Drift of the inclosed Farce being a low Ridicule or Sarcasm upon the Emperor of Morocco, & containing besides some Allusions to titles & Persons, of the improper Tendency of which, in a political or personal View, it is impossible that I should be a competent Judge.'[53] While this particular 'Emperor of Morocco' was the fictional creation of O'Keeffe, his real-life counterpart had cropped up in April's London newspapers because of a 'very troublesome' prospective alliance with France when it was feared Morocco was about to attack Spanish outposts in Africa, potentially necessitating British intervention.[54]

Jenny's Whim was situated in a continuum of Haymarket plays about the Middle East, with its manager the author, George Colman the Younger, having had some success with his own comedy, *Turk and No Turk* (1785). The significance of the O'Keeffe and Colman plays lies in the degree of awareness both writers had of the political contexts within which their dramas were situated. In *Turk and No Turk*, the basic plot of an Englishman coming home disguised as a Turk in order to surprise his relatives is very typical of its period in encompassing within its dialogue a figuring of the range of global types Britain encountered as its empire expanded. The culture of exchange and encounter of people from remote regions, most notably typified by Omai (*c*. 1753–*c*. 1780), the first Tahitian visitor to England, had by the 1780s become a commonplace, worthy of parody on the stage. Sir Simon Simple's preposterous 'Cabinet of Curiosities' included, much to Lady Simple's chagrin, living specimens, 'people you have maintain'd in your house by way of rarities'. However, it turns out that the nobleman only accommodates other noblemen, with Colman's text unconsciously demonstrating that the reception of racial difference in late Georgian England was intersected by deference towards class boundaries, a circumstance fully cognate with the reception of the actual Turkish ambassador in 1794. Indeed, Sir Simon's 'Cabinet' was closely modelled on Sir Ashton Lever's Holophusikon museum near the Haymarket in Leicester Square, representing not only competition Colman might want to ridicule but also, in 1785, an enterprise by then financially stricken. *Turk and No Turk*'s portrayal of 'foreigners ... of the first families and professions. Tawneys of rank, and blacks of a fair reputation. Indian kings, gentoo generals, and barbarous chiefs from the friendly islands', and the 'connoisseurs coming to consult – gaping with sleep and wonder! Watching the thick lips, without hearing a word pass thro 'em – asking about their customs and manners – and finding their custom is to have no manners at all!' at Sir Simon's house says much about London as a centre of a commercial and imperial power reaching from India to Cook's Friendly Islands in the Pacific.[55]

Not least, lurking within the starkness of Colman's effortlessly racialized language, the text of *Turk and No Turk* also contains an exact understanding of the nature of Britain's relationship with the regions it encountered. As Sir Simon says to his wife by way of defending his extravagance in providing board and lodging for his multiethnic noble 'foreigners', 'We rob 'em of all their luxuries, why shou'd not the poor devils partake of ours? Zounds, I'll have 'em over in bunches, like their own black grapes, and to a good taste they'll prove as acceptable.'[56] The precision of Colman's assessment of the fractured morality of a global economy where the East is recognized as containing luxuries otherwise unobtainable in the West, except by pillage, is remarkable, not least on account of its location buried deep within the unlikely setting of *Turk and No Turk*. As with many other plays of the late Georgian era, such analyses of the morality of imperial expansion are so uncomplicated as to be almost disarming.

For Larpent carrying out his role as Examiner in 1794, the proposed staging of *Jenny's Whim* carried the risk of the Turkish ambassador seeing a fictionalized 'Emperor of Morocco' ridiculed on the stage right in front of him. Much of the effort put into maintaining and developing diplomatic, commercial and military relations with the Ottomans would be put in jeopardy. O'Keeffe's play drew upon the fullest reaches of comedy to portray the Emperor of Morocco cajoled into working in his own palace kitchens at the behest of Jenny (this was the 'Jenny's Whim' of the title). Larpent marked the entire passage for deletion:

> SCENE III. *A Chambr in the Palace, Fire, and duck roasting. The Emperor discovered sitting on a stool and turning the Spit.*
> Emperor: Pho, this is hot work I find now its better to be an Emperor than a Cook. Strange fancy this of my charmer to have her dinner dresst in her own apartment she's the most whimsical Enchanting but I must comply with all her flights or I shall never soften her mind to love me. . . .If I leave it its spoilt then I displease my Love yet I wouldn't for a Kingdom that even the meanst of my Slaves was to see me in this Ridiculous situation I must prepare to receive the Spanish Ambassador Spain's a proud Nation I must Strike him with an Idea of my Magnificence . . .

Of course, by the end of the summer of 1794, relationships between the real Emperor of Morocco and Spain were already perceived from London as strained. Worse still, O'Keeffe's farce reiterated the well-founded allegations of Barbary slaving attacks on European shipping, almost certainly one of the issues the new diplomatic links were meant to diminish. *Jenny's Whim Or The Roasted Emperor* was supposed to open showing:

> *A Beech [sic] Storm Enter Busra followed by several Moors, rolling in Trunks Chests Bales etc. (crys & shouts of Joy) . . .*

BUSRA: This Ship is a good prize, besides the Cargo, I think the Crew will make a
full shew in our Slave market Enter Moors driving in English Mariners.

Staging *Jenny's Whim* with scenes such as these, quite apart from its
portrayal of Ottoman vassal dignitaries, would have been a diplomatic
disaster, and the Haymarket farce was stopped in its tracks.

While *Jenny's Whim* was not submitted for licensing until August 1794,
the authorities would have been aware as early as May that Yusuf Agha
Effendi had begun a series of visits to London's theatres and other places of
entertainment. As it happened, this period also coincided with a series of
British victories against the French. The relationship between ideas
of nationhood and Britain's engagement in virtually non-stop military
conflicts has been stressed throughout this book. By the mid 1790s, theatres
had become adept at expressing how Britain's armed forces possessed the
ideological commitment and stoical virtue with which to mount determined and successful military campaigns. Throughout the spring and
summer of 1794, changes in military fortune meant that Yusuf Agha
Effendi was greeted with a series of dramas and spectacles underlining
British military prowess.

Right from the start of his season of playhouse visits, the material capacity
of theatres to mount, before considerable audiences, ideologically loyal
dramas is a striking feature of the physical and organizational complexity
of the contemporary theatrical assemblage. Another feature of the ambassador's visits was his apparent willingness to sponsor or endorse performances.
Whatever reward (or none) the playhouses or performers received, his
expected presence was always puffed in the newspaper advertising. On 7
May, Yusuf Agha Effendi attended a Covent Garden performance billed as
'By Desire of His Excellency the Ambassador from the Sublime Porte'. His
choice was Thomas Holcroft's *The Road to Ruin* (a play which he saw once
again in June; see below) coupled with 'a Grand New Historical Spectacle'
called *The Soldier's Festival; or, The Night Before the Battle*. The latter
appears to have been a simple variation on *The Sailor's Festival*, an
'Interlude' shown in the same playhouse on the previous day. Four days
earlier, Covent Garden had also introduced another new 'Interlude', *Naples
Bay; or, The British Seamen at Anchor*, which, one assumes, itself incorpo-
rated scenery recycled from their 3 May new piece, *Love and Honor; or,
Britannia in Full Glory at Spithead* (the latter of which is discussed in
Chapter 5). In contrast to this plethora of specifically nautical dramas,
The Soldier's Festival; or, The Night Before the Battle emphasized recent
British victories by land, probably specifically aiming at blazoning the

recent Battle of Landrecy (26 April 1794), but with the piece also apparently, wildly anachronistically winching in 'an exact Representation of The Siege of Quebec, and the Death of General Wolfe' together with the singing of 'General Wolfe's favourite Song'. Elsewhere that night, over the Thames at Astley's Amphitheatre, audiences could see the equestrian spectacle of *The Storming and Surrender of Forts Royal and Bourbon, in the Island of Martinque* followed by a 'New Pantomimical Sketch, called The Ensuing Campaign, or, The Combined Forces in Motion', which incorporated 'A Panorama of the Grand Armies'. This was followed, astonishingly, by 'A Comic Grotesque Pantomime' called *Mirth and Magic. Or, Harlequin's Whim*, featuring the music of 'Whittington and His Cat'.

In other words, this kind of mixing and fusing of different types of entertainment, many of them specifically or broadly militaristic, but with much variation and nuance across different theatres and different genres, was not uncommon. The spectacle of *The Soldier's Festival; or, The Night Before the Battle* that the Turkish ambassador witnessed, with its grafting on of material referring to the siege of Quebec, was programmed by Covent Garden with a specific rationale in mind. Their apparent concertinaing of historical sequence, where the Battle of Landrecy, one of Britain's earliest wartime victories, had reinvigorated an allusion to the siege of Quebec of 1759, can only by explained by reference to the theatrical assemblage's ability to shuffle, redeploy and represent on stage newly emergent intersections of collective memory. Topical and long-term national ideological meanings were compounded in the Georgian playhouse to a degree difficult for us to recover today but which presumably worked as a set of near-automatic temporal adjustments in the audience as they picked up inflected meanings and nuances. Indeed, even taken on its own, the celebration of Landrecy in 1794, alongside Quebec in 1759, provides a fascinating example of how non-linear historical narrative could be assimilated by audiences at an everyday level.

Although pretty unambiguously marking the success at Landrecy, as part of its *Soldier's Festival; or, The Night Before the Battle*, Covent Garden deliberately chose to refer back to the siege of Quebec. This was mainly on account of a specific historical incident which occurred a few weeks after the battle. This specificity and topicality, however, was compounded by more strategic references to military or heroic parallels from antiquity. In the programme for 6 May (not a night when the ambassador was there), *The Sailor's Festival* had been played as an afterpiece appended to a revival of Nathaniel Lee's *Alexander the Great; or, The Rival Queens* (1715), a production billing a prominent 'Grand Triumphal Entry of Alexander into

Babylon'. Such juxtapositions fulfilled straightforward ideological objectives in comparing and contrasting Britain's current circumstances against the favourable backdrop of previous imperial eras. In *The Soldier's Festival*'s staging of 'an exact Representation of The Siege of Quebec, and the Death of General Wolfe', Covent Garden may have been imitating (if not downright plagiarizing) Astley's Amphitheatre's successful 1790 'Grand Heroic and Historical Pantomime ... The Siege of Quebec; or, The Death of General Wolfe' (complete with 'English and French Soldiers, Indian Warriors, Scalpers &c'), a production possibly timed to evoke belligerently French failure at the beginnings of the Revolution.[57] However, it is much more likely that Covent Garden's *Siege of Quebec* was referencing one of the later, now obscure, incidents which occurred directly after the end of the siege of Valenciennes (13 June–28 July 1793), a significant British campaign led – more or less – by Prince Frederick, Duke of York, and later commemorated by the theatrical scene painter Philippe-Jacques de Loutherbourg's oil painting *The Siege of Valenciennes*, which was exhibited at the Historic Gallery, Pall Mall, from 2 March 1795.

Although news of the victory quickly reached London, and was rapidly (in just under two weeks) represented by Sadler's Wells as 'An Entirely New Historical ... Spectacle' called *The Honours of War; or, The Siege of Valenciennes*, news did not filter through to London that Lieutenant Colonel James Moncrieff (1744–1793) of the Royal Engineers, an important aide to the Duke of York, who had played a crucial role in the conflict, had died at the siege of Dunkirk a few weeks later in early September. Following the capitulation of Valenciennes, the Duke of York had diverted his siege army to Dunkirk, but progress there was slow and muddled. During a second, abortive, attempt to storm the town, Moncrieff was shot through the head by grapeshot on 5 September. News of the severity of his wounds was trailed in the London newspapers by 9 September, and readers were made aware of his death on the 12th, two days after his actual burial.[58] Amidst the constant flow of military incident within a swiftly moving tide of warfare, the London theatrical scene quickly reconfigured their shows.

Astley's Amphitheatre near Westminster Bridge had already been staging, since 2 September, an ambitious 'new, grand Military Spectacle' entitled *The Siege of Valenciennes; or, The Entrance of the British Troops into France*. What was special about Astley's production was that Philip Astley senior (1742–1814), who had in 1783 opened a Parisian outpost – the Amphithéâtre Astley – to match his London equestrian venue, was able to bring his own eyewitness experiences of the Valenciennes battlefield site. Following an earlier career in the army, at the age of fifty Astley re-enlisted at the outbreak of war in 1793, serving in Flanders with the Duke of York and later writing accounts of his experiences. He also took the opportunity to visit the Dunkirk and the Valenciennes battlegrounds, in the latter instance making the drawings (puffed as 'on the spot') which formed the basis of *The Siege of Valenciennes* 'Spectacle' at his Westminster Bridge premises, managed in his absence by his son, John.[59] From its very first performances, the Astley *Siege of Valenciennes* had included a representation of 'the British Battery; constructed by the ingenious Col. Moncrieff'.[60] In other words, as a result of the contingencies of war, the victory at Valenciennes – in which Moncrieff had played a prominent part in directing the siege batteries – was overshadowed by his death at Dunkirk barely a month later.

Picking out this personal tragedy as a theatrical cue, where the destiny of personal heroism could be linked to final military success, Astley's continued to perform their *Siege of Valenciennes* well into the autumn – with Moncrieff's battery featured in its billing – before fading light and the necessities of not infringing the patent-house monopolies halted the Amphitheatre's restricted season of performance.[61] Covent Garden made a similar judgement although one more subtle in its elaboration. When the Turkish ambassador saw *The Soldier's Festival* played alongside 'The Siege of Quebec, and the Death of General Wolfe', the Ottoman diplomat was witnessing a further twist to this new deformation of national history equating Wolfe's death at Quebec at the hour of victory with Moncrieff's death in the weeks following the victorious siege of Valenciennes. With both the Sadler's Wells 'Spectacle' of *The Honours of War; or, The Siege of Valenciennes* and Astley's longer-running *Siege of Valenciennes* already well known to London audiences, Covent Garden's incorporation of the Wolfe piece as an adjunct to *The Soldier's Festival* allowed them to modulate between topical pieces while retaining the broader context of developing some sense of a larger national ideological purpose in which battlefield military success could also portray a native resilience able to accommodate individual setbacks and defeats.

In other words, the theatrical spectacles, interludes and 'loyal effusions' Yusuf Agha Effendi attended would have revealed a metropolis with an enormous built theatrical infrastructure capable of representing Britain's changing military fortunes and either consolidating them against the heroics of antiquity or swiftly modulating them to encompass the unexpected and topical. With his background in the Ottoman admiralty, and assisted by his Turkish interpreters, it is very probable the ambassador would have understood the full significance and topical nuances of the 'The Siege of Quebec, and the Death of General Wolfe' when it played in front of him in tandem with *The Soldier's Festival*.

As May 1794 passed into June, however, the military situation was about to change. Out in the Atlantic, on 1 June the British and French fleets locked in combat in the battle which became known as The Glorious First of June (or 'The Third Battle of Ushant', as the French termed it). Although London newspapers were aware by 31 May from Admiralty dispatches that the fleets had sighted each other, with one British ship – forced to abandon the engagement early due to damage – bringing fragmentary news back by 7 June, full reports of the victory were not published until 9 June. In the middle of this momentous engagement, Yusuf Agha Effendi visited Covent Garden. On 3 June he saw, for the second time, Thomas Holcroft's *Road to Ruin* (1792), presumably oblivious of the author's radical political connections, which were to lead to his indictment for high treason that summer. This was accompanied by a 'Pantomimic Ballet', devised by James Byrne (1756–1845), called *The Shipwreck; or, French Ingratitude*, a development of Byrne's October 1790 *The Provocation!* (discussed in Chapter 5).[62]

Amidst this intricate multiplicity of developing programming, the particular version of *The Shipwreck; or, French Ingratitude* the ambassador witnessed was one newly revised to cover the capture of Martinique from the French in March 1794. Of course, the morphing of the theatrical genotype is very clear in this example, with the May 1794 *Shipwreck* a distant derivation from *Nootka Sound; Or, Britain Prepar'd* of 1790. As billed, the ballet pantomime now included a spectacle showing 'an Engagement between an English and a French Man of War, a Shipwreck, and a Grand Military Procession, as it passed, when the French Colours, taken by the British Army, were conveyed from St James's to St Paul's Cathedral'. The ceremony of the captured flags was held at St Paul's on 17 May, when the French colours captured at Martinique were taken by military procession and put on show to the public after they had first been presented to George III at St James' Palace.[63] In other words, the Covent Garden performances provided materialized extensions of public memory of this event through reiterated, high-density audience and performer populations. Just how thoroughly and easily this type of revision could be incorporated into Covent Garden's working schedules can be considered by taking note of the casual reference to how the spectacle portrayed the procession '*as it passed*' (my italics) on its way to St Paul's. Some of these entertainments could be very quickly mounted because, as most probably in this case, they redeployed existing stage properties. The scenes used in the 'spectacle' contained within *The Shipwreck* probably redeployed streetscapes dating at least as far back as the spring 1789 *St. George's Day; or, Britons Rejoice!*, which had needed to show the environs of St Paul's.

From a theoretical perspective, quite apart from this constant mutation of the original theatrical genotypes emerging in the possibility spaces of successive Covent Garden performances, one of the capacities structured into scenery of this type was its ability as a material signifier to reference other signifieds. With a two-thirds-full house of around 2,000 people, the Covent Garden component of the assemblage was a very efficient distributor of ideological messages. As well as this type of simple incorporation of old scenery in new dramas, entertainments produced to illustrate one event produced a collective knowledge network in the audience which could then be taken as the starting point for other entertainments. Again, this capacity for emergence, stored in the new performance of reiterated, actualized, texts is a parameter embodied within these types of theatrical assemblages.

One of the heroes of the Martinique campaign implicitly referenced in *The Shipwreck; or, French Ingratitude* was Captain Robert Faulknor (1763–1795), a figure already discussed in Chapter 5 with respect to Covent Garden's later 'Musical Interlude', *The Death of Captain Faulkner* [*sic*]*; or, British Heroism* of May 1795.[64] In the action at Martinique in March 1794 which resulted in the capture of the French colours, Faulknor had landed from his sloop, the *Zebra*, onto the beach below the crucial tactical obstacle of Fort Louis and had then helped take the fortress despite being hit by grapeshot. Although there is nothing to suggest this incident formed part of *The Shipwreck; or, French Ingratitude*, the performances act as a series of complex assemblages, storing narratives of British military success ready to be rematerialized in later performances, deterritorialized of their original meaning and recoded at their new performance venue with new topicalities of meaning. Other components of the assemblage similarly stored the same narrative, reinforcing its presence although lacking in immediacy and density. Such an example would be the painting, *The Capture of Fort Louis, Martinique, 20 March 1794* (1795; oil on canvas, National Maritime Museum, Greenwich) by the Royal Academician William Anderson. Again, the time lag between the theatrical production and the painting is noticeable. In Faulknor's case, by the time Anderson had completed his painting, the naval officer was already dead, shot in the skirmish with the French off Guadaloupe in January 1795, an event which had already been the subject of *The Death of Captain Faulkner* [*sic*]*; or, British Heroism*. These transportations of meaning across materialized performances at specific dates are excellent examples of how knowledge and reputations about military exploits were stored and relayed to outlier networks, including the eventual spectators of the painting. As with Colonel Moncrieff's death at Dunkirk, while stage representations could be swiftly modified and morphed, the painting took time to catch up.

Back in the spring of 1794, however, what Yusuf Agha Effendi would have witnessed in the new variant *The Shipwreck; or, French Ingratitude* would have been an impressive celebration of the results of British naval military power in the West Indies. From a British perspective, the Ottoman ambassador's witnessing of *The Shipwreck* ballet – together with the actual ceremony of processing captured French flags through the streets of London – would all have acted as a reminder of how British naval power could be projected to the other side of the Atlantic. As it happened, within a few days the military situation itself underwent rapid change as news of Howe's victory of 1 June flooded into London, but, meanwhile, the playgoing and other activities of the ambassador continued, with the newspapers regularly reporting issues as diverse as his fondness for women at the Mansion House ball in April and, by August, picking up the story of an unnamed Turkish 'domestic' attached to his entourage whose gold watch and money were stolen by 'a *nymph* of the Public Haram' at Hungerford Market.[65]

Two days after he had seen *The Road to Ruin* and *The Shipwreck; or, French Ingratitude* on 3 June, *The World* newspaper reported an apparently flirtatious encounter in Kensington Gardens between the ambassador and Lady Eglantine Wallace – later the author of the banned play *The Whim* (1795) – before he attended Sydney Smith's dancing 'breakfast' on the frigate *Diamond* the next day.[66] By 13 June all the London newspapers were carrying reports of the Glorious First of June victory, and on that day too the Turkish ambassador made another visit to Covent Garden. On this occasion he saw Hugh Kelly's *School for Wives* (1774), a standard repertoire piece but now pieced together with an elaborately detailed and referenced 'Loyal Effusion' based on the Howe victory. Kelly's drama, as much as anything else, provides a good idea of the kind of modernizing Western perspectives on the social roles of women which was not only an integral aspect of a playhouse context in which female actors readily became celebrities in their own right, but also a reminder that much late eighteenth-century drama was, in fits and starts, debating and refiguring new roles for women.

In the case of Kelly's *School for Wives*, Yusuf Agha Effendi would have encountered not only an example of the recurrent portrayals in Georgian drama of quarrelsome Irishmen (here the duel-prone lawyer, Leeson, and his manservant, Connolly) but also, more unusually, an example of a growing range of outspoken female characters. Kelly's *School for Wives* not only flirted with infidelity when Belville attempts to seduce his niece, Miss Leeson, a would-be actress he hopes to impress, but the play also featured from the outset an assertive female role. As was the custom, the Prologue was delivered by a male actor, but, in *The School for Wives*, the speech is disrupted by an actress. In the original production, Elizabeth Younge (who played Miss Leeson) interrupts the Prologue in mid delivery – here played by Thomas King (1730–1805), who doubled as the comically militaristic General Savage:

YOUNGE: Pray give me leave – I've something now to say.
KING: Is't at the School for Wives, you're taught this way? The School for Husbands teaches to obey.[67]

Younge's interruption crystallized emerging metropolitan attitudes to women's new social roles. Within the reception model, this performance captures Yusuf Agha Effendi's exposure to the Western changes in gender roles gradually emerging in everyday life, and for which he was an important and official channel for communication back to Constantinople. Younge's stage-grabbing female ('I've something now to say') revealed a far different mode of female conduct than that which prevailed in general in the Ottoman Empire.

In addition to this exposure to new attitudes towards gender, Yusuf Agha Effendi would also have been impressed by that night's 'Loyal Effusion'. With the news of the outcome of the Glorious First of June naval engagement now disseminated throughout London via the newspapers, the battle's projection on stage would have materialized through its spectacle – suited to non-native speakers – the conduct of the two embattled navies. The 'Loyal Effusion' took the form of 'a Representation of the Engagement and Defeat of the French Navy, By the British Fleet, Under the Command of Lord Howe, on the Glorious First of June; With the bringing in [of the ships] La Juste, Sans Pareille, L'America, L'Achille, Northumberland, le Impeteux, and the Sinking of Le Vengeur – With the Song and Chorus of Rule Britannia'.[68] No doubt, Covent Garden's 'Loyal Effusion' yet again recycled scenery from *The Shipwreck; or, French Ingratitude*, but this time the British victory was on a more strategic scale than was the case with quickly retaken Caribbean islands. Of the various ships represented, the 'Sinking of Le Vengeur' (or 'Vengeur du Peuple', an old vessel renamed to suit republican tastes) gave rise to the legend of the crew going down with their ship. A year later, after the time lag seemingly typical for such paintings, 'Le Vengeur' became the principal subject in de Loutherbourg's picture, *The Battle of the First of June, 1794* (1795; oil on canvas, National Maritime Museum, Greenwich). With Britain's capture of the six prize ships and the sinking of *Le Vengeur*, the Turkish ambassador would have been left in no doubt as to Britain's ability to win a large-scale naval conflict in the mid Atlantic.

Not long after seeing the spectacle of the captured ships in Covent Garden's 'Loyal Effusion', as the winter-season houses closed, the Turkish ambassador went to Astley's Amphitheatre and witnessed, almost inevitably, yet another 'Naval Scene' projecting British glory.[69] What the Turkish ambassador was exposed to until his recall in late 1795, yet not by any design or prior arrangement, was the ability of London's theatres to demonstrate the ideological cohesion of Britain and a remarkable ability to develop, revise and redefine its own history. As the war unfolded, oscillating between defeats and sudden victories, London's ability rapidly to materialize and narrate the national destiny through stage representation was enabled by the massive physical and organizational structure of its theatres. Although the entire episode has been overlooked, this chapter has captured one strategic figure, Yusuf Agha Effendi, the Ottoman ambassador to London, at an important moment when the Muslim East was making diplomatic overtures to Europe, while, with infinitely more urgency, Britain sought military and commercial alliances capable of outflanking its French enemies in the eastern Mediterranean and the overland routes to the Indian empire.

Above all, what the ambassador experienced in the playhouse was an ideological assemblage of assemblages. The multiplicity of the plays Yusuf Agha Effendi witnessed – together with the dramas discussed in Chapter 5 – constituted a theatrical assemblage constructed (and carefully sharpened by the interventions of censoring dramas such as *Jenny's Whim*) around the ideological basis of loyalism. As DeLanda writes, although it is a commonplace-enough proposition for a country perceiving itself under the threat of invasion, 'The reality or threat of armed conflicts is itself a powerful territorializing force, making people rally behind their governments and close ranks with each other.'[70] Loyalism was clearly a reiterated expressive component of these particular, mid-1790s theatrical assemblages, with the non-human agency of monopoly ensuring the economic viability of the two patent playhouses that efficiently materialized these expressions before hundreds of thousands of the London population annually. Ultimately, whatever the symbolic registers of the plays, individuals needed to be willing to die for their country. From *The Soldier's Festival*, with its specially added 'Siege of Quebec, and the Death of General Wolfe' of 1794 to *The Death of Captain Faulkner; or, British Heroism* that he went to in 1795, the Ottoman ambassador would have encountered, exactly as outlined here and in Chapter 5, a theatrical assemblage of fully materialized social complexity fully committed to representing British distinctiveness and military valour.

CHAPTER SEVEN

Historicizing the theatrical assemblage: Marie Antoinette and the theatrical queens

On another of his theatrical excursions, on the night of 10 May 1794 the Turkish ambassador went to Covent Garden to see *Hamlet*. That evening it was paired with a now obscure one-act drama by Edward Jerningham, *Margaret of Anjou: An Historical Interlude* (1777). Hamlet was played by the Irish actor and painter, Alexander Pope (1763–1835), a Covent Garden stalwart, with the whole evening forming the programme of his benefit for the 1793–4 season. The title role in the three-handed *Margaret of Anjou* was played by his wife, Elizabeth Younge (1739×45–1797), then billed in the style of the day as 'Mrs. Pope'. Since the entire evening's programme was advertised as performed 'At the Particular Desire of His Excellency the Ambassador from the Sublime Porte', and Alexander Pope was to play Hamlet for just that one night, it is possible both pieces were, exactly as their billing claimed, played as specific requests of the ambassador. What is certain is that, until 2 May, Pope had been advertised to play the Earl in *The Countess of Salisbury*.[1] Although Pope's Hamlet went off without comment – he tended to specialize in serious roles and this portrayal would have been routine for him – it is Elizabeth Pope's portrayal of Margaret of Anjou, wife of Henry VI of England, which is the most interesting feature of that night's bill.

The conjunction of *Margaret of Anjou* and Yusuf Agha Effendi is a remarkable example of the materialization of a new reception context for Jerningham's seventeen-year-old drama, a context that night reconfigured and deterritorialized as part of a post-French Revolutionary, self-determinedly pro-Ottoman, theatrical assemblage. Whatever its original performance meaning, that night *Margaret of Anjou* spoke powerfully of the fate of Marie Antoinette, Queen of France, mirroring the emotive rhetoric of Edmund Burke's *Reflections on the Revolution in France* (1790) within a deterritorialized context of a playhouse location where at least one individual within its assemblage population, the Ottoman ambassador, embodied British hopes for vital new strategic alliances little imagined in Burke's ruminations on the French queen.

Although now neglected, *Margaret of Anjou* and other contemporary repertoire plays associated with Henry VI's queen comprise a component of the theatrical assemblage whose stagings and contemporary resonances have been overlooked. While Chapters 5 and 6 gave some idea of the density, stability and solidarity of London's theatrical assemblage in the mid 1790s, with all of these properties capable of synthesis through examination of their exterior relations, this chapter proposes that the extent and organizational complexity of this particular assemblage requires interpretive revisions substantially modifying recent scholarship.[2]

The operation of the assemblage as a market provides some kind of preliminary purchase on the material status of this extraordinary performance of *Margaret of Anjou*. At that time, Elizabeth Pope was Covent Garden's highest-paid actress, the theatre's account books showing that, at the end of the 1793–4 season, she was earning £18 per week in contrast to her husband Alexander's £10 per week. Situated at the top of the benefit-night pecking order, Elizabeth, unlike her husband, had already taken her benefit in early April 1794, playing in George Colman the Younger's *The Jealous Wife* (1775) coupled with *The Sailor's Festival*, Covent Garden's alternating version of *The Soldier's Festival*, the show which a month or so later would be extensively upgraded to form the basis of *The Glorious First of June*. Their choice of the *Hamlet/Margaret of Anjou* programme was a case of the crowd-drawing wife supporting the lesser-talented husband, although, of course, they were both operating as a thespian unit, maximizing their combined leverage on the monopolistic system of the London playhouses. While Covent Garden's accounts (as a matter of their accountancy practices) do not reveal the benefit-night house charges, so making accurate comparisons difficult, Elizabeth's benefit was much more financially successful than that of her husband, with the latter's night triggering a £52. 7s. 0d. deficiency payment.[3]

Billed before her marriage as 'Miss Younge', Elizabeth Pope's career stretched back to Garrick's Drury Lane. In 1774 she originated the role of Miss Leeson in Hugh Kelly's *School for Wives*, the play the Turkish ambassador went to see on 16 June. In the early 1780s, and before her marriage to Alexander Pope, poems addressed to her beauty and professional powers as an actress had been written by John Philip Kemble ('*Eliza*, Nature's Daughter, makes us feel').[4] The previous season, she had performed *Margaret of Anjou* on 18 March 1793, pairing it with her role as Lady

Amaranth in John O'Keeffe's *Wild Oats*. Although records do not survive to give her income for that season, other account books reveal that in her benefit for the 1791–2 season (when she risked playing Medea) she not only took the first spot of the season but also earned £115. 17*s*. in benefit receipts.[5]

The day before her husband's benefit, a significant piece of contextual information concerning the contemporary reception of *Margaret of Anjou* had been carried in *The Oracle and Public Advertiser*. In the lead-up to a benefit night, the Popes would have been especially assiduous at forewarning friendly newspapers such as *The Oracle* about the contents of their benefits, probably not only giving them advance information of the Turkish ambassador's attendance ('the presence of the Turkish Ambassador, will no doubt occasion an overflow to-morrow evening at Covent-Garden Theatre'), but also supplying the full contents of the playbill. Commenting on *Margaret of Anjou* as a 'Monologue, relieved at intervals by music, and recited by Mrs. Pope', *The Oracle* crucially went on to say that 'it gains, no doubt, an additional interest from the resemblance of the sorrows of MARGARET to those of the late QUEEN OF FRANCE!'[6]

On the night of the ambassador's visit in May 1794, with Marie Antoinette having been executed on 16 October 1793, the cultural meaning of *Margaret of Anjou* had suddenly shifted. Although now neglected, *Margaret of Anjou* exemplifies the capacity for reception meanings to change in relation to different temporal locations. As *The Oracle* put it, although in the repertoire for nearly twenty years, in a little over six months *Margaret of Anjou* was suddenly perceived to bear 'resemblance of the sorrows of MARGARET to those of the late QUEEN OF FRANCE!' That the Popes had fully appreciated the possibilities of this new context, even before Marie Antoinette's execution, is borne out by Covent Garden's licensing on 16 March 1793 (two days before Elizabeth Pope's benefit performance in the 1792–3 season) of 'Additions to the Historical Interlude of Margaret of Anjou'. As Jerningham was still actively writing for the theatre (his new work, *The Siege of Berwick*, ran for five nights at Covent Garden from 13 November 1793), this version is likely to have been an authorial revision. Although Marie Antoinette was still alive when the text of the revision was submitted to the Lord Chamberlain, Louis XVI had been executed on 21 January. The 'Additions' voice Margaret's isolation rather more clearly ('Dethron'd, oppress'd, forsaken of all hope'), but substantial new text written for the Robber provides a remarkable overview of conservative British perspectives on the Revolution: 'Behold how Anarchy with Giant steps stalks o'er the trembling Land! At her approach, the sumptuous Palace falls – The Norman Castle stretches its lonely ruin down the

Mountain's side – With louder vehemence the civil Deluge rolls, and rushes thro' the portals of the Sanctuary – The Temples are prophaned; the hallowed Walls dismantled, the Choirs deformed; the Altars overthrown, – The Ministers, amidst their awful duties, massacred! Their snowy Vestments drench'd in blood.'[7]

This new 1793 acting version of the 1777 *Margaret of Anjou* is another example of how theatrical texts modulate, diverging and developing from their original genotype ready to be reterritorialized by new audiences in determinable temporal and spatial locations where new political and ideological meanings are in the process of emerging. As for retrieving a sense of contemporary public reaction to the fate of the French monarchs as exhibited by theatre audiences, the diary of the censor's wife, Anna Larpent, provides a remarkably vivid account of the news of the execution of Louis XVI and how it reached Covent Garden during what was billed to be a Royal Command performance of Frederick Reynolds' new comedy, *Notoriety* (1793) (paired with Fielding's *Tom Thumb*) just two days after the actual event: 'We went to see the Royal Family at the play. Scarce were we entered when we were informed that the family did not come to the play on account of the news from France. This News was that of the Kings Murder – The Audience was Confused, most were agitated, others unfeeling yet scared from seeing others feel. The manager wished to stop the play – but the house was too much disappointed at the Absence of the family to hear further disappointment. The play was not given up. yᵉ Curtain rose "God Save the King" sang. The effect was Awful.'[8]

However, perhaps the most significant context for this aspect of *Margaret of Anjou*'s likely impact after 1789 comes in the reassessment which must now be given to Edmund Burke's famous description of Marie Antoinette's maltreatment in his *Reflections on the Revolution in France*. While there is no evidence Burke ever attended a performance of *Margaret of Anjou*, its role in providing a template for Burke's theatricalized description of Marie Antoinette in the *Reflections* needs to be assimilated as a consequence of Burke's awareness of the cultural possibilities of the contemporary London theatrical assemblage, of which he was an enthusiastic audience member.

Elizabeth Younge had been performing *Margaret of Anjou* as one of her regular benefit-night pieces since 1777 when Jerningham wrote it for her to premiere at Drury Lane, perhaps specifically tailoring it to be used in her benefit performances.[9] In his short introduction printed in his *Fugitive Poetical Pieces* (1778), Jerningham specifically praises Younge's 'excellence of acting' and the 'spirit and colouring' she brought to its premiere; indeed, its genesis may have been the product of a real-life romantic relationship between author and actress.[10] In any event, *Margaret of Anjou* stayed in Younge's repertoire from then on, but the 10 May 1794 performance was apparently her last. It is difficult to quantify the number of performances she gave of *Margaret of Anjou* during that seventeen-year period. Quite early in her career, like many others able to leverage their careers through their status on London's monopolistic stage, she established a pattern of summer provincial touring, taking advantage of the patent houses' closed season. Between 1771 and 1778, for example, she is known to have made tours to Bristol, Edinburgh, Birmingham, Liverpool, and Cork (*ODNB*). A posting in London's *Public Advertiser* of an adulatory poem commemorating what appears to be an Edinburgh performance of *Margaret of Anjou* in the summer of 1786 ('Thy mind, like hers, with inborn genius great, / Impresses, speaks and dignifies the Queen') suggests that Jerningham's interlude continued to form part of her regular touring repertoire, perhaps particularly where she was able to negotiate a provincial benefit night.[11] If anything, *Margaret of Anjou* was likely to have increased in its attractiveness after her 1785 marriage to Alexander Pope, because the couple were able to double up roles for benefit performances, as they did on the night the Turkish ambassador attended. *Margaret of Anjou*'s longevity in Younge's repertoire and its ability to acquire new cultural meanings through repeated performances means that it should be factored into representations of that other queen from France, Marie Antoinette, in the context of Edmund Burke's celebrated description of her in *Reflections on the Revolution in France*.

Burke's highly theatricalized description of the forced removal of the French royal family from Versailles has become a critical *cause célèbre*:

> History will record, that on the morning of 6 October 1789, the king and *queen* of France, after a day of confusion, alarm, dismay, and slaughter, lay down, under the pledged security of public faith, to indulge nature in a few hours of respite, and troubled melancholy repose. From this sleep the *queen* was first startled by the voice of the centinel at her door, who cried out to her, to save herself by flight – that this was the last proof of fidelity he could give – that they were upon him, and he was dead. Instantly he was cut down. A band of cruel ruffians and assassins, reeking with his blood, rushed into the chamber of the queen, and pierced with an hundred strokes of bayonets and poniards the bed, from whence this persecuted woman had but just had time to fly almost naked, and through ways unknown to the murderers had escaped to seek refuge at the feet of a king and husband, not secure of his own life for a moment.[12]

If nothing else, Burke's description – taken together with his explanation later in the book (quoted below) that his responses to this event mirrored the affective power of Garrick's or Siddons' tragic acting – is an important expression of the pre-eminent cultural status of the rhetoric and discourse of theatricality in Georgian metropolitan society. With sales of the *Reflections* reaching 18,000–20,000 copies by its twelfth edition in 1792, and with much contemporary excerpting of its contents and ideological critiquing, Burke's description of the French queen has become a kind of founding moment of modern historiography, synthesizing different branches of both sympathetic loyalism and radical scepticism about the national foundations of monarchy, religion and the social order.[13]

On the Turkish ambassador's night, there was the usual mixing of genres in the programme together with, at least partly dictated by the economics of benefit performances, a doubling of some roles. With the Queen in *Hamlet* played by Pope's wife (nearly twenty years his elder), a 'dirge' was added to the last act and a number of miscellaneous songs were also performed that night, including some by Charles Dibdin, with the evening concluding with a ballet by the ubiquitous Byrne.[14] As well as Mrs Pope playing the Queen in *Hamlet* and Margaret of Anjou, and her husband playing Hamlet and the Robber in *Margaret of Anjou*, the piece's one remaining part (that of the Prince) was played by the juvenile actress, Miss Standen (*fl.* 1790–9).[15] Not only was this a carefully constructed programme but also the Popes might even have prompted its new political context of the French queen's death as a point of comment to *The Oracle* newspaper. Certainly, they needed to maximize their audience. Georgian theatre was constructed around the simple proposition that audiences paid cash up front, the basic arrangement which made acting as attractive to provincial *ad hoc* strollers as it did to well-established patent house performers. Under the benefit-night system, actors hired the theatre for their night. Managing costs so as to increase profits was axiomatic to taking a benefit. By doubling up their roles for *Hamlet* and *Margaret of Anjou*, Pope and his wife minimized their expenditure to other actors. Miss Standen's role, for example, would probably have required only a child's rate of pay and, of course, it is entirely possible the Popes' receipts were boosted by money or gifts from Yusuf Agha Effendi.

Although the Turkish ambassador's 'Particular Desire' to see a performance of *Hamlet* is interesting enough (and might be viewed as a lucky excursion from the season of patriotic interludes he had embarked on), Jerningham's long-forgotten *Margaret of Anjou* ('with Alterations and Additions, interspersed with Music, after the manner of Rousseau's *Pygmalion*') represents one of the most recognizable models for Burke's influential description of the forsaken and victimized Marie Antoinette in *Reflections on the Revolution in France*. Modern understanding of Burke's theatrical rhetoric in the *Reflections*, particularly the Marie Antoinette passage, has been impelled by a series of major critical insights begun in the essays of Frans De Bruyn, Tom Furness and Christopher Reid gathered in Steven Blakemore's *Burke and the French Revolution* (1992).[16] The extract above, together with Burke's further comments in the *Reflections* comparing his emotional responses to the memory of seeing Garrick's and Siddons' tragic acting has helped situate Burke's *Reflections* firmly within the context of contemporary rhetorics and cultures of theatre:

> Some tears might be drawn from me, if such a spectacle were exhibited on the stage. I should be truly ashamed of finding in myself that superficial, theatric sense of painted distress, whilst I could exult over it in real life. With such a perverted mind, I could never venture to shew my face at a tragedy. People would think the tears that Garrick formerly, or that Siddons not long since, have extorted from me, were the tears of hypocrisy; I should know them to be the tears of folly.[17]

While it would be an exaggeration to say that all recent studies of Burke's rhetoric stem from the notoriety of these two passages, even a cursory glance at recent research demonstrates that they have generated an unusually high number of inquiries.[18] The overall position is best summarized by Anne Mallory: 'From Thomas Paine to the present day, critics have sought the key to Burke's overdetermined political stance in the theatricality of the *Reflections*.'[19]

Worryingly, some recent studies of Burke fail to appreciate the sheer volume and diversity of eighteenth-century theatre. Some have considered Shakespeare the only source of his dramatic allusion.[20] Others have verged on the simplistic.[21] Occasionally, reviewers imagine Edmund Burke (1729–1797) witnessed the acting of Edmund Kean (1789–1833).[22] Antagonistic contemporaries such as Tom Paine quickly learned to view his writing as a 'dramatic performance', 'very well calculated for theatrical representation', while his early biographers similarly noted that 'The amusement in which he most delighted was the theatre.'[23] However, despite Christopher Reid's ground-breaking essay of 1992, little further has been added about Burke and the London stage. Of course, long before the *Reflections*, Burke's theatrical rhetorical style and personal connections with London theatre were well known. By the time of the Warren Hastings trial in 1788 and Burke's descriptions of the atrocities committed by Devi Singh at Rangpur, his oratory was already drawing many figures connected with the theatre.[24] The Devi Singh speech was said to have caused Mrs Sheridan to faint, while another contemporary commentator originated the detail that, on the same occasion, Mrs Siddons was seen to be in tears.[25] Burke had known Siddons personally, at least as early as 1784 when he was reported to have taken a close interest in the progress of Reynolds' painting, *Mrs. Siddons as the Tragic Muse*. Nor was it only celebrity actresses who came to hear him. In a typical mix of contemporary politics, theatre, sociability and the concerns of empire, in February 1788 Elizabeth Inchbald, taking a day off from acting in the Covent Garden company, attended 'from nine till four at the Trial of Mr. Hastings' before going on to see the East India Company director James Cobb's new comic opera, *Love in the East*, at the rival Drury Lane theatre.[26]

Burke's reference to Siddons in the *Reflections* implies that he saw her act fairly recently ('Siddons not long since ... extorted from me ... tears'). Almost at face value, this has been sufficient to fix her as the sole Burkean tragic muse. Certainly, Burke's tearful response correlates with well-corroborated, eyewitness accounts of Siddons' affective power. Siddons was undoubtedly an unusually powerful actress. A week before seeing Siddons in October 1783 and observing a nearby member of the audience swoon, the future American president, John Quincy Adams, had attended a Drury Lane *Hamlet* and thought it 'not well acted', ascribing this to a vein of 'affectation throughout the actors', their delivery sometimes inaudible and taking a quarter of an hour to speak twenty lines.[27] Performances by other actresses, such as Mary Stephens Wells (referred to above), who praised Siddons' 'every Gesture, Movement, look Divine' at her own benefit in April 1784 on the same stage, serve to remind us that '[E]very social entity is shown to emerge from the interactions among entities operating at a smaller scale.' In other words, repeated or reiterated performances (particularly those which are textually modulating) alter the overall configuration of the theatrical assemblage.[28] In their several ways, both Adams and Wells alert modern readers to Siddons as a contemporary acting phenomenon, but, even in Wells' example, it is clear that the London stage was continually evolving, precisely developing as an assemblage of assemblages reactive to changes in contemporary taste, manners and politics as well as, not least, different career phases. Even when measured against the yardstick of some of her greatest roles, as in Garrick's Isabella, Siddons ultimately took her turn with those who, like Wells, were tackling the challenge of regaining their professional confidence and building their own careers in the shadow of Siddons.

With Siddons having reached national status only after 1782, and with a miscarriage and illness meaning that she missed the winter season of 1789–90 (which opened mid September), Burke's last chance to have seen her act on the professional stage before he began writing the *Reflections* would have been no later than 11 May 1789, when she appeared as Juliet in *Romeo and Juliet* at Drury Lane.[29] On that occasion (her benefit night), she reappeared at the end of the evening, after the farce, dressed as Britannia ('imagine the astonishment of the spectators, when ... she sat down in the exact attitude of Britannia as impressed upon our copper coin') to recite an ode specially written by the radical Della Cruscan poet, Robert Merry, to mark the King's return to mental health.[30] It seems unlikely to have provoked the kind of emotions Burke recollected in the *Reflections*. Christopher Reid was the first to note that Siddons remembered Burke's attending her performances. The post-Garrick stage still placed Shakespeare as a staple rather than as an icon, and Siddons' tragic acting did not always refer to her performances of Shakespeare. Reid's essay is a valuable reminder of the roles with which Siddons was most often associated: 'If she could be said to have had a typical part it was that of a virtuous matron, often separated from her husband by force of circumstance and exposed to the threats of violent, lustful, and ambitious men.' Siddons' roles of this type included Calista in Nicholas Rowe's *The Fair Penitent* (1703), the title role in Rowe's *Tragedy of Jane Shore* (1714) and Euphrasia in Arthur Murphy's *The Grecian Daughter* (1772).[31]

Indeed, of the roles that made Siddons famous, none seem to approximate the mixture of personal predicament and national allusion suggested in the description of Marie Antoinette at Versailles in the *Reflections*. Nevertheless, Burke obviously considered as a basic assumption of his writing that the heroic dimensions of Marie Antoinette's plight referenced his readers' knowledge of contemporary drama. However, many of Siddons' most famous roles do not readily equate with Marie Antoinette's predicament as queen. In *Isabella; or, The Fatal Marriage*, Isabella's victimhood is all too readily acknowledged and becomes her *modus operandi* throughout the play:

> Let Women all take Warning at my Fate;
> Never resolve, or think they can be safe,
> Within the Reach and Tongue of tempting Men.
> Oh! had I never seen my *Biron*'s Face,
> Had he not tempted me, I had not fall'n.[32]

At the end of the play, Isabella suffers violence at her own hands, stabbing herself to death. As Christopher Reid notes, Siddons' roles often portrayed nobility in suffering, gendering it as the resilient and stoical trait of the female.[33] In other roles, however, Siddons played more resistant and triumphant women. Siddons' role of Euphrasia in Murphy's *The Grecian Daughter* involved her killing Dionysus, the tyrant, with a concealed dagger (in an etching to Bell's edition of 1785, the moment of her drawing the weapon is captioned, 'Now one glorious effort!'), thereby releasing Rome's slaves and restoring their natural rights:

> (*Stabs him.*) Dionysus: Detested fiend! – Thus by a woman's hand! – (*He falls.*)
> Euphrasia: Yes . . .
> A woman's vengeance tow'rs above her sex . . .
> Behold, all Sicily behold! – The point
> Glows with the tyrant's blood. Ye slaves . . .
> . . . the blow for freedom
> Gives you the rights of men![34]

Even in these two plays, outstanding vehicles for Siddons' tragic acting, it is clear they are divergent enough to give ample scope for not only a passionate demeanour but also the syntax of rhetorical gestures best encapsulated by Wells' flattering Epilogue comment that 'Siddons pictures Isabella's Woes / In every Gesture, Movement, look Divine.'

   None of these dramas, however, quite seem to match the circumstances of the female isolation or sheer brutality of the incident at Versailles or to capture its resonance for the future of British constitutional monarchy. The exact connection Burke seems to have made between recollecting the pathetic and melodramatic power of Siddons and the predicament of Marie Antoinette seems to lie in Jerningham's *Margaret of Anjou: An Historical Interlude* (1777). Jerningham's source was David Hume's *The History of England, from the Invasion of Julius Caesar to the Revolution in 1688* (1763). Hume's enormously popular *History* described the events of 1462, during the turmoil of the Wars of the Roses, when Margaret was trying to restore her husband, Henry VI, to the throne. After landing unsuccessfully in Northumberland, she escaped capture in the vicinity of Bamburgh Castle before being forced to flee to Flanders with her son, Prince Edward. According to some of the sources, she owed her escape to a robber she met in the Northumberland forests. With Margaret and Henry well known to have been forced to spend many years apart, it is not difficult to see how Hume's description acquired new cultural parameters given Marie Antoinette's circumstances in October 1789:

> The fate of the unfortunate royal family, after this defeat, was very singular. Margaret, flying with her son into a forest, where she endeavoured to conceal herself, was beset, during the darkness of the night, by robbers, who either ignorant or regardless of her quality, despoiled her of her rings and jewels,

and treated her with the utmost indignity. The partition of this rich booty raised a quarrel among them; and while their attention was thus engaged, she took the opportunity of making her escape with her son into the thickest of the forest, where she wandered for some time, over-spent with hunger and fatigue, and sunk with terror and affliction. While in this wretched condition, she saw a robber approach with his naked sword; and finding that she had no means of escape, she suddenly embraced the resolution of trusting entirely for protection to his faith and generosity. She advanced towards him; and presenting to him the young prince, called out to him, *Here, my friend, I commit to your care the safety of your King's son.* The man, whose humanity and generous spirit had been obscured, but not entirely lost, by his vicious course of life, was struck with the singularity of the event, and charmed with the confidence reposed in him; and he vowed, not only to abstain from all injury against the princess, but to devote himself entirely to her safety and protection. By this means she dwelt some time concealed in the forest, and was at last conducted to the sea-coast, whence she made her escape into Flanders.[35]

At just about every point, Margaret of Anjou's circumstances contrast illuminatingly with those of Marie Antoinette as described by Burke. Separated from their husbands, both queens are at the mercy of armed men. One is the queen of France; the other is the French queen of England. Both are victims of struggles to control kingdoms. But there are also crucial differences. In the context of Burke's *Reflections*, these differences point to the key characteristics which defined their distinctive and collective national sentiment.

The most vivid of these contrasts is that whereas the 'centinel' of Marie Antoinette, who 'cried out to her, to save herself by flight', was 'Instantly . . . cut down', in *Margaret of Anjou* the confrontation between queen and Robber quickly moves from the threat of violence ('Give me thy treasure, or I'll slay the Child') to the provision of protection and assistance, despite the Robber's own desperate circumstances: 'Thanks to my God / I'm not so lost in vice, so deep-ingulph'd / In woe, but that my Sovereign's distress / Obliterates my own.'[36] In the new context of the French Revolution, the British perception of which was so influentially shaped by Burke's *Reflections*, Jerningham's three-handed interlude appeared to dramatize sharply both the similarities and the differences between the positions of two isolated queens threatened with physical violence, danger to their children and the loss of their husbands and state.

However, it is not simply that Marie Antoinette's execution in October 1793 had re-evaluated *Margaret of Anjou*'s meaning along the lines *The Oracle and Public Advertiser* implied. It is probable that the extensive sales and distribution of Burke's *Reflections* in early 1790s Britain would also have helped resituate Jerningham's piece, but only as part of what Anne Mallory has queried as Burke's bafflingly ambiguous positions: 'Is Burke writing tragedy or comedy? making history or plays? His manic self-presentation makes it difficult to know.'[37] However, the presence of the Ottoman ambassador in the May 1794 Covent Garden audience was a powerful public signal of the vast changes in Britain's perception of its political and military position subsequent to the French Revolution. *Margaret of Anjou*'s performance longevity, dating back to 1777, over which time it must have accumulated tens of thousands of theatre-going people, was sufficient for it to have helped produce contemporary metropolitan and provincial attitudes towards distressed female rulers, eventually including contemporary British reactions to those events occurring at Versailles in 1789. Certainly, Margaret of Anjou's recognition of her predicament, 'amid the horrors of this hour, / Reft of a crown, husband, ev'ry friend', mirrors the position of Marie Antoinette.[38] Burke's description pictures her narrowly escaping 'A band of cruel ruffians and assassins . . . through ways unknown to the murderers', while Jerningham's Margaret had similarly escaped her pursuers but still remained exposed and in danger. Both accounts are filled with the imagery of violence and potential regicide: 'Margaret: Yet what avail these momentary triumphs! / Ev'n while I speak perchance my Henry lies / Extended on the plain, deform'd with wounds, / While o'er his sacred corse the hostile band / Irreverently pass, and with vile taunts/Upbraid his overthrow.'[39]

Such was the dissemination of other theatrical representations of Margaret of Anjou that it is unlikely Burke would have been unaware that other dramatists had adapted his friend David Hume's narrative of the story in his best-selling *The History of England*. More or less on the eve of his writing the *Reflections*, the chief success of the summer season Haymarket theatre in 1789 had been George Colman the Younger's *The Battle of Hexham* (1789), a work quickly mirrored by a Crow Street theatre, Dublin, production. Like *Margaret of Anjou*, Colman's *Battle of Hexham* was based on Hume's story of the queen's debacle in the Northumberland area. Its treatment as a comedy fitted in well with the Haymarket's licence, which, rather erratically, permitted some level of discretion for presenting the spoken word but generally meant that the playhouse needed to introduce a fairly high ratio of song.[40] The twist in Colman's plot was that it now featured not just one robber but a band of robbers led by Gondibert, a heroic patriot living in disguise in the forest and sought by Adeline, his cross-dressed wife, who is accompanied by their servant, Gregory Gubbins. With the Gondibert/Adeline narrative essentially becoming a comic subplot, Margaret's role (played by Priscilla Kemble) emphasized her own heroic stature, striving against the military and political setbacks she had shared with her husband: 'Well on *me* must rest the load of war. Assist me then ye powers of just revenge – fix deep the memory of injured majesty – heat my glowing fancy, with all the glittering pride of high dominion, that when we meet the traitors who usurp'd it, my breast shall swell with manly indignation, and spur me on to enterprize.'[41] Given the originating template of Hume's *History*, the plot predictably allowed not only Margaret's salvation at the hands of Gondibert but also his reunion with Adeline (she recognizes him by his dagger). Colman's excellent relations with the press ensured a steady amount of newspaper commentary, including the presence at an August performance of the bungling, eccentric Clotworthy Skeffington, 2nd Earl of Massereene, barely a month after he had been freed from a Parisian debtors' prison by the revolutionary mob (*ODNB*).[42]

Not only did the Haymarket version survive having Prince Edward played by a 'little girl', but also Colman's *Battle of Hexham* was surprisingly successful. Twenty-five years later when the misfit actor Edward Cape Everard turned up with his strollers at the actual town of Hexham seeking an audience, 'I found, to my regret, that not only "The Battle of Hexham", but many other plays had been performed here by a small company in this small town, who had staid [*sic*] here above two months, till the town was tired and drained . . . nobody came; the town, for the present was surfeited, and could not bear to look at any thing like a play-bill.'[43] As with other parts of the Georgian repertoire, *The Battle of Hexham* reached America no later than June 1794 and similarly lodged itself for many years in the American repertoire.[44] The dissemination of the Margaret of Anjou story to theatre audiences, even in its *Battle of Hexham* format, was extremely extensive. Indeed, Colman's 1789 encapsulation of Margaret's heroic stature ('Well on *me* must rest the load of war') had itself already been figured in Thomas Francklin's tragedy, *The Earl of Warwick* (1766).

Francklin's *Earl of Warwick* presented another incarnation of the story and dealt with Margaret of Anjou's circumstances at a historical point rather later than her escape into the Northumberland woods and flight to France. Francklin locates Margaret at a time datable to around 1471 after the defeat of her cause at the Battle of Tewkesbury, although actually conflating a number of historical details to maximize dramatic incident. In the play, Margaret is portrayed as being deceived by her ally, the Earl of Warwick, and left to attempt to ensure the survival of her son, Prince Edward, against the machinations of her husband's successor, Edward IV. Francklin's play also became a repertoire staple, in the mid 1780s receiving a significant boost when the Margaret of Anjou role was taken up by Sarah Siddons.[45] Far from being exclusive to Siddons, on Tate Wilkinson's Yorkshire-to-Edinburgh circuit, as well as in London, it was also performed well into the 1780s with Mary Anne Yates (1728–1787) as Margaret.[46] In other words, by the time Burke came to write the *Reflections*, and given his interest in the theatre, it is likely he would have known that there were three versions of the Margaret of Anjou story still regularly featuring on the London and provincial stage.

The most remarkable feature of Francklin's Margaret – something picked up in Colman's later *Battle of Hexham* but not in Jerningham's interlude – was her resilience and resourcefulness. In Francklin's play, Margaret fatally wounds Warwick, although his death agonies are prolonged and include having him, in his final entrance, being brought on stage supported by two soldiers before entering into an incredibly lengthy dialogue. However, it is Margaret's unexpected reappearance before King Edward which was among the most memorable of her performances. George F. Bartley (1782?–1858), who must have acted with Siddons at the very end of her career close to her retirement in 1812, provided Siddons' contemporary biographer, Thomas Boaden, with a vivid description of her at this moment in the play:

> I happened to personate the character of King Edward the Fourth ... The scene had a large archway, in the centre, at the back of the stage. She was preceded by four guards, who advanced rapidly through the archway, and divided, two and two on each side, leaving the opening quite clear. Instantly, on their appearing, the giantess burst upon the view, and stood in the centre of the arch motionless. So electrifying was the unexpected impression that I stood for a moment breathless ... Her head was erect, and the fire of her brilliant eyes darted directly upon mine ... This, with the flashing eye, and fine smile of appalling triumph, constituted all the effort which usually produced an effect upon actors and audience never surpassed, if ever equalled.[47]

After Siddons started playing the role in 1784, it quickly became a regular feature of her career. In 1786, 'A Lady of Distinction' recorded her impressions in *The Beauties of Mrs. Siddons: or, a Review of her Performance of the Characters of Belvidera, Zara, Isabella, Margaret of Anjou, Jane Shore – And Lady Randolph*, a title which itself acts as a reminder of the modern unfamiliarity with the Georgian repertoire. Quite clearly, if Burke witnessed Siddons in this role, it was a very different one from the forlorn victims she often otherwise had to play and, certainly, different from the representation of the historical Margaret of Anjou by Jerningham or even by Colman, and different again from the *Reflections'* description of Marie Antoinette.

Bartley's striking description of Siddons as a 'giantess' correlates well with contemporary accounts which emphasized her physical stature, both facial and bodily, as being slightly larger, perhaps more statuesque, than average. Bartley's account of her sudden and dramatic appearance makes sense of the triumphant account she gives of her wounding of Warwick:

> Press'd by surrounding multitudes, and made
> A slave, they dragg'd me to the conqu'ror's tent,
> There the first horrid object I beheld,
> Was the pale corse of my poor bleeding child:
> There – as th' insulting Warwick stood, and seem'd
> To triumph o'er him – from my breast I drew
> A poniard forth, and plung'd it in his heart.[48]

Earlier commentators had described how in this role 'Mrs Siddons's mien strongly marked the haughty Queen; she walked as if she trod her enemies beneath.'[49] Mary Anne Yates, Siddons' predecessor in tragic roles, was similarly described as portraying 'the haughty, injured, vindictive, Margaret of Anjou' of Francklin's play.[50] These sharply divergent representations of the historical Margaret were also typical of attitudes in the general public print culture, reminding us that this French queen of England had an enduring contemporary resonance.

Not only had the Regency crisis of 1788–9 generated renewed debate about the role of the royal consort, insofar as it concerned the gendered positions of King and consort, but also, more widely, the crisis forced meditation about the constitutional authority for substituting a different national leader, and here recollection of Margaret of Anjou's role as queen figured as a precedent.[51] For one commentator, Margaret was the ideal English queen, 'a pattern of heroism and maternal attachment'. In a parallel which appeared to mirror the circumstances of the Regency crisis, it was remembered that Margaret had upheld the claim of her son, Edward, Prince of Wales, against the incoming power of King Edward IV. In the midst of a national crisis spared only by George's return to health, by the end of the 1780s it was felt keenly that Edward IV's reign had led swiftly to that of 'the bloody tyrant king Richard Third', and that, had it been more fortunate and effective, Margaret's influence would have ameliorated the country's political strife.[52] As Burke began the process of composing and publishing the *Reflections*, the cultural presence of Margaret of Anjou remained a potent force in the factual and fictional historiography of the national culture. For his part, Edward Jerningham was a staunch loyalist, although one who figured only slightly in Burke's social circle, with their meetings apparently casual even though they remained in intermittent correspondence by letter.[53] In November 1790 Jerningham had expressed approval of the *Reflections*, eliciting Burke's pleasure at his support for his 'endeavours to prevent some enthusiasts from running the Country into confusion and barbarism'.[54] Although one must treat Burke and Jerningham as only slight acquaintances, the poet's political views clearly harmonized with Burke's. Jerningham's anti-Foxite *Peace, ignominy, and destruction: a poem. Inscribed to the Rt. Hon. Charles James Fox* (1796) ascribed looming national ruin to the machinations of radical politicians.

The cultural context of Margaret of Anjou as both a historical personage and a theatrical figure in performance is informed by the immense distribution and consumption of her story by theatre audiences. In Jerningham's case, this was assisted by his important (and overlooked) developments in the generic innovations he included in its theatrical form. The introduction had noted that *Margaret of Anjou* was 'interspersed with Music, after the manner of Rousseau's Pygmalion'. This derivation is of immense significance. Jean-Jacques Rousseau's lyric opera *Pygmalion* (Geneva, 1771) had been available in an English translation (by Horace Coignet), with at least some of its music available since a *Pigmalion, Monologue* edition of 1772. Although it is not clear whether Jerningham actually witnessed a performance himself (he simply says it was 'form'd upon the same plan'), he clearly followed its pattern, describing the Rousseau piece as 'a new species of dramatic Entertainment, consisting of a Monologue that is often suspended by the interposition of Music, which must sympathize with the passions and feelings of the personage who is supposed to speak'.[55] In other words, the dramaturgy of *Margaret of Anjou* was supported by music composed by the prolific Vauxhall Gardens composer, James Hook (1746–1827), aimed at mirroring its textual meaning. This incorporation of an expressive role for music makes it the earliest English melodrama, preceding by some twenty-five years Thomas Holcroft's *A Tale of Mystery* (1803).

While *A Tale of Mystery* (with music by Thomas Busby) was instantly recognized as an importation of the French melodramatic mode, Jerningham's *Margaret of Anjou* interlude unequivocally used music as an expressive textual accompaniment much earlier, making Jerningham a very early British adopter of experiments exploring the projection and meaning of emotional sensibility that Rousseau was conducting towards the end of his working life.[56] Not only does Jerningham explicitly state that he aimed to use music to 'sympathize with the passions and feeling' of the characters – and interrupted his texts with 'Astericks' to show where the music was to go – but also contemporary reviewers were clearly struck by Jerningham's attempts to match the music to the emotion. A negative first-night review condemned it as 'the strangest novelty ever served up in an English theatre. Without beginning, middle, or end – a mere French, frigid, piece of foolery', viewing Margaret's predicament as that of a 'madwoman'. However, *The Morning Chronicle and London Advertiser* noted that 'at every climax of passion, the fiddles strike up, and give us a tune accordant to the madwoman's phrenzy.' In other words, it is quite clear from this account that *Margaret of Anjou* was a melodrama, its musical expressivity explicitly mirroring and matching meanings inherent in its spoken dialogue. As if to round off the newspaper's recognition of the nationalist implications of this new genre, the review added that, although 'We have heard indeed of something in this strange stile on the French stage . . . we profess ourselves such firm Antigallicans, that we heartily wish never again to be witnesses of any thing so truly ridiculous in an English Theatre.'[57] These demarcations between native and French melodramatic tendencies are significant, not least because of Rousseau's growing reputation for sensual decadence.

Although Hook's music has been lost, judging by the huge appetite for melodrama belatedly initiated by Holcroft's *Tale of Mystery* at the century's turn, it seems highly likely that a considerable part of *Margaret of Anjou*'s affective power was due to its novel ability to combine musical expressivity with dramatic linguistic meaning. If it is true, as has been argued by others, that Rousseau's *Pygmalion* was an attempt to create a musicalized language using theatricalized public space as a founding type of social community, there was much at stake.[58] The reaction of the expressly 'Antigallican' *Morning Chronicle and London Advertiser* reviewer was instinctive, summarizing unease towards the expressivity of sensibility yet also signalling the growing presence of Rousseau's influence on British culture. Burke's highly theatricalized description of Marie Antoinette written nearly twenty years later was by then fully assimilated into the registers of appropriate emotional responses available to the British public coming to terms with the predicament of an endangered French queen.

Even if one takes into account only the two Elizabeth Pope *Margaret of Anjou* benefits in the seasons 1792–4 and draws on the records of the box-office receipts, the performances must have been witnessed by 4,000–6,000 people. However, precisely because of theatre's structure as an assemblage connected across emergent components and populations, in addition to the patent-house performances at Covent Garden and Drury Lane, there are likely to have been an unknowable number of private performances. In a demonstration of *Margaret of Anjou*'s repertoire longevity and ability to reach into such domestic performance spaces, Elizabeth Craven,

Margravine of Brandenburg-Anspach-Bayreuth (1750–1828), produced it at Brandenburg House, Hammersmith, in 1795. At that performance it was programmed as part of an evening's entertainment preceded by a 'Prologue' masque in which the Goddess of Taste descended from the heavens and after which, 'Mr. Jerningham's interlude of Margaret of Anjou, a French Comedy and an Italian Pastoral followed.'[59] Predictably, the British drama won the laurels dispensed by Taste. Indeed, although such private festivities of upper-class metropolitan society remain largely inscrutable, the hostess of the Brandenburg House theatricals, Elizabeth Craven, had developed a network of contacts in her travels across the Ottoman Empire in the late 1780s, which were detailed in her book, *A Journey through the Crimea to Constantinople . . . Written in the year MDCCLXXXVI* (1789). Given the extent of her social circle, which reached out beyond continental Europe, as well as the documented continuation of the Ottoman embassy into 1795, it is just possible Yusuf Agha Effendi attended.

It is worth quoting DeLanda at length to give a perspective on the methodological processes of this chapter: 'The identity of any assemblage at any level of scale is always the product of a process (territorialization and, in some cases, coding) and it is always precarious, since other processes (deterritorialization and decoding) can destabilize it. For this reason, the ontological status of assemblages, large or small, is always that of unique, singular individuals. In other words, unlike taxonomic essentialities in which genus, species and individual are separate ontological categories, the ontology of assemblages is flat since it contains nothing but differently scaled *individual singularities* (or *hacceities*).'[60] The reassessment of Burke's acclaimed theatricalization of Marie Antoinette in the *Reflections* claimed here is dependent on reconfiguring the cultural status of theatre in contemporary Georgian society, returning the associative power of resonant stage roles to their likely reception communities and, as part of that process, stripping away Siddons' reified ranking as *par excellence* celebrity tragic actress and emotional arbiter for a generation of affective feeling. Again, the emphasis is on the organizational complexity of the theatrical assemblage, its populations, scale and the gradients of difference between its components, all of which enabled the emergence of new possibility spaces surrounding the cultural reception of the distressed queen of France.

CHAPTER EIGHT

The regulatory assemblage: The Roman Actor
and the politics of self-censorship

The analytical methodologies of the previous chapters have mainly been aimed at describing theatrical assemblages from a straightforwardly materialist basis, analysing the distribution of metropolitan and provincial playhouses through to examining ensembles of performers, clusters of performance text or even flattening celebrity profiles in the light of the overall theory. However, assemblage theory inevitably also has to be viable as a theory applicable to multiple types of social complexity. The basic formulation is that, given the perpetuation of difference in the materiality of the assemblage (as a consequence of the scale and complexity of its population gradients), capacities permitting the emergence of new interactions (both real or virtual and actual) are always present. The ontological status of these possibility spaces bears a relationship to the presence of the human and non-human dimensions in which emergence can take place as a process of actualization. In the 1790s, political upheavals in Britain brought about by reactions to the French Revolution, the outbreak of war, sporadic civil unrest and pressures for radical reform engendered arrays of possibility spaces in which unusually sharp social differentials were in operation. Many of these differentials were at their most vivid in London. Unlike other contemporary strata of ideological or epistemological possibility space with tendencies to remain in real or virtual symbolic registers (categories which would include novels, political treatises and poetry), London theatres provided spaces where capacities for emergence could become actualized with meaningful densities of reception and population co-presence. Predictably enough, one of the aims of the government in this period was to ensure that places such as theatres, where dissonant voices might become actualized, were rigorously policed. Indeed, the contemporary practice of permitting plays to be printed even though they had been censored for stage representation, is a good example of how the British government instinctively separated real or virtual texts from their actualized counterparts.

In this chapter examples in the theatrical assemblage will be described which were not fully materialized into performance, and yet were structured as components otherwise capable of completing their process of actualization. Of course, they have left ample traceable associations of their exterior relations. Dealing with semi- or non-emergence within the theatrical assemblage should not worry us too much, since, as long as the materialized components of their identities can be traced, the existence of the overall assemblage confers the necessary diagram of connectivity. Or, as DeLanda puts it in giving a résumé of the philosophical history of emergence in *Philosophy and Simulation: The Emergence of Synthetic Reason*, 'the structure of possibility spaces plays as great a role in the explanation of emergence as do mechanisms.'[1] This chapter delineates such a set of possibility spaces linked to capacities composed of both symbolic and materialized expressive registers by examining a single sequence of interactions within London's theatrical assemblage relative to one play, John Philip Kemble's textually remixed version of Philip Massinger's Jacobean tragedy, *The Roman Actor* (1629).

Kemble's *Roman Actor* was prepared for the 1794–5 Drury Lane season but withdrawn by them from scheduling, apparently as an act of self-censorship. If one were to assume that playhouses were run under the direction of single people, it would be feasible to apportion much of what happened to the increasingly theatrically dysfunctional Drury Lane proprietor, Richard Brinsley Sheridan. Sheridan had been questioned by the Privy Council in May 1794 about his knowledge of the indicted Irish nationalist traitor, the Revd William Jackson, but Drury Lane was a complex organization and not the perquisite political space of any individual.[2] While the individual agency of Sheridan was probably contributory in pushing it forward for production, it cannot have been decisive. In any case, *The Roman Actor* was devised and licensed by Kemble, possibly in consort with Sheridan but ultimately aimed to be part of the playhouse's overall schedule.

As conceptualized here, the assemblage consists of a network of material activities mirroring *The Roman Actor*'s real (or virtual) existence as an undeployed capacity. In other words, it existed in an extremely molecular phase of possibility space within the assemblage: 'The dimensions of the possibility space are the relevant ways of changing for an assemblage, that is, its degrees of freedom. If there are interactions between these degrees of freedom the diagram is nonlinear, possessing multiple singularities of different types, whereas if there are no interactions, the diagram is linear, structured by a single singularity of the steady-state type.'[3] The play's withdrawal during a period of regulatory anxiety and political turmoil conforms to a pattern of non-linearity within its historical presence. Crucially, the traceable associations of *The Roman Actor*'s exterior relations remain historically actualized even though the play in Kemble's precise version had a deferred performance history.

On 16 October 1794 John Philip Kemble (1757–1823), the manager of the Drury Lane theatre, signed and sent off for licensing to John Larpent, the Lord Chamberlain's Examiner of Plays, a shortened – 'compressed' as he described it – version of Massinger's tragedy, *The Roman Actor*.[4] It was an odd move. Not least, what arrived on Larpent's desk was a manuscript Kemble had caused to be laboriously copied by scribes within the play-house. Having already been in the repertoire, *The Roman Actor* did not really need licensing or the payment of the Examiner's 2-guinea fee. The original printed title page clearly announced it as already 'with good allowance acted, at the private play-house in the *Black-Friers*, by the Kings Majesties Servants'. Indeed, at some time between 1695 and 1705, the actor Thomas Betterton (*c.* 1635–1710) had revived – and acted in – a version of it at the theatre in Lincoln's Inn Fields, and it was his adaptation which was eventually printed in 1722 (dutifully recorded as 'reviv'd with alterations'). If Kemble really felt he needed the Examiner's approval, the presence of a printed edition in the public domain would have been a far easier option for enclosure to facilitate the licensing application. Indeed, it is clear from the Larpent copy that Kemble had not introduced large amounts of newly composed text. By the time of Kemble's revision, *The Roman Actor* was something of a repertoire staple with Betterton's championing of it well known to contemporary compilers of British performance history.[5] Significantly, Kemble himself already knew the play extremely well, having performed sizeable extracts of it in Yorkshire theatre manager Tate Wilkinson's dramatic medley, *Humours and Passions; or, A Theatrical Fête*, which had toured to York, Leeds and Edinburgh in 1781. Tate even remembered that Kemble had been 'particularly impressive' in the role of Paris.[6]

What was so different about Drury Lane's plan to stage this radically altered version of *The Roman Actor* in the autumn of 1794? After all, not only had custom and practice established a number of precedents for its place in the repertoire of the London playhouses, but also Kemble's 'compressed' version of Massinger's drama introduced no new verbal material for the licenser to license. However, what proved to be politically explosive – too explosive for Drury Lane to handle in 1794 – was that Kemble's *Roman Actor* began with a striking transposition of Massinger's text. The play now had a markedly different opening, repositioning a speech otherwise buried away and placing it as the opening lines. It was the potential impact of this new opening which reversed Drury Lane's plans to stage the play and made it imperative to postpone its first outing. In a decision which exemplifies the highly charged relationship between drama and London politics, having licensed *The Roman Actor* on 16 October, the playhouse decided not to perform it until May 1796, when Kemble took the role of Paris in a single benefit night performed on behalf of his actress wife, Priscilla, on the occasion of her retirement from the stage.[7] In contrast with its normal practices, the playhouse's pulling of *The Roman Actor* was unprecedented.

Licensing records show that the average time delay in the 1790s between Drury Lane's obtaining the Lord Chamberlain's authority and producing a play was about two weeks. Given the Georgian practice of staging two plays a night, and with runs of consecutive nights being rare at this time, the pressure to programme new material often impelled frantic scrambles to get the plays onto the boards. At Drury Lane, as with Covent Garden or the Haymarket, plays were usually produced within a couple of days of their licensing with some, on occasion, actually being staged the next day.[8] The problem Kemble sensed about *The Roman Actor* in 1794 prefigured a similarly telling occasion of self-censorship concerning another Drury Lane production already in the performance repertoire. One year later, in a process illuminatingly described by John Barrell, Drury Lane also pulled from performance its new production of Thomas Otway's *Venice Preserv'd: Or, A Plot Discover'd* (1681). After playing its third night on 29 October 1795, Drury Lane withdrew *Venice Preserv'd* amidst an atmosphere of increasing political tension subsequent to the 'Pop-Gun Plot' when, a few days earlier, someone had allegedly thrown a stone or fired an air gun at the King on his way to the opening of Parliament.[9] Such was the universal recognition of the immediate political implications of this act of withdrawal that within seven weeks news had crossed the Atlantic and the Pennsylvanian *Aurora General Advertiser* was unambiguously announcing that *Venice Preserv'd* was 'prohibited in England as of *treasonable and seditious tendency*'.[10]

Not only did the incident of *The Roman Actor*'s deferral occur a full year earlier than Drury Lane's abandoning of *Venice Preserv'd*, but also the circumstances of its postponement now make it clear that the latter incident marks a second occasion on which Drury Lane had attempted to perform a seventeenth-century repertoire standard – a play taken from the stable of canonical writing – only for the playhouse to realize that it intersected uncomfortably with the contemporary political situation. The problem *The Roman Actor* posed for Drury Lane in the autumn of 1794 lay in its very opening lines. In Kemble's version it began like this:

> Act 1 Scene 1 Lamia's House Enter Lamia Rusticus, Marcus and Sura
> Lam[ia]: What times are these!
> To what is Rome fall'n! May we being alone
> Speak our thoughts freely of the Prince and State,
> And not fear the Informer?
> Rust[icus]: Noble Lamia,
> So dangerous the age is and such bad acts
> Are practis'd every where, we hardly sleep
> Nay, cannot dream, with safety; to be virtuous
> Is to be guilty.[11]

In its new configuration, Kemble's Massinger had suddenly become a play starkly dramatizing the exact state of the national political psyche concerning the outcome of the London Corresponding Society (LCS) treason trials, in which several of its leading members had already been indicted on charges engineered by the machinations of an authoritarian government, a complicit judiciary and supposedly incriminating evidence fuelled by *agents provocateurs*.[12] The trial's formal proceedings had started on 2 October, barely a fortnight before Drury Lane had applied for the Massinger licence. Kemble was intending to stage *The Roman Actor* amidst almost palpable national tension, with the much-heralded trial of one of its chief indictees, the shoemaker Thomas Hardy, about to begin. Hardy's trial began on 28 October in 'the longest trial and most expensive trial for high treason that had ever been heard in Britain'.[13] On the day Kemble dispatched the manuscript to the Examiner of Plays, the capital's network of newspapers were carrying, as they had done on many previous days, the latest stages of that autumn's growing alarm and concern about an apparent epidemic of treasonous plots, which was paralleled by a debate about the manipulation of the country's legal system and its meaning for the British constitution.

In the 1790s, theatre and its ancillary worlds of politics and cultural life were merged in a way which can be conceptualized along the lines suggested by DeLanda's idea of an *intensive* map.[14] Much of London's metropolitan culture, the very aspects of its social and political life which made it a metropolis, was based on the operation of a small but highly focused group of winter- and summer-season theatres operating as complex cartels with distinctive features within their financial and labour markets. With the big, winter-season playhouses being public spaces where all social classes could see each other and be seen, the nightly movement in the 1790s of 6,000–9,000 people converging onto one small area meant that the capital's West End theatre land was a place teeming with Londoners, ranging, quite literally, from princes to prostitutes. In an area rather less than a quarter of a square mile in area, bounded along the axis of the Strand, which paralleled the north side of the Thames, but reaching a westward limit only as far as Charing Cross, and eastward only to the end of Fleet Street, this was a highly compacted urban space.

On occasion after occasion, playhouses became flashpoints for disturbances and incidents of public expression almost as if the very idea of British national identity was embodied night after night among the actors on stage and the spectators crushed within their boxes, galleries and pits, even spilling out into the general theatre environs. Where national identity was already under challenge, as in colonial America, civic leaders made greater causal connections between theatres and riots than was possible under English law. As early as 1700, the Pennsylvania General Assembly enacted a statute 'against Riots, Rioters, and Riotous Sports, Plays and Games', threatening with fines or imprisonment anyone introducing 'into this province and territories . . . stage-plays, masks, revels, bull-baitings, cock-fightings, bonfires'.[15] In London, productions at the winter-season playhouses had enormous potential to provoke highly visible public expressions of unrest precisely because of their concentration into such a tightly defined area of West End London and their ability to materialize real (or virtual) ideological tendencies. The patent theatres' monopoly over spoken drama in London scarcely afforded opportunities for variant or emergent performance venues offering different ideological perspectives or for emerging actors to access new opportunities to develop their art within the metropolis. With spoken word stage performance tightly concentrated in such a small area of West End London, deviations from regular patterns were quickly noticed and form the principal discursive features of a homogeneous assemblage.

The omission of 'God Save the King' at a single Drury Lane performance in July 1794 had been enough to cause newspaper comment. Although usually led from the stage or orchestra pit, audiences expected to join in singing the loyal anthem. Even though generic hybridity was rampant on the patent stages, the repetition of nightly patterns of behaviour tended to make anything exceptional stand out. Covent Garden and Drury Lane drew on fairly settled companies of actors of established familiarity. Their main-pieces and farce or pantomime afterpieces were also regularly interspersed with songs both within and between the dramas, and the theatres tended to follow a predictable formula of plays being prefixed by a prologue and concluded with an epilogue. In most cases performer roles for prologues and epilogues had even become gendered, with men speaking the prologue and women taking the epilogue, decorously provoking, reproving or titillating the audience. In contrast to this formulaic pattern adopted by the theatres as businesses deeply connected to their marketplace, audiences acquired looser social or communal conventions, behaving as active participants within the performances. Georgian London audiences learned techniques of manipulating these conventions in order to create audience-led counter-theatricality.

These actions of intermittent collective popular agitation are what the social historian Charles Tilly calls *repertoires of contention*.[16] Although Tilly's historical modelling is not defined from a predictive perspective, DeLanda has found Tilly's 'repertoire' idea a useful precursor of assemblage theory.[17] Tilly's *Popular Contention in Great Britain 1758–1834* (1995) even offers a key-date, historically specific 'calendar of contention', itemizing disturbances such as naval mutinies, bread riots and mass jailbreaks together with fleeting references to the 'Pop-Gun' Drury Lane agitation and an audience break-in at the Royal Circus in 1807.[18] With startling prescience, and a long time before actor-network-theory, Tilly, writing in 1995, articulated this thesis, using explicit metaphors drawn from theatricality, and visualizing something approximating to concepts of individual singularities and universal singularities as materialized economies of difference working within assemblage-like structures. He is worth quoting at length:

> Like their theatrical counterparts, repertoires of collective action designate not individual performances but means of *inter*action among pairs or larger sets of actors. A company, not an individual, maintains a repertoire. The simplest set consists of one actor (say a group of workers) making collective claims, and another actor (say the workers' boss) becoming the object of those claims ... Repertoires have several different levels: action, performance, campaign, and array of performances ... Actions, performances, campaigns, and repertoires have their counterparts in the dialogues, plays, play cycles, and whole arrays of dramas available to the interacting players of a particular drama company.[19]

Finally, Tilly also approached a tentative articulation of non-linearity, stressing that his book would 'focus on claim-making in which people gather, act together, and then disperse – that is, *discontinuous* claim-making'.[20] Tilly's research is important because it is both centred on civil disturbances in Britain around 1800 and modelled on a prototype of assemblage theory.

Disturbances at Covent Garden following the 'Pop-Gun Plot' against the King in October 1795 confirm the existence of these elaborate repertoires of communal theatricality and counter-theatricality centred on the singing of loyal songs within playhouse spaces: 'Even in the Playhouse [when] rebellious noises were drowned, by the loyal shoutings, of all that were admitted ... all the *Servants* of the House, and the whole *Band of Music* ... were forced to repeat the well known sounds of *God save the King*, till the ears of the facetious were made to tingle.'[21] James Sayers' etching, *A peep behind the curtain at Drury Lane* (1789), although actually referring to Sheridan's alleged response to George III's recovery from madness, is a good example of this type of repertoire of contention (Figure 8.1). The right both to assert and contest political expression during theatrical performances was deeply embedded in audiences' understanding of the theatre as a legitimate space in which to deploy their own repertoires of disruptive performance. The intervention by a section of the audience to coerce a repetition of orchestral sound, in this case music performed by 'the whole *Band of Music*', should not mask the realization that the theatre band was itself merely a vehicle hijacked for the purpose of fulfilling the audience's desire to exercise its powers of appropriation. The making of the 'ears of the facetious ... to tingle' was actually the specific objective of this commandeering of orchestral sound. In other words, Covent Garden had been appropriated as a public space where the needs of the contending political ideologies circulating within that night's audience had temporarily displaced the role of the theatre performers as mediators of the night's external political context. Within these intricacies of reaction to the 'Pop-Gun Plot' lies an array of theatrical and counter-theatrical activities in which the intentions and interventions of the audiences were as nuanced as the more familiar command over the theatricalities exercised by playwrights, actors or theatre managers.

Tilly's ideas of social repertoires can be modified to accommodate, in the state of their activity, assemblages where cultural meanings are successively territorialized and deterritorialized – in this example, as exchanges of difference about the ownership of public space, the appropriation of music or the authority of competing factions. Operating at different levels within the population gradients of the assemblage, the context of the plays and theatre disturbances described in this chapter operate as parameters of territorialization, and deterritorialization engendered by disputes around permissible degrees of coding and decoding of theatre as an assemblage. As DeLanda puts it, 'Territorialization refers not only to the determination of the spatial boundaries of a whole – as in the territory of a community, city, or nation

8.1 James Sayers, *A peep behind the curtain at Drury Lane JS f.,* in script balloons, 'Play God save the King', 'D——n em don't play God save the King', Thomas Cornell, 14 January 1789, etching and aquatint. Contested commands in theatres for playing the national anthem were fairly common. Sayers' print shows the Whig politician and Drury Lane manager, Richard Brinsley Sheridan, allegedly opposing its playing on the occasion of George III's recovery from mental ill health.

state – but also to the degree to which an assemblage's component parts are drawn from a homogeneous repertoire, or the degree to which an assemblage homogenizes its own components.'²² The pressure on the Drury Lane orchestra to play 'God Save the King' and abnormal sensitivity around *Every One has his Fault* (see below) are both demonstrations of active social and political network exerting an increasing degree of territorialization in a time of military conflict.

However, if this post-'Pop-Gun Plot' incident indicates the specific presence of contesting layers of political faction within Covent Garden on that particular evening, one must be cautious when attributing instant political reaction within London theatres to incidents occurring contemporaneously in topical politics even if, at first sight, they appear directly linked to topical events. Many apparently precipitate or coincident examples of popular expression within Georgian theatres are, on closer analysis, actually continuations of pre-existing customs connected to the appropriation or counter-appropriation of public theatrical spaces for political ends. If the devising of Kemble's *Roman Actor* shows that theatre managers were extremely attuned to shifts in their contemporary moment, it is also important to bear in mind that late eighteenth-century London theatres had highly evolved public cultures. While, at their most raucous, this could result in the commandeering of theatrical spaces by the audiences as discussed above, the incessant production of the Georgian theatrical repertoire helped create normative and non-normative precedents for commentary. Not only did the post-'Pop-Gun' omission of 'God Save the King' provoke a reaction because of its sudden withdrawal from the recognized content and sequence of the evening's theatrical entertainment, but also playwrights could find themselves infringing long-standing customs and practices of legitimate and illegitimate comment. The capital's playhouses had well-developed conventions of political reference which might be successfully traversed, but could not always be assumed to be without risk.

A good case history can by analysed by following the context of Elizabeth Inchbald's references in *Every One has his Fault* to the current high prices of food ('Provisions are so scarce!') and the censure she received from *The True Briton* newspaper after its opening night on 29 January 1793.²³ While Inchbald's play was immediately condemned by the newspaper, it had already passed into legitimate, licensed status with no substantive revisions being required.²⁴ This may be because the Examiner of Plays, unlike *The True Briton*, recognized that *Every One has his Fault* represented a continuation of, rather than a divergence from, the precedents of legitimate theatrical comment. The wider cultural licensing of critical allusions to both scarcity and conspicuous excess was commonplace in the theatre. Inchbald was probably right to make the professional judgement that her play's references to food scarcity were likely to be viewed as acceptable extensions of permissible commentary rather than contingent negative reactions to the turbulent contemporary political scene.[25] In the event, the first production of her play was postponed for three days to await an evaluation of the political climate following the execution of Louis XVI on 21 January 1793, but, as the play had already been licensed (on the 12th), it clearly caused no official alarm. Indeed, as the inevitable reader of the latest plays, the Examiner was in a prime position to judge whether *Every One has his Fault* could be placed within the boundaries of legitimate comment, and, quite clearly, he acceded to the play's place within such traditions. As it happened, Inchbald's recently published diaries show that although word had evidently reached Covent Garden about the fate of Louis XVI on the same day he died (whereupon Inchbald noted 'my Play postponed a few days'), she still recorded herself as 'very very happy' with its reception on the day *The True Briton* published its review and, moreover, 'still happier', the day following.[26]

Every One has his Fault can be situated along a continuum of theatrical allusions to high food prices and conspicuous consumption, a social fault-line within the capital's moral economy which remained unresolved as to its acceptable cultural treatment. To the macro-parameter of territorialization exerted by the controlling powers of the Lord Chamberlain can now be added a micro-parameter, that of processes of decoding. Objections to *Every One has his Fault* had erupted after licensing, beyond formalized attempts by the state to confer homogeneity and conformity, as, for example, from the licensing of the spoken word permitted under the patent to the Lord Chamberlain's scrutiny of the play text. However, quite clearly, *The True Briton*'s response also represents a particular type of decoding engendered by these degrees of territorialization. Indeed, the presence of reactionary responses, just as much as politically radical responses, demonstrates the workings of this assemblage model comprising different gradients of population within metropolitan London of 1793. The datable and locatable qualities of these responses, materialized at the playhouse and its immediate networks of newspaper comment, demonstrate the functionality of this particular assemblage, although it is possible to add further layers of territorialization and decoding.

As Sarah Lloyd has shown, even the convivial fund-raising dinners of eighteenth-century London charities oscillated uneasily between approval and condemnation of extravagant festivities in the support of social

benevolence.[27] The philanthropist Jonas Hanway's particular condemnation of the effeminate turn of such gatherings (which it was feared were
displacing the spirited masculinity of civic-inspired benevolence) sat
uncomfortably with the close relationship between his own Marine
Society and London theatre. In the late 1780s, shortly before his death,
Hanway's boys paraded on stage at the Royalty Theatre during a benefit
night on the charity's behalf and, even more surprisingly, later appeared in
similar guise as part of the finale of Covent Garden's *Nootka Sound; or,
Britain Prepared* (1790), a drama featuring a cross-dressed actress masquer-
ading as a sailor.[28] Again, the complexity of these cultural responses,
particularly because they were materialized at a playhouse location, are
evidence of the degree of complexity and presence of multiple populations
within the assemblage.

Given such unclear demarcations between philanthropy and frugality,
theatres had become well suited to providing commentaries as the prices of
provisions waxed and waned. An unperformed prelude, sent to the Examiner
of Plays by an unknown London playhouse (but internally datable to 14
August 1785), entitled *The Inquiry; or, Cause of the Present High Price of
Provisions* contains a typical allusion to a Lord Mayor's 'Livery Feast', referring
to the City aldermen's allegedly habitual series of civic dinners. *The Inquiry*
was probably much too sharply satirical on the 'superfluous consumption of
Animal Food, or Eating more than is necessary', complete with its grasping
physician, Dr Guttle ('I always ... pay my Rent out of what I get by a Lord
Mayor's Day'), to stand much likelihood of being staged, and the piece was
probably also quietly withdrawn from prospective performance in much the
same way as *The Roman Actor*.[29] Whatever the intentions behind this
unlicensed text, the Haymarket theatre the very next day performed *The
Feast of Thalia; or, A Dramatic Olio*, whose 'Bill of Fare ... [served] every
Dish belonging to the Drama', and followed it (as 'a Relish') with *Westminster
Hall in an Uproar*.[30] Indeed, the association of aldermen and the City with
excessive consumption provided sets of instantaneously recognizable allusions
for London theatre audiences. Indicatively, John O'Keeffe's Covent Garden
pantomime, *Lord Mayor's Day; or, A Flight from Lapland* (1782), featured the
characters Mr and Mrs Gobble.[31] In other words, Inchbald's evocation of
food scarcities in *Every One has his Fault* played into this pre-existing context
of theatrical allusion. Pushing the limits of permissible commentary to their
furthest reaches, some of these plays imply the presence of self-censorship (as
with the mystery of whatever happened to the staging of *The Inquiry*) or else
conscious avoidance of direct reference to politically sensitive areas, as with
The Feast of Thalia.

The wrath Inchbald experienced at the hands of *The True Briton* probably had as much to do with the newspaper's general sense of the bounds of patriotic decorum being breached within Covent Garden's public spaces as with any concern with specific sensitivities about the precise nature of Inchbald's individual politics. The pairing of plays should also be taken into account. This practice produced nightly variations of compounded intertextuality, which, inevitably, resulted in shifting interpretations arising out of the collision of the texts played out on stage. *Every One has his Fault* was not the only play Covent Garden staged on its first night. Paired with Inchbald's new drama was John O'Keeffe's *The Farmer* (1787), a play restating the virtues of Kentish rustic solidity and the 'spirit of a yeoman' embodied in Farmer Blackberry. But O'Keeffe's text was also – much like *Every One has his Fault* – located more darkly at the end of the American War of Independence, subtly hinting at the disastrous conflict's social fallout by referencing 'some Relation [who has] made a huge Fortune in America by Army Contracts'.[32] Haunting by past imperial defeats must have been lucid on the evening *The True Briton* attended. As well as castigating Inchbald's allusions to that winter's high food prices, *The True Briton* had also specifically found 'very exceptionable' Inchbald's portrayal of Irwin, an officer disbanded specifically from the American campaign, now fallen on hard times in London and, in his desperation, tempted to become both footpad and potential suicide.[33] *The True Briton* reviewer clearly witnessed both plays in tandem, neither of them perhaps instilling the brand of patriotic loyalty the newspaper expected to find. This standard Georgian theatrical practice of doubling a mainpiece with an afterpiece compounds all perceived political contexts within the plays performed. The doubling of texts and mixing of intertextual discursive economies often resulted in a dizzyingly intricate compounding of meaning, a complex deterritorialization of any intentionality of meaning attached to the night's principal drama. On the next two nights, for example, Covent Garden programmed *Every One has his Fault* paired with William Pearce's *Hartford Bridge; or, The Skirts of the Camp* (1792), a Sheridan *Camp* derivative, which, on its first night, had similarly been perceived by *The Evening Mail* as 'objectionable' on the grounds of its allusions to the fiasco of the erroneous assumption in the spring of 1792 that Lord Cornwallis had defeated and killed Tippoo Sultan.[34] In short, there was little wonder that contemporary perceptions of Inchbald's radicalism had become considerably magnified and distorted.

As well as the compounding of political meanings arising from *Every One has his Fault*'s successive pairing with *The Farmer* and *Hartford Bridge*, at

other times there were more general cultural contexts of performance. Some
of these can be readily connected to specific events, but they are often ones
having widely disseminated meanings verging more on national, mass-
cultural attitudes than on reactions to particular collisions of temperament
or moment. The early phases of the Napoleonic Wars, carrying their twin
fears of revolution and invasion, together with an unprecedented military
mobilization including voluntary associations, amounted to a national
moment when it is possible to speak of mass-consensual movements. In
the spring and summer of 1794, it seemed as if the nation's entire vocabulary
of public discourse had swung around an outpouring of celebration for
Admiral Howe's victory in the deep Atlantic against the French in the battle
known simply as The Glorious First of June. Again, an event as easily
datable and as historically significant as this (the war's first cataclysmic naval
engagement between the French and British Grand Fleets) rapidly generated both specific and general changes in Britain's public culture of patriotism. Inevitably, these changes were rapidly theatricalized. As outlined in
Chapter 5, Drury Lane mounted a large-scale *Glorious First of June* entertainment on 2 July, but as early as 13 June Covent Garden had interpolated a
'Loyal Effusion' (consisting of 'a representation of the Engagement and
Defeat of the French Navy . . . on the Glorious first of June') between Hugh
Kelly's *The School for Wives* (1774) and that night's pantomime afterpiece,
Harlequin and Faustus. By 19 June, Ranelagh Gardens was taking advantage
of the improving weather (and the magistrate's licence) to mount a benefit-
night concert in aid of 'the Wounded Seamen . . . Widows and Children of
the Brave Men who Fell in the late Glorious Naval Victory of the First of
June'.[35] Elsewhere, at the King's Theatre Opera House in the Haymarket on
the 21 June, a concert performance of patriotic music was accompanied by
transparencies of Admiral Howe and George III.[36]

   This mass theatricalization of commemoration for the victory is difficult
to overestimate, in terms of both its scale and its diversity. Public benefit
nights for First of June sailors, widows and orphans went on well into
October, perhaps the most remarkable of these being, in effect, a blackface
evening in slave-trading Bristol, where Richard Cumberland's *The West
Indian* (1771) was performed alongside Isaac Bickerstaffe's *The Padlock*
(1768). The event raised £156 for 'the Relief of the Widows and Orphans
of the gallant Tars who died in defence of their Country during the glorious
Action of the First of June'. That evening's crudely racial stereotyping is
suggested not only by the choice of plays but also by the fact that, driven by
an 'impulse of patriotism', '[Mr.] Weeks, the Landlord of the Bush Tavern',
played Mungo, *The Padlock*'s principal blackface part.[37] The enthusiasm for

charitable performance on behalf of British servicemen and their dependants became an established feature of the national culture, energized by the victories of Valenciennes and the First of June, and precipitating regular outbursts of public patriotism.

These developments in the display of public loyalty in the summer and autumn of 1794 were not just rapid but also comprehensive. They involved what may best be described as a contemporary cultural dynamic of patriotism operative throughout the metropolis and percolating into the provinces, where paying audiences had become not only increasingly receptive to the idea of loyalist interventions in playhouse spaces but also more inclined to the display of patriotic benevolence. Again, they are features of a theatrical assemblage connected through materialized networks across the nation.

Typical of the intensity of that summer's political temperature was that, shortly after the initial benefit nights of *The Glorious First of June*, Sheridan felt obliged to join the managers of Norwich and Liverpool theatres in pledging other benefit performances for Howe's widows and orphans, expressly committing himself to future winter-season benefits even though his playhouse, at that moment, was closed for the summer.[38] In this context of a heightened climate of public awareness, even Sheridan's local judicial commitments as a Bow Street magistrate played a role in highlighting his profile as a liberal whose political disposition was brought to local metropolitan prominence when he helped contain the worst effects of that August's 'crimp-house' riots in Charing Cross.[39] Sheridan's intervention in helping clear the area of 'crimp gangs' (press gangs) after the death and imprisonment of one of its victims in a local backstreet no doubt enhanced this reputation.

However, again, it is important to emphasize that theatricality permeated the national culture not only within the narrow sense of London's patent theatres but also across a wider range of venues across the assemblage, both marginal to Westminster and reaching into the provinces. For example, those demands reported in London newspapers regarding Drury Lane's omission of 'God Save the King' can also be located within a wider cultural context, telling us much about the national distribution of patriotic sentiment at public performances. Even circus-goers at James Handy's equestrian exhibitions in Leicester Square, at the height of the autumn of 1794 treason trials, witnessed a boy playing 'God Save the King' on a violin while riding on horseback.[40] The theatrical reiteration of the music was not confined to more established venues but passed easily into the more rough-edged sounds of the circus. Out in the provinces, at Rochester,

Kent, that July a riot took place at the theatre when a group of Royal Irish Artillery officers from the nearby Chatham garrison demanded the playing of the same tune. In the ensuing battle between members of the audience and the soldiers, 'the officers . . . sprung from the boxes into the pit', one of them drawing his sword and wounding a civilian.[41]

It was not just that, in the strained political atmosphere of the 1790s, the theatres had become places where the morality of patriotic benevolence was constantly paraded and debated. Plays were powerful vehicles for representing transformational cultural attitudes or the modification of certain patterns of behaviour. Clearly, Inchbald's comments on high food prices, in common with the satires of her predecessors on City excesses, formed one such type of critique, but there were many others.

Among the most revealing type are the clusters of entertainments celebrating George III's apparent recovery from madness in the spring of 1789. Just a few months before the storming of the Bastille, expressions of British loyalism in the theatre were taking a number of variant and intriguing forms. What they particularly demonstrate is not only the massive distribution of theatricalized loyalist sentiment into the two, 3,000-seat, royal patent playhouses but also their diffusion into provincial England. In addition, at least some of the loyalist dramas had the capacity to present surprisingly nuanced versions of what it meant to be patriotic. This is especially true of theatrical commemorations based on St George's Day (23 April), when George III, Queen Charlotte and members of the Corporation of London made their annual procession to St Paul's Cathedral for a thanksgiving service. In 1789, this ceremony also became one of the means of celebrating the King's recovery. On 30 April 1789, some days after the saint's anniversary, Drury Lane had produced John Bannister's monologue *British Loyalty; or, A Squeeze for St. Paul's*, while the Royal Circus performed, mixed in with its ordinary medley of entertainments, *St. George's Day; or, Britannia's Joy* (with 'grand Transparencies, and a magnificent Firework' – together with 'God Save the King') as another thanksgiving entertainment.[42]

The distribution of loyalist sentiment in public entertainments celebrating the King's return to health not only covered the larger metropolitan area (the Royal Circus' premises were located on the Surrey side of the river) but also spread much further afield. The chance survival of a playbill (*c.* 1789) for an unknown itinerant company (possibly visiting Norwich) offers some further hints as to their contemporary reception of such pieces. In this provincial production, Bannister's original Drury Lane piece was now performed as 'a new Epilogue, called, British Loyalty; or, A Squeeze for

St. Paul's (Written on the late happy occasion of his Majesty's Recovery)' appended to Samuel Foote's comedy, *The Minor* (1760), here subtitled as 'The Tricks of London Exposed'. As the whole evening's performance was billed as a *Divertissement; or, A Dramatic Olio* in three parts, it is likely these pieces would have been performed in abbreviated formats, with that evening's programming structure apparently aiming to make comic highlights of rural versus urban social mores by additionally featuring a version of Isaac Bickerstaffe's *The Recruiting Serjeant* (1770) with its timid, yokel, Countryman character (here subtitled 'Or, the Way to Enlist'). Perhaps more surprisingly, *The Recruiting Serjeant* was itself appended by 'An Epilogue on Slavery, in the Character of a Negro', a piece possibly designed to project something of the 'foreign [*sic*] wars' Bickerstaffe's Countryman fears, but which also – albeit in blackface – may be indicative of the penetration of types of abolitionist sentiments into the rural theatrical circuits, not least through the provincial popularity of Colman's *Inkle and Yarico* (1787).[43] This obscure piece of rural theatricality can be quite certainly dated on account of its 'Song, in the Character of a Runaway Frenchman from the Bastile', which, together with the verifiable dating of *British Loyalty; or, A Squeeze for St. Paul's* and that event's celebration of the King's improved mental state, most probably places it in the latter half of 1789.

   Indeed, the obscure, itinerant theatrical troupe who devised *Divertissement; or, A Dramatic Olio* encapsulates the breadth and variety of theatrical representation in the country, even its fielding of Foote's *Minor* representing an example of a once controversial play (arguably originally permitted default licensing due to the Lord Chamberlain's strategic negligence), which reflected changes in popular sentiment by ridiculing religious enthusiasm and Methodism in particular.[44] What the itinerant *Divertissement* demonstrates above all is the flexibility and distribution of an apparently metropolitan-based culture into the provinces and its functionality as an assemblage. By the play's touching on issues as diverse as slavery, the King's recovery, the French Revolution, Methodism, army recruitment and rustic manners, provincial audiences – in however sketchy a form – were updated on changes within their society. The theatrical critique of public behaviour disseminated via playhouses, both provincial and metropolitan, to their audiences meant that expressions of political sentiments such as loyalism were not only widely available but also inevitably remarkably nuanced and specific to different segments of the population component. While not specifically educational in its remit, British theatre kept the population supplied with an indicative range of

political and social concerns which became the subject of further discussion or meditation. This degree of sophistication, even within as loyalist a
topic as the King's health, was never less apparent than in the spring of
1789 amidst the multiple convergences of public entertainments celebrating the King's recovery. Present within at least some of these dramas was
the notion of a moral economy of patriotism.

Although Covent Garden billed it for 24 April, the day after St George's
Day, their anonymous one-act *St. George's Day; or, Britons Rejoice!* was
actually deferred until the 30th, possibly to act as spoiler to the competitor
productions discussed above. Specifically aimed to mark a saint's day, it had
only one performance, but its requirement to be licensed by the Lord
Chamberlain has secured its survival, capturing a remarkable transitional
moment in national history. National relief was evoked not only by the
personal aspects of the King's improved health but also by the realization
that a crisis around the constitutional position of a Regency had been
averted. A print by Thomas Rowlandson captures the event, but, more
especially, it particularly shows the windows of the streets lining the
procession filled with exuberant onlookers.[45] Covent Garden took these
crowded windows as its starting point, setting its location at the house of
Mr Nutmeg, a City shopkeeper joyfully telling his daughter about his success
at renting his windows out to people eager to see the King and Queen go past:

NUTMEG: I get so much Money by it, Oh! What a lucky circumstance that my
House stands so charmingly situated for a full view of the procession up and
down; – I have let the whole front of my Shop, and yet the Shop Tax repeal'd;
Oh! Pretty, if I had twenty Windows more, I cou'd let them all at Twenty
Guineas a Peice [*sic*] – I shall never more, abuse the minister for the window
Tax, when he has thus so nobly enabled me to pay it.

No doubt Nutmeg's sympathies for the notorious window tax (originating
in 1696), as well as the more recent shop tax of 1785, were sufficient
immediately to satirize his position, but what is most striking about
St. George's Day; or, Britons Rejoice! was that it did not specifically attempt
to replicate the spectacle.[46] Instead of being a re-enactment of the event, the
drama was a satiric analysis of conflicting public attitudes. Other contemporary dramas, even those also showing processions to St Paul's (such as one
performed in York in 1800), are quite clear that they hope to provide 'an
exact Representation of The Royal Procession to St. Paul's, On account of
the National Thanksgiving for the Three great Naval Victories achieved by
our Gallant Tars, under the respective Commands of Lords Howe,
St. Vincent, and Duncan'.[47] Instead of a celebration intertwining the

stabilities of monarchy, church and military, *St. George's Day; or, Britons Rejoice!* focused on the social issues provoked by the procession, specifically admonishing the rapacity of those charging money to see the King and Queen traversing the street. Within this moral economy of the public spectacle, Nutmeg's rebuke is addressed directly and forcefully to him by his daughter, Harriott: 'Places and Tickets! Lord Sir, one wou'd think you was a Box Keeper of the Playhouse, it's a great meanness for the sake of a few Guineas to hire your dwelling house out, and turn it into a mere Sadlers Wells.' Of course, although Covent Garden's supplementary meaning was slanted to imply the generosity of its own activities (charging fairer prices), the piece's sudden introduction of two sailors unable to find a viewing place, and too poor to buy one, forms the centrepiece of the final scene:

> Scene the 4th A Street before Nutmegs House (his Shop and Windows laid out in Seats the West Front of St Pauls with Steps. Platform &c. in the back Mob, Streets lin'd with the Artillery Company several occasional Characters, great confusion ringing of Bells &c. Enter Lieutenant Jack and Gunnel.

Into this 'confusion' walk the two sailors, home on leave from their ship, one of them the sweetheart of Nutmeg's daughter, whose father's self-serving can now be witnessed as having precluded them from viewing the procession. To contemporary audiences, Jack and Gunnel's exclusion would have been an incident of the day all too recognizable from their knowledge of how the procession was conducted. A contemporary print in *The Lady's Magazine*, showing specially installed, steeply raked tiers of seats in St Paul's some ten rows high, reinforces the sense of the ordinary contemporary populace removed from the sights to which *St. George's Day; or, Britons Rejoice!* alluded.[48]

Instead of the piece's aiming to be a simple simulacrum of the event, its ideological meaning, upon analysis, has very little to do with re-enacting or even celebrating the spectacle of the procession. Indeed, it rather chooses to show the apparent disorder of the procession (a 'Mob' and 'great confusion ringing of Bells &c.') and the irritating social turbulence it engendered among London's inhabitants. Prevented from witnessing the parade, the dialogue between Jack and Gunnel articulates a much larger context of national patriotic meaning noticeably distanced from the emotions and spectacle of the procession:

JACK: [S]o though I shou'd not be Bless'd with a sight of my Royal Master this
    Day, yet the glorious occasion must give true delight to the Soul of every
    honest Englishman.
GUN: Ah, Jack the reason why we rejoice is because we are all his Subjects.

JACK: No, its not.
GUN: Well then, its because he [*sic*] our king.
JACK: No its not, we rejoice because our king is a good man, and heaven has
    restor'd him to his People.
    [Air] Where our King is our Friend we in simplicity mourn
    Each ill that his peace might destroy
    So in sweet gratitude we hail healths return.

The stoicism of the men serving in the armed forces is a recurrent feature of
the representation of soldiers and sailors in Georgian Britain, but what is
important about this particular exchange is how carefully the ideology was
nuanced and articulated. What this piece of dialogue spells out is that, just
as the King does not automatically deserve deference or obedience (it being
a quality which arises naturally from his goodness), so too Nutmeg's
rapacity is worthy of criticism precisely because, as Gunnel says, 'we are
all his Subjects' who 'in simplicity mourn / Each ill that his peace might
destroy.' With the sailors excluded from entrance to both the tiered benches
of St Paul's, on account of their low social status, and Nutmeg's windows –
even at roof level ('Nutmeg: No places left, I suppose? Has Dick! [*sic*] Sold
all the Tickets for the Garrets') – it is only the outright shaming of Nutmeg
at the end of the drama which restores civic equilibrium. In short, harmony
is restored by the play's requiring that the shopkeeper perform financial
penance for his errors. The elaboration of this rationale within the drama's
moral economy of loyalism is worth detailing because it illustrates the range
of social issues implicitly resolved by Nutmeg's reformation:

NUTMEG: I'll remember my Friends, they are the poor and Miserable; I make this
    day by the hire of my House, just three hundred & forty Pounds, every
    shilling of which I shall as I all along intended appropriate to the discharge of
    such wretched Debtors in Fleet whose imprisonment has proceeded only
    from their misfortune. As a Citizen of London the highest Comp[limen]t.
    I cou'd Pay, a Monarch, of our Land of Liberty is by giving freedom to the
    distress'd the loyal Subject . . . God Save the King.

Of course, the drama pillories Nutmeg's belated charity through its feeble
timing ('as I all along intended') but allows him to make the perennially
populist gesture of freeing Fleet prison debtors, allowing the moral corrective of the rich giving liberty to the poor. Considering that *St. George's Day;
or, Britons Rejoice!* was a one-off, it was loaded with these precise interventions representing and critiquing a number of aspects of contemporary
behaviour, stretching from Jack's educative dialogue with Gunnel, patiently
explaining the unique constitutional proximity of the British monarch to
his people, to the denunciation and reformation of Nutmeg.

If any of these theatrical messages remained unclear, the inevitable doubling of mainpiece with afterpiece reinforced their collective meaning and, presumably, formed part of an overall programming rationale. In the case of *St. George's Day; or, Britons Rejoice!*, which seems to have been intended for only a single performance, the drama it was appended to was Richard Steele's repertoire staple, *The Funeral; or, Grief A La Mode* (1701), part of a benefit performance for the veteran actress Isabella Mattocks (1746–1826). Again, there appears to have been a certain amount of thematic continuity employed in deciding on this particular pairing, especially given that the dramas had wildly remote dates of origin. If *St. George's Day; or, Britons Rejoice!* was a satire on grasping shopkeepers, Steele's comedy was a grotesque satire on the rapacity of funeral directors and the vanity of mourners ('the poor Dead are deliver'd to my Custody, to be Embalm'd, Slash'd, Cut, and Drag'd about, not to do them Honour, but to satisfy the Vanity or Interest of their Survivors').[49] Like *St. George's Day; or, Britons Rejoice!*, Steele's *The Funeral; or, Grief A La Mode* lay in a clear continuum of critical commentary on social mores. The authority of precedence permitted the critiquing of deviant behaviour from the stage.

This emerging picture of late eighteenth-century British drama reveals an intricate network of theatrical performances, each interlocking in new and unexpected ways and forming a series of assemblages with distinct ordinal points. Inchbald's apparent breaching of *The True Briton*'s interpretation of loyal behaviour in the early 1790s had as much to do with that newspaper's perspective on the interplay of existing conventions of legitimate comment within the theatres as it did with the immediate political occasion of *Every One has his Fault*'s first-night performance. Yet for all of its apparent transience, *St. George's Day; or, Britons Rejoice!* shows that even when dramas might have been expected to be at their most loyal or at their most subservient to a nationally important occasion, their texts reveal a centring on more enduring groups of issues surrounding the moral economy of patriotism, whether that was the ironic exclusion of servicemen from seeing their monarch to the social harmony tardily restored by Nutmeg's freeing of the Fleet debtors via the redistribution of the fees he had collected. Within this context, *St. George's Day; or, Britons Rejoice!* is particularly interesting because its timing, performed shortly after the King's recovery but before the onset of the French Revolution in July 1789, situates it prior to an entirely new sequence of deeply felt, highly contested re-evaluations of the 1790s.

Amidst the new setting of a war against France and domestic turmoil within a country anxious at the possibility of pro-revolutionary radicals stalking the streets, the gentle satires and innuendoes of pre-Revolution *St. George's Day; or, Britons Rejoice!* were rapidly forgotten. Theatres continued to function as both public and private spaces where divergent ideologies could be manifested. Although details would not become available to the general newspaper-reading public until his treason trial in December 1794, the London Corresponding Society activist John Thelwall had raised the possibility during a Globe Tavern lecture of hijacking a performance of Thomas Otway's *Venice Preserv'd: Or, A Plot Discover'd* (1681) in order to appropriate parts of its political message in the radical cause. A witness testified to having been 'at the Play-house on the night the Play was represented, and saw the Prisoner [Thelwall] with about fifteen or twenty of his friends, in the Pit; the Play was represented in the usual manner, and the Prisoner and his friends attempted to encore those passages, but without effect.'[50] The passage Thelwall aimed to contest, taken from Act I, came from an exchange between Jaffier and Pierre criticizing the state's 'domestic spoilers, / That make us slaves, and tell us, 'tis our charter.' According to Thelwall's later account in *The Tribune* journal, he was 'joined with a great part of the house in applauding these passages'.[51] Nearly a year later, on 29 October 1795 when Drury Lane produced *Venice Preserv'd* in the days following the 'Pop-Gun Plot', it was Kemble who took the role of Jaffier (opposite Sarah Siddons' Belvedira) during this later episode of heightened audience sensitivity to exactly the same speeches. Fearing a recurrence of an attempted appropriation of the lines, in an apparent attempt to wrest the evening away from radical factions, Kemble (presumably still dressed for his part) instructed the pit orchestra to strike up 'God Save the King'. Farcically, too few of the musicians were then at their instruments and the anthem's music swayed uncertainly amidst the volatilities of the various audience factions.[52] This was an example of a recurrent phenomenon in eighteenth-century England, an audience who collectively embodied an alert awareness of the implicit political references which might be contextualized from hearing Georgian play texts spoken on stage. The examples of the *Venice Preserv'd* productions of 1794 and 1795 are not isolated and, even in their own topical context, are not features exclusive to Otway's play. Two days later, George III attended a performance of Sheridan's *The Rivals* at Covent Garden, and when Captain Anthony Absolute spoke the words, 'Sir, I serve his Majesty', as he is about to fight a duel with Sir Lucius O'Trigger, the audience spontaneously called out for 'God Save the King.'[53] The commotion in the playhouse reached such an 'alarming degree' that a Bow Street officer 'walked on the stage . . . and placed himself opposite to the King's Box', while *The Star* reported that Absolute's words 'shot through every heart like the electrical spark' (although one newspaper also reported that, when the loyal anthem was encored for a third time, it 'provoked a few hisses').[54] The Bow Street officer's sudden appearance on the Covent Garden stage itself underlines the way in which theatrical spaces had become understood as flashpoints for discontent and official intervention.

Within this whirling tide of politics and emotion, the realities of policing theatres as parts of London's general public spaces should not be overlooked. The King attended Covent Garden in order to exert his authority and reassure the populace about his survival following reports of an apparent attempt made upon his life. To reach the theatre, he took an unusually tortuous route along Long Acre, guarded by '200 horse and 300 footguards ... who, sparing neither age nor sex, used the authority vested in them much to the injury of his Majesty's subjects, many of whom suffered greatly by being trod under foot by the horses, and the wounds they received from their sabres.'[55]

It is not difficult to perceive the abrupt reversal by 1795 of the sentiments exhibited in *St. George's Day; or, Britons Rejoice!* Criticism of the crowd has now become criticism of the monarch, actually materialized in *Venice Preserv'd*, and potentially materialized in *The Roman Actor.* The Bow Street constable who mounted the stage during *The Rivals* was an ex-Clare Market hatter called Patrick Macmanus. Not only had he been a subpoenaed witness at Thomas Hardy's trial a year earlier but also he was now a newly created, close-attendance bodyguard of the King.[56] His appearance on stage at Covent Garden was indicative of the new dimensions envisaged by both the government and the King regarding the public safety of the monarch's person and the dangers posed to the state's stability if he were injured or killed. Of the playhouse hissers, a number were arrested that night but later released as merely drunk.[57] This concentration of official effort into controlling public spaces in and around the theatres can be added to other emerging configurations of political pressure on the playhouses, whose expressive roles had been realized because of their ability to materialize symbolic and linguistic criticisms of the monarch.

Given this recognition of the expressive role of the theatrical assemblage, it was not surprising that the government would seek to manipulate its outlier social networks in the print culture, attempting to replicate some of the authority they could exert through control of speech on the London stage. Two days before the 'Pop-Gun Plot', a new London-based, pro-government newspaper, *The Tomahawk or Censor General*, began publication ('The Tomahawk is not an instrument of a dastardly nature, like the

Italian stiletto; but is a manly weapon, used by manly nations; and boldly thrown, in the broad face of day, at the foes of their freedom').[58] Its publisher, Joseph Downes, also printed the papers of the Association for Preserving Property Against Republicans and Levellers as well as other loyalist titles – such as Patrick Colquhuon's *Observations and Facts Relative to Public Houses* (1794) – which were particularly energetic in targeting London's popular entertainments. Downes' *Anti-Levelling Songster* (1793), issued in two editions, and *Anti-Gallican Songster* (1793), issued in three, were intended as ideological interventions against the radical movement, and, much like Hannah More's later Cheap Repository Tracts series, they were aimed at the labouring classes in London's public houses newly located and quantified by Colquhuon.

A particular feature of *The Tomahawk* was its suspicion of all things theatrical but, in particular, Sheridan's role as both Whig politician and the manager of Drury Lane. Even in its first issue on 27 October, it had weighed in against 'Theatrical Patents' and published a complaint from a disgruntled Drury Lane employee (who 'never had one *civil* word from Kemble'). Sensing that the production was making a scandalous equivalence, *The Tomahawk* also condemned Drury Lane's new production of Otway's *Venice Preserv'd: Or, A Plot Discover'd* (1681) because its 'satire . . . was [originally] aimed at the greatest tyrannical oligarchy, the French convention excepted, that ever yet existed on earth.' Indeed, the first issue's parting shot was that Drury Lane's *Venice Preserv'd* production was an abuse of 'Patent Rights incroaching upon the very Basis of their Tenure!'[59] By the fourth issue, *The Tomahawk* was also corralling into its anti-theatrical polemics the disparate dangers of 'Plays, Debating Societies, Field Meetings, and Newspapers' while noting that 'French anarchy was accelerated as much by Destructive Dramatic Performances as by Seditious Clubs.' *The Tomahawk*'s targets are as good a guide as any to the structural features comprising the theatrical assemblage and its immediate networks. However, it also mounted carefully nuanced attacks aimed specifically at Sheridan.

In this fourth issue, *The Tomahawk* observed how 'the Lord Chamberlain, *attached to his Majesty's person*, refused a licence to a musical entertainment, because it might diminish the receipts of Drury Lane Theatre; which licence did not directly interfere with the patent of the Play house, and was demanded by one of his Majesty's most loyal subjects.'[60] *The Tomahawk*, in a move that remodels the most archaic features of the state legitimacy, conspicuously reminded Sheridan that Drury Lane owed its patent monopoly to the physical continuation of royal authority (technically, the patent lapsed on the death of the reigning monarch), whose official surrogate was the Lord Chamberlain. The fudging of the distinction between the incumbent of national authority (the body of the King) and the office (the Lord Chamberlain) embodying that deterritorialized authority is accomplished in the phrase '*attached to his Majesty's person*'. *The Tomahawk*'s fussy prose also buried within it a deeper allusion to Drury Lane's spoiling of its would-be competitors. The 'refused . . . licence' for 'a musical entertainment' appears to refer to Lady Eglantine Wallace's comedy, *The Whim* (1795), which was intended to have been produced at Margate theatre that September, but which had been halted only a few hours before its first performance because its licence application had been rejected.[61] Again, the connectivity across the assemblage between the metropolitan patent theatre and the provincial outlier competing to access some of its privileges is striking. Wallace elaborated the circumstances of the licence refusal (for a charity performance) when she later had the play printed accompanied by her defence of its contents. Although most of her comments were levelled at Larpent's powers of interdiction (she named him personally), she happens to mention that Larpent originally 'found no objections to it' but had specifically requested that the licence be 'signed by a Patentee', a wary ploy on Larpent's part in order to shift responsibility onto the royal theatre owners.[62] *The Tomahawk*'s account tallies with Wallace's own version insofar as it implies that Sheridan refused to sign-off on *The Whim* when requested to do so by Larpent. Of course, *The Tomahawk*'s attacks hit at the very basis of Drury Lane's prerogative (held in common with Covent Garden) over the enunciation of speech in the London theatres. *The Whim* could scarcely be described as 'a musical entertainment', but it did contain yet another song about Lord Howe's victory of 1 June over the French ('Britons . . . / . . . turned – and shew'd them Howe'), deftly signalling that *The Tomahawk* was aware that Sheridan's monopolistic playhouse with its royal monopoly on spoken drama absolutely relied on the continuance of the constitutional status quo.[63] The newspaper was clearly aware that by blocking *The Whim*, Sheridan was himself stretching the limits of his prerogative over speech, because – upon more minute analysis – Wallace's play contained just about enough music (especially of a patriotic nature) for it to pass muster as the type of musical entertainment a local magistrate could license. *The Tomahawk*'s implicit point, that the Margate theatre was not competing to the detriment of Drury Lane's audience catchment, was underlined by an implicit allusion to the patentees' most feared scenario, that the Lord Chamberlain would license rival theatres in London and permit them to perform the more musical forms of burletta, comic opera and burlesque.

These attempts at the appropriation and counter-appropriation of the political use of theatrical space were constants and express the physical identities of the metropolitan and provincial playhouses as occupying steeply differing positions of legitimacy between their gradients of population. *The Tomahawk*'s anti-theatrical stance was a major feature of its editorializing, ultimately shying away from (quite outrageously) naming Sheridan as personally involved in the 'Pop-Gun Plot', but otherwise also warning its readers of 'the secret influence of the theatre'. In effect, *The Tomahawk* mounted a personal campaign against both Sheridan and Kemble, predicting that 'A cloud is ready to burst, in the theatrical hemisphere of the most tremendous nature', as it harried them with allegations that the generous expansion in Drury Lane's size following its demolition in 1791 and subsequent reopening in 1794 constituted an infringement of its patent.[64] Confident in deploying a parodic feint in campaigning for a relaxation of the patent theatre monopolies, *The Tomahawk* was an unequivocal component in the government's anti-republican stance, an instrument in the dissemination of loyalist ideology, storing its perspectives at the nodes of each issue and along its distribution network.

What Thelwall cannot have known is that the government had already secured the services of the musician and playwright Charles Dibdin in its efforts to diffuse the audiences for Thelwall's radical lectures by displacing some of the density of his prospective audience. Dibdin operated the Sans Souci theatre off the Strand, close to the premises in Beaufort Buildings used by Thelwall for his political lectures subsequent to his acquittal in the 1794 treason trials. It seems clear that Dibdin's own loyalism suited the government. Although he is ambiguous about the precise circumstances of the government's intervention, the Sans Souci was heavily advertised as licensed by the Lord Chamberlain, despite its clear competition with the patent houses, a factor which usually raised some degree of fuss from the patentees, especially as it coincided with their winter seasons and was situated in close proximity. In this case, however, the patentees kept quiet. Dibdin specifically referred in his memoirs to the proximity of Thelwall's lecture venue, although it was more probably his explicit loyalist song-writing of the invasion scare years of 1802–3 which eventually secured his (highly unusual) £200 government pension.[65] Again, the absolute coincidence of performer, performance and venue establishes that some degree of organized counter-theatricality took place and, quite certainly, Dibdin included a comic sketch about 'Club Oratory' in his *Will of the Wisp* entertainment in October 1795 on the same night Thelwall was speaking in Beaufort Buildings on the motion that 'Corruption of the Representative

Body is the principal Source of Unjust and Ruinous Wars'. Of course, a crucial difference between them was that Dibdin's cheapest seats were 2s. (in the gallery), whereas entrance to Beaufort Buildings was just 6d.[66]

This degree of counter-theatricality – ultimately innocuous in the case of Dibdin versus Thelwall – typifies the extraordinary degree of both attention and intervention which went into the London politics of theatre in the 1790s. The convergence of theatre and politics was a pervasive feature of metropolitan public discourse in late eighteenth-century British culture, not least visible in the newspapers, which, of course, were also the principal vehicles for advertising playhouse bills. At the time of the 1794 treason trials, *The Star* newspaper, on 16 October, carried a single portmanteau column interspersing theatrical reportage with news about the impending trials. *The Star* covered the previous night's Covent Garden performances of *Richard III* and *Tom Thumb* – 'not a crowded house' – alongside puffs for Sarah Siddons' forthcoming appearances in Drury Lane's production of Lessing's *Emilia Galotti* (1772), before going on to bring the latest news about what became known as 'Pitt's Reign of Terror'.[67] Directly after commenting on the new 'dresses' and 'beautiful scenery' promised for Covent Garden's *Romeo and Juliet*, *The Star* reported that the execution of the Edinburgh treason indictee, David Downie, had been respited for one month, while that of his accomplice, Robert Watt, was soon to proceed ('at the west end of the Tolbooth') subsequent to a plot being uncovered after the discovery of a trunkful of pikes at Musselburgh. As far as developments in the metropolis were concerned, the column then went on to carry the news that printed 'indictments for High Treason' had been served on London Corresponding Society members Thomas Hardy and John Thelwall, then confined in the Tower, and legal papers on the same indictment had been served on the successful playwright and friend of Elizabeth Inchbald, Thomas Holcroft, then held in Newgate. Finally, the column reported that James Upton, 'the principal Informer' involved with the 'Pop-Gun Plot' against the King, was believed (erroneously) to be on the verge of being charged with perjury as a device to ensure his own protection.[68] Even within the confines of one newspaper column, readers encountered sudden juxta-positions of secret plots, espionage and counter-espionage in Britain's political life, directly interspersed with the kinds of 'Theatrical Intelligence' sections which publications such as *The Star*, *The Public Advertiser* and *St James's Chronicle* had made regular features.

The degree to which even fragments of dramatic texts could provoke immediate, even volatile, effects in theatre audiences has already been evidenced in relation to Thelwall's plan to hijack the iteration of lines in

Venice Preserv'd that February, but straightforwardly loyalist appropriations were equally energetically pursued and can be gauged by reactions to Covent Garden's staging of *Hamlet* on 27 September. When Claudius came to the lines (misquoted), 'There's a divinity doth hedge a King, / That Treason cannot reach him', *The True Briton* reported 'the audience, struck by their application to the discovery of the horrid plot which has just come to light, applauded them with a degree of emotion and enthusiasm which did honour to the feelings of Britons, and which we hope and trust will ever be their proudest characteristic.' According to *The London Packet*, 'the performance was interrupted for the space of ten minutes.'[69] Significantly, it was not Joseph Holman's Hamlet or even James Middleton's Laertes which provoked comment but simply the public iteration of such resonating lines before a sophisticated and alert audience.[70]

Kemble's transposition of sections of Massinger's text from late in *The Roman Actor*'s first scene to its very beginning, making them the play's opening lines, radically resituated the play's meaning, referencing it unmistakably to the politics of the day. It would have been a play whose text resonated fully with its audience. With its commentary about, 'What times are these! . . . / May we being alone / Speak our thoughts freely of the Prince and State, / And not fear the Informer?', Massinger's drama echoed the febrile atmosphere outside the playhouse where informers like Upton were thought to stalk public political meetings. Not only had Drury Lane steeply radicalized the play's potential reference to arguably the hottest domestic legal and political controversy of the decade but the theatre was also choosing to mount a drama which was itself an assertion of the civic role of theatre in promoting virtue by chastising political corruption. In Massinger's original beginning, the play had opened with a troupe of Roman actors ('Aesop: What do we act to day?') discussing the Senate's suppression of theatre's role in political commentary, all set amidst a climate of government vindictiveness against players fuelled by the reports of spies:

AESOP: 'Tis given out lately,
    The Consul *Aretinus* (*Caesar*'s Spy)
    Said at his Table, E'er a Month expir'd
    (For being gall'd in our last Comedy)
    He would silence us for ever.[71]

Kemble himself was completely aware of *The Roman Actor*'s place in the Georgian theatrical repertoire as a piece articulating theatre's civic centrality as a forum for reflecting public disquiet and satirizing changing patterns in social and cultural behaviour. When Tate Wilkinson had toured its excerpted version in the north of England, bannered on its playbills as 'A Defence of the Stage . . . in answer to an accusation brought against it by the Senate', it had been Kemble who had played the role of Paris, the actor who speaks in defence of his fellow players at the invitation of the suspected spy, the Senator Aretinus.[72] Again, these parts of Massinger's *Roman Actor* must have appeared to Kemble to mirror the heady atmosphere of the autumn of 1794:

ARETINUS: Stand forth.
  In thee, as being the chief of thy Profession,
  I do accuse the Quality of Treason,
    As Libelers against the State and *Cæsar.*
PARIS: Meer Accusations are not Proofs my Lord,
  In what are we Delinquents?
ARETINUS: You are they
  That search into the Secrets of the time,
  And under fain'd Names, on the Stage, present
  Actions not to be touch'd at.[73]

At that moment, the metropolis' newspapers were interacting with the theatre, law courts and government to form a complex network of information, dissemination and public reception in an assemblage with definable populations, nodes of storage of information and capacities for emergence.

Holcroft's recent indictment for high treason would have played a major part in Drury Lane's decision to drop *The Roman Actor*, details of which were readily available in the newspapers.[74] *The St. James's Chronicle or British Evening Post* had been quick off the mark to condemn wholesale – ahead of any formal charges – 'Mr. Holcroft, the play-wright and performer, pretty well known for the democratical sentiments which he has industriously scattered through the lighter works of Literature'.[75] On the day Kemble sent off *The Roman Actor*, the playwright Elizabeth Inchbald was reported to have visited Holcroft in Newgate. *The True Briton* newspaper, bursting with innuendo about their political sympathies, observed drily of the visit that it 'was nothing more than friendly in a *congenial* Muse'.[76] However, in reality she may have gone to Newgate simply to swap professional notes with Holcroft, who also did a lot of work for Covent Garden (although that month Inchbald would have been working on *The Wedding Day*, a comedy whose licence was applied for on 30 October and produced at Drury Lane on 1 November, three days before the spectacular collapse of Thomas Hardy's trial).[77] By this time, nearly two years had passed since the hostile reception (in the same *True Briton* newspaper) for her *Every One has his*

Fault, when it had been censured after opening in January 1793 as 'very exceptionable', with a 'highly objectionable' 'tendency' on account of its 'Allusions . . . to the dearness of provisions in this Metropolis; and in several sentences the *Democrat* displays a cloven foot.'[78] Two days later, in a revealing move prefiguring the political climate of 1794, Inchbald wrote to *The World* newspaper (founded by the occasional playwright, Edward Topham), remonstrating that although she had been 'accused of conveying seditious sentiments to the Public', she guaranteed that she had not 'expunged those sentences which were of [a] dangerous tendency'.[79] With the option of self-censorship obviously having been contemplated (and dismissed) by Inchbald, Drury Lane's decision to drop *The Roman Actor* falls into a now familiar reaction to the various modulations of intimidation, riposte and innuendo.

Holcroft's appearances in the London newspapers that autumn arrived thick and fast as the capital's print culture, amidst a growing popular atmosphere suspicious of traitorous conspiracies, connected his name with the world of theatre. As early as 30 September, he was having to deny allegations that he had been charged with sedition.[80] Just two weeks earlier, on 15 September, his new prelude, *The Rival Queens; or, Drury Lane & Covent Garden*, had kicked off Covent Garden's winter schedule ('The house was very full . . . all the performers were loudly applauded').[81] Although it was politically innocuous, Holcroft's *Rival Queens; or, Drury Lane & Covent Garden* satirized the two patent playhouses' luxurious refurbishments ('Chandeliers & mahogany doors, & fluted what-ye-call-ums-pillar-asters [*sic*]') with Covent Garden's summer makeover designed to pre-empt Drury Lane's rebuild opening.[82] With a long season to look forward to, both of the patent monopolies openly vied with each other for audiences. For his part Holcroft ridiculed their clientele, figured by Mr and Mrs Town, two 'fashionably dress'd' but indiscriminately ignorant theatre-goers, who, 'if Otway, Congreve, or even Shakespeare himself grace the Scene, 'tis ten to one but . . . [they] are to be found at some gambling Club, some City-feast, or, perhaps, on a party to a Puppet-shew.' Once again, although the piece escaped censure or comment, the conspicuous consumption of the 'City-feast' highlighted the same territory less luckily satirized by Inchbald one year earlier. However, what particularly characterized *The Rival Queens; or, Drury Lane & Covent Garden* was its reflection of the kind of mob rule that seemed to threaten London that year. In Holcroft's surrogate configuration of the external disquiet outside the theatre, the stagehands of the two playhouses scuffle as the playhouses compete for audience:

Scene Changes. The Carpenters and Servants of both houses with the Stagemen in their new Liveries, arm'd with various Weapons, rang'd on opposite sides in great Tumult, flourish their Clubs & ready to fight – others interfering to keep the peace.

D[RURY]. LANE MOB: Down with 'em! }
PEACE-MAKERS: Nay, but, Gentlemen! } all in tumult
COV[ENT]. G[ARDEN]. MOB: Fall on! }

Although this was a mock battle of the patentees, its tumultuous mobs mirrored fears of clashes on the streets. Holcroft had not even spared Covent Garden (his sponsor) as he glanced at the destitution found in nearby Vinegar Yard, Little Russell Street, pillorying and parodying even the 'Queen' of the 'Covent Garden Procession' looking down on her grandly refurbished surroundings:

> Oh! Vinegar Yard! Renown'd for drab & dirt
> For many a sleeveless Coat, and ragged Shirt,
> For roofless Straw, where Pat and Sawney lig
> Where tatter'd Nymphs with Breechless Britons Jig,
> Oh Vinegar Yard! How vast was thy surprise,
> At once to see me tow'ring to the Skies. . .

With the two patent houses' stagehands confronting each other ('C.G. Man . . . and I tell you (*pulling up his breeches*) You are no Gentleman. 1st D.L. Man: And I tell you (snapping his fingers in his face) you don't know good [*sic*]'), *The Rival Queens*, as much as anything else that autumn, theatricalized the consequences of competitive monopolies and steep social divisions within a disharmonious society. While its content was symbolic rather than topical or specific, the prelude served as an important surrogate for many of that autumn's civic tensions. As ever, a winter-season premiere audience of approaching 3,000 people could have witnessed it. Ultimately, it is within this context of heightening tension that Drury Lane quietly shelved *The Roman Actor*.

To close this chapter and to step out of the viciousness of the national climate of distrust reflected in the treason trials of 1794 and the anti-Drury Lane, anti-Sheridan, machinations of *The Tomahawk*, it is necessary to gain some perspective and to look back to 1789 and the time of the King's recovery. Whereas in 1795, the country thought someone was trying to kill the King, back in 1789 the nation had been worried and concerned about his state of health. As much as anything, this chapter has analysed the ways in which increasing anxiety about the war and radical agitation came to be reflected in London's theatres. If, in 1795, Drury Lane was perceived as a focus for anti-government sentiment, back in 1789 the same playhouse had adopted an altogether more patriotic stance, producing an adulatory masque celebrating the King's recovery. If *St. George's Day; or, Britons Rejoice!* had registered Covent Garden's particular perspective on the events surrounding the King's recovery, Drury Lane's later offering (similarly for one night only) is even more striking on account of the solemnity and formality with which the same set of national emotions was commemorated. Drury Lane's *Laoeudaimonos; or, A People Made Happy* performed on 19 May 1789 was a masque of remarkable obeisance.[83]

Formal masques, although echoing an earlier age, were not considered redundant theatrical genres. As late as 1795, on the marriage of the Prince of Wales to Caroline of Brunswick, Drury Lane had attached a masque 'in honour of the Royal Nuptials' to the comic opera, *Jack of Newbury*.[84] Just two months before the storming of the Bastille, *A People Made Happy* featured a masque including scenery portraying a 'Cavern of Despair ... Hygeia's Grove[; and a] Temple of Gratitude' and with it scenes populated by 'Britannia[; the] Genius of England[;] Hope[;] Hygeia' and sundry 'Britons'. The presence of Hygeia and her grove (the classical goddess of health and cleanliness) is indicative not only of a country whose monarch was troubled by intermittent bouts of apparent madness but also of a nation generally ill at ease with itself. The masque moves quite literally from the Cavern of Despair through Hygeia's Grove to the restoration of Britannia's place in the Temple of Gratitude, whence she is escorted by Hope and the Genius of Britain. Significantly, the masque also included a scene showing 'Albion's Cliffs with Britains Navy riding at Anchor', a typical projection of the confidence and reassurance the country took in its military might and the certainty of its imperial position. Although the licensing copy noted that it was 'In Commemoration of the Restoration of His Majesty's Health', the piece emphasized a sombre setting for its opening scene in the Cavern of Despair, where 'Britannia [is] discover'd seated in a disconsolate posture.' About a week earlier Sarah Siddons had recited 'an Ode on the recovery of his Majesty in the character of Britannia', but this was obviously thought insufficient to mark the occasion.[85] The masque's sense of national malady ('Britannia: When will affliction quit th' unhappy Isle?') is pervasive. Displaying a general atrophy of Britain's commercial, scientific and cultural life, 'Plenty throws down her Horn desponding Genius / Afflicted mourns her patrons dire distress', while Britannia grieves, 'Must the Ships be all moor'd in each road / Must the Arts be all scatter'd around / And shall Commerce grow sick of her Tide[?]' Not unexpectedly, the view of Britain that *A People Made Happy* ultimately projected was that of a commonwealth whose natural buoyancy and optimism had been temporarily compromised by a mentally impaired patriarch. Within the curious psyche of the masque, the 'patron' king is ill and his daughter, Britannia, in response herself sickens with hopelessness, the sickness of the patriarch displacing itself onto the female warrior genius of the island. Figured into the resilience of the nation expressed in this drama was the reassuring capacity of its military. The navy was pictured in a transparency showing ships riding under Albion's cliffs, as 'a party of Soldiers & Sailors each headed by an Officer' escort Britannia, assisted by Hope and Hygeia, as they join to sing the finale: 'The King is living / Bend the knee & God adore / Heav'n't this greatest bounty giving / Wafts our Joy from shore to shore / Happy Monarque who Surviving / Views the future by the past / Feels their pleasure e'en in Lying / To be lov'd unto the last.' The impact of the King's weakness (literally 'Lying' ill) was obviously strongly felt among the nation, and even an ode recited by Sarah Siddons at the height of her career was not enough to reflect and connect with national anxiety. Given the context of concerns about a regency, Drury Lane's decision to stage a masque allowed it neatly to repackage Britain not as a nation verging on constitutional confusion, but, rather, as one proudly embodied by the parallel existence of a symbolic Britannia, ageless, timeless and now sacramentally presented to Drury Lane's audience restored to health.

The sheer simplicity of *Laoeudaimonos; or, A People Made Happy* is revealing, particularly in its apparent ability not only to entertain but also to comfort and reassure. What is most striking are the ways in which these important messages about loyalty were presented in digestible form. In *St. George's Day; or, Britons Rejoice!*, the naval officer Jack's homilies to his sailor subordinate ('we rejoice because our king is a good man, and heaven has restor'd him to his People') are dressed up around the comic absurdities of shopkeeper Nutmeg's sale of window space. In *A People Made Happy*, the solemn message of the masque was almost certainly sugared by having its female cast playing dishabille, with Hygeia and Britannia representing the rejuvenating spirits of a national genius now conspicuously feminized by the absence of its ailing patriarch.[86] Indeed, although both dramas are centred on absent kings (because of illness, because of crowds), they also signal his ready presence as a presiding ruler, loved and adored by his subjects. By contrast, six years later – with George III very much present in the theatre – the Bow Street officer Patrick Macmanus had to take up position on the Covent Garden stage opposite the royal box in order to quell anti-monarchist unrest during *The Rivals*. Somewhere in the middle of this, alarmed at the possibility of the loyalist backlash its own productions – and many others – had helped engender, Drury Lane quietly dropped *The Roman Actor* with its devastating opening lines:

> What times are these!
> To what is Rome fall'n! May we being alone
> Speak our thoughts freely of the Prince and State,
> And not fear the Informer?

Conclusion

Anyone who has read *Celebrity, Performance, Reception* all the way through will have been left in no doubt as to the sheer scale of eighteenth-century London's theatrical assemblage. The volume of its audiences, the level of its organizational ability and its highly evolved functions as a market are beyond doubt. By conceptualizing British theatre as a diagram of connectivity linked across both its human and material components, the exterior relations of contemporary drama in performance can be traced with a high degree of certainty. The recovery of the assemblage's markets, spatial and temporal locations, densities of performance and co-present audience populations, together with a sense of their social networks, offers the possibility of redefining the cultural role of Georgian theatre in its national cultural context.

Britain's theatrical infrastructure brought with it considerable degrees of social change, some of it attached to pressures on the surviving archaisms of earlier eras, such as the patent system's vestment of authority in the life of the monarch, but also much which was notably socially progressive. Theatre was a marketplace where pay for women, if only on an irregular and sporadic basis, sometimes exceeded that of men. Crucially, the presence of women in considerable numbers as a significant proportion of the workforce precipitated the gender configuration of the theatrical funds, which, in turn, were founded on a vigorously entrepreneurial capitalism protectively embedded in an old-fashioned monopoly. Even taken on their own, the benefit provisions of the theatrical funds represent a major social innovation in the area of gender equality in the workplace. The Drury Lane Fund's codicil declaring that 'married subscribers to the Fund shall be considered as separate parties', together with the presence of its high annual income threshold on cohabitation before annuities were rescinded, requires a comprehensive rebalancing of our knowledge of the legal precedents relating to contemporary gender equality, particularly relative to marriage and to the cultural workplace. One might call this the issue of Elizabeth Inchbald's 1*s*. 6*d*.

The assemblage model's predictive qualities have the benefit of establishing a higher probable mean for actors' and actresses' earnings by returning celebrity cultural status (and the pay which went with it) much nearer to the general profile of the profession as a whole. Garrick, Siddons and Kean, each in their different ways in relation to the historical specificity of the theatrical assemblages in which they worked, were the products of voluminous social reception networks as fascinating and varied as the celebrities themselves. As DeLanda puts it, '[I]t is *the pattern of recurring links*, as well as the properties of those links, which forms the subject of study, not the attributes of the persons occupying positions in a network.'[1] By contrast with celebrity, we might call this the issue of 'Mr Fector's good Acting'.

The assemblage model also allows the theatre visits of Yusuf Agha Effendi to be placed precisely among these networks, not as a linear function of a historical process precipitating some exact causal effect, but, rather, as an identifiable component within London's enormous audience populations. The ambassador was one among many who went to see dramas enacting and memorializing a sequence of British naval and army victories against the French. Nevertheless, the Turkish ambassador's personal interest in theatre-going should be considered an emergent characteristic capable of interacting with Anglo-Ottoman geopolitical relations. We might call this *The Death of Captain Faulkner; or, British Heroism*, 'By Special Desire of His Excellency the Turkish Ambassador'.

All of these descriptions, which comprise the contents of this book, are predicated on following through the logic of DeLanda's primary insight, 'The identity of an assemblage is not only embodied in its materiality but also expressed by it.'[2] The historical specificity of an assemblage invokes materiality as the principal means through which the exterior relations of social actions should be investigated. For literary studies, there are a number of significant questions raised by assemblage theory, principally about how the symbolic registers of texts can be related to materiality where densities of population are diffuse. Assemblage theory's proposition of a 'single flat ontology with two sides, one side populated by virtual problems and the other by a divergent set of actual solutions to those problems', radically displaces symbolic registers (such as text) by determining them as coefficients of their material exterior relations.[3] This structure is consonant with DeLanda's formulation that, 'in assemblage theory expressivity cannot be reduced to language and symbols'.[4]

While congregated population density may exist only fleetingly at the site of performance, cultural meaning mutates rapidly with every performance reiteration to different co-present audiences, who, in turn, have different receptions because they are in different locations. In the Georgian, the materially massive theatrical infrastructure accommodated multiple gradients of population, all of them capable of relaying heterogeneous or mutated messages across the assemblage as well as along its networks. DeLanda's formulation is that, 'Once a large scale assemblage is in place, it immediately starts acting as a source of limitations and resources for its components ... downward causality is needed to account for the fact that most social assemblages are composed of parts that come into existence after the whole has emerged.'[5] By following the assemblage model, even the molecular components of the assemblage, its individual singularities, can be meaningfully integrated with their macro or universal singularities as new and emergent capacities structured within an existing possibility space.

In *Celebrity, Performance, Reception*, the obscure, immigrant D'Egville family of dancers emerged into their specific ideological being after performing in *The Glorious First of June*. Choosing not to contribute – as most Drury Lane performers had done – to the benefit performance in aid of the widows and orphans of the victorious British fallen, the D'Egvilles comprised a dissonant element within the national celebrations whose dissent is captured by the transactions recorded within the theatrical marketplace. We might call this the issue of the D'Egvilles' *6s. 8d.*

Above all, stretched out beyond London's giant 3,000-seat patent theatres stood the national inventory of regional and provincial playhouses partially recorded in Winston's *Theatric Tourist*. These were the ordinal points of a vast contemporary theatrical network. Out in rural East Anglia in the 1780s, a now irrecoverable troupe touring the (still) tiny villages of Laxfield, Suffolk, and Attleborough, Norfolk, distributed their crude playbills now deposited in Manchester's John Rylands Library. They offered John Gay's '*The begGars* [*sic*] *Opera*', the pantomime of *The Elopement or, Harlequin Triumphant*, and the comedies of George Farquhar's *The Beaux' Stratagem* (1707) and Garrick's *Miss in Her Teens* (1747). The presence of this live and varied repertoire in two rural hamlets conclusively demonstrates the absolute multiplicity of theatrical possibility spaces reaching across Georgian Britain, where performance meaning stood ever ready to mutate. Whether measured by extension or intensity, the contemporary theatrical assemblage existed as a materialized presence on a scale unequalled by any other cultural form.

Actor-network-theory

Bruno Latour's actor-network-theory (ANT), set out in *Reassembling the Social: An Introduction to Actor-Network-Theory* (2005), promises to model the fluctuating and transactional behaviour of human populations. ANT has been readily taken up by those advising modern retailers and manufacturers needing to understand the behaviour of changing cohorts of consumers, who are often increasingly linked to transient cultures of fashion and, today, it is usually mobilized to explain interactive electronic networks. ANT is also useful for understanding political behaviour, not only within democracies. ANT can also offer a transhistorical model well suited to describing the evolution of many types of global social and political conditions, including those encountered during the slower rates of social and cultural change experienced in Georgian Britain. ANT's structure for understanding the parameters of political, gender, class and racial topography is applicable to the Georgian but perhaps with the major caution that early modern and modern societies tend towards displaying greater degrees of cultural homogeneity. In particular for its relevance to this book, Latour's method of explaining ANT in *Reassembling the Social* consciously adapts imagery and metaphors drawn from theatre in order to explain the anthropology of a range of social functions, not all of them connected to human agency.

Although Latour's analytical concerns are not especially directed towards the particular cultural roles of theatres or actors, ANT sets out to 'reactivate the metaphors implied in the word actor', in order to 'retrieve its multiplicity'. He writes, '[T]he very word actor directs our attention to a complete dislocation of acting.' 'Play-acting puts us immediately into a thick imbroglio' of questions: 'Is this for real? Is it fake? Does the audience's reaction count? What about the lighting? What is the backstage crew doing? Is the playwright's message faithfully transported or hopelessly bungled? Is the character carried over? And if so, by what? . . . Where is the prompter?' The allure of the acting analogy is that it allows Latour to take advantage of the proposition within acting as a metaphor that 'action is *dislocated*'.[1] Latour notes that he has been attracted by what he perceives as the more liberal critical terminologies deployed in literary theory, and his employment of the word 'actor' seems principally to be based on its general level of accessibility (substituting for the more technical word 'actant').[2] Similarly, the attraction of the word 'network' lies in another set of metaphorical and analogical allusions also drawing on commonplace notions. For Latour, the network in ANT is 'a point-to-point connection ... which is physically traceable and thus can be recorded empirically'. He describes these networks as like a fisherman's net, a structural system which 'leaves *empty* most of what is *not* connected'. This overall idea of non-linear, intermittently broken, but substantially connected arrays of social networks again draws upon one of the most accessible of global metaphors, this time based on traditional methods of fishing with nets. One of its advantages is that the image of the net facilitates an almost universal sense of labour and of loss or, as Latour puts it, 'as any fisherman knows when repairing it on the deck', 'this connection is not made for free.'[3] According to Latour, these features of dislocated connectedness, or non-linearity, comprise the dominant structural features of social assemblage which ANT sets out to describe. To defend these notions pre-emptively, he also sets out a striking pathology of cautions against the assumption of stable subjectivity found within more fixed models of the social.[4]

In other words, ANT's basic proposition is that society comprises sets of fleeting, elusive compositions of assemblies coming into being as collective groups functionally (or dysfunctionally) through the agency of their constituent actors in which space, distance, the built environment and other non-human agencies all play important roles and are fully capable of being integrated within it. Theatrical spaces, players in theatre companies, or spectating, socializing audiences at theatrical performances appear to approximate very closely to the types of assemblages visualized in Latour's descriptions of the social: 'ANT ... is the name of a type of momentary association which is characterised by the way it gathers together into new shapes.'[5]

More waywardly, wishing to deconstruct fixed cores of social solidity or essentialist stability, Latour seems conscious that the theatrical metaphor is particularly well suited to integration within the types of gnomic methodology of pedagogy incorporated into several of the discourses in *Reassembling the Social*. For example, Latour's recourse to an amusingly fictionalized, neo-Socratic dialogue between a London School of Economics professor and an exasperated research student ('S[tudent]:

Sorry, but are you playing some sort of Zen trick here? . . . Can't ANT help me with this mass of data? I need a framework!') suggests the pervasiveness of the everyday social dramas which are, quite precisely, not constitutive of linear or fixed identity ('P[rofessor]: ANT is a method, and mostly a negative one at that; it says nothing about the *shape* of what is being described with it. S[tudent]: This is confusing!').[6]

In other words, Latour's central insight can be summarized as a distributed model of social and non-social actors evolving society through their own interactions with themselves and with their material environment. With Georgian society arguably more homogeneous, less fragmented and more likely to involve itself in customs or collective acts of social gathering, such as church or theatre-going, than our own, ANT offers a workable theoretical model for understanding the mix of Georgian materialities located in theatrical venues, performers and their performance texts. Moreover, as Latour argues with reference to speed bumps and scallop-fishing fields (or, one might add, working theatres), non-social actors as much as human agencies determine the shape of the social.[7] Georgian London's two big theatres, Covent Garden and Drury Lane, each with a 3,000-seat capacity and a dizzying programme of two productions per night per playhouse, were enormous contributors to the shaping of a range of metropolitan social perspectives, and not least to the shaping of the West End.

Of course (and to avoid the anxiety acted out by the research student), Latour's is actually a negative method. ANT describes a set of processes at work in society which, as long as there exist human and non-human actors, never falls back into stabilization or cessation. Social actors (human and non-human) are always in play (like processes of difference), existing in complex interactions of exterior relationships. As far as proposing a method is concerned, however, Latour, at best, simply announces the scope of a project: '[T]here is no society, no social realm, and no social ties, *but there exist translations between mediators that may generate traceable associations.*' This formulation is particularly helpful in establishing that 'translations' ('a connection that transports, so to speak') between actors (or, in Latour's sense, actor mediators) leave behind 'traceable associations' which generate or articulate the shape of the social.[8] Although my book is very largely concerned with social networks of human actors (audiences and players in playhouses), it is also intrinsically concerned with the range of roles performed by non-social actors. These non-social actors include not only the different playhouses (particularly as distinct, built environments of eighteenth-century London and the provinces) but also the effects on social assemblage of distance (on the Georgian touring circuits, or across a metropolis or national region). These explicit physical environments in which the social takes place can also be linked to the transformational forces of capitalist market economics, agencies which are connected to human social formations but not controlled or determined by them. *Celebrity, Performance, Reception* goes to some lengths to determine the complexity of the market forces in Georgian theatre which, along with other agencies of social assemblage, might be involved in accounting for things such as the attribution of personal theatrical celebrity or the income and expenditure calculations many performers became adept at in order to mount successful benefit nights. This type of historical method mirrors the already successful incorporation of Latour's work into modern business economics.[9]

Notes

INTRODUCTION: THEATRE, PERFORMANCE AND SOCIAL ASSEMBLAGE THEORY

1. DeLanda's key sections include *A New Philosophy of Society: Assemblage Theory and Social Complexity* (London: Continuum, 2006), Introduction and Chapters 1–3, pp. 1–67; *Deleuze: History and Science* (New York and Dresden: Atropos Press, 2010), 'Assemblage Theory and Human History', pp. 3–27; and *Philosophy and Simulation: The Emergence of Synthetic Reason* (London: Continuum, 2011), Appendix, pp. 184–203.

2. Conversely, sociologist Charles Tilly's 'repertoires of contention' model (see Chapter 8, below) is a methodology for analysing social formations by using metaphors of theatricality. Frequently focused on British eighteenth-century history, Tilly, arguably, foreshadows assemblage theory but without its typical schematized features such as non-linearity, materialized agency, emergent differences, spaces of possibility, individual and universal singularities, and population gradients. However, some of Tilly's later works, such as *Regimes and Repertoires* (University of Chicago Press, 2006) and the posthumous *Contentious Performances* (Cambridge University Press, 2008), introduce categories which seem overly crude; e.g. 'No Repertoire … Weak Repertoire … Strong Repertoire … Rigid Repertoire', Tilly, *Contentious Performances*, p. 15. However, for an excellent bibliography of 'performance' and 'repertoire' metaphors in sociological discourse, see Tilly, *Contentious Performances*, p. 14, n. 1.

3. For a study of such variants, partly linked to DeLanda's work, see Carsten Strathausen, 'Epistemological Reflections on Minor Points in Deleuze', *Theory & Event* 13:4 (2010), E-ISSN: 1092–311X.

4. DeLanda, *Philosophy and Simulation*, p. 200.

5. DeLanda, *New Philosophy of Society*, p. 19.

6. *Ibid.*, p. 118.

7. Some will find post-Deleuzian critical discourse remorselessly ahistorical, non-materialized and non-specific; see Martin Fuglsang and Bent Meier Sørensen (eds.), *Deleuze and the Social* (Edinburgh University Press, 2006). The collection includes an essay by DeLanda, 'Deleuzian Ontology and Assemblage Theory', pp. 250–66.

8. For an early transposition of DeLanda into performer-oriented (rather than reception-oriented) performance theory within a less materialist perspective, see

Susan Melrose, 'Bodies Without Bodies', in Susan Broadhurst and Josephine Machon (eds.), *Performance and Technology: Practices of Virtual Embodiment and Interactivity* (Basingstoke: Palgrave Macmillan, 2006), pp. 1–17. The concepts of performance included in Laura Cull (ed.), *Deleuze and Performance* (Edinburgh University Press, 2009), raise the possibility of several categories of theatricality and extra-theatricality beyond the scope of this book but which do not seem essentially inimical to it.

9. For an indicative bibliography, see Freddie Rokem, *Philosophers and Thespians: Thinking Performance* (Stanford, CA: Stanford University Press, 2010), p. 198, n. 1. Confusingly, modern 'performance theory' tends to focus on performers in performance rather than audiences in theatres. See, as representative, Philip Auslander, *Theory for Performance: A Student's Guide* (London: Routledge, 2008). For more materialized, non-linear, proto-assemblage perspectives on performance theory, see Richard Schechner, *Between Theater and Anthropology* (Philadelphia: University of Pennsylvania Press, 1985); *Performance Theory* (London: Routledge, [1977, 1988] 2003, rev. edn); 'Invasions Friendly and Unfriendly: The Dramaturgy of Direct Theatre', in Janelle G. Reinelt and Joseph R. Roach (eds.), *Critical Theory and Performance* (Ann Arbor, MI: University of Michigan Press, 1992), pp. 88–106.

10. For the vigour of the philosophical debate around ANT, see Graham Harman, *Prince of Networks: Bruno Latour and Metaphysics* (Prahan: Re.press, 2009).

11. Tony Bennett has usefully summarized 'the varied strands of assemblage and actor-network-theory [and their] . . . commitment to flat ontologies, in which texts, devices, knowledges, techniques, and technologies interact with each other in complexly articulated material ensembles', 'Sociology, Aesthetic, Expertise', *New Literary History* 41 (2010), pp. 253–76.

12. Similar investigative problems connected to twenty-first-century creative industries are encountered in Manuel Tironi's ANT and field-based ethnographic analysis of Chilean experimental music venues ('from electronica to folk, from *musique concrète* to hiphop'), 'Gelleable Spaces, Eventful Geographies: The Case of Santiago's Experimental Music Scene', in Ignacio Farias and Thomas Bender (eds.), *Urban Assemblages: How Actor-Network Theory Changes Urban Studies* (London and New York: Routledge, 2010), pp. 27–52, at p. 32.

13. DeLanda, *Deleuze: History and Science*, p. 104. The implications of assemblage theory for disciplines involved in the interactions of human beings and built material space are evident in new developments in urban planning theory. For an indicative essay which is also an excellent primer to DeLanda's version of assemblage theory, see Joris E. Van Wezemael, 'Modulation of Singularities – A Complexity Approach to Planning Competitions', in Jean Hillier and Patsy Healey, *The Ashgate Research Companion to Planning Theory: Conceptual Challenges for Spatial Planning* (Farnham: Ashgate, 2010), pp. 273–89.

14. For epistemological critiques of DeLanda, see Strathausen, 'Epistemological Reflections'; Graham Harman, 'Realism Without Materialism', *SubStance* 40 (2011), pp. 52–72.

15. William Dunlap, *A History of the American Theatre* (New York: 1832), p. 285.
16. DeLanda, *New Philosophy of Society*, p. 12.
17. 13 December 1800; 16, 17, 18 December 1807.
18. David O'Shaughnessy, *William Godwin and the Theatre* (London: Pickering & Chatto, 2010), p. 13; Victoria Myers, David O'Shaughnessy and Mark Philp (eds.), *The Diary of William Godwin* (Oxford Digital Library, 2010) (http://godwindiary.bodleian.ox.ac.uk). Godwin almost exclusively visited Covent Garden and Drury Lane in the winter and the Haymarket and Astley's Amphitheatre in the summer.
19. The contrast with church-going, another mass Georgian activity, is instructive. Both represent considerable components of the contemporary material culture. Places of worship and playhouses share the same characteristics of being available to all classes and with all classes being immediately visible, even if the flow between the classes was impeded by church pews or theatre boxes. However, there is no theatrical equivalent to the cultural status within church liturgies of the role of the Bible or Book of Common Prayer. Sermons, as a form of church performance, were regularly published but those printings represent only a tiny fraction of all the sermons given, and nearly all of them would have been dominated by references to British Christianity's two major texts. There are major problems with recovering the content of the average Georgian Sunday sermon, although the places, capacities and inferred dates of congregated worship are perfectly recoverable. On the other hand, hymn singing, a liturgical phenomenon originating with the Moravian and Welseyan movements in eighteenth-century England, makes a better comparison with theatre-going, particularly as congregations were specifically invited to join in with singing. The Wesleyan movement was also particularly conscious of its composition as a newly emerging social assemblage. However, theatres are quite distinctive in requiring the outlay of disposable income to gain admittance, the playhouses providing their public, in return, with an unusually diverse array of texts, multiple performers, music, dancing, and solo and ensemble singing as well as colourful costumes and scenery and a wide range of other audible and visual experiences.
20. For a thoughtful critique of Butler, see Julia A. Walker, 'Why Performance? Why Now? Textuality and the Rearticulation of Human Presence', *Yale Journal of Criticism* 16 (2003), pp. 149–75.
21. Alexander Dick and Angela Esterhammer, 'Introduction: Romantic Spheres of Action', in Dick and Esterhammer (eds.), *Spheres of Action: Speech and Performance in Romantic Culture* (University of Toronto Press, 2009), pp. 3–18, at p. 8.
22. Lilla Maria Crisafulli and Keir Elam, 'Introduction', in Crisafulli and Elam (eds.), *Women's Romantic Theatre and Drama: History, Agency, and Performativity* (Farnham: Ashgate, 2010), pp. 1–17, at p. 16.
23. For the issues at stake, see Janelle G. Reinelt, 'The Politics of Discourse: Performativity Meets Theatricality', *SubStance* 31 (2002), pp. 201–15; Walker, 'Why Performance? Why Now?'; Mikko Tuhkanen, 'Performativity and Becoming', *Cultural Critique* 72 (2009), pp. 1–35.

24. William St Clair, *The Reading Nation in the Romantic Period* (Cambridge University Press, 2004), pp. 367–73.

25. *Ibid.*, pp. 660–4.

26. H.J. Jackson, *Romantic Readers: The Evidence of Marginalia* (New Haven, CT: Yale University Press, 2005), pp. 4–6, 43. Jackson (pp. xxii–xxiii) examined 1,800 marginally annotated books, 400 annotated by Samuel Taylor Coleridge.

27. 4, 5 January, 4 February 1792, W.b. 294, Folger Shakespeare Library, Washington, DC. These performances were at the slightly smaller Haymarket, the Drury Lane company's temporary home during its rebuild.

28. St Clair, *Reading Nation*, p. 173; Drury Lane account book, 24, 27 February, 3 March 1767, Folger W.b. 273, Folger Shakespeare Library.

29. Bruno Latour, *Reassembling the Social: An Introduction to Actor-Network-Theory* (Oxford University Press, 2005), p. 108 (Latour's emphasis).

30. DeLanda, *New Philosophy of Society*, p. 10 (DeLanda's emphasis).

31. For a critical-creative study absorbed by the absolute lack of persistence of Georgian performance yet signalling its allure, see Judith Pascoe, *The Sarah Siddons Audio Files: Romanticism and the Lost Voice* (Ann Arbor, MI: University of Michigan Press, 2011).

32. DeLanda, *Philosophy and Simulation*, p. 188.

33. Newspapers were reliable carriers of theatre advertising, but, otherwise, newspaper and periodical reportage about theatres should be treated with caution. Colman's probable manipulation of copy for *The Separate Maintenance* (below), *The Public Advertiser*'s gross inflation of Sarah Siddons' touring earnings (Chapter 4), and the vehemently pro-government, anti-theatrical perspective of *The Tomahawk or Censor General* (Chapter 8) give some idea of the range of contemporary infidelities.

34. Remembering that 'in assemblage theory expressivity cannot be reduced to language and symbols', DeLanda, *New Philosophy of Society*, p. 12.

35. *Ibid.*, p. 19.

36. *Ibid.*, p. 17.

37. 'The identity of an assemblage is not only embodied by its materiality but also expressed by it', DeLanda, *Philosophy and Simulation*, p. 200.

38. Manuel DeLanda, *A Thousand Years of Nonlinear History* (New York: Swerve Editions, 1997), p. 147.

39. Scott Paul Gordon, 'Reading Patriot Art: James Barry's King Lear', *Eighteenth-Century Studies* 36 (2003), pp. 491–509; Sonia Massai, 'Nahum Tate's Revision of Shakespeare's *King Lears*', *SEL Studies in English Literature, 1500–1900* 40 (2000), pp. 435–50.

40. For a Boxing Day performance of *George Barnwell* paired with an unidentified 'pantomime' on 26 December 1797, see *The Thespian Oracle, or Monthly Mirror*, vol. 1, no. 1 (Philadelphia: 1798).

41. Joseph Roach, *Cities of the Dead: Circum-Atlantic Performance* (New York: Columbia University Press, 1996), p. 4.

42. Kathleen Wilson, 'Pacific Modernity: Theatre, Englishness, and the Arts of Discovery, 1760–1800', in Colin Jones and Dror Wahrman (eds.), *The Age of*

Cultural Revolutions: Britain and France, 1750–1820 (Berkeley, CA: University of California Press, 2002), pp. 62–93; 'Rowe's *Fair Penitent* as Global History: Or, a Diversionary Voyage to New South Wales', *Eighteenth-Century Studies* 41 (2008), pp. 231–51.

43. DeLanda, *Philosophy and Simulation*, p. 9 (DeLanda's emphasis).

44. *Ibid.*, pp. 7–21.

45. See, indicatively, James Sayers, *A Peep Behind the Curtain at Drury Lane* (etching and engraving), 14 January 1789; Thomas Rowlandson, *Pidgeon hole: a Convent Garden contrivance to coop up the gods* (etching), 20 February 1811.

46. Diaries of John Marsh, 1 June 1791, HM 54457, vol. XIII, Huntington Library, San Marino, California.

47. Ten years later, James Winston noted, 'The [Chichester] Theatre is rather small but scenes [*sic*] are hansome [*sic*] & well painted ... the Drama is respectable conducted here by a little active Manager', *Theatric Tourist* MS, TS 1335.21, Folio 69, Harvard Theatre Collection, Harvard University. On *The Theatric Tourist* (1804–5), see Chapter 2.

48. Diaries of John Marsh, 9 July 1805, HM 54457, vol. XXV, Huntington Library.

49. Jacob Beuler, *Songs, Humorous and Satirical, To Popular Tunes* (1829), pp. 27, 29.

50. Undated and unidentified newspaper clipping, *c.* November 1817; bill of sale, 13 June 1820, 'East London Theatre, and East London Gas Work', Royalty Theatre clippings, Harvard Theatre Collection.

51. DeLanda, *Deleuze: History and Science*, p. 12 (DeLanda's emphases).

52. The brevity of their season meant that the Haymarket did not always print their new plays, but the Lord Chamberlain's licensing manuscript is still extant. Colman revived it several times in updated versions (with a new prologue and other revisions) between 1779 and 1783.

53. Larpent 490, Huntington Library.

54. James Cobb, *English Readings; a Comic Piece, in one act. Inscribed to George Colman, Esq.* (1787), p. 5; see also Larpent 780, Huntington Library.

55. DeLanda, *New Philosophy of Society*, p. 98.

56. *Public Advertiser*, 1 September 1779.

57. Sybil Rosenfeld, 'A Georgian Scene Painter at Work', *British Museum Quarterly* 34 (1969), pp. 33–6, at p. 35.

58. *Public Advertiser*, 1 September 1779.

59. The original 'two Kings' referred to Charles II and his brother, James, Duke of York. George Villiers, *The Second Volume of Miscellaneous [sic] works, written by George, late Duke of Buckingham. Containing a Key to The Rehearsal* (1705, 2 vols.), vol. II, p. 2.

60. DeLanda, *Philosophy and Simulation*, p. 199.

61. Alfred L. Nelson and Gilbert. B. Cross (eds.), *Drury Lane Journal: Selections from James Winston's Diaries 1819–1827* (London: Society for Theatre Research, 1974), p. 9.

62. *St. James's Chronicle or British Evening Post*, 31 August 1779; *Morning Post and Daily Advertiser*, 1 September 1779.

CHAPTER ONE THEATRICAL ASSEMBLAGES
AND THEATRICAL MARKETS

1. *Prologue Written for the Re-opening of the Theatre at Brandenbourgh House, after it was embellished and enlarged in the Year 1795* (1795).
2. DeLanda, *New Philosophy of Society*, p. 16.
3. For anecdotes of social exclusivity in private theatricals, see Anthony Pasquin (pseud. John Williams), *The Life of the Earl of Barrymore, Including a history of the Wargrave Theatre and Original Anecdotes of Eminent Persons* (1793), pp. 300–3.
4. 'All of these processes are recurrent, and their variable repetition synthesizes entire populations of assemblages. Within these populations other synthetic processes, which may also be characterized as territorializations or codings but which typically involve entirely different mechanisms, generate larger-scale assemblages of which some of the members of the original population become component parts', DeLanda, *New Philosophy of Society*, p. 19.
5. DeLanda, *Philosophy and Simulation*, p. 184.
6. *Ibid.*, p. 187.
7. Samuel Whyte, *A Collection of Poems, on Various Subjects, including The Theatre, a didactic essay* (Dublin: 1792 [1794]), pp. 60–6.
8. Theresa Lewis (ed.), *Extracts of the Journals and Correspondence of Miss Berry From the Year 1783 to 1852* (London: Longmans, Green and Co, 1865), pp. 194–8; Mary Berry, *The Fashionable Friends; A Comedy, In Five Acts; As Performed . . . At the Theatre Royal, Drury-Lane* (1802), p. 12; *Morning Post and Gazetteer*, 26 April 1802; Andrew Elfenbein, 'Lesbian Aestheticism on the Eighteenth-Century Stage', *Eighteenth-Century Life* 25 (2001), pp. 1–16.
9. *Morning Post and Gazetteer*, 23 April 1802.
10. *The Director: A Weekly Literary Journal*, 11 April 1807, p. 360.
11. DeLanda, *Philosophy and Simulation*, p. 200.
12. W. Cutspear [pseud.], *Dramatic Rights: Or, Private Theatricals, and Pic-Nic Suppers, Justified by Fair Argument. With a few Whip-Syllabubs for the Editors of Newspapers* (1802), p. 19; David Worrall, *The Politics of Romantic Theatricality, 1787–1832: The Road to the Stage* (Basingstoke: Palgrave Macmillan, 2007), pp. 39–46.
13. *Rules and Regulations for the Lambs Conduit Private Theatre* (1799), p. 4.
14. Leman Thomas Rede and William Thomas Rede, *The Road to the Stage; Or, The Performer's Preceptor* (1836), p. 13.
15. James Henry Lawrence, *Dramatic Emancipation, or Strictures on the State of the Theatres, And the Consequent Degeneration of the Drama* (1813), p. 380. Lawrence's figures derive from an article in *The Morning Chronicle*, 29 February 1812. The number of seats is not related to the number of possible performances.
16. Rede and Rede, *Road to the Stage*, pp. 12–13.
17. *The Stage*, vol. 1, no. 4, 8 December 1814, p. 78; no. 11, 26 January 1815, p. 230.
18. *Ibid.*, no. 5, 15 December 1814, p. 99.

19. *The British Stage, and Literary Cabinet*, 25 March 1818, p. 293.
20. *The Stage*, vol. 1, no. 8, 5 January 1815, p. 187. This is John Dryden and Sir William Davenant's *The Tempest, or The Enchanted Island* (1670).
21. 'Books Borrowed from the Theatre Royal, Lyceum', prompter's journal, Drury Lane, 1812–18, Folger W.b. 381, Folger Shakespeare Library.
22. Typical is a payment to 'Mr. Younger a Bill for writing parts £2.12.5.', 17 October 1761, account book, Covent Garden Theatre, Folger W.b. 2, Folger Shakespeare Library.
23. James Winston cites a performance at Andover where the company were clearly prepared to perform a comedy with little or no knowledge of 'a syllable as printed', *The Theatric Tourist; Being A Genuine Collection Of Correct Views, With Brief And Authentic Historical Accounts Of All The Principal Provincial Theatres In The United Kingdom* (1805), pp. 9–10.
24. *No. 3. Lincoln Dramatic Censor, Saturday, November 13, 1809* (Lincoln: 1809), pp. 38–41.
25. For interesting comments on the consequences of entrepreneurial lack of confidence in the state's position with regard to grand theatre building ventures in London, see Judith Milhous, 'Built and Unbuilt Opera Spaces in Eighteenth Century London', in Joseph Roach (ed.), *Changing the Subject: Marvin Carlson and Theatre Studies, 1959–2009* (Ann Arbor, MI: University of Michigan Press, 2009), pp. 83–117.
26. Cheryl Wanko's discussion of 'value' in the celebrity market would be an example of such a reification, despite her valuable detailing of a small number of actual marketplace transactions; *Roles of Authority: Thespian Biography and Celebrity in Eighteenth-Century Britain* (Lubbock, TX: Texas Tech University Press, 2003), 'Chapter 7: Parable of the Talent(s): The Economics of Acting Authority', pp. 161–86. Despite its being addressed to the literary domain, Matthew Rowlinson's *Real Money and Romanticism* (Cambridge University Press, 2010) makes no reference to the economics of theatre.
27. DeLanda, *New Philosophy of Society*, p. 17.
28. R.B. Sheridan's struggles with the Duke of Bedford over Drury Lane's indebtedness are all too recognizable in their structured provisions: 'He [Sheridan] undertakes to settle the demand with the Duke of Bedford ... And that all the Rec[eip]t[s]. Of the theatre shall be regularly paid to Messrs. Hammersley &c [bankers] in the following manner ... 1st. £15 a night [of earnings], ~~10L of which~~ to be appropriated for the Duke of Bedford's Bank, 10L towards the accruing payment–& 5L towards the arrears', *c.* 1802, Folger Y.d. 614 12/84, Folger Shakespeare Library.
29. On the benefit-night system, see St Vincent Troubridge, *The Benefit System in the British Theatre* (London: Society for Theatre Research, 1967); Robert D. Hume, 'The Origins of the Actor Benefit in London', *Theatre Research International* 9 (1984), pp. 99–111; Matthew J. Kinservik, 'Benefit Play Selection at Drury Lane 1729–1769: The Cases of Mrs. Cibber, Mrs. Clive, and Mrs. Pritchard', *Theatre Notebook* 50 (1996), pp. 15–28.

30. George Parker, *A View of Society and Manners in High and Low Life; Being the Adventures In England, Ireland, Scotland, Wales, France, &c. of Mr. G. Parker. In which is Comprised a History of the Stage Itinerant* (1781), p. 53.

31. Manuel DeLanda, 'Molar Entities and Molecular Populations in Human History', in Jeffrey A. Bell and Claire Colebrook (eds.), *Deleuze and History* (Edinburgh University Press, 2009), pp. 225–36, at pp. 228–9, 233.

32. *The Monitor; or, Green-Room Laid Open; With Remarks Thereon, Which occasioned the Letter to Mr. Spatter* (1767), p. 2.

33. Charles Tilly, *Durable Inequality* (Berkeley, CA: University of California Press, 1998), p. 159.

34. For similar conclusions about early modern religious drama, see Paul Whitfield White, *Drama and Religion in English Provincial Society, 1485–1660* (Cambridge University Press, 2008), p. 11. See also Richard Foulkes (ed.), *Scenes from Provincial Stages: Essays in Honour of Kathleen Barker* (London: Society for Theatre Research, 1994); Adrian Edwards, 'Provincial Theatre in Britain, 1773–1808: The Burney Playbills Examined', *Theatre Notebook* 57 (2003), pp. 136–42.

35. A sampling of venues drawn from James Winston's contemporary survey includes seasonal theatres at Andover, Ashton Under Lyme, Beverley, Bolton, Boston, Bowness, Bridgenorth, Bristol, Cardiff, Carmarthen, Castle Town (Isle of Man), Chelmsford, Chester, Chichester, Circencester, Cockermouth, Coleshill, Coventry, Croydon, Doncaster, Douglas (Isle of Man), Exeter, Glasgow, Gosport, Grantham, Guildford, Halifax, Harrogate, Hereford, Honiton, Huntingdon, Keswick, Leominster, Lincoln, Litchfield, Louth, Lowestoft, Ludlow, Macclesfield, Manchester, Market Drayton, Maryport, Newberry, Newcastle, Oxford, Peterborough, Plymouth, Plymouth Dock, Preston, Richmond (North Yorkshire), Richmond (Surrey), Scarborough, Shrewsbury, Stamford, Stourbridge, Totnes, Truro, Ulverston, Wakefield, Whitby, Wigton, Windsor, Wisbech, Wolverhampton and York: James Winston, *Theatric Tourist* MS (*c.* 1802–4), Harvard Theatre Collection, TS 1335.211, Houghton Library, Harvard University. For an indicative programme, see 'By Desire of the Grooms and Jockeys of Newmarkett', the performances *c.* 1780 on one night of David Garrick's *The Clandestine Marriage* (1766) and Isaac Bickerstaffe's *The Padlock* (1768), 'By Mr. Hounslow's Company of the Comedians' in 'the Theatre, At the Cock Pit Royal, Newmarket' (playbill), John Rylands Library, Manchester.

36. Two sample playbills dating to *c.* 1780 for Laxfield, Suffolk, and Attleborough, Norfolk, demonstrate this quite clearly. These villages have never had populations larger than between one and two thousand people, yet they appear to have supported productions, advertised on roughly printed, undated, playbills, of John Gay's 'The begGars [*sic*] Opera'; the generic pantomime, *The Elopement or, Harlequin Triumphant* (probably derived from a 1750s original); George Farquhar's *The Beaux' Stratagem* (1707); and Garrick's *Miss in Her Teens* (1747) (playbills, no date; Attleborough and Laxfield), John Rylands Library, Manchester.

37. See playbill, private theatre, Leith (*c.* 1822), for how 'a Select Part of Young Gentlemen' joined with 'A few Professional Gentlemen', Folger Bill Box G5 L53pt 1822 a & b, Folger Shakespeare Library.

38. This is calculated as 195 nights of performance for Covent Garden and Drury Lane, both at 3,000-seat capacity, plus around 12 weeks at 4 nights of performance per week at the 1,800-seat capacity Haymarket. Capacities are taken from Lawrence, *Dramatic Emancipation*, p. 380. Pascoe gives Drury Lane's capacity in 1794 as 3,611, which is considerably larger than the figure used here, but gives no direct source, *Sarah Siddons Audio Files*, p. 57. In addition, the Opera House – open much less often – had a capacity of 2,500 to 3,000; see Milhous, 'Built and Unbuilt Opera Spaces'.

39. John Landers, *Death and the Metropolis: Studies in the Demographic History of London, 1670–1830* (Cambridge University Press, 1993).

40. Theatre capacity as a raw number of annual 'seats for sale' is the methodology adopted by the Society of London Theatre. The annual capacity in 2009 was 19,666,766. The population of London at the official 2001 Census was 7,172,091. *Society of London Theatre Box Office Data Report 2009*, Figure 1; Office for National Statistics (www.statistics.gov.uk/census2001/pyramids/pages/h.asp).

41. Unidentified clipping, Horace Walpole, *A Collection of prologues and epilogues and other pieces relative to the stage in the reign of King George the Third, from the year 1780*, LWL 49 1810 58, Lewis Walpole Library, Farmington, Connecticut.

42. DeLanda, *New Philosophy of Society*, pp. 29–30.

43. Playbill records and newspaper advertising are patchy up to the 1740s, but the only types of theatrical performances of stage plays which cannot now be determined concern those taking place within the private theatres which grew up, mainly in the 1810s, in London's West End fringes.

44. 'An annual exhibition, open to qualified artists, was expected to fund an academy of design, and possibly the relief of artists in need; should the society's income be insufficient, the king was asked to assist', Holger Hoock, *The King's Artists: The Royal Academy of Arts and the Politics of British Culture, 1760–1840* (Oxford: Clarendon Press, 2003), p. 23.

45. The figures were assembled by Edward Warren, one of two assistant treasurers, and comprise a 'Statement of the Number of Persons [who] Paid at the Theatre this Season' plus the number of 'Free Persons' admitted, the latter being a diverse group who would have included the Lord Chamberlain's officials, playwrights with whom the playhouse had an association, and a sprinkling of the socially influential. Keats' friend, Charles Armitage Brown, was given free admittance after his successful comic opera, *Narensky*; see Edward Warren, August 1814, Folger W.a. 12. Warren compiled a similar set of figures for Kean's 1814–15 season performances, 'Sundry Averages for 220 Nᵗˢ. Season 1814–15 [dated 8 July 1815]', Folger Art Vol. b8, Folger Shakespeare Library.

46. The Theatre Royal Company in Lincoln's Inn Fields in the 1720s and 1730s sometimes performed only one show, but two pieces soon became standard.

47. Folger W.a. 104 (8), Folger W.a. 104 (10), Folger Shakespeare Library.

48. Hoock, *King's Artists*, p. 35, Figure 2, 'Royal Academy of Arts exhibitions: number of paid visits, 1769–1820'.
49. *Ibid.*, p. 36, Figure 3, 'Royal Academy of Arts: total annual income, 1769–1818'.
50. This is derived by subtracting booked expenditure (£44,096. 2*s*. 8*d*.) from booked turnover. There is no way of knowing whether the surplus covered Drury Lane's obligations to its creditors, Drury Lane account book 1795–6 season, Folger W.b. 298, Folger Shakespeare Library.
51. Drury Lane account book 1776–7, Folger W.b. 319, Folger Shakespeare Library.
52. Kalman A. Burnim, 'The Drury Lane Theatre Theatrical Fund 1766–1798', *c*. 2005, unpublished manuscript, Garrick Club, Garrick Street, London, p. 1. On Garrick's involvement with the fund, see Robert D. Hume and Judith Milhous, '*A Bundle of Prologues* (1777): The Unpublished Text of Garrick's Last Rehearsal Play', *Review of English Studies* 58 (2007), pp. 482–99.
53. Winston, *Theatric Tourist*, p. 5.
54. Wendy Trewin, *The Royal General Theatrical Fund: A History, 1838–1988* (London: Society for Theatre Research, 1989), p. 4; *The Act of Parliament together with the Rules and Regulations of the Society Established for the Relief of Indigent Person, Belonging to His Majesty's Company of Comedians of the Theatre Royal, Drury Lane* (1777).
55. Reply to Susan Greville, 9 December 1782, 'Proceedings of the [Drury Lane Theatrical] Fund 7 October 1781–31 December 1789', Garrick Club.
56. *The Fund, For the Relief of Indigent Persons Belonging To His Majesty's Company of Comedians of the Theatre Royal Drury Lane. Established, Endowed and Incorporated, By that Great Master of his Art, David Garrick, Esq. 1777* (1813), p. 5, Article II, Article VI.
57. 31 December 1783, 'Proceedings of the [Drury Lane Theatrical] Fund'. The Covent Garden fund held £4,300 at its incorporation, Trewin, *Royal General Theatrical Fund*, p. 4. In 1810 this fund held bond investments totalling £11,200 in addition to income from subscriptions, *Theatrical Fund, Instituted at the Theatre Royal, in Covent-Garden, December 22, 1765, And Confirmed by Act of Parliament, 1776* (1811), p. 4. At Incorporation, the Drury Lane Fund held 'Four Thousand Pounds, or thereabouts', *Fund, For the Relief of Indigent Persons*, p. 8.
58. Felicity Nussbaum, *Rival Queens: Actresses, Performance, and the Eighteenth-Century British Theater* (Philadelphia: University of Pennsylvania Press, 2010); Helen E.M. Brooks, 'Negotiating Marriage and Professional Autonomy in the Careers of Eighteenth-Century Actresses', *Eighteenth-Century Life* 35:2 (2011), pp. 39–75.
59. *Fund, For the Relief of Indigent Persons*, Article III.
60. Clive Emsley, Tim Hitchcock and Robert Shoemaker, 'London History – Currency, Coinage and the Cost of Living', Old Bailey Proceedings Online (www.oldbaileyonline.org, version 6.0, 16 November 2011).
61. *Fund, For the Relief of Indigent Persons*, Article XV.

62. The Covent Garden Fund's articles are tortuously worded but amount to the same terms: 'Article XII. If any contributor, whose wife also is a contributor, should, from sickness, or any other cause, appear to the committee a proper claimant, he shall be admitted as such, without consideration of the wife, and the same *vice versâ.*' This was helpfully glossed, 'Husband and wife claim independently of each other', *Theatrical Fund, Instituted at the Theatre Royal.*
63. Elizabeth Inchbald diary, 1781, Folger M.a. 151, Folger Shakespeare Library. Inchbald's payments conform to the Covent Garden Fund's levy of 6*d* in the pound of earnings, *Theatrical Fund, Instituted at the Theatre Royal*, Article II. The minimum weekly salary for entry into the Drury Lane Fund was £1, *Fund, For the Relief of Indigent Persons*, Article I.
64. A milkmaid earned between £6 and £8 per year, a footman around £8 per year, Clive Emsley, Tim Hitchcock and Robert Shoemaker, 'London History – Currency, Coinage and the Cost of Living'.
65. Philip H. Highfill, Jr, Kalman A. Burnim and Edward A. Langhans, *A Biographical Dictionary of Actors, Actresses, Musicians, Dancers, Managers & Other Stage Personnel in London, 1660–1800* (Carbondale and Edwardsville, IL: Southern Illinois University Press, 1973–93, 16 vols.), vol. VI, pp. 122–6.
66. The death in Westminster of Mr Pilliner, apothecary, is recorded for 19 April 1814, *European Magazine*, April 1814, p. 371.
67. 28 October, 29, 30 November, 4 December 1783, 26 January 1784, 'Proceedings of the [Drury Lane Theatrical] Fund.
68. *Fund, For the Relief of Indigent Persons*, Article XII.
69. Charles Durang, MS notes for 'The Philadelphia Stage; from 1749–1854', *Philadelphia Sunday Dispatch*, first series, 7 May 1854 to 1860 (7 vols.), vol. II, 18 July 1794, Harvard Theatre Collection, Harvard University. Durang notes that the attempt was abortive.
70. *Heads of a Plan for a Private Theatre . . . 1st March 1811* (1811).
71. Between 1766 and 1806, the largest individual donations to the Drury Lane Fund were by David Garrick (£505. 5*s*. 0*d*.) and General John Burgoyne, author of *The Maid of the Oaks*, (£205), *Fund, For the Relief of Indigent Persons*, pp. 5–6.
72. 19 May 1783, 'Proceedings of the [Drury Lane Theatrical] Fund'.
73. 17 May 1783 (playbill), Drury Lane. This playbill advertised *Isabella; or, The Fatal Marriage*.
74. 26 May 1783, 'Proceedings of the [Drury Lane Theatrical] Fund'.
75. Siddons donated £50 to the fund in 1797, *Fund, For the Relief of Indigent Persons*, p. 6.

CHAPTER TWO GEORGIAN PERFORMANCE AND THE ASSEMBLAGE MODEL

1. 'In this extended sense the term "individual" has no preferential affinity for a particular scale (persons or organisations) and refers to any entity that is *singular*

and unique . . . here all entities exist at the same ontological level differing only in scale. The human species, for example, is every bit as historical an individual as the organisms that compose it. Like them, it has a date of birth (the event of speciation) and, at least potentially, a date of death (the event of extinction). In other words, the human species as a whole exists "alongside" the human organisms that compose it, alongside them in an ontological plane that houses only historically individuated entities', DeLanda, 'Molar Entities and Molecular Populations', pp. 225–36, at p. 227 (DeLanda's emphasis).

2. DeLanda, *New Philosophy of Society*, p. 28.
3. *Ibid.*, p 29 (DeLanda's emphasis).
4. Judith Milhous, 'Reading Theatre History from Account Books', in Michael Cordner and Peter Holland (eds.), *Players, Playwrights, Playhouses: Investigating Performance, 1660–1800* (Palgrave Macmillan: Basingstoke, 2007), pp. 101–34.
5. 16, 17, 18 January 1792, Drury Lane account book, Folger W.b. 294, Folger Shakespeare Library, Washington, DC; Larpent 698, Huntington Library.
6. 12 March, 2 April 1796, Drury Lane account book, Folger W.b. 298, Folger Shakespeare Library.
7. Samuel Birch, *Songs, duets, trio, and choruses, in The Mariners, a musical entertainment, in two acts. As performed at the King's Theatre, Hay-Market* (1793); Thomas Attwood, *The Mariners, a Musical Entertainment in Two Acts . . . composed by T. Attwood* (1793). A year later, Attwood also published *The Additional Song, Duett and Trio in the Mariners* (1794).
8. Jean Marsden, 'Performing the West Indies: Comedy, Feeling, and British Identity', *Comparative Drama* 42 (2008), pp. 73–88.
9. Marsden, 'Performing the West Indies', refers to Lord Kames, but does not use this citation; John Adams, *Curious Thoughts on the History of Man; chiefly abridged or selected from the celebrated works of Lord Kaimes, Lord Monboddo, Dr. Dunbar, and the immortal Montesquieu* (1789), p. 50.
10. Gilles Deleuze and Félix Guattari, *A Thousand Plateaus: Capitalism and Schizophrenia*, trans. Brian Massumi (London: Continuum, 2004), pp. 349, 365, 371.
11. *Ibid.*, p. 360.
12. DeLanda, *Philosophy and Simulation*, p. 200.
13. Deleuze and Guattari, *A Thousand Plateaus*, pp. 342–86, at pp. 352, 353, 367 (Deleuze and Guattari's emphasis).
14. Folger M.a. 151, Elizabeth Inchbald diary, 1781, Folger Shakespeare Library.
15. *Candid and Impartial Strictures on the Performers belonging to Drury-Lane, Covent-Garden, and the Haymarket Theatres* (1795), pp. 22–3.
16. Lawrence, *Dramatic Emancipation*, p. 380.
17. Robert W. Jones, 'Sheridan and the Theatre of Patriotism: Staging Dissent During the War for America', *Eighteenth-Century Life* 26 (2002), pp. 24–45.
18. 'The main territorializing process providing the assemblage with a stable identity is *habitual repetition*', DeLanda, *New Philosophy of Society*, p. 50 (DeLanda's emphasis).

19. Larpent 983, Huntington Library.
20. Mary A. Favret, *War at a Distance: Romanticism and the Making of Modern Wartime* (Princeton University Press, 2010), p. 10.
21. The repertoire comic sketch known as 'Hippisley's Drunken Man', a monologue in which a supposedly inebriated actor reads and comments on newspaper articles, was quite popular. The original version was performed by the Bristol actor manager, John Hippisley, no later than the 1740s, *For the Benefit of a Widow, and a Large Family, under Great Difficulties. The Theatrical Museum; or, Fugitive Repository: being a collection of very choice and pleasing interludes, both serious and comic. . . . . To the whole is prefixed, The much and long-desired Interlude of The Celebrated Hippesley's drunken man* (1776); *The Catch Club: A Collection of All the Songs, Catches, Glees, Duets, &c. As sung by . . . Mr. Leoni . . . at the Royalty Theatre, Well-Street, Goodman's-Fields: To which is Added Hippesley's Drunken-Man, As altered and spoken by Mr. Lee Lewes (c. 1787).*
22. Folger W.b. 423, Folger Shakespeare Library.
23. Kathleen Wilson, *The Island Race: Englishness, Empire and Gender in the Eighteenth Century* (London and New York: Routledge, 2003), pp. 63, 70.
24. 'The Killigrew and Davenant Patents', *Survey of London: Volume 35: The Theatre Royal, Drury Lane, and the Royal Opera House, Covent Garden* (1970), pp. 1–8 (www.british-history.ac.uk/report.aspx?compid=100226).
25. DeLanda, *Philosophy and Simulation*, p. 188.
26. These ideas are suggested by my reading of Manuel DeLanda, 'Materiality: Anexact and Intense', in Lars Spuybroek (ed.), *Nox: Machining Architecture* (London: Thames and Hudson, 2004), pp. 370–7.
27. Winston, *Theatric Tourist*, p. 46.
28. *Ibid.*, p. 6.
29. James Winston and Daniell Havell, *The Theatric Tourist*, vol. II (1805), unused drawings, Fol. 8, Harvard Theatre Collection, Harvard University.
30. Other, less systematized, methods of analysis have reached similar conclusions, possibly more suggestively than outlined here. See Marvin Carlson, *The Haunted Stage: The Theatre as Memory Machine* (Ann Arbor, MI: University of Michigan Press, 2001), Chapter 5: 'The Haunted House', pp. 131–64.
31. George Parker, *A View of Society and Manners in High and Low Life; Being the Adventures In England, Ireland, Scotland, Wales, France, &c. of Mr. G. Parker. In which is Comprised a History of the Stage Itinerant* (1781), p. 53. Flip was beer and spirits sweetened with sugar and heated with a hot iron (*OED*).
32. Samuel Birch, *Songs, duets, trio, and choruses, in The Mariners, a musical entertainment, in two acts. As performed at the King's Theatre, Hay-Market* (1793), p. 7.
33. *Regulations for the Prussian infantry. Translated from the German original* (1754); *Regulations for the Prussian cavalry. Translated from the German original by Capt. William Faucitt* (1757). Although the Larpent manuscript is the only extant text, it appears 'Fozbourg' was further anglicized into 'Flintbourg' in the production version; Birch, *Songs, duets, trio, and choruses*, p. 4.

34. As early as 1761, a theatre company in Portsmouth performed *King Lear* in tandem with *The Revels of Winchester Camp*, 'In which will be introduc'd the Prussian Exercise', playbill, New Theatre, Portsmouth, 5 August 1761.
35. For changing adaptations of *The Fair Quaker of Deal*, see Patricia Howell Michaelson, *Speaking Volumes: Women, Reading, and Speech in the Age of Austen* (Stanford, CA: Stanford University Press, 2002).
36. Larpent 54, Huntington Library; Anonymous broadside, *The Female Volunteer: or, an Attempt to make our Men STAND* (1746); *General Advertiser*, 17, 18 March 1746.
37. John O'Keeffe, *Songs, Duets, Trios, &c. in The Siege of Curzola, a comic opera, performed at the Theatre-Royal in the Hay-Market* (1786), p. 4.
38. *The Female Duellist: An After Piece. With Songs Set To Music By Mr. Suett As It Was Performed At The King's Theatre, In The Haymarket, By His Majesty's Company From The Theatre Royal, Drury-Lane* (1793), p. 50.
39. Larpent 743, Huntington Library.
40. *Public Advertiser*, 9 August 1786.
41. DeLanda, *Deleuze: History and Science*, p. 104.
42. Highfill *et al.*, *Biographical Dictionary*, vol. I, pp. 273–6.
43. *Ibid.*, vol. XIII, pp. 265–7. For a higher figure puffed in the newspapers, see Judith Milhous and Robert D. Hume, 'Opera Salaries in Eighteenth-Century London', *Journal of the American Musicological Society* 46 (1993), pp. 26–83. By 1791, she was included in an enterprise to help performers who had not had benefit nights, and her career seems to have ended in the same year; 'King's Theatre, Haymarket. For the Benefit of such of the Principal Dancers as have not distinct nights, and all the figurants. On Monday next, June 6, 1791, will be given a new selection of serious and comic music' (playbill, 1791).
44. Joseph Haslewood, *The Secret History of the Green Room: containing authentic and entertaining memoirs of the actors and actresses in the three Theatres Royal* (1790, 2 vols.), vol. I, pp. 247–51. Cuyler played Kitty in George Colman the Younger's *The Separate Maintenance* (1779), for example.
45. Frank Dawes, 'William: or the Adventures of a Sonata', *Musical Times* 106 (1965), pp. 761–4.
46. Highfill *et al.*, *Biographical Dictionary*, vol. VI, pp. 154–8.
47. John Oldmixon, *Apollo Turn'd Stroller; or, Thereby Hangs a Tale. A musical pasticcio. In two parts. As performed, with the most unbounded Applause, at the Royalty-Theatre* (1787); playbill, Royalty Theatre 31 January 1788.
48. O'Keeffe, *Songs, Duets, Trios*, pp. 17–18.
49. Samuel Arnold, *The Siege of Curzola: A Comic Opera ... Adapted for the Voice & Harpsichord. The Words by Mr. O'Keefe* (1786).
50. *The Green-Room Mirror. Clearly delineating our present theatrical performers* (1786), p. 44; Joseph Haslewood, *The Secret History of the Green Room: containing authentic and entertaining memoirs of the actors and actresses in the three Theatres Royal* (1790, 2 vols.), vol. II, p. 272.
51. Gilli Bush-Bailey, *Treading the Bawds: Actresses and Playwrights on the Late-Stuart Stage* (Manchester University Press, 2006), pp. 81–2.

52. Haslewood, *Secret History of the Green Room*, vol. II, pp. 152, 154.

CHAPTER THREE THEATRICAL CELEBRITY AS SOCIAL ASSEMBLAGE: FROM GARRICK TO KEAN

1. David Minden Higgins, *Romantic Genius and the Literary Magazine: Biography, Celebrity and Politics* (London: Routledge, 2005); Mary Luckhurst and Jane Moody (eds.), *Theatre and Celebrity in Britain, 1660–2000* (Basingstoke: Palgrave Macmillan, 2006); Tim Mole (ed.), *Romanticism and Celebrity Culture, 1750–1850* (Cambridge University Press, 2009); Ghislaine McDayter, *Byromania and the Birth of Celebrity Culture* (Albany, NY: SUNY Press, 2009).
2. Deleuze and Guattari, *Thousand Plateaus*, pp. 349, 365, 371.
3. Wanko, *Roles of Authority*; Laura Engel, *Fashioning Celebrity: Eighteenth-Century British Actresses and Strategies for Image Making* (Columbus, OH: Ohio State University Press, 2011).
4. Edmund Curll, *Faithful Memoirs of the Life, Amours and Performances, Of That Justly Celebrated, And Most Eminent Actress Of Her Time, Mrs. Anne Oldfield* (1731), pp. 144, 210.
5. *Authentick Memoirs Of The Life Of That Celebrated Actress Mrs. Ann Oldfield. Containing a genuine account of her transactions from her infancy to the time of her decease. The third edition, with large additions and amendments* (1730), p. vii.
6. For a completely opposite perspective, see Pascoe, *Sarah Siddons Audio Files*.
7. DeLanda, *New Philosophy of Society*, p. 56 (DeLanda's emphasis).
8. *Ibid.*
9. DeLanda, *Deleuze: History and Science*, p. 12 (DeLanda's emphasis).
10. *Ibid.*
11. Siddons played Isabella several times that season, including 2 March 1784 and 11 May 1784, directly after Wells' benefit.
12. *Morning Chronicle and London Advertiser*, 30 April 1784.
13. *Morning Herald and Daily Advertiser*, 1 May 1784.
14. *Morning Chronicle and London Advertiser*, 1 May 1784.
15. Larpent 655, Huntington Library.
16. DeLanda, *Deleuze: History and Science*, p. 12.
17. Still useful in showing the diversity of this eighteenth-century phenomenon is Elbridge Colby, 'A Supplement on Strollers', *Publications of the Modern Language Association* 39 (1924), pp. 642–54.
18. Mark Moore, *The Memoirs And Adventures of Mark Moore, Late and Officer in the British Navy, Interspersed With a Variety of original Anecdotes, selected from his Journals, when in the Tuscan, Portuguese, Swedish, Imperial, American, and British Service, in each of which he bore a commission . . . As the Author has been at Intervals the Manager of a respectable Company of Comedians, in several of the principal Towns of England, France, and Flanders, he has also added some original Sketches of several Theatrical Characters, who now rank high in the Thespian Corps* (1795), pp. 86, 122–6.

19. Undated playbill, 'Mr. Kent most respectfully acquaints the Ladies and Gentlemen of this Town and its Vicinity . . .', printed Whitechapel Road, London, John Rylands Library, Manchester.

20. DeLanda, *Deleuze: History and Science*, 'Intensive and Extensive Cartography', pp. 115–40.

21. Richard Hill, *A Letter from Richard Hill, Esq; To His Friend near Shrewsbury, containing Some Remarks on a Letter signed by A Player Which Letter is also prefixed . . . sold for the Benefit of the Prisoners in Shrewsbury Goal* (Shrewsbury: 1767), p. 7.

22. DeLanda, *Deleuze: History and Science*, p. 130.

23. *Ibid.*, p. 130 (DeLanda's emphasis).

24. This also seems to be the conclusion reached in Manuel Tironi's study of disaggregated clusters of exceptionally creative, non-economically motivated, musicians in present-day Santiago, 'Gelleable Spaces, Eventful Geographies: The Case of Santiago's Experimental Music Scene', in Farias and Bender (eds.), *Urban Assemblages*, pp. 27–52.

25. Assemblage models of behavioural practices are intrinsic to economically efficient market theory. Key papers are Eugene F. Fama, 'Efficient Capital Markets: A Review of Theory and Empirical Work', *Journal of Finance* 25 (1970), pp. 383–417; Sanford J. Grossman and Joseph E. Stiglitz, 'On the Impossibility of Informationally Efficient Markets', *American Economic Review* 70 (1980), pp. 393–408.

26. Covent Garden receipts, 4, 22 October 1746, BL Egerton MS 2,268.

27. *Ibid.*, 21 October 1746.

28. 30 May 1776, Folger W.a. 104 (13), Folger Shakespeare Library.

29. Prompt deficiency payment was an evolving practice. Wignell did not pay his £6. 13*s*. 9*d*. benefit deficiency dating from 12 May 1760, the previous season, until 20 November 1760, Covent Garden Theatre Accounts September 1760–September 1761, Garrick Club.

30. 29 April 1796, fol. 66 recto, Folger W.b. 423, Folger Shakespeare Library. Folger W.b. 423 itemizes the bare house charge to King as £200, plus Jordan (£10. 10*s*. 0*d*.) and Siddons (£20. 0*s*. 0*d*.), plus 1*s*. 6*d*. for stage properties and £1. 5*s*. 6*d*. for 'Supernum[eraries]' (e.g. dressers), plus 10*s*. 6*d*. payment for tuning the kettledrum, making King's actual costs £232. 7*s*. 6*d*.; see also Folger W.b. 298.

31. *Morning Chronicle and London Advertiser*, 1 May 1784.

32. Drury Lane account book 1796–9, Folger W.b. 423, Folger Shakespeare Library.

33. DeLanda, *New Philosophy of Society*, p. 17.

34. *Ibid.*

35. For information about interpreting Georgian theatre account books, see Milhous, 'Reading Theatre History from Account Books'.

36. Elizabeth Pope's salary fluctuated at other times in other years, also apparently in line with benefit seasons, Covent Garden account book, 1790–1, BL Egerton MS 2,291.

37. Ann Barry is not to be confused with the actress/manager Elizabeth Barry (*c.* 1656–1713). Abington's clothing allowance (no doubt as a retention incentive) was paid to her at the rate of £1 or £2 per week; 29 May 1775, Drury Lane account book, Folger W.b. 277, Folger Shakespeare Library.
38. Covent Garden account book, 4 April 1791, BL Egerton MS 2,291.
39. Covent Garden ledger book, 1 and 6 November 1746, BL Egerton MS 2,268.
40. Cross-Hopkins diaries, 22 February 1748, Folger W.a. 104 (1), Folger Shakespeare Library.
41. *Ibid.*, 14 March 1748.
42. For an entirely different interpretation of Garrick's celebrity, see Wanko, *Roles of Authority*, Chapter 8, 'The Authority of the Celebrity: David Garrick', pp. 187–213.
43. William Hopkins diary, 3 February 1776, Folger W.a. 104 (13), Folger Shakespeare Library.
44. *Ibid.*, 5 February 1776.
45. A list of benefit performances in the Folger Shakespeare Library records 'A Riot on this Night on Account of the Blackamoor. & no farce Performd'; 5 February 1776, Folger W.a. 39, Folger Shakespeare Library.
46. 14 November 1749, Folger W.a. 104 (1); 30 October 1812, Folger W.b. 381, Folger Shakespeare Library.
47. Leigh Woods, 'Actors' Biography and Mythmaking, the Example of Edmund Kean', in Thomas Postlewait and Bruce A. McConachie (eds.), *Interpreting the Theatrical Past* (Iowa City, IA: University of Iowa Press, 1989), pp. 230–47, at p. 244.
48. Jeffrey Kahan, *The Cult of Kean* (Aldershot and Burlington, VT: Ashgate, 2006).
49. Tracy C. Davis, '"Reading Shakespeare by Flashes of Lightning": Challenging the Foundations of Romantic Acting Theory', *English Literary History* 62 (1995), pp. 933–54.
50. The keeper of the Folger's Drury Lane prompter's journal (Folger W.b. 381) must be Thomas John Dibdin, engaged at £520 per year. See *The Reminiscences of Thomas Dibdin* (1827, 2 vols.), vol. II, p. 3.
51. Dibdin's duties included writing a new pantomime each year, in this case published as *Sketch of the New Melo-Dramatick Comick Pantomime, called Harlequin and Humpo; or, Columbine by Candlelight etc.* (1812).
52. Drury Lane prompter's journal, 3–26 December 1812, Folger W.b. 381, Folger Shakespeare Library.
53. *Ibid.*, 11–26 December 1813.
54. *Ibid.*, 2 October–29 December 1813.
55. *Ibid.*, 25 January 1814.
56. *Ibid.*, 26 January 1814.
57. London Green, 'Edmund Kean's Richard III', *Theatre Journal* 36 (1984), pp. 505–24; see pp. 507ff. Green notes that the myth, not least, was perpetuated by Kean himself in conversation with David Garrick's widow.
58. Drury Lane prompter's journal, 26 January 1814, Folger W.b. 381, Folger Shakespeare Library.

59. Deleuze and Guattari, *Thousand Plateaus*, pp. 349, 365, 371.
60. Joseph W. Donohue, Jr, 'Hazlitt's Sense of the Dramatic: Actor as Tragic Character', *SEL Studies in English Literature, 1500–1900* 5 (1965), pp. 705–21; James Mulvihill, 'William Hazlitt on Dramatic Text and Performance', *Studies in English Literature, 1500–1900* 41 (2001), pp. 695–709.
61. William Hazlitt, *A View of the English Stage; or, A Series of Dramatic Criticisms* (1821), pp. x–xi. Hazlitt's Preface is dated by him to 24 April 1818.
62. Drury Lane account book, 26 January 1814, Folger W.b. 327, Folger Shakespeare Library.

CHAPTER FOUR CELEBRITY NETWORKS: KEAN AND SIDDONS

1. DeLanda, *New Philosophy of Society*, p. 53 (DeLanda's emphasis).
2. Lawrence, *Dramatic Emancipation*, p. 378.
3. 6 September 1789, HM 54457, vol. XIII, Huntington Library.
4. George B. Bryan, *American Theatrical Regulation 1607–1900 Conspectus and Texts* (Metuchen, NJ and London: Scarecrow Press, 1993), pp. 229–30.
5. David Grimsted, *Melodrama Unveiled: American Theater and Culture, 1800–1850* (Berkeley, CA: University of California Press, 1968), p. 11.
6. *The Cynick*, vol. V, 19 October 1811, p. 81.
7. DeLanda, *Deleuze: History and Science*, p. 15.
8. Edward Warren, 8 July 1815, Folger Art Vol. b 8. Warren's Drury Lane office title is given at Folger W.b. 381, fol 50 recto, Folger Shakespeare Library.
9. Edward Warren, 'Statement of the Nightly Receipts, arranged according to the largeness of the Sum, beginning with the greatest', August 1814, Folger W.a. 12, Folger Shakespeare Library.
10. Advertisement, *Liverpool Mercury*, 1 September 1815.
11. 21 February 1814, Folger Z.e. 16, Folger Shakespeare Library.
12. Advertisement, *Morning Post*, 29 April 1814; 'P.G.P.', 'Mr Kean's Othello', *The Examiner*, 15 May 1814.
13. 16 January 1819, *The Inspector, A Weekly Dramatic Paper*, no. 3, p. 6.
14. 10 February, 1, 10, 11 March 1814, Drury Lane prompter's journal, Folger W.b. 381, Folger Shakespeare Library.
15. William Hazlitt, *Characters of Shakespeare's Plays* (1848/1817), p. 15.
16. See entry, 'Hon Mr Kinnaid [*sic*]', 26 January 1814, Drury Lane box book, Folger Z.e. 16, Folger Shakespeare Library. Kinnaird is shown as a frequent attender at Kean's performances in subsequent weeks.
17. Kahan, *Cult of Kean*, pp. 50–5; Edward Ziter, 'Kean, Byron and Fantasies of Miscegenation', *Theatre Journal* 54 (2002), pp. 607–26.
18. 19 February 1814, *Diary of William Godwin*, ed. Myers *et al.*
19. The odd sixpence is probably accounted for by the purchase of some extra service, such as food or drink, taken into the box. Folger Z.e. 16, Folger Shakespeare Library.

20. John Kandl, 'Plebeian Gusto, Negative Capability, and the Low Company of "Mr Kean": Keats' Dramatic Review for the *Champion* (21 December 1817)', *Nineteenth Century Prose* 28 (2001), pp. 130–41.

21. Jonathan Mulrooney, 'Keats in the Company of Kean', *Studies in Romanticism* 42 (2003), pp. 227–50.

22. Drury Lane prompter's journal, 27 January 1814, Folger W.b. 381, Folger Shakespeare Library.

23. 12 March 1814, Drury Lane ledger, Folger W.b. 316, Folger Shakespeare Library.

24. 19 February 1814, Drury Lane box book, Folger Z.e. 16, Folger Shakespeare Library; William Godwin diary, 19 February 1814 (http://godwindiary.bodleian.ox.ac.uk/diary/18140219.html).

25. 24 February 1814, Drury Lane box book, Folger Z.e. 16, Folger Shakespeare Library.

26. 4, 5, 7, 9, 11, 12 February 1814, Drury Lane prompter's book, Folger W.b. 381, Folger Shakespeare Library.

27. 19, 29 October, 4 November 1814, Drury Lane delivery book, Folger W.b. 382, Folger Shakespeare Library.

28. John Quincy Adams, diary 9, 31 October 1783, Massachusetts Historical Society, online edition (www.masshist.org/jqadiaries/diaries.cfm).

29. Wu-Chi Liu, 'The Original *Orphan of China*', *Comparative Literature* 5 (1953), pp. 193–212; Hsin-yun Ou, 'Gender, Consumption, and Ideological Ambiguity in David Garrick's Production of *The Orphan of China* (1759)', *Theatre Journal* 60 (2008), pp. 383–407.

30. HM 54457, vol. IX, March 1785, Huntington Library.

31. DeLanda, *New Philosophy of Society*, p. 21.

32. Leman Thomas Rede, *The Road to the Stage; Or, The Performer's Preceptor. Containing Clear and Ample Instructions for Obtaining Theatrical Engagements* (1827), p. 16.

33. *Ibid.*, p. 17.

34. BL Egerton MS 2,279, 23 October 1776.

35. Troubridge, *Benefit System*.

36. *The General Advertiser*, 29 June, 1, 12 July 1750; Janine Barchas notes how Snell portraiture modulated into more feminized versions in the later Georgian period, 'Prefiguring Genre: Frontispiece Portraits from *Gulliver's Travels* to *Millenium Hall*', *Studies in the Novel* 30 (1998), pp. 260–86.

37. *Gazetteer and New Daily Advertiser*, 22 December 1779. This unknown woman in soldier's uniform provokes many questions about the actual percentage of females infiltrating the armed services.

38. Pope's name is printed in the cast list of Henry Jones, *The Earl of Essex. A Tragedy . . . Adapted for theatrical representation, as performed at the Theatre-Royal, in Covent-Garden. Regulated from the prompt-books* (1791).

39. *The Oracle* and *The World*, 11 April 1791.

40. Shearer West, 'The Public and Private Roles of Sarah Siddons', in Robyn Asleson (ed.), *A Passion for Performance: Sarah Siddons and Her*

Portraitists (Los Angeles, CA: J. Paul Getty Museum, 1999), pp. 1–40; Heather McPherson, 'Painting, Politics and the Stage in the Age of Caricature, in 'Robyn Asleson (ed.), *Notorious Muse: The Actress in British Art and Culture, 1776–1812* (New Haven, CT and London: Paul Mellon Centre for Studies in British Art, 2003), pp. 171–94.

41. Heather McPherson, 'Picturing Tragedy: Mrs. Siddons as the Tragic Muse Revisited', *Eighteenth-Century Studies* 33 (2000), pp. 401–30; Robyn Asleson, '"She Was Tragedy Personified": Crafting the Siddons Legend in Life and Art', in Asleson (ed.), *Passion for Performance*, pp. 41–96.

42. McPherson, 'Picturing Tragedy', pp. 401–30, at p. 422.

43. Reproduced in Asleson (ed.), *Passion for Performance*, Figure 22.

44. DeLanda, *Deleuze: History and Science*, p. 12.

45. *Ibid.*

46. Milhous, 'Reading Theatre History from Account Books'.

47. Thomas Campbell, *Life of Mrs Siddons* (1839), p. 203.

48. *Ibid.*, p. 325.

49. *Public Advertiser*, 26 May 1785.

50. HM 33780, fol. 84 verso, citing 'London Chronicle [*sic*]'; that is, *Public Advertiser*, 26 May 1785, Huntington Library.

51. 22 December 1784, 24 April 1785, Folger W.b. 286, Folger Shakespeare Library.

52. John Jackson, *The History of the Scottish stage, from its first establishment to the present time; with a distinct narrative of some recent theatrical transactions* (Edinburgh: 1793), pp. 126, 129.

53. *Report from the Select Committee on Dramatic Literature: With The Minutes of Evidence. . . 2 August 1832*, Parliamentary Papers (1831–2), vol. VII, Question 66.

54. Siddons already knew the theatre, having first appeared there on 18 December 1776, J.L. Hodgkinson and Rex Pogson, *The Early Manchester Theatre* (London: Anthony Blond for the Society of Theatre Research, 1960), p. 84.

55. *Ibid.*, p. 79.

56. *Ibid.*, p. 115.

57. Playbill, Liverpool Theatre, 25 September 1820.

58. Michael R. Booth repeats Jackson's figures; 'Sarah Siddons', in Michael R. Booth, John Stokes and Susan Bassnett (eds.), *Three Tragic Actresses: Siddons, Rachel, Ristori* (Cambridge University Press, 1996), pp. 10–65, at p. 16.

59. *Morning Chronicle and London Advertiser*, 23 May 1785.

60. Winston, *Theatric Tourist* MS, Harvard Theatre Collection, TS 1335.211, fol. 80.

61. Manchester Theatre Royal MS account book, 1784–5, TS 996.900, Harvard Theatre Collection.

62. John Bernard, *Retrospections of the Stage* (1830, 2 vols.), vol. II, pp. 73–4.

CHAPTER FIVE A WORKING THEATRICAL ASSEMBLAGE:
1790S REPRESENTATIONS OF NAVAL CONFLICT

1. DeLanda, *New Philosophy of Society*, p. 50 (DeLanda's emphasis).

2. Joseph Roach, *Cities of the Dead: Circum-Atlantic Performance* (New York: Columbia Univesity Press, 1996), p 4; Kathleen Wilson, *The Island Race: Englishness, Empire and Gender in the Eighteenth Century* (London and New York: Routledge, 2003), pp. 63, 70.

3. DeLanda, *New Philosophy of Society*, p. 56 (DeLanda's emphasis).

4. Given further research and the ability to compute £.*s.d.* into box-office charges per seating area, it would be possible to render exact audience figures for most (non-benefit) Covent Garden and Drury Lane performances of this era.

5. Kathleen Wilson's comments refer specifically to de Loutherbourg and O'Keeffe's Covent Garden pantomime, *Omai, or a Trip round the World* (1785), *The Island Race*, pp. 63, 70.

6. The definitive contemporary eyewitness is an 1802 New York performance, William B. Wood, *Personal Recollections of the Stage, Embracing Notions of Actors, Authors, and Auditors, during a Period of Forty Years* (Philadelphia: Henry Carey Baird, 1855), p. 87.

7. Lucyle Werkmeister, *A Newspaper History of England, 1792–1793* (Lincoln, NE: University of Nebraska Press, 1967), pp. 360, 376, 456–7.

8. *Great news from Lord Howe, by Express, from the London Gazette* (1794), *Bristol Journal Extraordinary, printed by J. Rudhall, from the London Gazette extraordinary, of Wednesday, June 11, 1794* (Bristol: 1794).

9. Peter Howell, 'Burke, Paine, and the Newspapers: An "Archaeology" of Political Knowledge 1789–93', *Studies in Romanticism* 43 (2004), pp. 357–98.

10. Sometimes 'Byrn'.

11. *Official papers relative to the dispute between the courts of Great Britain and Spain, on the subject of the ships captured in Nootka Sound* (1790), p. 1.

12. For the thesis of pre-1800 Asian economic global dominance, see André Gunder Frank, *ReOrient: Global Economy in the Asian Age* (Berkeley, CA: University of California Press, 1998); Kenneth Pomeranz, *The Great Divergence: China, Europe, and the Making of the Modern World Economy* (Princeton University Press, 2000); B.M. Gough, 'India-Based Expeditions of Trade and Discovery in the North Pacific in the Late Eighteenth Century', *Geographical Journal* 155:2 (1989), pp. 215–23.

13. Add MS 29,946, British Library. The benefit was a shared performance for four actors, Cubit, Macready, Thompson and Boyce.

14. *Authentic copy of the memorial to the Right Honourable William Wyndham Grenville, & by Lieutenant John Mears, & dated 30th April, 1790* (1790), p. 4.

15. John M. Norris, 'The Policy of the British Cabinet in the Nootka Crisis', *English Historical Review* 70 (1955), pp. 562–80.

16. Larpent 872, Huntington Library.

17. Gillian Russell, *The Theatres of War: Performance, Politics, and Society 1793–1815* (Oxford: Clarendon Press, 1995), pp. 95–121.

18. HM 54457, vol. XIII, Huntington Library.

19. *Ibid.*, entry for June 1790; Marsh must have seen it on 9 or 14 June 1790; Frederick Reynolds, *The Life and Times of Frederick Reynolds* 2nd edn (1827, 2 vols.), vol. II, pp. 54–5.

20. *Woodfall's Register*, 5 June 1790.
21. *The World*, 4 October 1790.
22. *The Gazetteer and New Daily Advertiser*, 8 October 1790.
23. Larpent 743, Huntington Library; Samuel Birch, *Songs, duets, trio, and choruses, in The Mariners, a musical entertainment, in two acts. As performed at the King's Theatre, Hay-Market* (1793), p. 10.
24. Playbill, 3 June 1794.
25. Eugene H. Jones adds a few more details about the New York *Nootka* but does not mention the Covent Garden version, *Native Americans as Shown on the Stage, 1753–1916* (Metuchen, NJ: Scarecrow Press, 1988), pp. 13–14.
26. This discussion amplifies Gillian Russell, *The Theatres of War: Performance, Politics, and Society 1793–1815* (Oxford: Clarendon Press, 1995), pp. 60–3. Mary Robinson also contributed a song. See *A Compendious History of the English Stage, from the earliest period to the present time. Containing a candid analysis of all dramatic writings* (1800), p. 123.
27. Stephen Storace, *O'er the vast Surface of the Deep. A Favorite Song in the Glorious First of June, etc.* (1794); Richard Brinsley Sheridan *et al.*, *Songs duetts, choruses, &c. in a new and appoiate [sic] entertainment, called The glorious first of June. Performed, for the first time, by His Majesty's servants, at the Theatre Royal, Drury-Lane, on Wednesday, July 2nd. 1794 for the benefit of the widows and orphans of the brave men who fell in the late engagements under Earl Howe* (1794). The authoritative modern edition is Cecil Price (ed.), *The Dramatic Works of Richard Brinsley Sheridan* (Oxford: Clarendon Press, 1973, 2 vols.), vol. II, pp. 751–74.
28. DeLanda, *New Philosophy of Society*, p. 50 (DeLanda's emphasis).
29. Pieter Van der Merwe, 'The Glorious First of June: A Battle of Art and Theatre', in Michael Duffy and Roger Morriss (eds.), *The Glorious First of June 1794: A Naval Battle and Its Aftermath* (University of Exeter Press, 2001), pp. 132–58, at p. 153.
30. *The Times*, 25 June 1794.
31. 8 July 1794, W.b. 296, Folger Shakespeare Library.
32. Van der Merwe, 'Glorious First of June', pp. 132–58.
33. Cobb had joined the East India Company in 1771; he became assistant secretary in 1792 and secretary in 1814; H.V. Bowen, *The East India Company and Imperial Britain, 1756–1833* (Cambridge University Press, 2006), p. 145.
34. Admiralty instructions to Howe are reprinted verbatim in Duffy and Morriss (eds.), *Glorious First of June 1794*, pp. 43–5.
35. Larpent 1032, Huntington Library.
36. Timothy Jenks, *Naval Engagements: Patriotism, Cultural Politics, and the Royal Navy 1793–1815* (Oxford University Press, 2006), pp. 36–42, at p. 40.
37. Chace's ship would have been identifiable as the 60-gun, fourth-rate *Dreadnought*, built in 1742 and sold in 1784; Brian Lavery, *The Ship of the Line – The Development of the Battlefleet 1650–1850* (London: Conway Maritime Press, 1983, 2 vols.), vol. I, p. 171.

38. Clive Emsley, 'Repression, "Terror" and the Rule of Law in England During the Decade of the French Revolution', *English Historical Review* 100 (1985), pp. 801–25.

39. Clive Emsley, 'Hardy, Thomas (1752–1832)', *Oxford Dictionary of National Biography* (*ODNB*) (Oxford University Press, 2004) (www.oxforddnb.com/view/article/12291).

40. Larpent 1414, Huntington Library.

41. DeLanda, *Philosophy and Simulation*, p. 188.

42. Playbills, 25 April, 6 May 1794, Theatre Royal, Covent Garden, London.

43. *The Times*, 19 April 1794.

44. See the 'perfect models . . . made with such minute beauty' referred to by *The Salopian Journal*, 9 July 1794, quoted in Cecil Price (ed.), *The Dramatic Works of Richard Brinsley Sheridan* (Oxford: Clarendon Press, 1973, 2 vols.), vol. II, pp. 756–7.

45. Larpent 1022, Huntington Library.

46. *The Times*, 9 April 1794.

47. Playbills, Covent Garden, 9 May 1794.

48. The play derives from Dibdin's novel, *Hannah Hewit; or, the Female Crusoe. Being the history of a woman of uncommon, mental, and personal accomplishments; who, & was cast away* (1792, 3 vols.).

49. Larpent 1210, Huntington Library.

50. Mark Philp (ed.), *Resisting Napoleon: The British Response to the Threat of Invasion, 1797–1815* (Aldershot: Ashgate, 2006).

51. *The Times*, 14 February, 20 April 1798.

52. *The Times*, 25 April 1798. See also, 'A Correct Plan and Elevation of the Famous French Raft &' (*c.* 1798), PU4060, NMM, Greenwich.

53. Larpent 1202, Huntington Library. Douglas A. Reid observes that 'Saint Monday' helped fill theatres, 'The Decline of Saint Monday, 1766–1876', *Past and Present* 71 (1976), pp. 76–101, at p. 84.

54. G.N. Reynolds is not to be confused with the prolific playwright, Frederick Reynolds. G.N. Reynolds is the attributed author of the broadside, 'Monody on Louis, [*sic*] XVI. late King of France' (Dublin: 1793).

55. *Morning Chronicle*, 11 January 1797; *The Times*, 12 January 1797.

56. The Royalty figures are based on the four advertised performances I have located to date, and assume two-thirds-full houses based on its 1813 seating capacity of 1,600 persons; Lawrence, *Dramatic Emancipation*, p. 380.

57. *Oracle and Public Advertiser*, 21 February 1797.

58. G.N. Reynolds, *Bantry Bay, or the Loyal Peasants* (1797), pp. 8, 16–17, 24.

59. Susan B. Egenolf, 'Maria Edgeworth in Blackface: *Castle Rackrent* and the Irish Rebellion of 1798', *English Literary History* 72 (2005), pp. 845–69.

60. Larpent 1154, Huntington Gallery; Reynolds, *Bantry Bay*, p. 8.

61. By ingenuity, meteorological providentiality was also incorporated into official discourse, James Porter, *Wind and Weather. A sermon on the late providential storm which dispersed the French fleet off Bantry Bay. Preached to the Congregation*

of Gray-Abbey on Thursday the 16th February, being the Fast Day Appointed by Government for Thanksgiving (Belfast: 1797).

62. DeLanda, *Deleuze: History and Science*, p. 12.

63. *The Observer*, 30 April 1797.

64. *The Times*, 28 March 1797. The Spithead mutiny (in the Solent) began on 16 April, with news reaching *The Times* by 21 April 1797.

65. Michael Duffy, *Soldiers, Sugar, and Seapower: The British Expeditions to the West Indies and the War Against Revolutionary France* (Oxford: Clarendon Press, 1987), p. 269.

66. *Ibid.*, p. 275.

67. Mark Lonsdale, *Songs, &c. in Naval triumph; or the Tars of Old England, A new entertainment, founded on the late victory obtained by Earl Howe over the French* (1794), p. 9.

68. Larpent 1166, Huntington Library.

69. Contemporary knowledge about the conquest is uncertain. Michael Duffy refers to the key role in the capture of Trinidad played by the white officer, Lieutenant-Colonel Soter, who had experience of commanding a Negro corps on Martinique, but a Negro pilot called Sharper was also crucial in navigating British warships round the treacherous Dragon's Teeth rocks in the Gulf of Paria, western Trinidad. However, these details remained for many years within documents held at the War Office and the Admiralty department. Duffy, *Soldiers, Sugar, and Seapower*, p. 278.

70. Richard B. Sheridan, *Sugar and Slavery, an Economic History of the British West Indies, 1623–1775* (St Lawrence, Barbados: Caribbean Universities Press, 1974), p. 46.

71. P.C. Emmer, 'The Dutch and the Making of the Second Atlantic System', in Barbara Lewis Solow (ed.), *Slavery and the Rise of the Atlantic System* (Cambridge University Press, 1992), pp. 75–96, at p. 91; Richard B. Sheridan, 'The Crisis of Slave Subsistence in the British West Indies and After the American Revolution', *William and Mary Quarterly* 33 (1976), pp. 615–41, at p. 628.

72. Navy Officer, *A Letter to the Right Hon. Lord Rodney, K.B. & on the subject of the St. Eustatius prize money. Containing a plan for the speedy and final division of it, &c.* (1788).

73. Playbills, Drury Lane, 31 March 1781.

74. Larpent 552, Huntington Library.

75. Matthew Mulcahy, *Hurricanes and Society in the British Greater Caribbean, 1624–1783* (Baltimore, MD: Johns Hopkins University Press, 2005), pp. 111–12.

76. Jay Barnes, *Florida's Hurricane History* (Chapel Hill, NC: University of North Carolina Press, 2007), p. 50.

77. George Colman the Younger, *Inkle and Yarico: an Opera, in Three Acts. As performed at the Theatre-Royal in the Hay-Market, on Saturday, August, 11th, 1787* (Dublin: 1787), p. 6; Daniel O'Quinn, 'Mercantile Deformities: George Colman's *Inkle and Yarico* and the Racialization of Class Relations', *Theatre Journal* 54 (2002), pp. 389–409.

78. The shipboard amateur theatricals in *Nootka Sound; or, Britain Prepar'd* had specified 'Enter two Sailors one as an english [*sic*] Seaman The other in an awkward Spanish dress', Larpent 872, Huntington Library.
79. News of the attack reached London within a week, *The Times*, 23 March 1796. D.K. Broster, 'Sir Sidney Smith and Frotté in 1796', *English Historical Review* 23 (1908), pp. 534–7.
80. Playbills, Covent Garden, 15 April, 3, 18 May 1796.
81. It was first performed on 15 April 1796 literally as an interlude, alongside George Colman the Younger's *Inkle and Yarico* (1787) and Arthur Murphy's *Three Weeks After Marriage* (1775), as part of Margaret Martyr's benefit. Takings of £298. 10*s*. 6*d*. suggest that the two-thirds-full house estimate is a reasonable one.
82. Larpent 1124, Huntington Library.
83. William James, *The Naval History of Great Britain: From the Declaration of War by France in 1793 to the Accession of George IV* (1837), pp. 234–5; N.A.M. Rodger, *The Command of the Ocean: A Naval History of Britain 1649–1815* (London: Allen Lane in Association with the National Maritime Museum, 2004), p. 433.
84. John Flaxman, *A Letter to the Committee for Raising the Naval Pillar, or Monument, under the patronage of His Royal Highness the Duke of Clarence* (1799); Malcolm Campbell, 'An Alternative Design for a Commemorative Monument', *Record of the Art Museum, Princeton University* 17 (1958), pp. 65–73; Nicholas Penny, '"Amor Publicus Posuit": Monuments for the People and of the People', *Burlington Magazine* 129 (1987), pp. 793–800.
85. Thomas John Dibdin, *The Naval Pillar: A Musical Entertainment, As Performed at the Theatre Royal Covent Garden* (1799), pp. 7, 12.
86. *Ibid.*, p. 24.
87. Timothy Jenks, *Naval Engagements: Patriotism, Cultural Politics, and the Royal Navy 1793–1815* (Oxford University Press, 2006), pp. 77–87.
88. Rodger, *Command of the Ocean*, pp. 428–9; Duffy, *Soldiers, Sugar, and Seapower*, pp. 83–4. Guadeloupe was retaken by the French three months later.
89. Naval dispatches giving these details were reprinted in *Bulletins of the Campaign 1795* (1796), pp. 43–6. Despite Faulknor's personal heroism, the occupation of Guadeloupe and the other French Windward Islands was strategically counterproductive. As with Rodney's invasion of St Eustatius, the islands had been plundered, and the originally receptive French plantationer population turned against the British, despite their being alienated by a French government decree of February 1794 ordering them to emancipate their slaves.
90. *Oracle and Public Advertiser*, 6 May 1795.
91. BL Egerton MS 2,293, British Library Department of Manuscripts.
92. François Arnould-Mussot, *The Death Of Captain Cook; A Grand Serious-Pantomimic-Ballet* (1789), p. 17.
93. 2, 8, 18 July 1794, W.b. 296, Folger Shakespeare Library.
94. Highfill *et al.*, *Biographical Dictionary*, vol. IV, pp. 266–76.
95. *Old Bailey Proceedings Online* (www.oldbaileyonline.org, version 6.0, 23 November 2011), May 1800, trial of John Wilson (t18000528-39).

96. DeLanda, *Philosophy and Simulation*, p. 202 (DeLanda's emphasis).

CHAPTER SIX THEATRICAL ASSEMBLAGE
POPULATIONS: THE TURKISH AMBASSADOR'S VISITS
TO LONDON PLAYHOUSES, 1794

1. DeLanda, *Philosophy and Simulation*, p. 202 (DeLanda's emphasis).
2. DeLanda, *New Philosophy of Society*, p. 39.
3. Arnold Hare, *The Georgian Theatre in Wessex* (London: Phoenix House, 1958), pp. 41–2.
4. 24, 27 November 1761, Folger W.b. 2, Folger Shakespeare Library. Theatre visits by British royalty similarly triggered payments to their servants and are frequently recorded in the ledger books.
5. Malyn Newitt, *A History of Mozambique* (London: C. Hurst, 1995), pp. 157–9; 27 April, 2, 3 May 1721, Folger W.a. 32, Folger Shakespeare Library.
6. The existence of the embassy is not noted, for example, in Gerald Maclean, *Looking East: English Writing and the Ottoman Empire Before 1800* (Basingstoke: Palgrave Macmillan, 2007). Harriet Guest, *Empire, Barbarism, and Civilisation: James Cook, William Hodges, and the Return to the Pacific* (Cambridge University Press, 2007), pp. 182–4, comments on the embassy with respect to the late work of William Hodges, noting the rapid change in Anglo-Turkish relations, *vis-à-vis* Russia by 1794, which affected the reception of Hodges' painting, *The Effects of Peace and the Consequences of War*, exhibited in December 1794. Earlier work by Thomas Naff and, more recently, that by G.R. Berridge (see below) are the best guides to the diplomacy.
7. Thomas Naff, 'Reform and the Conduct of Ottoman Diplomacy in the Reign of Selim III, 1789–1807', *Journal of the American Oriental Society* 83 (1963), pp. 295–315.
8. This probably explains the much-delayed formal 'entrance' of the ambassador into the court of St James on 5 January 1795. See *The True Briton*, 2 January 1796. The best-known British ambassador to the Ottoman Empire was Sir Edward Wortley Montagu (1678–1761), who served from 1716 to 1718. Double funding from the Levant Company and the Sultan made these lucrative postings, and the ambassador's exemption from duties on wine and jewellery permitted the development of a personal miniature import/export trade in those commodities. G.R. Berridge, *British Diplomacy in Turkey, 1583 to the Present: A Study in the Evolution of the Resident Embassy* (Leiden and Boston: Martinus Nijhoff, 2009), p. 29.
9. Yusuf Agha, *Account of the Mission of Yusuf Agha, Ambassdor from Turkey to the British Court. Written by Himself.* Translated from the Turkish by the Ritter Joseph Von Hammer (1833).
10. No account of the theatre-going is provided in Yusuf Agha, *Account of the Mission*.
11. HM 54457, vol. XVI, July 1794, Huntington Library.

12. The viability of land routes between the eastern Mediterranean and India was a key feature of British diplomacy. See Edward Ingram, 'From Trade to Empire in the Near East. I. The End of the Spectre of the Overland Trade, 1775–1801', *Middle Eastern Studies* 14 (1978), pp. 3–21.

13. For the Russian background, see A.I. Baggis, *Britain and the Struggle for the Integrity of the Ottoman Empire: Sir Robert Ainslie's Embassy to Istanbul 1776–1794* (Istanbul: Isis Yayimcilik, 1984).

14. Constantin-François Chasseboeuf, comte de Volney, 'It [Egypt] contains all the productions of Europe and Asia, such as corn, rice, cotton, flax, indigo, sugar, saffron, &c. &c. &c. and, possessed of that country alone, we may give up all our other colonies: lying almost at the door of France, ten days would carry our fleets from Toulon to Alexandria . . . Through Egypt we would get to India, we would engross all the commerce of the Red Sea, we would restore the ancient route of Suez,and cause the passage round the Cape of good [*sic*] Hope to be deserted', *Considerations on the War with the Turks* (1788), p. 73.

15. S.W. Fores, 3 April 1791.

16. *A Comparative Estimate of the Advantages Great Britain would derive from a Commercial Alliance with the Ottoman, in preference to the Russian empire* (1791), p. 4.

17. *Observations on the Commerce of Great Britain With the Russian and Ottoman Empires, and on the Projects of Russia Against the Ottoman and British Dominions* (1801), pp. 29, 47.

18. Rajani Sudan, 'Mud, Mortar, and Other Technologies of Empire', *The Eighteenth Century: Theory and Interpretation* 45 (2004), pp. 147–69.

19. Daniel Orme, after Mather Brown, *His Majesty King George III and the Officers of State Receiving the Turkish Ambassador and his Suit*, S.W. Fores, 1 January 1797, stipple engraving. Jean-Jacques-François Le Barbier (1738–1826) exhibited *The Turkish Ambassador* at the Royal Academy in April 1794, but, given Le Barbier's interest in Oriental themes, the picture is likely to have been generic rather than a specific portrait of Yusuf.

20. *Pocket Magazine* (1794), pp. 289–90, Plate v.

21. James Gillray, *Presentation of the Mahometan Credentials – or – The Final Resource of French Atheists* (26 December 1793); Isaac Cruikshank, *A Peep at the Plenipo-!!!* (1 January 1794), reproduced in Guest, *Empire, Barbarism and Civilization*, Plates 7.3 and 7.4.

22. The previous year, Kambra had written *The Siege of Valenciennes for the Piano Forte or Harpsichord* (1793). Cope's work included marches 'in Honor of the Loyal Association of the Parish of St. Saviour, Southwark' (1798) and various songs performed at Vauxhall Gardens.

23. James Cobb, *The Siege of Belgrade; a comic opera, in three acts; as it is performed at the Theatres Royal in London and Dublin* (Dublin: 1791), p. 46.

24. Storace's music drew considerably on the Spanish-located, two-act opera by Martin y Soler, *Unca Cosa Rara* (Venice: 1787), to a libretto by Da Ponte but including music adapted from Mozart's 'Turkish Rondo' (K. 331); Jane

Girdham, *English Opera in Late Eighteenth-Century London: Stephen Storace at Drury Lane* (Oxford: Clarendon Press, 1997), p. 207.

25. Richard P. Sodders, 'The Theatre Management of Alexandre Placide in Charleston, 1794–1812' (Louisiana State University and Agricultural and Mechanical College, Ph.D. dissertation, 1983, 2 vols.), vol. II, calendar for 19, 24 March, 9 April 1802.

26. *The Siege of Belgrade: an Historical Novel. Translated from a German manuscript* (*c.* 1791), p. 1. The title page is misdated in Roman numerals as '1741', but its publisher, H.D. Symonds, was a well-known publisher of the 1790s.

27. Hannah Brand, *Plays and Poems* (Norwich: 1798).

28. Richard Harding Graves, *Quarrelling Duet ... words by J. Cobb* (London: J. Curwen & Sons, 1950).

29. Cobb, *Siege of Belgrade*, pp. 11–12.

30. The current *ODNB* entry (lightly revised from the previous version) dismisses his work as a playwright, but he was well placed and highly productive, and, today, his dramas tell us much about contemporary attitudes to the East. By the time he became company secretary, a principal executive role, he was beset by the ultimately successful campaign to de-monopolize the East India Company. On his work as a playwright, see my *Harlequin Empire: Race, Ethnicity and the Drama of the Popular Enlightenment* (London: Pickering & Chatto, 2007), pp. 25, 92, 102, 116, 117.

31. Adam Smith, *An Inquiry Into The Nature And Causes Of The Wealth Of Nations* (1784, 3rd edn, 3 vols.), vol. III, pp. 108–16.

32. *A Short Reply to Mr. Eton's observations respecting the establishment of the Levant Company* (1799); *An Answer to Mr. Eton's charges against the Turkey Company* (1799).

33. Berridge, *British Diplomacy in Turkey*, pp. 28–9. Ainslie gave up his post in 1793 but stayed on in Constantinople for a further year.

34. In the late 1770s Ainslie's powerful role in Constantinople had brought to a halt a maverick attempt by the governor of Bengal, Warren Hastings, and the explorer of Ethiopia, James Bruce, to set up a 'Suez Company' trading by ship into the Red Sea. Partially through the agency of Ainslie, the Levant Company and the East Indian Company managed to disrupt threats to their monopolies. See David Kimche, 'The Opening of the Red Sea to European Ships in the Late Eighteenth Century', *Middle Eastern Studies* 8 (1972), pp. 63–71.

35. Brand, *Plays and Poems*, p. 56.

36. On Smith's slightly later popular reputation, see *Glorious Defeat of the French Gun-boats! A true and particular Account of the Total Defeat of the Grand French Flotilla, At the Island of St. Marcou ... To which is added, A true and circumstantial Account of the Escape of that Gallant Hero Sir Sidney Smith ... By a Perusal of this Book it may be seen how little Old England has to fear from the boasted French Invasion* (*c.* 1798).

37. There is no scholarly biography, but Smith appears to have joined the Turkish navy as a volunteer. See *Memoirs of Admiral Sir Sidney Smith* (1839, 2 vols.),

vol. i, p. 41, and Tom Pocock, *A Thirst for Glory: The Life of Admiral Sir Sidney Smith* (London: Aurum Press, 1996), p. 20.

38. Thomas Naff, 'Ottoman Diplomacy and the Great European Powers, 1789–1802', Ph.D. thesis, University of California, 1961, pp. 39–40. See also Naff, 'Reform and the Conduct of Ottoman Diplomacy in the Reign of Selim III, 1789–1807', *Journal of the American Oriental Society* 83 (1963), pp. 295–315.

39. Berridge, *British Diplomacy in Turkey*, p. 43.

40. *ODNB*, quoting *St James's Chronicle*, 9 December 1790.

41. Dispatch of 1781, cited in Berridge, *British Diplomacy in Turkey*, p. 27.

42. Naff, 'Ottoman Diplomacy', pp. 72–3.

43. *Ibid.*, p. 72.

44. Naff, 'Reform and the Conduct of Ottoman Diplomacy', pp. 295–315, at pp. 303–5.

45. Paul E. Klopsteg, *Turkish Archery and the Composite Bow: A Review of an Old Chapter in the Chronicles of Archery, and a Modern Interpretation* (Manchester: Simon Avery Foundation, 1987, 3rd edn), pp. 17–18.

46. Martin Johnes, 'Archery, Romance and Elite Culture in England and Wales, *c.* 1780–1840', *History* 89 (2004), pp. 193–208.

47. See also the S.W. Fores print etching, *The Graces of Archery or Elegant Airs, Attitudes & Lady Traps*, January 1794.

48. Roger Ascham, *Toxophilus, the Schole, or Partitions, of Shooting* (Wrexham: 1788), p. vii.

49. HM 54457, vol. xiv, Huntington Library.

50. *Sun*, 22 April 22, 1794; *Oracle and Public Advertiser*, 6 May 1794.

51. *True Briton*, 8 July 1795.

52. *Pocket Magazine* (1794), pp. 289–90, Plate v.

53. Larpent 1037, enclosure, Huntington Library.

54. *Morning Post*, 10 April 1794.

55. Peter A. Tasch (ed.), *The Plays of George Colman the Younger* (New York and London: Garland Publishing, 1981), p. 18.

56. *Ibid.*, p. 19.

57. *The World*, 26 April 1790.

58. *London Packet or New Lloyd's Evening Post*, 9 September 1793; *Gazetteer and New Daily Advertiser*, 11 September 1793; *General Post*, 12 September 1793.

59. Philip Astley, *A Description And Historical Account, Of The Places Now The Theatre Of War In The Low Countries* (1794), pp. 28–30, 50–2.

60. *Public Advertiser*, 2 September 1793.

61. Advertising in *The True Briton* shows that Astley's *The Siege of Valenciennes* played at least until 2 November 1793.

62. The version of *The Shipwreck; or, French Ingratitude* the ambassador saw was a development from a piece of the same title first performed in May 1793; *The Star*, 20 May 1793.

63. *London Chronicle*, 20 May 1794.

64. Duffy, *Soldiers, Sugar, and Seapower*, pp. 86–7.

65. *Oracle and Public Advertiser*, 23 April, 4 August 1794.

66. *The World*, 5 June 1794; *Oracle and Public Advertiser*, 6 June 1794.
67. Hugh Kelly, *The School for Wives. A comedy. As it is performed at the Theatre-Royal in Drury-Lane* (1774), p. x. In the preface Kelly claimed his play had no connection with Molière's *School for Husbands*.
68. As billed in *The World*, 13 June 1794.
69. *Morning Post*, 23 June 1794.
70. DeLanda, *New Philosophy of Society*, p. 92.

CHAPTER SEVEN HISTORICIZING THE THEATRICAL ASSEMBLAGE: MARIE ANTOINETTE AND THE THEATRICAL QUEENS

1. *Morning Post*, 2 May 1794; *The World*, 2 May 1794.
2. On density, stability and solidarity as aspects of the networks connecting assemblages, see DeLanda, *New Philosophy of Society*, pp. 56–7.
3. Elizabeth Pope's gross benefit receipts were £405. 16s. 0d.; Alexander Pope's gross receipts, £228. 14s. 0d., minus the 'Benefit Deficiency' of £52. 7s. 0d. Taken in conjunction with the 'Ticket' money receipted, this suggests house charges of around £150; 7 April, 10 May, 2 June 1794. Folger W.b. 436, Folger Shakespeare Library.
4. 'To Miss Younge', John Philip Kemble, Dublin, 10 July 1782, Folger Y.d. 448 (8), Folger Shakespeare Library.
5. BL Egerton MS 2,292, 26 March 1792. The 'house' took another £151. 4s., but, as with several of these accounts, the charge made by the playhouse against Mrs Pope's earnings (effectively for the hire of the playhouse) is not easily determined.
6. *Oracle and Public Advertiser*, 9 May 1794.
7. Larpent 974, Huntington Library.
8. 23 January 1793, diaries of Anna Larpent, HM 31201 (16 vols.), vol. 1, Huntington Library.
9. *Public Advertiser*, 11 March 1777.
10. Edward Jerningham, *Fugitive Poetical Pieces* (1778), p. v. It was reprinted in his *Poems* (1779), which reached six editions by 1781 and was reissued in new editions of 1786, 1790 and 1796.
11. The wording of the poem is ambiguous. It may also refer to the role of Margaret of Anjou in Thomas Francklin's *The Earl of Warwick* (1766), which Sarah Siddons had established in 1784, as discussed below. As the poem was headed 'Lines addressed to Mrs. Pope, on her leaving the Edinborough [*sic*] Theatre; where she had performed for twelve Nights to crouded Audiences with an uncommon Degree of Applause', it very much makes Elizabeth Pope (*née* Younge) its centre. I have not been able to locate a playbill for these performances. *Public Advertiser*, 4 August 1786; James Boaden, *Memoirs of Mrs. Siddons* (Philadelphia: 1827), p. 248.
12. Edmund Burke, *Reflections on the Revolution in France, and on the proceedings in certain societies in London relative to that event. In a letter intended to have been sent to a gentleman in Paris* (1790), pp. 105–6.

13. St Clair, *Reading Nation*, Appendix 9, p. 583.
14. The playbill is set out in *The World*, 8 May 1794.
15. Highfill *et al.*, *Biographical Dictionary*, vol. XIV, p. 237.
16. Christopher Reid, 'Burke's Tragic Muse: Sarah Siddons and the "Feminization" of the Reflections'; Frans De Bruyn, 'Theater and Counter-Theater in Burke's Reflections on the Revolution in France'; and Tom Furniss, 'Stripping the Queen: Edmund Burke's Magic Lantern Show', all in Steven Blakemore (ed.), *Burke and the French Revolution: Bicentennial Essays* (Athens, GA and London: University of Georgia Press, 1992), pp. 1–27, 28–68, 69–96. See also Julie A. Carlson, *In the Theatre of Romanticism: Coleridge, Nationalism, Women* (Cambridge University Press, 1994), pp. 10–1, 136–44; Geraldine Friedman, *The Insistence of History: Revolution in Burke, Wordsworth, Keats, and Baudelaire* (Stanford, CA: Stanford University Press, 1996), pp. 12–43, 51–6; Robert Kaufman, 'The Madness of George III, by Mary Wollstonecraft', *Studies in Romanticism* 37 (1998), pp. 17–25; Robert Kaufman, 'The Sublime as Super-Genre of the Modern, or Hamlet in Revolution: Caleb Williams and His Problems', *Studies in Romanticism* 36 (1997), pp. 541–74; and Peter H. Melvin, 'Burke on Theatricality and Revolution', *Journal of the History of Ideas* 36 (1975), pp. 447–68.
17. Burke, *Reflections on the Revolution*, p. 120.
18. Paddy Bullard, 'The Meaning of the "Sublime and Beautiful": Shaftesburian Contexts and Rhetorical Issues in Edmund Burke's *Philosophical Enquiry*', *Review of English Studies* 56 (2005), pp. 169–91. For representative recent studies of rhetorical and performative types of analysis, see Katherine O'Donnell, 'Edmund Burke's Political Poetics', in Nessa Cronin, Seán Crosson and John Eastlake (eds.), *Anáil an Bhéil Bheo: Orality and Modern Irish Culture* (Newcastle upon Tyne: Cambridge Scholars Publishing, 2009), pp. 175–87; Betsy Bolton, 'Imperial Sensibilities, Colonial Ambivalence: Edmund Burke and Frances Burney', *English Literary History* 72 (2005), pp. 871–99; Daniel O'Quinn, *Staging Governance: Theatrical Imperialism in London, 1770–1800* (Baltimore, MD: Johns Hopkins University Press, 2005), pp. 164–221; Fran De Bruyn, 'William Shakespeare and Edmund Burke: Literary Allusion in Eighteenth-Century British Political Rhetoric', in Peter Sabor and Paul Yachnin (eds.), *Shakespeare and the Eighteenth Century* (Aldershot: Ashgate, 2008), pp. 85–102.
19. Anne Mallory, 'Burke, Boredom, and the Theater of Counterrevolution', *Publications of the Modern Language Association* 118 (2003), pp. 224–38, at p. 224.
20. Paul Hindson and Tim Gray, *Burke's Dramatic Theory of Politics* (Aldershot: Avebury, 1988), pp. 158–72.
21. 'Siddons was also the favorite of Edmund Burke, whose tearful spectatorship inspired him to write his infamously excessive idealization of Marie Antoinette in *Reflections on the Revolution in France*', Linda Brigham, 'Joanna Baillie's Reflections on the Passions: The "Introductory Discourse" and the Properties of Authorship', *Studies in Romanticism* 43 (2004), pp. 417–37, at p. 417.

22. Harry E. Shaw, book review, *Victorian Studies* 48 (2006), pp. 549–51.
23. Tom Paine, *The Rights of Man* (1791), pp. 24, 39; Robert Bisset, *The Life of Edmund Burke. Comprehending an impartial account of his literary and political efforts* (1798), p. 154.
24. The best account, and one which provides a close analysis of Burke's rhetoric, is O'Quinn, *Staging Governance*, pp. 164–221.
25. *The World*, 19 February 1788; Major John Scott, *A letter to the Right Honourable Charles James Fox, on the extraneous matter contained in Mr. Burke's Speeches, in Westminster-Hall* (1789), p. 52.
26. In November 1783, Inchbald had contemplated visiting India, Ben P. Robertson (ed.), *The Diaries of Elizabeth Inchbald* (London: Pickering & Chatto, 2007, 2 vols.), vol. II, pp. xiv, 220, 227. Cobb's working title for *Love in the East* was *Calcutta; or, Twelve Hours in India*, Larpent 796, Huntington Library.
27. John Quincy Adams, diary 9, 27 October 1783, Massachusetts Historical Society, online edition www.masshist.org/jqadiaries/diaries.cfm.
28. DeLanda, *New Philosophy of Society*, p. 118; Larpent 655, Huntington Library.
29. Playbills, Drury Lane, 11 May 1789.
30. Boaden, *Memoirs of Mrs. Siddons*, p. 327.
31. Reid, 'Burke's Tragic Muse', pp. 2, 6–7.
32. David Garrick, *Isabella; or, The Fatal Marriage* (1757), p. 9.
33. Reid, 'Burke's Tragic Muse', pp. 1–27, at pp. 6–7.
34. Arthur Murphy, *The Grecian Daughter* (1772), p. 70.
35. David Hume, *The History of England, from the Invasion of Julius Caesar to the Revolution in 1688* (1763, 8 vols.), vol. III, pp. 233–4.
36. Jerningham, *Fugitive Poetical Pieces*, p. 10.
37. Mallory, 'Burke, Boredom', pp. 224–38, at p. 235.
38. Jerningham, *Fugitive Poetical Pieces*, p. 11.
39. *Ibid.*, p. 4.
40. Samuel Arnold's music was published by the music publishers, Longman and Broderip, *The Overture, Songs, Chorusses &c in the Battle of Hexham or Days of Old* (1789).
41. George Colman the Younger, *The Battle of Hexham. A Comedy, In Three Acts, As Peformed at the Theatre-Royal, Crow-Street* (Dublin: 1790), pp. 17–18.
42. The first review appeared in *English Chronicle or Universal Evening Post*, 11 August 1789. A rather more impartial review ran in *The World* the next day. *Diary or Woodfall's Register*, 14 August 1789.
43. Edward Cape Everard, *Memoirs Of An Unfortunate Son Of Thespis; Being A Sketch Of The Life Of Edward Cape Everard, Comedian* (1818), p. 261.
44. It was performed at Philadelphia, *Pennsylvania Gazette*, 5 June 1794.
45. Siddons first played the role on 4 November 1784, Boaden, *Memoirs of Mrs. Siddons*, p. 248.
46. Tate Wilkinson, *The Wandering Patentee; Or, A History Of The Yorkshire Theatres, From 1770 To The Present Time* (York: 1795, 4 vols.), vol. II, p. 187.
47. Thomas Campbell, *Life of Mrs. Siddons* (1834, 2 vols.), vol. I, pp. 286–7.

48. Thomas Francklin, *The Earl of Warwick, a tragedy, as it is perform'd at the Theatre Royal in Drury-Lane* (1766), p. 66.
49. *The Beauties of Mrs. Siddons: or, a review of her performance of the characters of Belvidera, Zara, Isabella, Jane Shore – And Lady Randolph* (1786), p. 33.
50. *The Bristol and Bath Magazine: or, Weekly Miscellany* (Bristol: 1782–3, 3 vols.), vol. II, p. 284.
51. See Denis O'Bryen's pamphlets, *The Prospect Before Us. Being a series of papers upon the great question which now agitates the public mind. To which is added a new postscript* (1788), p. 70, and *The Prospect Before Us, on the present momentous crisis, addressed to every friend of the constitution* (Dublin: 1789), p. 55.
52. *Reflexions on the Consequences of His Majesty's recovery from his late indisposition* (1789), pp. 24–5.
53. Jerningham had written to a friend, 'Nothing . . . respecting the commotions in France will have any weight with me', 25 March 1790, Lewis Bettany, *Edward Jerningham and His Friends: A Series of Eighteenth Century Letters* (London: Chatto & Windus, 1919), pp. 314–15.
54. Burke to Jerningham, 18 November 1790, Bettany, *Edward Jerningham and His Friends*, p. 37.
55. Jerningham, *Fugitive Poetical Pieces*, p. v.
56. See Jacqueline Letzter and Robert Adelson, 'French Women Opera Composers and the Aesthetics of Rousseau', *Feminist Studies* 26 (2000), pp. 69–100. For the context of the uptake of Rousseau's ideas in Britain, see James H. Warner, 'The Basis of J.-J. Rousseau's Contemporaneous Reputation in England', *Modern Language Notes* 55 (1940), pp. 270–80.
57. *Morning Chronicle and London Advertiser*, 12 March 1777.
58. Tracy B. Strong, 'Theatricality, Public Space, and Music in Rousseau', *SubStance* 25 (1996), pp. 110–27.
59. *Prologue Written for the Re-opening of the Theatre at Brandenbourgh House, after it was embellished and enlarged in the Year 1795* (c. 1795), p. 12.
60. DeLanda, *New Philosophy of Society*, p. 28 (DeLanda's emphasis). 'Haecceity' is a non-qualitative property of individuation first outlined by John Duns Scotus (1266–1308). See Richard Cross, 'Medieval Theories of Haecceity', in Edward N. Zalta (ed.), *Stanford Encyclopedia of Philosophy* (Fall 2010 edn) (http://plato.stanford.edu/archives/fall2010/entries/medieval-haecceity/).

CHAPTER EIGHT THE REGULATORY ASSEMBLAGE: *THE ROMAN ACTOR* AND THE POLITICS OF SELF-CENSORSHIP

1. DeLanda, *Philosophy and Simulation*, p. 5.
2. A. Norman Jeffares, 'Sheridan, Richard Brinsley (1751–1816)', *ODNB*, online edn, January 2008 (www.oxforddnb.com/view/article/25367).
3. DeLanda, *Philosophy and Simulation*, p. 189.
4. Larpent 1040, Huntington Library.
5. David Erskine Baker, *The Companion to the Play-House: or, an historical account of all the dramatic writers (and their works) that have appeared in Great Britain*

and Ireland . . . *Composed in the form of a dictionary* (1764, 2 vols.), vol. 1, pp. 243–4. A collected edition of Massinger's plays appeared in 1761.

6. Tate Wilkinson, *The Wandering Patentee; or, a History of the Yorkshire Theatres, from 1770 to the present time: interspersed with anecdotes respecting most of the performers . . . from 1765 to 1795* (York: 1795, 4 vols.), vol. 11, pp. 107–8.

7. Playbill, 23 May 1796, Drury Lane. Priscilla Kemble only acted in the after-piece, *Celadon and Florimel; Or, The Happy Counterplot*, a relicensed adaptation by John Philip Kemble of Dryden and Cibber's *The Comical Lovers*, Larpent 1133, Huntington Library. An apparent anomaly is that Priscilla's 'Address . . . On Occasion of Her Retiring from the Stage' was either unlicensed or simply purloined from Drury Lane's stock of similar texts licensed on previous occasions.

8. A definitive list of Drury Lane plays of the 1790s performed (prior to *The Roman Actor*) with gaps longer than two weeks before staging includes Miles Peter Andrews, *Better Late than Never*, licensed 25 March 1790, produced 17 November 1790, Larpent 863; Sophia Lee, *Almeyda, Queen of Granada*, licensed 19 February 1796, produced 20 April 1796, Larpent 1113; Robert Jephson, *The Conspiracy*, licensed 30 March 1796, produced 15 November 1796, Larpent 1120, Huntington Library.

9. John Barrell, *Imagining the King's Death: Figurative Treason, Fantasies of Regicide, 1793–1796* (Oxford University Press, 2000), pp. 567–8.

10. *Aurora General Advertiser*, 24 December 1795.

11. Larpent 1040, Huntington Library.

12. A close analysis of the sequence of events is given in Barrell, *Imagining the King's Death*.

13. *Ibid.*, p. 318.

14. DeLanda, *Deleuze: History and Science*, 'Intensive and Extensive Cartography', pp. 115–40.

15. Bryan, *American Theatrical Regulation*, p. 330.

16. Charles Tilly, *Popular Contention in Great Britain 1758–1834* (Cambridge, MA: Harvard University Press, 1995), pp. 41–62.

17. DeLanda, *New Philosophy of Society*, p. 92; *Deleuze: History and Science*, pp. 41–2.

18. Tilly, *Popular Contention in Great Britain*, pp. 73–87, at pp. 77, 79.

19. *Ibid.*, pp. 42–3 (Tilly's part italicization).

20. *Ibid.*, p. 16 (Tilly's emphasis).

21. *Truth and Treason! Or A Narrative of the Royal Procession To The House of Peers, October the 29th, 1795. To Which Is Added, An Account Of The Martial Procession To Covent-Garden Theatre, On the Evening of the 30th* (1795), p. 7.

22. DeLanda, *Deleuze: History and Science*, p. 13.

23. Elizabeth Inchbald, *Every One has his Fault: a comedy, in five acts, as it is performed at the Theatre Royal, Covent-Garden* (1793), pp. 10, 46; Katherine S. Green, 'Mr Harmony and the Events of January 1793: Elizabeth Inchbald's *Every One Has His Fault*', *Theatre Journal* 56 (2004), pp. 47–62.

24. Larpent 967, Huntington Library. Larpent dated his receipt of the play on 12 January 1793.

25. For a thorough evaluation of the wider political context, see Daniel O'Quinn, 'Bread: The Eruption and Interruption of Politics in Elizabeth Inchbald's *Every One Has His Fault*', *European Romantic Review* 18 (2007), pp. 149–57; Amy Garnai, 'Radicalism, Caution, and Censorship in Elizabeth Inchbald's *Every One Has His Fault*', *SEL Studies in English Literature 1500–1900* 47 (2007), pp. 703–22.

26. Robertson (ed.), *Diaries of Elizabeth Inchbald*, vol. II, pp. 296–7.

27. Sarah Lloyd, 'Pleasing Spectacles and Elegant Dinners: Conviviality, Benevolence, and Charity Anniversaries in Eighteenth-Century London', *Journal of British Studies* 41 (2002), pp. 23–57.

28. *Songs, &c. in the Deserter of Naples; or, Royal Clemency: To Which is Added, An Ode to Friendship, A Tale from Baker's Chronicle, Address for the Marine Society, Mr. Lee Lewes's Farewell Address, and other favourite Pieces Performed at the Royalty Theatre* (c. 1787); Larpent 872, Huntington Library.

29. Larpent 716, Huntington Library.

30. Playbill, Haymarket 16 August 1785.

31. Larpent 608, Huntington Library.

32. John O'Keeffe, *The Farmer: A Comic Opera, in Two Acts, as it is performed at the Theatres Royal in London and Dublin* (Dublin: 1788), pp. 7, 13.

33. *True Briton*, 30 January 1793.

34. *Evening Mail*, 2 November 1792; William Pearce, *Hartford-Bridge: or, the skirts of the camp. An operatic farce, in two acts. Performed at the Theatre-Royal, Covent-Garden* (1793), p. 38.

35. *Oracle and Public Advertiser*, 18 June 1794.

36. *Whitehall Evening Post*, 21 June 1794.

37. *The Sun*, 3 October 1794.

38. *Morning Chronicle*, 5 August 1794.

39. *Oracle and Public Advertiser*, 18 August 1794; on the riots, see John Barrell, *The Spirit of Despotism: Invasions of Privacy in the 1790s* (Oxford University Press, 2006), pp. 42–4.

40. *The Sun*, 28 October 1794.

41. *Oracle and Public Advertiser*, 31 July 1794.

42. *Morning Star*, 30 April 1789.

43. Isaac Bickerstaffe, *The Recruiting Serjeant, a musical entertainment as it is perform'd at the Theatre-Royal in Drury-Lane* (1770), p. 18.

44. Matthew J. Kinservik, 'The Censorship of Samuel Foote's *The Minor* (1760): Stage Controversy in the Mid-Eighteenth Century', *Studies in the Literary Imagination* 32 (1999), pp. 89–104.

45. Thomas Rowlandson, engraver and painter, *The Grand Procession to St Paul's on St George's Day 1789* (William Holland: 1789). For the impact on the Regency question, see also S.W. Fores, *The Funeral Procession of Miss Regency*, 29 April 1789.

46. Pamela Horne, 'An Eighteenth Century Battleground: The Shop Tax of 1785–1789', *Genealogists' Magazine* 28 (2006), pp. 479–86.

47. Playbills, York, 18 March 1800.

48. 'Their Majesties Procession in St. Pauls, Apl 23d 1789', *Lady's Magazine* (1789).

49. Richard Steele, *The Funeral: or, Grief a-la-mode. A comedy. As it is acted at the Theatre Royal in Drury-Lane, by His Majesty's Servants* (1702), p. 2.

50. *St. James's Chronicle or British Evening Post*, 2 December 1794. The performance referred to is likely to have been that held at Covent Garden on 4 February 1794. See also *Trials for High Treason; containing the whole of the proceedings at the Old-Bailey, from October 28, to December 5, 1794* (1795), p. 337.

51. John Thelwall, *The Tribune, a Periodical Publication, consisting chiefly of the political lectures of J. Thelwall. Taken in short-hand by W. Ramsey* (1795–6, 3 vols.), vol. III, p. 313. Contrary to the witness evidence in court, Thelwall claimed he was accompanied by only four or five people.

52. *Morning Chronicle*, 4 November 1795.

53. Richard Brinsley Sheridan, *The Rivals, A Comedy, As it is Acted at the Theatre-Royal in Covent-Garden* (1775), p. 97.

54. *London Packet or New Lloyd's Evening Post*, 30 October 1795; *Morning Chronicle*, 31 October 1795; *The Star*, 31 October 1795.

55. *The Star*, 31 October 1795.

56. Thomas B. Howell, *A Complete Collection of State Trials* (1818), vol. XXIV, p. 1391.

57. Steve Poole, *The Politics of Regicide in England, 1760–1850: Troublesome Subjects* (Manchester University Press, 2001), pp. 53–4, 108, 118, n. 70.

58. *The Tomahawk or Censor General*, 27 October 1795.

59. *Ibid*.

60. *Ibid.*, 31 October 1795.

61. Larpent 1093, Huntington Library. The manuscript is endorsed in Larpent's hand, 'Prohibited from being acted'.

62. Lady Eglantine Wallace, *The Whim, a Comedy, in three acts . . . With an Address to the Public, upon the Arbitrary and Unjust Aspersion of the licenser against its Political Sentiments* (Margate: 1795), p. 6. In a complex battle to outmanoeuvre Drury Lane over its loyalist sympathies, *The Whim* was not really 'a musical entertainment', but it did include a lengthy patriotic song about Admiral Howe's victory on 1 June 1794 against the French, a cause to which Sheridan had committed one night's Drury Lane takings (*Morning Chronicle*, 6 August 1794). Responsibility for interdicting Wallace's loyalist gesture could now be laid at the feet of Sheridan.

63. Wallace, *The Whim*, pp. 64–6.

64. *The Tomahawk or Censor General*, 2 November 1795.

65. Charles Dibdin, *The Professional Life of Mr. Dibdin, Written by Himself* (1803, 4 vols.), vol. IV, p. 6.

66. *Morning Post and Fashionable World*, 15 October 1795. An enclosure with the licensing application for Dibdin's *Hannah Hewit; or, The Female Crusoe*, staged at Drury Lane in 1798, makes it clear that he thought – mistakenly – that he had established a special relationship of precedence with the Lord Chamberlain and did not need his songs vetted. Larpent 1210, Huntington Library.

67. *The Star*, 16 October 1794.
68. Barrell, *Imagining the King's Death*, pp. 472–3.
69. *True Briton*, 1 October 1794; *London Packet or New Lloyd's Evening Post*, 29 September 1794.
70. Playbill, Covent Garden, 29 September 1794.
71. Philip Massinger, *The Roman Actor. A tragedy . . . reviv'd with alterations* (1722), p. 2.
72. Tate Wilkinson, *The Wandering Patentee; or, a History of the Yorkshire Theatres, from 1770 to the present time* (York: 1795, 4 vols.), vol. II, pp. 107–8.
73. Massinger, *Roman Actor*, p. 9.
74. Holcroft was named in the *London Evening Post* (4 October 1794), and the bills of indictment were printed in full on 15 October (*Oracle and Public Advertiser*).
75. *St James's Chronicle or British Evening Post*, 7 October 1794. On the same day, *The General Evening Post*, along with several other newspapers, carried verbatim reports of Holcroft's initial arraignment before the High Court.
76. *True Briton*, 16 October 1794.
77. Larpent 1044, Huntington Library. Inchbald knew Holcroft both socially and professionally. Although there are no records for 1794, they spent 'some time' together on 17 June 1793; she 'went to Mass' with him on 23 June 1793 and 'walked' with him on 3 July and 26 September 1793. Robertson (ed.), *Diaries of Elizabeth Inchbald*, vol. II, pp. 309, 310, 317.
78. *True Briton*, 30 January 1793.
79. *The World*, 2 February 1793. The day before, this 'unjust accusation' had been challenged by an anonymous correspondent to *The Morning Chronicle* (1 February 1793).
80. *Whitehall Evening Post*, 30 September 1794.
81. *Oracle and Public Advertiser*, 16 September 1794.
82. Larpent 1039, Huntington Library.
83. Larpent 833, Huntington Library. John Genest comments that the title is 'Playhouse Greek . . . somewhat unintelligible . . . [it] probably meant Laos eudaimon', *Some Account of the English Stage: From the Restoration in 1660 to 1830* (1832, 10 vols.), vol. VI, p. 540.
84. James Hook, *Songs, Choruses, &c. in Jack of Newbury, A comic opera, with a masque, in honour of the Royal Nuptials, performed by their Majesties servants, at the Theatre Royal, Drury Lane* (1795).
85. Genest, *Some Account of the English Stage*, vol. VI, p. 540.
86. A somewhat louche or Gothicized Hygeia was the figure chosen by Sir Joshua Reynolds under which to portray William Beckford's mistress and his cousin's wife (*Mrs Peter Beckford*, 1782; oil and canvas, Lady Lever Art Gallery, Liverpool).

CONCLUSION

1. DeLanda, *New Philosophy of Society*, p. 56 (DeLanda's emphasis).
2. DeLanda, *Philosophy and Simulation*, p. 200.

3. DeLanda, *Deleuze: History and Science*, p. 104.
4. DeLanda, *New Philosophy of Society*, p. 12.
5. DeLanda, *Deleuze: History and Science*, p. 12.

APPENDIX: ACTOR-NETWORK-THEORY

1. Latour, *Reassembling the Social*, p. 46.
2. *Ibid.*, pp. 54–5.
3. *Ibid.*, p. 132 (Latour's emphasis).
4. 'First, no interaction is what could be called *isotopic*. What is acting at the same moment in any place is coming from many other places, many distant materials, and many faraway actors . . . Second, no interaction is *synchronic* . . . Action has always been carried on thanks to shifting the burden of connection to longer- or shorter-lasting entities. Third, interactions are not *synoptic*. Very few of the participants in a given course of action are simultaneously visible at any given point . . . Fourth, interactions are not *homogeneous* . . . How many successive shifts in agencies should we have to detect if we wanted to move from the architect's cabinet, fifteen years ago, to the lecture hall [in which we now teach]? . . . Fifth, interactions are not *isobaric* . . . Some of the participants are pressing very strongly, requesting to be heard and taken into account, while others are fully routine customs sunk rather mysteriously into bodily habits . . . If any of the intermediaries mutates into a mediator, then the whole set up, no matter how solemn or controlled, may become unpredictable.' Latour, *Reassembling the Social*, pp. 200–2.
5. *Ibid.*, p. 65.
6. *Ibid.*, 'On the Difficulty of Being an ANT: An Interlude in the Form of a Dialog', pp. 141–56.
7. *Ibid.*, pp. 106–7.
8. *Ibid.*, p. 108 (Latour's emphasis).
9. See, indicatively, for the inclusion of DeLeuze and Latour on the 2003 power crises, Jane Bennett, 'The Agency of Assemblies and the North American Blackout', *Public Culture* 17 (2005), pp. 445–65; on the bombings in London on 7 July 2005, see Liza Potts, 'Using Actor Network Theory to Trace and Improve Multimodal Communication Design', *Technical Communication Quarterly* 18 (2009), pp. 281–301.

Bibliography

Unless otherwise indicated, the place of publication of all works published before 1850 is assumed to be London.

MANUSCRIPTS

British Library

Add MS 29,946
Egerton MSS 2,268; 2,279; 2,291; 2,292; 2,293

Folger Shakesepeare Library, Washington, DC

Folger Art Vol. b8
Folger Bill Box G5 L53pt 1822 a & b
Folger M.a. 151
Folger W.a. 12; W.a. 32; W.a. 39; W.a. 104 (1); W.a. 104 (8); W.a. 104 (10); W.a. 104 (13)
W.b. 2; W.b. 273; W.b. 277; W.b. 286; W.b. 294; W.b. 296; W.b. 298; W.b. 316;
    W.b. 319; W.b. 327; W.b. 381; W.b. 382; W.b. 423; W.b. 436
Folger Y.d. 448 (8); Y.d. 614 12/84
Folger Z.e. 16

Garrick Club, Garrick Street, London

Covent Garden Theatre Accounts September 1760–September 1761, Garrick Club, Garrick Street, London
Kalman A. Burnim, 'The Drury Lane Theatre Theatrical Fund 1766–1798', *c.* 2005, unpublished manuscript, Garrick Club, Garrick Street, London
'Proceedings of the [Drury Lane Theatrical] Fund 7 October 1781–31 December 1789', Garrick Club, Garrick Street, London

Harvard Theatre Collection, Harvard University

Charles Durang, MS notes for 'The Philadelphia Stage; from 1749–1854', *Philadelphia Sunday Dispatch*, first series, 7 May 1854 to 1860, 7 vols.

MS John Winston, *Theatric Tourist*, TS 1335.211
TS 996.900

Huntington Library, San Marino, California

Diaries of Anna Larpent, HM 31201
Diaries of John Marsh, HM 54457
HM 33780
John Larpent MSS 54; 490; 608; 655; 698; 716; 743; 780; 796; 833; 863; 872; 967;
    974; 983; 1037; 1039; 1040; 1044; 1093; 1113; 1120; 1124; 1210

Lewis Walpole Library, Farmington, Connecticut

LWL 49 1810 58

Massachusetts Historical Society

John Quincy Adams diary, online edition www.masshist.org/jqadiaries/diaries.cfm

Unpublished Ph.D. theses

Thomas Naff, 'Ottoman Diplomacy and the Great European Powers, 1789–1802',
    University of California, 1961
Richard P. Sodders, 'The Theatre Management of Alexandre Placide in
    Charleston, 1794–1812', Louisiana State University and Agricultural and
    Mechanical College, 1983, 2 vols.

PERIODICAL PRIMARY SOURCES

Acting Manager; or, The Minor Spy. A Weekly Review of the Public and Private Stage
    (1831)
Aurora General Advertiser (Philadelphia)
Bristol and Bath Magazine: or, Weekly Miscellany
British Stage, and Literary Cabinet
Cynick (Philadelphia)
Diary or Woodfall's Register
Director: A Weekly Literary Journal
English Chronicle or Universal Evening Post
European Magazine
Evening Mail
Examiner
Gazetteer and New Daily Advertiser
General Evening Post
General Post
Inspector, A Weekly Dramatic Paper
Lady's Magazine
Lincoln Dramatic Censor
Liverpool Mercury

London Chronicle
London Packet or New Lloyd's Evening Post
Morning Chronicle and London Advertiser
Morning Herald and Daily Advertiser
Morning Post and Daily Advertiser
Morning Post and Fashionable World
Morning Post and Gazetteer
Observer
Oracle and Public Advertiser
Pennsylvania Gazette
Pocket Magazine
Public Advertiser
St. James's Chronicle or the British Evening Post
Stage (1814–15) (ed. T.J. Wooler)
Star
Sun
Thespian Oracle, or Monthly Mirror (Philadelphia)
Times
Tomahawk or Censor General
True Briton
Whitehall Evening Post
Woodfall's Register
World

PRIMARY PRINTED SOURCES

Account of the Life of that Celebrated Tragedian Mr. Thomas Betterton. Containing A Distinct Relation of his Excellencies in his Profession, and Character in Private Life (1749)
Act of Parliament together with the Rules and Regulations of the Society Established for the Relief of Indigent Person, Belonging to His Majesty's Company of Comedians of the Theatre Royal, Drury Lane (1777)
Adams, John, *Curious Thoughts on the History of Man; chiefly abridged or selected from the celebrated works of Lord Kaimes, Lord Monboddo, Dr. Dunbar, and the immortal Montesquieu* (1789)
Answer to Mr. Eton's charges against the Turkey Company (1799)
Arnold, Samuel, *The Overture, Songs, Chorusses &c in the Battle of Hexham or Days of Old* (1789)
  The Siege of Curzola: A Comic Opera . . . Adapted for the Voice & Harpsichord. The Words by Mr. O'Keefe (1786)
Arnould-Mussot, François, *The Death Of Captain Cook; A Grand Serious-Pantomimic-Ballet* (1789)
Ascham, Roger, *Toxophilus, the Schole, or Partitions, of Shooting* (Wrexham: 1788)
Astley, Philip, *A Description And Historical Account, Of The Places Now The Theatre Of War In The Low Countries* (1794)
Attwood, Thomas, *The Additional Song, Duett and Trio in the Mariners* (1794)

The Mariners, a Musical Entertainment in Two Acts . . . composed by T. Attwood (1793)

Authentic copy of the memorial to the Right Honourable William Wyndham Grenville, . . . by Lieutenant John Mears, . . . dated 30th April, 1790 (1790)

Authentick Memoirs Of The Life Of That Celebrated Actress Mrs. Ann Oldfield. Containing a genuine account of her transactions from her infancy to the time of her decease. The third edition, with large additions and amendments (1730)

Baillie, Joanna, *Series of Plays: In Which it is Attempted to Delineate the Stronger Passions of the Mind – Each Passion Being the Subject of a Tragedy and a Comedy* (1798–1812, 3 vols.)

Baker, David Erskine, *The Companion to the Play-House: or, an historical account of all the dramatic writers (and their works) that have appeared in Great Britain and Ireland . . . Composed in the form of a dictionary* (1764, 2 vols.)

The Beauties of Mrs. Siddons: or, a Review of her Performance of the Characters of Belvidera, Zara, Isabella, Margaret of Anjou, Jane Shore – And Lady Randolph (1786)

Bernard, John, *Retrospections of the Stage* (1830, 2 vols.)

Berry, Mary, *The Fashionable Friends; A Comedy, In Five Acts; As Performed . . . At the Theatre Royal, Drury-Lane* (1802)

Beuler, Jacob, *Songs, Humorous and Satirical, To Popular Tunes* (1829)

Bickerstaffe, Isaac, *The Recruiting Serjeant, a musical entertainment as it is perform'd at the Theatre-Royal in Drury-Lane* (1770)

Birch, Samuel, *Songs, duets, trio, and choruses, in The Mariners, a musical entertainment, in two acts. As performed at the King's Theatre, Hay-Market* (1793)

Bisset, Robert, *The Life of Edmund Burke. Comprehending an impartial account of his literary and political efforts* (1798)

Boaden, James, *Memoirs of Mrs. Siddons* (Philadelphia: 1827)

Brand, Hannah, *Huniades; or, The Siege of Belgrade* (1791)
 Plays and Poems (Norwich: 1798)

Bristol Journal Extraordinary, printed by J. Rudhall, from the London Gazette extra-ordinary, of Wednesday, June 11, 1794 (Bristol: 1794)

Brownsmith, J., *The Dramatic Time-Piece: or Perpetual Monitor* (1768)
 Bulletins of the Campaign 1795 (1796)

Burke, Edmund, *Reflections on the Revolution in France, and on the proceedings in certain societies in London relative to that event. In a letter intended to have been sent to a gentleman in Paris* (1790)

Campbell, Thomas, *Life of Mrs Siddons* (1839)

Candid and Impartial Strictures on the Performers belonging to Drury-Lane, Covent-Garden, and the Haymarket Theatres (1795)

Catch Club: A Collection of All the Songs, Catches, Glees, Duets, &c. As sung by . . . Mr. Leoni . . . at the Royalty Theatre, Well-Street, Goodman's-Fields: To which is Added Hippesley's Drunken-Man, As altered and spoken by Mr. Lee Lewes (c. 1787)

Cobb, James, *English Readings; a Comic Piece, in one act. Inscribed to George Colman, Esq.* (1787)

The Siege of Belgrade; a comic opera, in three acts; as it is performed at the Theatres Royal in London and Dublin (Dublin: 1791)

Colman, George, The Elder, *The English Merchant* (1767)

Colman, George, The Younger, *Inkle and Yarico* (1787)
   The Battle of Hexham. A Comedy, In Three Acts, As Performed at the Theatre-Royal, Crow-Street (Dublin: 1790)

Colquhuon, Patrick, *Observations and Facts Relative to Public Houses* (1794)

Comparative Estimate of the Advantages Great Britain would derive from a Commercial Alliance with the Ottoman, in preference to the Russian empire (1791)

Craven, Elizabeth, *A Journey through the Crimea to Constantinople . . . Written in the year MDCCLXXXVI* (1789)

Curll, Edmund, *Faithful Memoirs of the Life, Amours and Performances, Of That Justly Celebrated, And Most Eminent Actress Of Her Time, Mrs. Anne Oldfield* (1731)

Cutspear, W. [pseud.], *Dramatic Rights: Or, Private Theatricals, and Pic-Nic Suppers, Justified by Fair Argument. With a few Whip-Syllabubs for the Editors of Newspapers* (1802)

Dibdin, Charles, *The Professional Life of Mr. Dibdin, Written by Himself* (1803, 4 vols.)

Dibdin, Thomas John, *The Naval Pillar: A Musical Entertainment, As Performed at the Theatre Royal Covent Garden* (1799)
   The Reminiscences of Thomas Dibdin (1827, 2 vols.)
   Sketch of the New Melo-Dramatick Comick Pantomime, called Harlequin and Humpo; or, Columbine by Candlelight etc. (1812)

Dodsley, Robert, *The King and the Miller of Mansfield* (1737)

Downes, Joseph, *Anti-Gallican Songster* (1793)
   Anti-Levelling Songster (1793)

Dunlap, William, *A History of the American Theatre* (New York: 1832)

Eton, William, *A Survey of the Turkish Empire* (1798)

Everard, Edward Cape, *Memoirs Of An Unfortunate Son Of Thespis; Being A Sketch Of The Life Of Edward Cape Everard, Comedian* (1818)

The Female Volunteer: or, an Attempt to make our Men STAND (1746)

Flaxman, John, *A Letter to the Committee for Raising the Naval Pillar, or Monument, under the patronage of His Royal Highness the Duke of Clarence* (1799)

For the Benefit of a Widow, and a Large Family, under Great Difficulties. The Theatrical Museum; or, Fugitive Repository: being a collection of very choice and pleasing interludes, both serious and comic. . . To the whole is prefixed, The much and long-desired Interlude of The Celebrated Hippesley's drunken man (1776)

Francklin, Thomas, *The Earl of Warwick, a tragedy, as it is perform'd at the Theatre Royal in Drury-Lane* (1766)

Fund, For the Relief of Indigent Persons Belonging To His Majesty's Company of Comedians of the Theatre Royal Drury Lane. Established, Endowed and Incorporated, By that Great Master of his Art, David Garrick, Esq. 1777 (1813)

Garrick, David, *Cymon* (1767)
   Isabella; or, The Fatal Marriage (1757)

Genest, John, *Some Account of the English Stage: From the Restoration in 1660 to 1830* (1832, 10 vols.)

Glorious Defeat of the French Gun-boats! A true and particular Account of the Total Defeat of the Grand French Flotilla, At the Island of St. Marcou . . . To which is added, A true and circumstantial Account of the Escape of that Gallant Hero Sir Sidney Smith . . . By a Perusal of this Book it may be seen how little Old England has to fear from the boasted French Invasion (c. 1798)

Godwin, William, *Antonio; or, The Soldier's Return* (1800)

   The Diary of William Godwin, ed. Victoria Myers, David O'Shaughnessy and Mark Philp (Oxford: Oxford Digital Library, 2010). http://godwindiary.bodleian.ox.ac.uk

   Faulkner (1807)

Great news from Lord Howe, by Express, from the London Gazette (1794)

Green-Room Mirror. Clearly delineating our present theatrical performers (1786)

Haslewood, Joseph, *The Secret History of the Green Room: containing authentic and entertaining memoirs of the actors and actresses in the three Theatres Royal* (1790, 2 vols.)

Hazlitt, William, *A View of the English Stage; or, A Series of Dramatic Criticisms* (1821)

Heads of a Plan for a Private Theatre . . . 1st March 1811 (1811)

Hill, Richard, *A Letter from Richard Hill, Esq; To His Friend near Shrewsbury, containing Some Remarks on a Letter signed by A Player Which Letter is also prefixed . . . sold for the Benefit of the Prisoners in Shrewsbury Goal* (Shrewsbury: 1767)

Hook, James, *Songs, Choruses, &c. in Jack of Newbury, A comic opera, with a masque, in honour of the Royal Nuptials, performed by their Majesties servants, at the Theatre Royal, Drury Lane* (1795)

Howell, Thomas B., *A Complete Collection of State Trials* (1818)

Hume, David, *The History of England, from the Invasion of Julius Caesar to the Revolution in 1688* (1763, 8 vols.)

Inchbald, Elizabeth, *Every One has his Fault: a comedy, in five acts, as it is performed at the Theatre Royal, Covent-Garden* (1793)

   Modern Theatre (1811)

Jackson, John, *The History of the Scottish stage, from its first establishment to the present time; with a distinct narrative of some recent theatrical transactions* (Edinburgh: 1793)

James, William, *The Naval History of Great Britain: From the Declaration of War by France in 1793 to the Accession of George IV* (1837)

Jerningham, Edward, *Fugitive Poetical Pieces* (1778)

   Margaret of Anjou: An Historical Interlude (1777)

   Peace, ignominy, and destruction: a poem. Inscribed to the Rt. Hon. Charles James Fox (1796)

   Poems (1779)

Jones, Henry, *The Earl of Essex. A Tragedy . . . Adapted for theatrical representation, as performed at the Theatre-Royal, in Covent-Garden.* Regulated from the prompt-books (1791)

Kelly, Hugh, *The School for Wives. A comedy. As it is performed at the Theatre-Royal in Drury-Lane* (1774)

Kemble, John Philip, *Love in Many Masks* (1790)

Knolles, Richard, *General History of the Turks* (1638)

Lawrence, James Herny, *Dramatic Emancipation, or Strictures on the State of the Theatres, And the Consequent Degeneration of the Drama* (1813)

Le Mesurier, Havilland, *Thoughts on a French Invasion, with Reference to the Probability of its Success, and the Proper Means of Resisting It* (1798)

Lillo, George, *The London Merchant, or The History of George Barnwell* (1731)

Massinger, Philip, *The Roman Actor* (1629)

   The Roman Actor. A tragedy . . . reviv'd with alterations (1722)

   Monitor; or, Green-Room Laid Open; With Remarks Thereon, Which occasioned the Letter to Mr. Spatter (1767)

Moore, Edward, *The Foundling* (1748)

Moore, Mark, *The Memoirs And Adventures of Mark Moore, Late an Officer in the British Navy, Interspersed With a Variety of original Anecdotes, selected from his Journals, when in the Tuscan, Portuguese, Swedish, Imperial, American, and British Service, in each of which he bore a commission . . . As the Author has been at Intervals the Manager of a respectable Company of Comedians, in several of the principal Towns of England, France, and Flanders, he has also added some original Sketches of several Theatrical Characters, who now rank high in the Thespian Corps* (1795)

Murphy, Arthur, *The Grecian Daughter* (1772)

O'Bryen, Denis, *The Prospect Before Us. Being a series of papers upon the great question which now agitates the public mind. To which is added a new postscript* (1788)

   The Prospect Before Us, on the present momentous crisis, addressed to every friend of the constitution (Dublin: 1789)

O'Keeffe, John, *The Farmer: A Comic Opera, in Two Acts, as it is performed at the Theatres Royal in London and Dublin* (Dublin: 1788)

   The Jene Scai Quoi a New Song (c. 1786)

   Songs, Duets, Trios, &c. in The Siege of Curzola, a comic opera, performed at the Theatre-Royal in the Hay-Market (1786)

Observations on the Commerce of Great Britain With the Russian and Ottoman Empires, and on the Projects of Russia Against the Ottoman and British Dominions (1801)

Official papers relative to the dispute between the courts of Great Britain and Spain, on the subject of the ships captured in Nootka Sound (1790)

Old Bailey Proceedings Online (www.oldbaileyonline.org, version 6.0)

Oldmixon, John, *Apollo Turn'd Stroller; or, Thereby Hangs a Tale. A musical pasticcio. In two parts. As performed, with the most unbounded Applause, at the Royalty-Theatre* (1787)

Paine, Tom, *The Rights of Man* (1791)

Parker, George, *A View of Society and Manners in High and Low Life; Being the Adventures In England, Ireland, Scotland, Wales, France, &c. of Mr. G. Parker. In which is Comprised a History of the Stage Itinerant* (1781)

Pasquin, Anthony (pseud. John Williams), *The Life of the Earl of Barrymore, Including a history of the Wargrave Theatre and Original Anecdotes of Eminent Persons* (1793)

Pearce, William, *Hartford-Bridge: or, the skirts of the camp. An operatic farce, in two acts. Performed at the Theatre-Royal, Covent-Garden* (1793)

Prologue Written for the Re-opening of the Theatre at Brandenbourgh House, after it was embellished and enlarged in the Year 1795 (1795)

Rede, Leman Thomas, *The Road to the Stage; Or, The Performer's Preceptor. Containing Clear and Ample Instructions for Obtaining Theatrical Engagements* (1827)

Rede, Leman Thomas and William Thomas Rede, *The Road to the Stage; Or, The Performer's Preceptor* (1836)

Reflexions on the Consequences of His Majesty's recovery from his late indisposition (1789)

Regulations for the Prussian cavalry. Translated from the German original by Capt. William Faucitt (1757)

Regulations for the Prussian infantry. Translated from the German original (1754)

Report from the Select Committee on Dramatic Literature: With The Minutes of Evidence. . . 2 August 1832, Parliamentary Papers (1831–2)

Rousseau, Jean-Jacques, *Pigmalion, Monologue* (1772)

Rules and Regulations for the Lambs Conduit Private Theatre (1799)

Scott, John, Major, *A letter to the Right Honourable Charles James Fox, on the extraneous matter contained in Mr. Burke's Speeches, in Westminster-Hall* (1789)

Shadwell, Charles, *The Fair Quaker of Deal; or, The Humours of the Navy* (1710)

Sheridan, Richard Brinsley, *The Critic; or, A Tragedy Rehearsed* (1781)

The Rivals, A Comedy, As it is Acted at the Theatre-Royal in Covent-Garden (1775)

Short Reply to Mr. Eton's observations respecting the establishment of the Levant Company (1799)

The Siege of Belgrade: an Historical Novel. Translated from a German manuscript (c. 1791)

Smith, Adam, *An Inquiry Into The Nature And Causes Of The Wealth Of Nations* (1784, 3rd edn, 3 vols.)

Smith, Sidney, *Memoirs of Admiral Sir Sidney Smith* (1839, 2 vols.)

Snell, Hannah, *The Female Soldier; or, the Surprising Life and Adventures of Hannah Snell* (1750)

Songs, &c. in the Deserter of Naples; or, Royal Clemency: To Which is Added, An Ode to Friendship, A Tale from Baker's Chronicle, Address for the Marine Society, Mr. Lee Lewes's Farewell Address, and other favourite Pieces Performed at the Royalty Theatre (c. 1787)

Steele, Richard, *The Funeral: or, Grief a-la-mode. A comedy. As it is acted at the Theatre Royal in Drury-Lane, by His Majesty's Servants* (1702)

Suett, Richard, *The Female Duellist: An After Piece. With Songs Set To Music By Mr. Suett As It Was Performed At The King's Theatre, In The Haymarket, By His Majesty's Company From The Theatre Royal, Drury-Lane* (1793)

Tate, Nahum, *The History of King Lear acted at the Duke's theatre reviv'd with alterations* (1681)

Theatrical Fund, Instituted at the Theatre Royal, in Covent-Garden, December 22, 1765, And Confirmed by Act of Parliament, 1776 (1811)

'Their Majesties Procession in St. Pauls, Apl 23d 1789', *The Lady's Magazine* (1789)

Thelwall, John, *The Tribune, a Periodical Publication, consisting chiefly of the political lectures of J. Thelwall*. Taken in short-hand by W. Ramsey (1795–6, 3 vols.)

Trials for High Treason; containing the whole of the proceedings at the Old-Bailey, from October 28, to December 5, 1794 (1795)

Truth and Treason! Or A Narrative of the Royal Procession To The House of Peers, October the 29th, 1795. To Which Is Added, An Account Of The Martial Procession To Covent-Garden Theatre, On the Evening of the 30th (1795)

Villiers, George, Duke of Buckingham, *The Rehearsal* (1672)

The Second Volume of Miscellaneons [sic] works, written by George, late Duke of Buckingham. Containing a Key to The Rehearsal (1705, 2 vols.)

Volney, Constantin-François Chasseboeuf, comte de, *Considerations on the War with the Turks* (1788)

The Ruins; or, A Survey of the Revolutions of Empires (1792)

von Dittersdorf, Karl Ditters, *The Doctor and the Apothecary* (1788)

Wallace, Lady Eglantine, *The Whim, a Comedy, in three acts . . . With an Address to the Public, upon the Arbitrary and Unjust Aspersion of the licenser against its Political Sentiments* (Margate: 1795)

Whyte, Samuel, *The Theatre: A Didactic Essay. Including An Idea Of The Character Of Jane Shore, As Performed By A Young Lady In A Private Play, &C. &C* (Dublin: 1790)

The Theatre, A Didactic Essay, In The Course Of Which Are Pointed Out The Rocks And Shoals To Which Deluded Adventurers Are Inevitably Exposed (1793)

Wilkinson, Tate, *The Wandering Patentee; Or, A History Of The Yorkshire Theatres, From 1770 To The Present Time* (York: 1795, 4 vols.)

Winston, James, *The Theatric Tourist; Being A Genuine Collection Of Correct Views, With Brief And Authentic Historical Accounts Of All The Principal Provincial Theatres In The United Kingdom* (1805)

Wood, William B., *Personal Recollections of the Stage, Embracing Notions of Actors, Authors, and Auditors, during a Period of Forty Years* (Philadelphia: Henry Carey Baird, 1855)

Yusuf Agha, *Account of the Mission of Yusuf Agha, Ambassador from Turkey to the British Court*. Written by Himself (1833)

SECONDARY SOURCES

Asleson, Robyn, '"She Was Tragedy Personified": Crafting the Siddons Legend in Life and Art', in Asleson (ed.), *A Passion for Performance: Sarah Siddons and Her Portraitists* (Los Angeles, CA: J. Paul Getty Museum, 1999), pp. 41–96

Auslander, Philip, *Theory for Performance: A Student's Guide* (London: Routledge, 2008)

Baggis, A.I., *Britain and the Struggle for the Integrity of the Ottoman Empire: Sir Robert Ainslie's Embassy to Istanbul 1776–1794* (Istanbul: Isis Yayimcilik Ltd, 1984)

Barchas, Janine, 'Prefiguring Genre: Frontispiece Portraits from *Gulliver's Travels* to *Millenium Hall*', *Studies in the Novel* 30 (1998), pp. 260–86

Barrell, John, *Imagining the King's Death: Figurative Treason, Fantasies of Regicide, 1793–1796* (Oxford University Press, 2000)
    The Spirit of Despotism: Invasions of Privacy in the 1790s (Oxford University Press, 2006)

Bennett, Jane, 'The Agency of Assemblies and the North American Blackout', *Public Culture* 17 (2005), pp. 445–65

Bennett, Tony, 'Sociology, Aesthetic, Expertise', *New Literary History* 41 (2010), pp. 253–76

Berridge, G.R., *British Diplomacy in Turkey, 1583 to the Present: A Study in the Evolution of the Resident Embassy* (Leiden and Boston: Martinus Nijhoff, 2009)

Bettany, Lewis, *Edward Jerningham and His Friends: A Series of Eighteenth Century Letters* (London: Chatto & Windus, 1919)

Bolton, Betsy, 'Imperial Sensibilities, Colonial Ambivalence: Edmund Burke and Frances Burney', *English Literary History* 72 (2005), pp. 871–99

Booth, Michael R., 'Sarah Siddons', in Michael R. Booth, John Stokes and Susan Bassnett (eds), *Three Tragic Actresses: Siddons, Rachel, Ristori* (Cambridge University Press, 1996), pp. 10–65

Brigham, Linda, 'Joanna Baillie's Reflections on the Passions: The "Introductory Discourse" and the Properties of Authorship', *Studies in Romanticism* 43 (2004), pp. 417–37

Brooks, Helen E.M., 'Negotiating Marriage and Professional Autonomy in the Careers of Eighteenth-Century Actresses', *Eighteenth-Century Life* 35:2 (2011), pp. 39–75

Broster, D.K., 'Sir Sidney Smith and Frotté in 1796', *English Historical Review* 23 (1908), pp. 534–7

Bryan, George B., *American Theatrical Regulation 1607–1900 Conspectus and Texts* (Metuchen, NJ and London: Scarecrow Press, 1993), pp. 229–30

Bullard, Paddy, 'The Meaning of the "Sublime and Beautiful": Shaftesburian Contexts and Rhetorical Issues in Edmund Burke's *Philosophical Enquiry*', *Review of English Studies* 56 (2005), pp. 169–91

Bush-Bailey, Gilli, *Treading the Bawds: Actresses and Playwrights on the Late-Stuart Stage* (Manchester University Press, 2006)

Campbell, Malcolm, 'An Alternative Design for a Commemorative Monument', *Record of the Art Museum, Princeton University* 17 (1958), pp. 65–73

Carlson, Julie A., *In the Theatre of Romanticism: Coleridge, Nationalism, Women* (Cambridge University Press, 1994)

Carlson, Marpvin, *The Haunted Stage: The Theatre as Memory Machine* (Ann Arbor, MI: University of Michigan Press, 2001)

Colby, Elbridge, 'A Supplement on Strollers', *Publications of the Modern Language Association* 39 (1924), pp. 642–54

Crisafulli, Lilla Maria and Keir Elam (eds.), *Women's Romantic Theatre and Drama: History, Agency, and Performativity* (Farnham: Ashgate, 2010)

Cross, Richard, 'Medieval Theories of Haecceity', *Stanford Encyclopedia of Philosophy*, ed. Edward N. Zalta (Fall 2010 edition) (http://plato.stanford.edu/archives/fall2010/entries/medieval-haecceity/)

Cull, Laura (ed.), *Deleuze and Performance* (Edinburgh University Press, 2009)

Davis, Tracy C., '"Reading Shakespeare by Flashes of Lightning": Challenging the Foundations of Romantic Acting Theory', *English Literary History* 62 (1995), pp. 933–54

Dawes, Frank, 'William: or the Adventures of a Sonata', *Musical Times* 106 (1965), pp. 761–4

De Bruyn, Frans, 'Theater and Counter-Theater in Burke's *Reflections on the Revolution in France*', in Steven Blakemore (ed.), *Burke and the French Revolution: Bicentennial Essays* (Athens, GA and London: University of Georgia Press, 1992), pp. 28–68

    'William Shakespeare and Edmund Burke: Literary Allusion in Eighteenth-Century British Political Rhetoric', in Peter Sabor and Paul Yachnin (eds.), *Shakespeare and the Eighteenth Century* (Aldershot: Ashgate, 2008), pp. 85–102

DeLanda, Manuel, *Deleuze: History and Science* (New York and Dresden: Atropos Press, 2010)

    'Materiality: Anexact and Intense', in Lars Spuybroek (ed.), *Nox: Machining Architecture* (London: Thames and Hudson, 2004), pp. 370–7

    'Molar Entities and Molecular Populations in Human History', in Jeffrey A. Bell and Claire Colebrook (eds.), *Deleuze and History* (Edinburgh University Press, 2009), pp. 225–36

    A New Philosophy of Society: Assemblage Theory and Social Complexity (London: Continuum, 2006)

    Philosophy and Simulation: The Emergence of Synthetic Reason (London: Continuum, 2011)

    A Thousand Years of Nonlinear History (New York: Swerve Editions, 1997)

Deleuze, Gilles and Félix Guattari (1980), *A Thousand Plateaus: Capitalism and Schizophrenia* (London: Continuum, 2004)

Dick, Alexander and Angela Esterhammer, 'Introduction: Romantic Spheres of Action', in Dick and Esterhammer (eds.), *Spheres of Action: Speech and Performance in Romantic Culture* (University of Toronto Press, 2009), pp. 3–18

Donohue, Joseph W., Jr, 'Hazlitt's Sense of the Dramatic: Actor as Tragic Character', *Studies in English Literature, 1500–1900* 5 (1965), pp. 705–21

Duffy, Michael, *Soldiers, Sugar, and Seapower: The British Expeditions to the West Indies and the War against Revolutionary France* (Oxford: Clarendon Press, 1987)

Edwards, Adrian, 'Provincial Theatre in Britain, 1773–1808: The Burney Playbills Examined', *Theatre Notebook* 57 (2003), pp. 136–42

Elfenbein, Andrew, 'Lesbian Aestheticism on the Eighteenth-Century Stage', *Eighteenth-Century Life* 25 (2001), pp. 1–16

Emsley, Clive, Tim Hitchcock and Robert Shoemaker, 'London History – Currency, Coinage and the Cost of Living', Old Bailey Proceedings Online (www.oldbaileyonline.org, version 6.0, 16 November 2011)

Engel, Laura, *Fashioning Celebrity: Eighteenth-Century British Actresses and Strategies for Image Making* (Columbus, OH: Ohio State University Press, 2011)

Fama, Eugene F., 'Efficient Capital Markets: A Review of Theory and Empirical Work', *Journal of Finance* 25 (1970), pp. 383–417

Favret, Mary A., *War at a Distance: Romanticism and the Making of Modern Wartime* (Princeton University Press, 2010)

Foulkes, Richard (ed.), *Scenes from Provincial Stages: Essays in Honour of Kathleen Barker* (London: Society for Theatre Research, 1994)

Frank, André Gunder, *ReOrient: Global Economy in the Asian Age* (Berkeley, CA and London: University of California Press, 1998)

Friedman, Geraldine, *The Insistence of History: Revolution in Burke, Wordsworth, Keats, and Baudelaire* (Stanford, CA: Stanford University Press, 1996)

Fuglsang, Martin and Bent Meier Sørensen (eds.), *Deleuze and the Social* (Edinburgh University Press, 2006)

Furniss, Tom, 'Stripping the Queen: Edmund Burke's Magic Lantern Show', in Steven Blakemore (ed.) *Burke and the French Revolution: Bicentennial Essays* (Athens, GA and London: University of Georgia Press, 1992), pp. 69–96

Garnai, Amy, 'Radicalism, Caution, and Censorship in Elizabeth Inchbald's Every One Has His Fault', *SEL Studies in English Literature 1500–1900* 47 (2007), pp. 703–22

Girdham, Jane, *English Opera in Late Eigtheenth-Century London: Stephen Storace at Drury Lane* (Oxford: Clarendon Press, 1997)

Gordon, Scott Paul, 'Reading Patriot Art: James Barry's *King Lear*', *Eighteenth-Century Studies* 36 (2003), pp. 491–509

Gough, B.M., 'India-Based Expeditions of Trade and Discovery in the North Pacific in the Late Eighteenth Century', *Geographical Journal* 155:2 (1989), pp. 215–23

Graves, Richard Harding, *Quarrelling Duet ... Words by J. Cobb* (London: J. Curwen & Sons, 1950)

Green, Katherine S., 'Mr Harmony and the Events of January 1793: Elizabeth Inchbald's *Every One Has His Fault*', *Theatre Journal* 56 (2004), pp. 47–62

Green, London, 'Edmund Kean's Richard III', *Theatre Journal* 36 (1984), pp. 505–24

Grimsted, David, *Melodrama Unveiled: American Theater and Culture, 1800–1850* (Berkeley, CA: University of California Press, 1968)

Grossman, Sanford J. and Joseph E. Stiglitz, 'On the Impossibility of Informationally Efficient Markets', *American Economic Review* 70 (1980), pp. 393–408

Guest, Harriet, *Empire, Barbarism, and Civilisation: James Cook, William Hodges, and the Return to the Pacific* (Cambridge University Press, 2007)

Hare, Arnold, *The Georgian Theatre in Wessex* (London: Phoenix House, 1958)

Harman, Graham, *Prince of Networks: Bruno Latour and Metaphysics* (Prahan: Re.press, 2009)

'Realism Without Materialism', *SubStance* 40 (2011), pp. 5–72

Higgins, David Minden, *Romantic Genius and the Literary Magazine: Biography, Celebrity and Politics* (London: Routledge, 2005)

Highfill, Philip H., Kalman A. Burnim and Edward A. Langhans (eds.), *A Biographical Dictionary of Actors, Actresses, Musicians, Dancers, Managers & Other Stage Personnel in London, 1660–1800* (Carbondale and Edwardsville, IL: Southern Illinois University Press, 1973–93, 16 vols.)

Hindson, Paul and Tim Gray, *Burke's Dramatic Theory of Politics* (Aldershot: Avebury, 1988), pp. 158–72

Hodgkinson, J.L. and Rex Pogson, *The Early Manchester Theatre* (London: Anthony Blond for the Society of Theatre Research, 1960)

Hoock, Holger, *The King's Artists: The Royal Academy of Arts and the Politics of British Culture, 1760–1840* (Oxford: Clarendon Press, 2003)

Horne, Pamela, 'An Eighteenth Century Battleground: The Shop Tax of 1785–1789', *Genealogists' Magazine* 28 (2006), pp. 479–86

Howell, Peter, 'Burke, Paine, and the Newspapers: An "Archaeology" of Political Knowledge 1789–93', *Studies in Romanticism* 43 (2004), pp. 357–98

Hsin-yun Ou, 'Gender, Consumption, and Ideological Ambiguity in David Garrick's Production of *The Orphan of China* (1759)', *Theatre Journal* 60 (2008), pp. 383–407

Hume, Robert D., 'The Origins of the Actor Benefit in London', *Theatre Research International* 9 (1984), pp. 99–111

Hume, Robert D. and Judith Milhous, 'A Bundle of Prologues (1777): The Unpublished Text of Garrick's Last Rehearsal Play', *Review of English Studies* 58 (2007), pp. 448–99

Ingram, Edward, 'From Trade to Empire in the Near East. I. The End of the Spectre of the Overland Trade, 1775–1801', *Middle Eastern Studies* 14 (1978), pp. 3–21

Jackson, H.J., *Romantic Readers: The Evidence of Marginalia* (New Haven, CT: Yale University Press, 2005)

Jenks, Timothy, *Naval Engagements: Patriotism, Cultural Politics, and the Royal Navy 1793–1815* (Oxford University Press, 2006)

Johnes, Martin, 'Archery, Romance and Elite Culture in England and Wales, c. 1780–1840', *History* 89 (2004), pp. 193–208

Jones, Robert W., 'Sheridan and the Theatre of Patriotism: Staging Dissent During the War for America', *Eighteenth-Century Life* 26 (2002), pp. 24–45

Kahan, Jeffrey, *The Cult of Kean* (Aldershot and Burlington, VT: Ashgate, 2006)

Kandl, John, 'Plebeian Gusto, Negative Capability, and the Low Company of "Mr Kean": Keats' Dramatic Review for the *Champion* (21 December 1817)', *Nineteenth Century Prose* 28 (2001), pp. 130–41

Kaufman, Robert, 'The Madness of George III, by Mary Wollstonecraft', *Studies in Romanticism* 37 (1998), pp. 17–25

  'The Sublime as Super-Genre of the Modern, or Hamlet in Revolution: Caleb Williams and His Problems', *Studies in Romanticism* 36 (1997), pp. 541–74

Kimche, David, 'The Opening of the Red Sea to European Ships in the Late Eighteenth Century', *Middle Eastern Studies* 8 (1972), pp. 63–71

Kinservik, Matthew J., 'Benefit Play Selection at Drury Lane 1729–1769: The Cases of Mrs. Cibber, Mrs. Clive, and Mrs. Pritchard', *Theatre Notebook* 50 (1996), pp. 15–28

  'The Censorship of Samuel Foote's *The Minor* (1760): Stage Controversy in the Mid-Eighteenth Century', *Studies in the Literary Imagination* 32 (1999), pp. 89–104

Klopsteg, Paul E., *Turkish Archery and the Composite Bow: A Review of an Old Chapter in the Chronicles of Archery, and a Modern Interpretation* (Manchester: Simon Avery Foundation, 3rd edn, 1987)

Landers, John, *Death and the Metropolis: Studies in the Demographic History of London, 1670–1830* (Cambridge University Press, 1993)

Latour, Bruno, *Reassembling the Social: An Introduction to Actor-Network-Theory* (Oxford University Press, 2005)

Letzter, Jacqueline and Robert Adelson, 'French Women Opera Composers and the Aesthetics of Rousseau', *Feminist Studies* 26 (2000), pp. 69–100

Lewis, Theresa (ed.), *Extracts of the Journals and Correspondence of Miss Berry From the Year 1783 to 1852* (London: Longmans, Green and Co, 1865)

Lloyd, Sarah, 'Pleasing Spectacles and Elegant Dinners: Conviviality, Benevolence, and Charity Anniversaries in Eighteenth-Century London', *Journal of British Studies* 41 (2002), pp. 23–57

Luckhurst, Mary and Jane Moody (eds.), *Theatre and Celebrity in Britain, 1660–2000* (Basingstoke: Palgrave Macmillan, 2006)

Mallory, Ann, 'Burke, Boredom, and the Theater of Counterrevolution', *Publications of the Modern Language Association* 118 (2003), pp. 224–38

Marsden, Jean, 'Performing the West Indies: Comedy, Feeling, and British Identity', *Comparative Drama* 42 (2008), pp. 73–88

Massai, Sonia, 'Nahum Tate's Revision of Shakespeare's *King Lears*', *SEL: Studies in English Literature, 1500–1900* 40 (2000), pp. 435–50

McDayter, Ghislaine, *Byromania and the Birth of Celebrity Culture* (Albany, NY: SUNY Press, 2009)

McPherson, Heather, 'Painting, Politics and the Stage in the Age of Caricature', in Robyn Asleson (ed.), *Notorious Muse: The Actress in British Art and Culture,*

1776–1812 (New Haven, CT and London: Paul Mellon Centre for Studies in British Art, 2003), pp. 171–94

'Picturing Tragedy: Mrs. Siddons as the Tragic Muse Revisited', *Eighteenth-Century Studies* 33 (2000), pp. 401–30

Melrose, Susan, 'Bodies Without Bodies', in Susan Broadhurst and Josephine Machon (eds.), *Performance and Technology: Practices of Virtual Embodiment and Interactivity* (Basingstoke: Palgrave Macmillan, 2006), pp. 1–17

Melvin, Peter H., 'Burke on Theatricality and Revolution', *Journal of the History of Ideas* 36 (1975), pp. 447–68

Michaelson, Patricia Howell, *Speaking Volumes: Women, Reading, and Speech in the Age of Austen* (Stanford, CA: Stanford University Press, 2002)

Milhous, Judith, 'Built and Unbuilt Opera Spaces in Eighteenth Century London', in Joseph Roach (ed.), *Changing the Subject: Marvin Carlson and Theatre Studies, 1959–2009* (Ann Arbor, MI: University of Michigan Press, 2009), pp. 83–117

'Reading Theatre History from Account Books', in Michael Cordner and Peter Holland (eds.), *Players, Playwrights Playhouses: Investigating Performance, 1660–1800* (Basingstoke: Palgrave Macmillan, 2007), pp. 101–34

Milhous, Judith and Robert D. Hume, 'Opera Salaries in Eighteenth-Century London', *Journal of the American Musicological Society* 46 (1993), pp. 26–83

Mole, Tim (ed.), *Romanticism and Celebrity Culture, 1750–1850* (Cambridge University Press, 2009)

Mulrooney, Jonathan, 'Keats in the Company of Kean', *Studies in Romanticism* 42 (2003), 227–50

Mulvihill, James, 'William Hazlitt on Dramatic Text and Performance', *SEL Studies in English Literature, 1500–1900* 41 (2001), pp. 695–709

Naff, Thomas, 'Reform and the Conduct of Ottoman Diplomacy in the Reign of Selim III, 1789–1807', *Journal of the American Oriental Society* 83 (1963), pp. 295–315

Nelson, Alfred L. and Gilbert. B. Cross (eds.), *Drury Lane Journal: Selections from James Winston's Diaries 1819–1827* (London: Society for Theatre Research, 1974)

Newitt, Malyn, *A History of Mozambique* (London: C. Hurst, 1995)

Norris, John M., 'Bread: The Eruption and Interruption of Politics in Elizabeth Inchbald's *Every One Has His Fault*', *European Romantic Review* 18 (2007), pp. 149–57

'The Policy of the British Cabinet in the Nootka Crisis', *English Historical Review* 70 (1955), pp. 56–80

Nussbaum, Felicity, *Rival Queens: Actresses, Performance, and the Eighteeth-Century British Theater* (Philadelphia: University of Pennsylvania Press, 2010)

O'Donnell, Katherine, 'Edmund Burke's Political Poetics', in Nessa Cronin, Séan Crosson and John Eastlake (eds.), *Anáil an Bhéil Bheo: Orality and Modern Irish Culture* (Newcastle upon Tyne: Cambridge Scholars Press, 2009), pp. 175–87

O'Quinn, Daniel, *Staging Governance: Theatrical Imperialism in London, 1770–1800* (Baltimore, MD: Johns Hopkins University Press, 2005), pp. 164–221

O'Shaughnessy, David, *William Godwin and the Theatre* (London: Pickering & Chatto, 2010)

Pascoe, Judith, *The Sarah Siddons Audio Files: Romanticism and the Lost Voice* (Ann Arbor, MI: University of Michigan Press, 2011)

Penny, Nicholas, '"Amor Publicus Posuit": Monuments for the People and of the People', *Burlington Magazine* 129 (1987), pp. 793–800

Pocock, Tom, *A Thirst for Glory: The Life of Admiral Sir Sidney Smith* (London: Aurum Press, 1996)

Pomeranz, Kenneth, *The Great Divergence: China, Europe, and the Making of the Modern World Economy* (Princeton University Press, 2000)

Poole, Steve, *The Politics of Regicide in England, 1760–1850: Troublesome Subjects* (Manchester University Press, 2001)

Potts, Liza, 'Using Actor Network Theory to Trace and Improve Multimodal Communication Design', *Technical Communication Quarterly* 18 (2009), pp. 281–301

Reid, Christopher, 'Burke's Tragic Muse: Sarah Siddons and the "Feminization" of the *Reflections*', in Steven Blakemore (ed.), *Burke and the French Revolution: Bicentennial Essays* (Athens, GA and London: University of Georgia Press, 1992), pp. 1–27

Reinelt, Janelle G., 'The Politics of Discourse: Performativity Meets Theatricality', *SubStance* 31 (2002), pp. 201–15

Roach, Joseph, *Cities of the Dead: Circum-Atlantic Performance* (New York: Columbia Univesity Press, 1996)

Robertson, Ben P. (ed.), *The Diaries of Elizabeth Inchbald* (London: Pickering & Chatto, 2007, 2 vols.)

Rodger, N.A.M., *The Command of the Ocean: A Naval History of Britain 1649–1815* (London: Allen Lane in Association with the National Maritime Museum, 2004)

Rokem, Freddie, *Philosophers and Thespians: Thinking Performance* (Stanford, CA: Stanford University Press, 2010)

Rosenfeld, Sybil, 'A Georgian Scene Painter at Work', *British Museum Quarterly* 34 (1969), pp. 33–6

Rowlinson, Matthew, *Real Money and Romanticism* (Cambridge University Press, 2010)

Schechner, Richard, *Between Theater and Anthropology* (Philadelphia: University of Pennsylvania Press, 1985)

'Invasions Friendly and Unfriendly: The Dramaturgy of Direct Theatre', in Janelle G. Reinelt and Joseph R. Roach (eds.), *Critical Theory and Performance* (Ann Arbor, MI: University of Michigan Press, 1992), pp. 88–106

Performance Theory (London: Routledge, 2003, rev. edn)

Shaw, Harry E., book review, *Victorian Studies* 48 (2006), pp. 549–51

Society of London Theatre Box Office Data Report 2009; Office for National Statistics (www.statistics.gov.uk/census2001/pyramids/pages/h.asp)

St Clair, William, *The Reading Nation in the Romantic Period* (Cambridge University Press, 2004)

Strathausen, Carsten, 'Epistemological Reflections on Minor Points in Deleuze', *Theory & Event* 13 (2010), E-ISSN: 1092–311X

Strong, Tracy B., 'Theatricality, Public Space, and Music in Rousseau', *SubStance* 25 (1996), pp. 110–27

Sudan, Rajani, 'Mud, Mortar, and Other Technologies of Empire', *The Eighteenth Century: Theory and Interpretation* 45 (2004), pp. 147–69

Survey of London: volume 35: The Theatre Royal, Drury Lane, and the Royal Opera House, Covent Garden (1970), pp. 1–8 (www.british-history.ac.uk/report.aspx?compid=100226)

Tasch, Peter A. (ed.), *The Plays of George Colman the Younger* (New York and London: Garland Publishing 1981)

Tilly, Charles, *Contentious Performances* (Cambridge University Press, 2008)
   Durable Inequality (Berkeley, CA: University of California Press, 1998)
   Popular Contention in Great Britain 1758–1834 (Cambridge, MA: Harvard University Press, 1995)
   Regimes and Repertoires (University of Chicago Press, 2006)

Tironi, Manuel, 'Gelleable Spaces, Eventful Geographies: The Case of Santiago's Experimental Music Scene', in Ignacio Farias and Thomas Bender (eds.), *Urban Assemblages: How Actor-Network Theory Changes Urban Studies* (London and New York: Routledge, 2010), pp. 27–52

Trewin, Wendy, *The Royal General Theatrical Fund A History: 1838–1988* (London: Society for Theatre Research, 1989)

Troubridge, St Vincent, *The Benefit System in the British Theatre* (London: Society for Theatre Research, 1967)

Tuhkanen, Mikko, 'Performativity and Becoming', *Cultural Critique* 72 (2009), pp. 1–35

Van Wezemael, Joris E., 'Modulation of Singularities – A Complexity Approach to Planning Competitions', in Jean Hillier and Patsy Healey, *The Ashgate Research Companion to Planning Theory: Conceptual Challenges for Spatial Planning* (Farnham: Ashgate, 2010), pp. 273–89

Walker, Julia A., 'Why Performance? Why Now? Textuality and the Rearticulation of Human Presence', *Yale Journal of Criticism* 16 (2003), pp. 149–75

Wanko, Cheryl, *Roles of Authority: Thespian Biography and Celebrity in Eighteenth-Century Britain* (Lubbock, TX: Texas Tech University Press, 2003)

Warner, James H., 'The Basis of J.-J. Rousseau's Contemporaneous Reputation in England', *Modern Language Notes* 55 (1940), pp. 270–80

Werkmeister, Lucyle, *A Newspaper History of England, 1792–1793* (Lincoln, NE: University of Nebraska Press, 1967)

West, Shearer, 'The Public and Private Roles of Sarah Siddons', in Robyn Asleson (ed.), *A Passion for Performance: Sarah Siddons and Her Portraitists* (Los Angeles: J. Paul Getty Museum, 1999), pp. 1–40

White, Paul Whitfield, *Drama and Religion in English Provincial Society, 1485–1660* (Cambridge University Press, 2008)

Wilson, Kathleen, *The Island Race: Englishness, Empire and Gender in the Eighteenth Century* (London and New York: Routledge, 2003)

'Pacific Modernity: Theatre, Englishness, and the Arts of Discovery, 1760–1800', in Colin Jones and Dror Wahrman (eds.), *The Age of Cultural Revolutions: Britain and France, 1750–1820* (Berkeley, CA: University of California Press, 2002), pp. 6–93

'Rowe's *Fair Penitent* as Global History: Or, a Diversionary Voyage to New South Wales', *Eighteenth-Century Studies* 41 (2008), pp. 231–51

Woods, Leigh, 'Actors' Biography and Mythmaking, the Example of Edmund Kean', in Thomas Postlewait and Bruce A. McConachie (eds.), *Interpreting the Theatrical Past* (Iowa, IA: University of Iowa Press, 1989), pp. 230–47

Worrall, David, *Harlequin Empire: Race, Ethnicity and the Drama of the Popular Enlightenment* (London: Pickering & Chatto, 2007)

The Politics of Romantic Theatricality, 1787–1832: The Road to the Stage (Basingstoke: Palgrave Macmillan, 2007)

Wu-Chi Liu, 'The Original *Orphan of China*', *Comparative Literature* 5 (1953), 193–212

Ziter, Edward, 'Kean, Byron and Fantasies of Miscegenation', *Theatre Journal* 54 (2002), pp. 607–26

Index